A TRANSFORMATION IN AMERICAN NATIONAL POLITICS

A TRANSFORMATION IN AMERICAN NATIONAL POLITICS

THE PRESIDENTIAL ELECTION OF 2012

EDITED BY

DOUGLAS M. BRATTEBO

TOM LANSFORD

JACK COVARRUBIAS

The University of Akron Press
Akron, Ohio

20   19   18   17   16   5   4   3   2   1

LIBRARY OF CONGRESS CATALOGING-IN-PUBLICATION DATA
A transformation in American national politics : the presidential election of 2012 / edited by
Douglas M. Brattebo.
     pages cm
Includes index.
ISBN 978-1-62922-003-1 (pbk. : alk. paper) — ISBN 978-1-62922-005-5 (epub) —
ISBN 978-1-62922-004-8 (epdf)
1. Presidents—United States—Election—2012. 2. United States—Politics and government—2009–
I. Brattebo, Douglas M.
JK5262012 .T73 2015
324.973'0932—dc23

2015029033

The paper used in this publication meets the minimum requirements of American National
Standard for Information Sciences—Permanence of Paper for Printed Library Materials, ANSI
Z39.48–1984. ∞

A Transformation in American National Politics was typeset in Goudy with Avenir display by
Amy Freels, printed on sixty-pound natural, and bound by Bookmasters of Ashland, Ohio.

In memory of Byron "Bill" Daynes.

Thank you for your contributions to the study of the presidency, and for being a true gentleman.

Contents

Acknowledgments

This book is the product of a conference, "The Presidential Election of 2012," held at Hiram College on November 16 and 17, 2012, as the dust was just starting to clear from Election Day (Tuesday, November 6). One hundred and thirty-two years earlier, in November 1880, Hiram College had seen one of its very own elevated to the presidency. James A. Garfield—who in 1851 commenced two years as a student at what was then the Western Reserve Eclectic Institute, returned to the school in 1856 as an instructor and soon thereafter became its principal, and left the school in 1861 to embark upon a career in the Union Army and in government— became the 20th president of the United States. Appropriately, the conference participants enjoyed a private tour of the James A. Garfield National Historic Site in nearby Mentor, Ohio—an experience that fueled dinner conversation as nearly 40 scholars from the United States and Canada enjoyed the music of a string quartet.

The high quality of the scholarly chapters contained in this volume speaks for itself. The editors are enduringly grateful for the creativity, diligence, and patience that each author brought to his or her contribution. Graduate assistant Charlie Carlee provided valuable editorial assistance in assembling the manuscript. The University of Akron Press has been a steady partner on this project, and we have benefited mightily from the wise counsel and good work of Amy Freels, editorial and design coordinator; Carol Slatter, coordinator of print manufacturing and digital production; and director Thomas Bacher. However, neither the conference nor the resulting book would have been possible without the superb efforts of several other estimable people. Brittany Jackson was indefatigable in handling a wide range of planning and logistical challenges associated with the conference. Anita Stocz and Mary Landries ensured that there would be suitable lodging for the participants, that the venues for the panel discussions and meals would be appropriate, and that transportation to and from airports and the historic site would be seamless. Todd Arrington, Chief of Interpretation and Education at the James A. Garfield National Historic Site, and his National Park Service colleagues, epitomized professionalism and enthusiasm as they shared their knowledge of the Garfield family and the site with the conference attendees. Keynote speakers Shirley Ann Warshaw, Professor of Political Science at Gettysburg College, and Stephen Koff, Washington Bureau Chief of the *Cleveland Plain Dealer*, offered up insightful analysis of the Obama presidency and Ohio's role in presidential elections, respectively. And the Garfield Institute for Public Leadership provided generous support for the conference, underwriting nearly one-fifth of the conclave's budget.

The conference was a true team effort, so rewarding and productive that we surely will convene another such gathering in the future. Hiram College's new James A. Garfield Center for the Study of the American Presidency, whose mission is to cultivate in students a deep understanding of the institution of the presidency and the individuals who have held the office, surely will be the locus of that effort. We hope President Garfield would be proud.

Introduction

Chapter 1

Introduction

Douglas M. Brattebo, Hiram College, and
Tom Lansford, University of Southern Mississippi–Gulf Coast

There is no ceremony more splendid than the inauguration of an American President. Yet Inauguration is a ceremony of state, of the visible majesty of power. And though the powers of the office are unique, even more spectacular and novel in the sight of history is the method of transfer of those powers—the free choice by a free people, one by one, in secrecy, of a single national leader:
Whether Americans have chosen this leader well or badly is of the most immense importance not only to them but to the destiny of the human race. Yet, well or badly done, no bells ring at any given hour across the nation when the voting is over, nor do any purple-robed priests wait that night to anoint the man who will soon be the most powerful individual in the free world. The power passes invisibly in the night as election day ends; the national vigil includes all citizens; and when consensus is reached, the successful candidate must accept the decision in the same rough, ragged, and turbulent fashion in which he has conducted the campaign that has brought him to power.
—Theodore H. White, The Making of the President 1960

"I hear America singing, the varied carols I hear," wrote Walt Whitman in his poem of the same name as its opening phrase, published in *Leaves of Grass* in 1867, "…each singing what belongs to him or her, and to none else" (Whitman [1867] 1965, 308). The 2012 presidential election confirmed what many observers of American national politics had noted for several years, since before Barack Hussein Obama was first elected to the presidency in 2008. Namely, the choir of citizens whose voices make up the anthem of American life has come to look and sound different from what most of our grandparents, and even many of our parents, could ever have anticipated. The United States is being transformed. Yet the driving factors and complexity of this sweeping change are only now beginning to draw adequate attention, and the implications—for who Americans are, how they think of themselves, how their country divides or coheres along geographical and demographic boundaries, the manner in which presidential candidates communicate with them, the ways Americans decide how to cast their votes, and the ramifications for the making of national policy—could not be more important. The purpose of this book is to provide a series of insightful essays that will help readers understand the 2012 presidential election in all its intricacy. The volume is both retrospect and prospect, a snapshot in time and a projection into the future, seeking to chronicle America as a work in progress.

The inquiry unfolds in three parts.

Part One is made up of five chapters about campaigning and geography. Shirley Anne Warshaw looks at the exodus of senior Obama administration staff members in late 2010 and throughout 2011, a contrast with previous administrations, which had maintained a significant reelection operation in the White House, centered in the Office of Political Affairs (OPA). Warshaw concludes that the Obama administration's decision to close the OPA and transfer all reelection personnel to the Chicago campaign headquarters ensured that partisan decisions would not be intertwined with political decisions, but the departure of numerous senior staff members also meant a loss of policy continuity and institutional memory. Jewerl Maxwell and Andrew Travis explore the impact of vice presidential candidates Paul Ryan and Joe Biden during the 2012 general election campaign to assess whether each running mate enhanced or compromised his side's strategy. After examining the acceptance speeches of the two vice presidential candidates, the aftereffects of the vice presidential debate, and the use of the two running mates to target constituency groups and battleground states, Maxwell and Travis conclude that Paul Ryan did nothing to enhance Mitt Romney's chances of winning the White House. Chad Kinsella uses Geographic Information Systems (GIS) to analyze 2012 election results of all 50 states and their counties. Kinsella notes differences in voting patterns between 2008 and 2012 to pinpoint trends in geographic concentrations of partisans and finds that the electorate is increasingly polarized not only by ideology but also along geographical lines. Neal Allen observes that despite failing to win the White House, the Republican Party in 2012 solidified its hold on elected office in the South, thereby ensuring its majority in the House of Representatives. President Obama's relatively weak showing in the South, a continuation of the Democratic Party's decades-long decline with white Southern voters as its center of gravity moves north and west, underscores the party's likely long-term weakness in the region. Capping off the first section, Susan A. MacManus and David J. Bonanza examine the micro-targeting of voters by race/ethnicity, age, gender, religion, and geography in Florida, one of the nation's premier battleground states and one of the most complex in which to campaign due to its constantly changing demographics. MacManus and Bonanza find that the Obama campaign was more successful in its demographic-based micro-targeting, and that the 2012 presidential race in Florida was very likely a precursor of the 2016 presidential race there, with a deepening divide between the young (Democratic) and the old (Republican).

Part Two consists of four chapters on domestic and economic policy. Through a close analysis of the 2012 primaries, national party conventions, and presidential debates, Steve A. Stuglin demonstrates that the Obama campaign was able to control the narrative about the 2008–2009 government intervention in the auto industry that bailed out General Motors and Chrysler. Stuglin concludes that by appropriating the history of events, shaping those events into a success story, and using that account as a line of attack against Romney, the Obama campaign was able to win the crucial battleground state of Ohio, an important reminder of the power of controlling economic narratives in presidential elections. Michael K. Gusmano notes that the Patient Protection and Affordable Care Act (ACA) of 2010, the signature domestic policy achievement of President Obama's first term, was based on the 2006 Massachusetts health care reform law signed into law by then governor Mitt Romney.

Nonetheless, the 2012 presidential election did not lead to strong public consensus about the ACA or its future, but rather was merely a skirmish in the long and continuing battle over national health insurance in the United States. Richard S. Conley points out that regulatory issues became subsumed in the larger, partisan divide about the state of the economy and perceptions of the incumbent president's economic management. Conley finds that partisan voters on both sides fell back on their general predispositions regarding government regulation, with independents remaining divided on the president's regulatory strategy. Byron W. Daynes examines the curious situation by which climate change, despite its intensification as a major global threat, never became a big issue in the 2012 presidential contest. Daynes explains that neither Obama nor Romney was eager for climate change to become a central issue in the race because they were uncertain which way it would cut, but Obama nonetheless went on to highlight the gravity of climate change in his Second Inaugural Address and promise action to combat it.

Part Three encompasses four chapters on foreign policy. Stephen D. Wrage explores the concept of American exceptionalism by employing a "symbol, ritual, and myth" approach, derived in part from the work of anthropologists, and argues that an understanding of exceptionalism is expected by voters and should be part of any presidential campaign. Wrage discusses the ways that appeals of the concept of exceptionalism have figured in recent elections by candidates as different as Carter, Reagan, Obama, and Romney, but he finds that exceptionalism was given short shrift in 2012. Leonard Cutler observes that Romney found it extremely challenging to draw a sharp contrast with President Obama's national security strategy of flexible pragmatism, the light-footprint approach by which the United States strikes from a distance with drone technology, obviating the need for years-long military occupations. However, with an eye on his own ultimate legacy, Obama's challenge after reelection would be to bring legal checks and balances to bear upon the process of targeted killing, even as he continued to engage in it, so that it might become more consonant with America's professed values and more likely to augment rather than undermine the country's long-term national interests. Tom Lansford, Jack Covarrubias, and Robert J. Pauly, Jr., investigate the reasons that Homeland Security issues did not play a major role in the 2012 general election campaign. The authors find that the Obama administration already had moved toward the moderate Republican position on Homeland Security during the first term, and Romney, having won an intense skirmish over Homeland Security policy with the Libertarian wing of the Republican Party during the primaries, was left with little room to take a position that would strike a dramatic contrast with the president. Chris J. Dolan notes that, although domestic issues were most important in the minds of many voters in 2012, the Obama administration's approach to global issues figured prominently in news coverage during election season—in large part because the global system itself is experiencing considerable change. In the last presidential debate, Obama maintained that after more than a decade of war he was placing the United States in a more stable global position, but the president also had to parry claims by Romney that his diplomatic approach was too apologetic and entailed leading from behind.

Time will illuminate whether the changes portended by the 2012 presidential election come into being rapidly, slowly, or at all. Even the most profound tectonic shifts of the American polity can seem uncertain until accreting years confirm their magnitude. Yet, as we approach the 2016 election, for some the message appears to be "business as usual." Retiring *Daily Show* host Jon Stewart explained, "I'd covered an election four times, and it didn't appear that there was going to be anything wildly different about this one" (Gajewski 2015). The Clinton/Bush stronghold on American politics appears to be firmly entrenched as a new generation of Democrats and Republicans struggle to define themselves against the backdrop of Hillary Clinton, and to a lesser extent, the continued wash of the Bush years in the American presidency. Yet, the 2012 election was significant in serving as a reminder that structural issues continue to play an important and underappreciated role in election wins, despite the rhetoric of change and hope that political parties rest their campaigns on and a changing political landscape of issues and challenges for the American experience.

As we seek to understand the 2012 watershed event and project into the future, it is appropriate to bear in mind another astute observation of Theodore H. White concerning presidential elections: "Heroes and philosophers, brave men and vile, have since Rome and Athens tried to make this particular manner of transfer work effectively; no people has succeeded at it better, or over a longer period of time, than the Americans" (White 1967, 13). There is solace in White's reminder, but also a reminder that no practice or trend lasts forever. America remains all at once an aspiration, an experiment, a colossus, and the sum total of all the demons and angels its citizenry is able to muster. The possible outcomes of this enterprise span the gamut, summon our hopes and fears, and demand our curiosity. May it ever be so.

REFERENCES

Gajewski, Ryan. 2015. "Jon Stewart on 'Daily Show' Departure: I Didn't Want to Cover 2016 Election." *The Hollywood Reporter,* April 18. Retrieved from http://www.hollywoodreporter.com/news/jon-stewart-daily-show-departure-789949.

White, Theodore H. 1967. *The Making of the President 1960.* New York. The New American Library.

Whitman, Walt. (1867) 1965. *Leaves of Grass: Comprehensive Reader's Edition.* Harold W. Blodgett and Sculley Bradley, editors. New York: New York University Press.

I. Campaigning and Geography

Chapter 2

The Obama White House's Transition from Governing to Campaigning

Shirley Anne Warshaw, Gettysburg College

OVERVIEW

The announcement in September 2010 by David Axelrod, the political strategist in the White House, that he would be leaving his position in a few months set the stage for an exodus of other senior staff members to return to Chicago to work on the reelection campaign (Axelrod 2010). Axelrod's departure was followed by that of Press Secretary Robert Gibbs and, several months later, by Deputy Chief of Staff Jim Messina, Social Secretary Juliana Smoot, and Deputy Senior Advisor Stephanie Cutter. Dozens of others from the White House followed. The most senior members of the 2008 campaign, all of whom had taken senior White House positions, were now leaving the administration to focus on the 2012 campaign.

The administration intended the exodus of campaign staffers, along with other actions, to present an aura of transparency. Political decisions would not be made by White House staff, with the clear message transmitted to the electorate that partisan decisions would not be intertwined with policy decisions. Transparency had been a hallmark of the Obama administration, as it sought to distance itself from the Bush administration's pattern of secrecy in decision making. During the 2008 campaign, Obama often discussed the necessity for greater transparency in government, and, once in office, pledged on the White House website that "My administration is committed to creating an unprecedented level of openness in government" (White House).

Issues of transparency became equally prevalent during the 2012 reelection campaign, as the Obama administration sought to ensure that political decisions remained independent of policy decisions, a process that necessitated separating the political and policy decision makers. The separation process took two paths. Not only were senior staff members moved out of the White House into the campaign offices in Chicago, but the White House Office of Political Affairs was shuttered and its senior staff moved out of the White House (Zelany 2011). Patrick Gaspard, director of the Office of Political Affairs, moved to the Democratic National Committee (DNC) as executive director to guide the intersection of the national party and the reelection campaign. Officially, the White House did not have a liaison to either the campaign or to the DNC with Gaspard's departure and the closure of the Office of Political Affairs. Unofficially, newly hired senior advisor David Plouffe, the 2008 campaign strategist, would serve as the liaison to the campaign and the DNC.

Although Obama's commitment to transparency across government was often discussed in the 2008 campaign and reinforced after the election, the decision to remove so many staff from the White House payroll and formally move them to the campaign was driven primarily by Representative Henry Waxman (D-CA) and by decisions rendered by the Office of Special Counsel (OSC). Similarly, the decision to close the White House Office of Political Affairs, which had operated continuously since 1981, was driven by Waxman and OSC. While transparency was the public cover for the Obama administration's decision, fear of negative publicity from Waxman and OSC were paramount in the decision.

To replace these four and others from the White House who had moved to the Chicago headquarters from the White House, President Obama chose more junior members of the White House staff rather than moving staff members from the departments into the White House or bringing in outside experts. By 2011, the White House was divided among current White House staff members who had held mid-level positions in the 2008 election and new staff members moved in from the departments. However, with the House of Representatives under Republican control, the potential for new legislation to support the administration's agenda was negligible, thus lessening the necessity of a proactive White House staff. By promoting lower-level staffers into more senior positions, the president sought to maximize continuity of policy within his senior staff and, at the same time, ensure cohesiveness within the depleted ranks of the White House.

This chapter is divided into three sections. The first section examines how past administrations dealt with the reelection campaign within the White House. The primary question addressed is whether White House staff members became integrally involved in the campaign. Six recent administrations that dealt with a reelection campaign are examined: Nixon, Carter, Reagan, George H. W. Bush, Clinton, and George W. Bush. Each provides a similar archetype of how the White House staff prior to the Obama administration became embroiled in the reelection process. The second section examines the Obama administration, which operated rather differently from its predecessors. The final section compares the Obama and past administrations and offers thoughts on how White House staff will be used in future reelection campaigns.

EXAMINING PAST ADMINISTRATIONS: IS THERE A STANDARD OPERATING MODEL?

Examining how past administrations staffed their reelection offices provides an opportunity to gauge whether the Obama administration moved away from a standard operating mode or, indeed, whether any standard operating mode exists.

Richard Nixon and Gerald Ford

Richard Nixon had few qualms about engaging White House staff in his reelection efforts, nor apparently did the public. Unlike Obama who dismantled the internal political operations within the White House,

Nixon had White House staff openly engaging in political functions. Using White House staff to further the president's reelection campaign was neither questioned in the press nor the courts. As a result, few left the White House to join the Committee to Re-Elect the President (CREEP), preferring to work within the White House as liaisons between the two operations. Most of the senior staff, led by Chief of Staff Bob Haldeman and Domestic Advisor John Ehrlichman, were directly engaged in campaign activities, working closely with Nixon and with CREEP.

One of the few members of the staff to move to CREEP was Frederic Malek, special assistant to the president, named deputy campaign manager. Malek followed John Mitchell, named campaign manager, who resigned as attorney general to reprise his role as Nixon's campaign manager. Before Malek officially moved from the White House to CREEP, he devised a plan to encourage Nixon appointees within the departments and agencies to support positions that benefited Nixon's reelection efforts. Known as the "responsiveness program," the plan sought to have Nixon appointees direct federal funds to specific states, localities, and organizations that supported the president and, most importantly, would benefit the campaign. In a December 23, 1971, memo to White House chief of staff H. R. Haldeman, Malek set the stage for White House staff to work directly with departmental personnel to enhance Nixon's reelection as part of the "responsiveness program":

> Naturally, carrying out this program, even if done discreetly, will represent a substantial risk. Trying to pressure "non-political" civil servants to partisanly support the President's re-election would become quickly publicized and undoubtedly backfire. Consequently, the strategy should be to work through the top and medium-level political appointees who exercise control over most of the Departmental decisions and actions. Also, to minimize any direct links to the President, there should be no directions on this project in writing, and most of the initiative should come from the Department Heads themselves. (In fact, as this concept is refined further, I propose we stop calling it "politicizing the Executive Branch," and instead call it something like strengthening the Government responsiveness.) (Malek 1971)

Malek's memo notes that White House staff members could discreetly "pressure" civil servants to move programs toward presidential goals that would immediately benefit the campaign. There was a supposition from the memo that the White House would be involved in designing purely political initiatives that benefited the president's reelection. The term "responsiveness program" stems from the last two words in the memo, which urge a strengthening of government responsiveness.

Nixon had few reservations about bringing his staff directly into the fight for the presidency. When George McGovern, the Democratic Party's nominee, appeared to be receiving more favorable press, Nixon said to his staff that McGovern's "press is very good, ours is still lousy" (Ambrose 1989, 581). According to Nixon biographer Stephen Ambrose, "Nixon therefore instructed his aides to never let up on McGovern, to make him responsible for all his prenomination statements." Ambrose further noted, "Shortly after McGovern's nomination, Kissinger gave Nixon a four-page, single-spaced memorandum on McGovern's defense proposals" (Ambrose 1989, 581).

Haldeman, Nixon's chief of staff, played the most significant role on the staff throughout the reelection, meeting regularly with Nixon and delegating campaign-related jobs to other staff members. Haldeman held regular election strategy meetings for White House and campaign staffers. "We had our regular strategy meeting this afternoon for a couple of hours [October 24, 1972], with [John] Connally, E[hrlichman], [Clark] MacGregor, [Chuck] Colson, and [John] Mitchell" (Haldeman 1994, 522–523). Haldeman reviewed presidential decisions on domestic and foreign policy issues, and the Vietnam peace negotiations. To a significant extent, Haldeman was the central player in the campaign for the president, coordinating how the campaign would handle presidential positions and delegating assignments to both campaign and White House staff members. When Nixon wanted the White House press office to "keep a hard attack going on McGovern," Haldeman met with Press Secretary Ron Ziegler (Haldeman 1994, 523). Using the White House Press Office to attack McGovern was an acceptable use of staff time during the 1972 election.

While it was not unusual for White House staffers to be intertwined with the campaign in 1972, most employees of the executive branch were barred from similar activities. The 1939 Act to Prevent Pernicious Political Activities, or Hatch Act, barred federal employees from engaging in political activity in any government office and from using any government equipment for political activity.[1] Employees of the White House Office within the Executive Office of the President were the only federal employees exempt from the restrictions of the Hatch Act, although they were also barred from using federal funds (as were all federal employees) for political activity. They could, however, discuss political activity in their offices and use government equipment for communications on political matters. This exemption for White House staff members stemmed from the exemption in the Hatch Act for the president and the vice president. The framers of the law specifically exempted White House staffers since they were the personal aides of the president and thus were logically an extension of the exemption they had granted him.

Nixon's use of White House staff in the 1972 campaign was most egregiously seen during the Watergate affair, when it became inordinately clear that White House staffers were engaged in the cover-up of the break-in into the Democratic National Committee's headquarters. The famous Watergate audio tapes, which Nixon refused to release until mandated by the Supreme Court, provide ample record of conversations between Nixon and his staff concerning CREEP and the Watergate burglars. However, at no point during the 1972 campaign did Nixon designate a new office or did he provide a title to anyone on the White House staff specifically identified as the liaison to the campaign or as a liaison to the Republican National Committee (RNC). Haldeman and John Ehrlichman were often the liaisons, as both had worked on the 1968 campaign and knew Mitchell, Malek, and Senator Robert Dole (R-KS), who was serving as chair of the RNC. Dole, a first-term senator with little experience in national elections, was content to integrate his operations with both CREEP and the White House.

The Ford administration continued the tradition of having White House staff deeply engaged in the reelection effort. Intertwining political assignments into their official activities became routine for some White House staffers. The 1976 election, which pitted incumbent Gerald Ford against former Georgia governor Jimmy Carter, was largely managed from the White House. Neither newly appointed RNC chair Mary Louise Smith nor campaign manager Bo Callaway had been engaged in a presidential election and neither knew Ford well. Dick Cheney, Ford's chief of staff, became the de facto campaign manager, often using White House staffers to prepare political analyses and examine federal policies applicable to swing states. Although Cheney was the White House liaison to the President Ford Committee (PFC), he played a major role in guiding the campaign. John Robert Greene noted in his study of the Ford presidency that Cheney, as early as the primary phase, was guiding the campaign strategy from the White House:

> Cheney generally ignored Callaway, and instead dealt with his assistant Stuart Spencer.... By October Spencer was attending weekly meetings with Ford and Cheney... by the end of the year, Callaway had been completely moved aside.... It was Cheney, Spencer and pollster Robert Teeter of Michigan... who developed the strategy for the early primary races. (Greene 1995, 162–163)

Guiding the campaign strategy included positioning Ford to counter the conservative insurgency within the Republican Party, led by Ronald Reagan. Cheney was central in the decision to remove Nelson Rockefeller from the ticket and to replace Rockefeller with Senator Robert Dole of Kansas, a more conservative voice than New Yorker Nelson Rockefeller. Cheney had been at odds with Rockefeller throughout his tenure as vice president, frequently seeking to reverse Rockefeller's recommendations to Ford (Warshaw 1995, 71–73). Ford had also been at odds with campaign chair Bo Callaway and replaced him with Rogers Morton, who rarely challenged Cheney's control of the reelection campaign.

Jimmy Carter

Not until the Carter administration did the president formally designate a position in the White House to work with the national political party and state political organizations and to ensure policy decisions were reviewed for their political implications. Tim Kraft, the president's White House scheduler who was promoted to the more senior-level position of assistant to the president in 1978, was charged with overseeing an informal office of political affairs. This was done to relieve Chief of Staff Hamilton Jordan from an overburdened workload, but also in deference to Speaker of the House Thomas "Tip" O'Neill who had criticized the White House for a lack of political acuity (Tenpas 1996, 515). The Carter Presidential Library lists Kraft's sole role in the White House as dealing with "political matters in the White House" (Jimmy Carter Presidential Library). Presidential scholar Kathryn Dunn Tenpas interviewed Kraft in 1992, and he confirmed his role as "assistant to the president for political affairs and personnel" although his title was officially only "assistant to the president" (Tenpas 1996, 520).[2] With Kraft's appointment in 1978, the president was, for the first time, formally designating staff to oversee political relationships and to serve as a liaison with the reelection campaign.

Ronald Reagan and George H. W. Bush

With the nearly official recognition of a political office in the White House during the Carter administration, full recognition came with the Reagan administration. James A. Baker, whom Reagan appointed chief of staff, created the position of assistant to the president for political affairs specifically for Lyn Nofziger (Tenpas 1996, 515). A journalist by training, Nofziger had been deputy chairman of finance for the Reagan presidential committee. When James Brady was given the press secretary position by Reagan, Baker used the newly created political affairs position to keep Nofziger as part of the Reagan team in the White House.

Nofziger built the fledgling one-person office that Kraft had created three years earlier into a larger staff of three: Nofziger, Ed Rollins, and Lee Atwater. Rollins, a political strategist for Reagan in the 1980 campaign, and Atwater, a campaign strategist recommended by Senator Strom Thurmond (R-SC), expanded professional political management skills in the White House. For the first time, the president had in-house political staffers whose only role was to interact regularly with the political party, quietly conduct polling, and ensure that policy decisions did not alienate key constituent interests.

Two years later, Nofziger left the administration and Rollins moved into his position, continuing to serve as the White House political arm. This allowed Nofziger and Rollins to regularly collaborate on campaign issues. Chief of Staff James A. Baker III, who brought Nofziger and Rollins into the White House, ensured that the Office of Political Affairs was finely integrated into the White House apparatus. Nofziger, and later Rollins, was given the title assistant to the president. However, following Reagan's 1984 victory, the office was downgraded and moved under a deputy assistant to the president. Rather than serving as the assistant to the president for political affairs, the new title was deputy assistant to the president and director of the office of political affairs (U.S. Government Manual). Whether this was recognition that the office was no longer central to long-term planning or whether the new chief of staff, Donald Regan, wanted to make his own imprint, is uncertain.

With the Office of Political Affairs having a place in the White House at either the assistant or deputy assistant to the president level for eight years, George H. W. Bush chose to continue the office at the deputy assistant to the president level with James Wray at the helm. Wray had been involved in the 1992 Bush presidential campaign, serving as a field director and deputy director of the nominating convention. But, unlike Nofziger and Rollins for Reagan, Wray lacked the close ties to the inner circle of the presidential campaign, many of whom had been with Bush during his 1980 and 1988 presidential campaigns. Wray's position within the White House staff reflected his distance from the inner circle and the lack of influence he had in coordinating political and policy issues. Lee Atwater, Bush's 1988 campaign chair and newly appointed chair of the Republican National Committee, served as the coordinator between the White House staff, RNC, and other political interests. The close personal bond between Atwater and Bush allowed Atwater direct contact with Chief of Staff John Sununu and other senior members of the White House staff in coordinating political and policy decisions, minimizing the influence of Wray.

Kathryn Dunn Tenpas, in her study of the Office of Political Affairs, added the following insights:

> The office did not appear to be as influential as it was during the Carter and Reagan administrations for two reasons. First, the office was downgraded in size. Second, the head of the office was not a close confidant. Rather, President Bush's closest political advisers resided outside the White House: Robert Teeter (pollster), Atwater (RNC), and James Baker (State Department). (Tenpas 1996, 516)

Unquestionably Atwater's role at the RNC changed the character of the Office of Political Affairs and reduced its in-house involvement in political matters.

Bill Clinton

Bill Clinton's ascent on the national political scene in 1992, culminating with his capture of the White House that year, was the product of a carefully developed political plan by strategists James Carville and Paul Begala. Neither joined the White House staff, choosing to remain in the private sector, but the new coalitions fashioned by the two men during the campaign were protected by others in the White House. That role fell to Rahm Emanuel, the campaign finance director, who was named assistant to the resident and director of political affairs.

Unlike Reagan, who brought many of his senior campaign strategists into the White House, or Bush, who brought relatively few senior campaign strategists into the White House, Clinton sought a middle ground. Emanuel had played a major role in Clinton's campaign and leveraged that influence into a senior White House position as director of political affairs. In contrast, Carville, Begala, Mandy Grunwald, and others from the campaign remained private political advisers to Clinton. Tensions mounted and Emanuel eventually was moved to another position with his deputy, Joan Baggett, taking over his previous role. Baggett, who had little political capital of her own, was dwarfed in the White House with the 1993 addition of Assistant to the President and Deputy Chief of Staff Harold Ickes, whose primary role was to manage political relationships as the White House prepared for the reelection campaign.

Ickes became the campaign spokesman for the White House, rather than the director of the Office of Political Affairs. For example, on September 18, 1995, more than a year before the election, Ickes briefed the press on the reelection campaign's fundraising. "We expect to raise approximately $5 million in the series of fundraisers beginning with tonight going down to Miami then over to Denver" (Office of the Press Secretary 1995).[3] He continued to address the location of other fundraisers, the lack of primary challengers, and the decision of whether to accept matching funds from the federal government. It is notable that this press briefing was by the deputy chief of staff, not by the press secretary or by the director of the office of political affairs. Lines were blurred between politics and policy for White House staff.

Yet, 12 years after the office had been formally created by Reagan, two successive administrations, one Republican and the other Democratic, had an Office of Political Affairs at senior levels in the White House. Its degree of influence in the White House depended on who sat in the Oval Office.

George W. Bush

Following the path that his father had crafted, George W. Bush continued the Office of Political Affairs at the deputy assistant to the president level. Ken Mehlman, the national grassroots chair of the 2000 Bush/Cheney campaign, built a strong relationship with the key campaign strategist, Karl Rove. When both were brought into the White House, Mehlman and Rove worked to assess which political candidates the president should support, what policies were politically sensitive, and how the RNC could support the presidential agenda. The office, more influential than it had been under either George H. W. Bush or Bill Clinton, played a key role in gauging political operations and planning for the 2004 reelection campaign.

Following the reelection, Mehlman was named by Bush as chair of the RNC. Rove, who officially became deputy chief of staff in the second term, was given oversight over a number of White House offices, including political affairs. The Office of Strategic Initiatives, which Rove created in 2001, continued to work closely with the Office of Political Affairs throughout the entire eight years of the Bush presidency.

Mehlman's office became the center of political activity in the White House, handling the day-to-day operations while Rove's office focused on policy issues, both long- and short-term. Among the responsibilities that the Office of Political Affairs handled were vetting applicants for political appointments at federal agencies, assisting agencies with selecting individuals to serve as White House liaisons, and implementing a series of efforts, such as briefings at the White House and at the federal agencies, designed to keep political appointees connected to the White House and to boost morale (Office of Special Counsel, 40).

Barack Obama

Although both George H. W. Bush and George W. Bush downgraded the Office of Political Affairs to a deputy assistant to the president position, Barack Obama returned it to an assistant to the president position, as both Reagan and Clinton had positioned it. Patrick Gaspard, a labor leader with the Service Employees International Union who had directed the union's efforts for the Obama campaign, was named assistant to the president for political affairs. The office was closed in 2011 as the reelection effort formally began to separate the policy and other official staff from those related to campaign activity.

OFFICE OF SPECIAL COUNSEL: CHALLENGES TO WHITE HOUSE POLITICAL ACTIVITIES

Malek's efforts during the Nixon administration to use career civil service employees to move forward specific programs that would enhance Nixon's reelection were chronicled by the Senate Watergate committee. Gerald Ford did little to pursue the abuses during the Nixon administration, but Jimmy Carter began to explore how political appointees could work more efficiently, without political interference, with career employees.

To that end, Carter created in 1977 the President's Personnel Management Project, chaired by Dwight Ink. Their recommendation was for an overhaul of the Civil Service Commission, which the Democratically controlled Congress supported. Among the points noted by the commission was that "assaults on the merit system have taken place" (Civil Service Reform Act 1978, 745), a clear reference to the Nixon presidency. Soon after, Congress passed the Civil Service Reform Act of 1978, creating the Office of Personnel Management to replace the Civil Service Commission and, among other changes, an independent investigative agency, the Office of Special Counsel (OSC), which reviews and prosecutes violations of the act.

Among the responsibilities of the Office of Special Counsel is to oversee violations of the Hatch Act regulations that were codified by the Office of Personnel Management (OPM). Part 734 of the regulations, entitled "Political Activities of Federal Employees," included a section on "Special Provisions for Certain Presidential Appointees Paid from the Appropriation for the Executive Office of the President" (Special Counsel). Subsection 734.502, section (c) specifically allows political activity for presidential appointees in the Executive Office of the President "while he or she is on duty." According to the OPM regulations, "(c) An employee described in paragraph (a) of this section may participate, subject to any restrictions that may be imposed in accordance with § 734.104, in political activities: (1) While he or she is on duty" (Office of Special Counsel). The regulations, however, bar Senate confirmed officials from participating in political activity in the conduct of their official roles.

Following the 2006 midterm elections, Representative Henry Waxman (D-CA), chairman of the House Oversight and Government Reform Committee, charged the Bush White House with engaging in political activity in violation of the OPM regulations. Specifically, Waxman stated that Scott Jennings, deputy director of the Office of Political Affairs in the White House, had briefed political appointees in the General Services Administration on a number of close Republican races (Neal 2008). Jennings then had asked the political appointees how they could help in those races. The matter was forwarded by Waxman to the Office of Special Counsel for investigation.

In 2008, the Office of Special Counsel released a report, "Investigation of Political Activities by White House and Federal Agency Officials During the 2006 Midterm Elections," which concluded that Ken Mehlman and his staff in the Office of Political Affairs had operated outside of their protections in the Hatch Act by working with agency federal employees during work hours. In addition, Mehlman and his staff had encouraged the use of federal programs to benefit Republican candidates. No penalty was levied by OSC, which stopped at providing further clarification of the Hatch Act to OPM.

According to the OSC investigation, "OSC identified approximately 75 political briefings given by OPA employees to political appointees at 20 federal agencies between 2001 and 2007. Typically, these briefings were conducted by the OPA Director or Deputy Director" (Office of Special Counsel, 15). However, OSC found that the members of the Office of Political Affairs understood that they could not conduct political business with political employees during work hours. According to the OSC report:

> Ms. Sara Taylor testified that the White House Counsel's Office advised that political briefings should be held after 5:00 p.m. to avoid using government resources for political activity. The evidence shows that on June 30, 2005, an OPA Associate Director sent an e-mail to the White House liaison at the U.S. Department of Education (DOEd) stating that political briefings "MUST take place after hours due to content... [at] 5PM

or later." In spite of these warnings, between April 2005 and February 2007, OPA conducted 36 political briefings for political appointees at federal agencies. Of the 30 political briefings for which OSC was able to discern a specific time of presentation, 14 were held before 5:00 p.m.

The report concluded that "the evidence shows that in scheduling political briefings, it was routine for OPA to contact an agency's White House liaison to offer a political update, or for a White House liaison to request one directly from OPA" (Office of Special Counsel, 17).

After a detailed review, the Office of Special Counsel concluded that "many if not all of the political briefings were directed at the political success of the Republican Party . . . and thus consisted of political activity for Hatch Act purposes." It further noted that all federal employees, including PAS and high-level EOP employees, are prohibited from using their official authority to interfere with or affect the result of an election (Office of Special Counsel, 32).[4] The effect of the review was to affirm that employees in the White House could themselves have political conversations, but they could not have political conversations with agency political employees during the workday nor could they seek to influence the election using official actions.

OBAMA WHITE HOUSE STAFF, CAMPAIGNING, AND POLITICAL ROLES

Since the ruling by the Office of Special Counsel on the Bush administration, the Obama White House has been cautious in how the Office of Political Affairs engages in interactions with federal agencies. No red flags were waved by Republican members of Congress in the 2010 midterm elections nor did OCS conduct any investigations of OPA or other White House staff. But, because of the investigation into the OPA under Bush, the Obama White House has trod carefully about any negative publicity that would stem from an OCS investigation in an election year.

To mitigate any possibility of an investigation, Obama closed the Office of Political Affairs in 2011, and its director, Patrick Gaspard, moved to the Democratic National Committee as its executive director. Other White House offices were equally sensitive to the appearance of improper political behavior. The PBS *NewsHour* noted on October 1, 2012, that "White House officials have tried to draw a bright line between their duties and the functions and priorities of the Chicago-based Obama campaign—even limiting the kinds of press questions they answer, deferring many to campaign aides who recently began travelling aboard Air Force One" (Holman 2012).

Not only did Obama close the Office of Political Affairs, but a host of senior White House staff members resigned their positions to move to Chicago for the reelection campaign. The entire senior level of the campaign moved in 2011 from the White House to Chicago, including campaign manager Jim Messina, deputy campaign managers Juliana Smoot and Stephanie Cutter, and the principal campaign advisors, David Axelrod and Robert Gibbs.

The decision to move senior staff into the campaign was not unprecedented. Of the seven reelection campaigns from Nixon to George W. Bush, three had used current White House staff members (Carter, Reagan, George W. Bush). Of the remaining four administrations, one used a White House staff member from a former administration (George H. W. Bush), two used current administration departmental officials (Nixon and Ford), and one (Clinton) used an outside consultant. Carter moved Tim Kraft, who had served as the unofficial director of a White House political office, to the campaign. Both Reagan and George W. Bush shifted the director of the Office of Political Affairs into the campaign (Ed Rollins moved from the Reagan White House and Ken Mehlman moved from the Bush White House). George H. W. Bush used longtime Nixon political mastermind Frederic Malek. Ford used Howard "Bo" Callaway, his secretary of the army and a former Georgia congressman; Nixon used his attorney general, John Mitchell; Clinton used Dick Morris.

By moving Jim Messina to the campaign from the White House, Obama was following a practice used by both Democratic (Carter) and Republican (Reagan and George W. Bush) administrations. However, closing the Office of Political Affairs and moving numerous senior White House staff into the campaign had not been done in previous administrations.

Table 2.1 indicates which White House staff members moved to the campaign in 2011, the staff position each held, and the campaign position each held.

Table 2.1 White House Staff Members Who Moved to Obama Campaign in 2011

Name	White House Position	2012 Campaign Position	Date Left White House
Jim Messina	Deputy Chief of Staff	Campaign Manager	28 Jan 2011
David Axelrod	Senior Advisor	Consultant	28 Jan 2011
David Simas	Deputy to Axelrod	Director of Opinion Research	Jun 2011
Juliana Smoot	White House Social Secretary	Deputy Campaign Manager	Jan 2011
Stephanie Cutter	Assistant to the President; Deputy Senior Advisor	Deputy Campaign Manager	Jan 2011
Peter Newell	Director, White House Travel Office	Special Assistant to the Campaign Manager	11 Feb 2011
Marion Marshall	Deputy White House Liaison to the State Department	Deputy Field Director	5 Apr 2011
Robert Gibbs	Press Secretary	Senior Advisor	20 Feb 2011
Dan Kanninen	White House Liaison to EPA	Northeast Regional Director	NA
Buffy Wicks	Deputy Director, White House Office of Public Engagement	Project Voter Director	NA
Michael Blake	Deputy Associate Director, White House Office of Public Engagement	Project Vote Deputy Director	25 Apr 2011
Michael Wear	Executive Assistant to the Executive Director of the White House Office of Faith Based and Neighborhood Partnerships	Faith Vote Director	May 2012
Ben LaBolt	Assistant Press Secretary	Press Secretary	May 2011
Katie Hogan	Associate Director of Press Advance and Press Pool Wrangler	Deputy Press Secretary	May 2011
Jen Psaki	Deputy Communications Director	Traveling Press Secretary	May 2011
Elizabeth Javis-Shean	Director of Research	Research Director	NA
Lisa Kohnke	Director of Special Events, White House Office of Public Engagement	Director of Scheduling and Advance	NA
Joseph Reinstein	Deputy Social Secretary, Office of the First Lady	Director of Surrogates	NA
Allyson Laackman	CFO in the Executive Office of the President	Chief of Staff for the First Lady	NA

Name	White House Position	2012 Campaign Position	Date Left White House
Nora Cohen	Deputy Director of Advance for the Vice President	Director of Advance for Vice President	NA
Virginia Lance	Scheduler for Vice President	Scheduler for Vice President	NA

CONCLUSION

The decision by the White House staff to shutter the Office of Political Affairs and to shift a significant number of staff members to the reelection campaign was unprecedented. The explanation for the decision appears to stem from the investigation by the Office of Special Counsel into the political activities of Ken Mehlman's Office of Political Affairs in the 2006 midterm elections. Not wanting to attract any negative publicity to White House political operations in a hyperpartisan environment was fundamental to the decision. A somewhat parallel explanation stems from Obama's campaign promise in 2008 to have transparency in his administration. Such transparency would preclude members of the White House staff from engaging in political discussions with the reelection campaign.

Because the Obama administration concentrated so many campaign staffers from 2008 in the White House, rather than distributing them across the agencies, their departures in 2011 were noticeable and affected White House operations. Their departure created conspicuous vacuums in the White House and reduced the president's confidence in his own staff, changed relationships both within the White House and within the broader executive branch, and forced new learning curves.

REFERENCES

Ambrose, S. 1989. *Nixon: Triumph of a Politician, 1961–1972.* New York: Simon and Schuster.

"Axelrod Leaving White House in First Half." 2010. *Huffington Post,* November 14. Retrieved from http://www.huffingtonpost.com/2010/11/14/david-axelrod -leaving-whi_1_n_783228.html.

Civil Service Reform Act. 1978. Report of the Senate Committee on Governmental Affairs. July 10. Retrieved from http://www.flra.gov/webfm_send/562.

Greene, J. R. 1995. *The Presidency of Gerald R. Ford*. Lawrence: University of Kansas Press.

Haldeman, H. R. 1994. *The Haldeman Diaries*. New York: Putnam.

Holman, K. 2012. "White House Turns Over Debate Prep to Obama Campaign." *PBS NewsHour*, October 1.

Jimmy Carter Presidential Library, Atlanta, Georgia. Historical Materials in the Jimmy Carter Library. Retrieved from http://www.jimmycarterlibrary.gov /library/guide.pdf.

Malek, F. 1971. "The Responsiveness Program. Memo to Haldeman, H. R." *Senate Watergate Report*, Chapter III. December 23.

Neal, R. 2008. "Rep. Waxman Alleges Hatch Act Violations by White House." *Federal Times*, October 16.

Office of the Press Secretary, White House. 1995. Press Briefing by Deputy Chief of Staff Harold Ickes. September 18.

Office of Special Counsel. Retrieved from http://www.osc.gov/documents/hatchet /federal/5cfr734.pdf.

Tenpas, K. D. 1996. "Institutionalized Politics: The White House Office of Political Affairs." *Presidential Studies Quarterly* 26 (2) (Spring).

U.S. Government Manual, 1981, 1982, 1983, 1984, 1985, 1986, 1987, 1988. Washington, D.C.: U.S. Government Printing Office.

Warshaw, S. A. 1995. *The Domestic Presidency: Cabinet–White House Relations in the Modern Presidency*. New York: Allyn and Bacon.

White House. "Open Government and Transparency." Retrieved from http://www .whitehouse.gov/the_press_office/TransparencyandOpenGovernment.

Zelany, J. 2011. "White House Will Move Political Operations to Chicago." *New York Times*, January 20. Retrieved from http://www.nytimes.com/2011/01/21/us /politics/21obama.html.

NOTES

1. Pub. L. No. 76-252, 53 Stat. 1147 (codified as amended in scattered sections of 5 U.S.C.).

2. Footnote 28.

3. Online by Gerhard Peters and John T. Woolley, *The American Presidency Project*. Available at http://www.presidency.ucsb.edu/ws/?pid=59471.

4. The findings note: In addition to the political briefings addressed in the previous chapter, OSC's investigation uncovered evidence of a much broader involvement of OPA employees in on-duty political activities directed at the success of Republican candidates during the 2006 election season. The evidence shows that certain activities conducted by OPA employees constituted prohibited political activity under the Hatch Act. Specifically, OSC's investigation revealed that OPA was essentially an extension of the RNC in the White House. Thus, OPA:

- Worked with the RNC to develop a "target list" consisting of those Republican candidates involved in close races.

- Encouraged high-level agency political appointees to attend events with targeted Republican candidates in order to attract positive media attention to their campaigns, a practice called "asset deployment."
- Utilized the services of several RNC desk coordinators—who worked inside the White House—to help coordinate high-level political appointees' travel to both political and official events with Republican candidates.
- Kept track of Republican candidates' fundraising efforts as well as high-level agency political appointees' attendance at events with targeted candidates.
- Encouraged political appointees to participate in political activities.

Chapter 3

A Heartbeat Away
The Strategic Importance of Paul Ryan and Joe Biden in the 2012 Presidential Election

Jewerl Maxwell, Gordon College and Andrew Travis, Cedarville University

INTRODUCTION

The strategic importance of vice presidential selection is by no means a new topic of discussion or scholarly examination. Each election cycle brings talk of the potential for presidential nominees to use their vice presidential candidates to strike a geographic balance, or to at least ensure victory in a key swing state (Adkison 1982). But then we are left with the questions: In 2004, did George W. Bush choose Dick Cheney in order to win the key state of Wyoming, or to secure victory in the mountain west? Likewise, in 2008, did John McCain worry that voters would not turn out in Alaska, or did Barack Obama decide his success hinged on his ability to secure Delaware? Not likely. Perhaps it is ideological balance that drives campaigns (Natoli 1985). Or perhaps it is more than ideological balance, more that a candidate should find a running mate who will balance his "image." Nelson Polsby and Aaron Wildavsky (1991, 168) surmised that the two parties seek a ticket that creates "a composite image of forward-looking-conservative, rural-urban, energetic-wise leadership that evokes hometown, ethnic, and party loyalties among a maximum number of voters." Interestingly, analysts spend weeks, if not months, trying to gauge the potential effects of possible vice presidential nominees, yet it was 30 years ago that Danny Adkison (1982, 334) published his well-known article, "The Electoral Significance of the Vice Presidency," and concluded, "This study has shown that the tendency is for the vice presidential candidate to hurt rather than help the ticket." The major exception, according to Adkison, is when a presidential candidate can convince an "extremely popular" figure with a "loyal following" to join his ticket. Since it will be nearly impossible to find just such a person to accept the role, it is usually best to choose a "non-controversial, relatively unknown person for a running mate" (Adkison 1982, 334).

No matter what successes or failures campaigns have encountered in these regards, two recent developments have highlighted the increased importance of the selection of vice presidential candidates. First, Americans witnessed the central and controversial role of Dick Cheney in governing during the George W. Bush administration. As a result, supporters and detractors alike recognized the potential for the institutionalization of this newly developed position of importance in future administrations. This was highlighted by Democratic vice presidential nominee Joe Biden in the 2008 vice presidential debate, where he assailed Vice President Cheney as "one of the most dangerous vice presidents" in history (CNN 2008). This leads to the second development, the heightened scrutiny of John McCain's campaign for its selection of Sarah Palin. The choice of Governor Palin, a perceived "lightweight" in presidential politics, came at a time when the role of vice president seemed more extensive than ever, and when our country was still in the midst of two wars and an economic crisis.

Given these developments, this chapter explores the impact of vice presidential candidates Paul Ryan and Joe Biden in the 2012 presidential election. It examines how the vice presidential candidates enhanced or minimized the strategies of the two campaigns. How did the campaigns utilize their vice presidential candidates, and were these strategies successful? In particular, this chapter will examine the decisions by the presidential candidates to choose Paul Ryan and Joe Biden as their running mates, the acceptance speeches of the two candidates, the developments that resulted from the vice presidential debate on October 11, and the success (or lack thereof) in the constituency groups and states targeted by the vice presidential candidates.

THE SELECTION OF PAUL RYAN

In selecting Paul Ryan, chair of the House Budget Committee, as his running mate, political pundits agreed that Mitt Romney made a calculated, but uncharacteristically risky, campaign decision. Analysts identified several factors that likely contributed to the Romney campaign's decision, but chief among these factors seemed to have been a desire to focus the campaign squarely on the federal budget and the economy. Prior to the selection of Ryan, the Romney campaign conspicuously lacked policy specificity and had offered few concrete proposals to the electorate. In contrast, Ryan's political career had been marked by his willingness to articulate specific proposals to stem the rise of the federal deficit, namely his 2010 "Roadmap for America's Future" budget plan and the subsequent "Path to Prosperity." By choosing Ryan, Romney hoped that the federal deficit would be an impossible issue for the Obama campaign to ignore. Chris Cillizza (2012) of *The Washington Post* asserted that the Romney campaign bet its success on the fact that the American electorate would embrace the Republican vision for America's economic future and decide that the budget deficit must be addressed sooner rather than later. Echoing the mantra of his fellow Republicans who took the House of Representatives in 2010, Ryan sent the message that America could no longer ignore its deficit problem. In a speech at Miami University in Ohio, Ryan confirmed this, saying, "We want this debate. We need this debate. And we will win this debate" (Sonmez and Gardner 2012).

By aligning himself with the controversial but articulate Ryan, Romney made the distinction between himself and Obama far clearer. With Ryan, the Romney campaign gained an indisputable vision for the future, one that offered the American electorate a referendum on whether it would embrace the vision set forth by Obama or that of Romney and Ryan. As Dan Balz (2012b) pointed out, Romney did not run on Ryan's specific budget plan, but he aligned himself with the individual who produced that plan. Ryan was renowned for his proactiveness in seeking policy modifications, and Romney hoped to communicate that he would be equally proactive as president.

The speculation surrounding vice presidential nominations inevitably examines how a candidate will appeal to particular demographics, and the selection of Paul Ryan also faced such scrutiny. Like Romney, Paul Ryan was a white male, so Romney did not intend to diversify his ticket in terms of race or gender. Ryan, however, did differ from Romney in several key ways. During the grueling Republican nomination process, Romney's Mormon faith was a much-discussed topic. The social conservative faction of the Republican Party consisted primarily of Christians, and particularly evangelicals. As a practicing Catholic, Ryan did not belong to the ranks of conservative evangelicals, but his pious commitment to his faith greatly appealed to that demographic, along with Catholics in key battleground states throughout the Rust Belt—or at least so Romney hoped. Peter Nicholas and Mark Peters (2012) noted that "The Romney campaign likely believes that Ryan's faith will be a political asset, particularly in battleground states such as Wisconsin, Michigan and Pennsylvania, with heavy Catholic populations." In many ways, the selection of Paul Ryan allowed Governor Romney to appeal to those who had supported Rick Santorum in the primaries.

More skeptical pundits have proposed that Romney chose Ryan out of anxiety because he was trailing Obama in the polls. At the time of the selection, *The New York Times* cited Romney as trailing Obama by three points nationwide (Silver 2012). Romney took a considerable risk in selecting the controversial Ryan, but he also gained the potential to reinvigorate his campaign and energize the Republican base. Undoubtedly, after weeks of speculation about who Romney would choose, the Romney campaign did not select Ryan without full awareness of the risks involved. As conservative columnist Ross Douthat (2012) noted, "Romney's choice of Ryan looks a lot like Ryan's own policy positioning: It was more politically risky than the alternatives, but it was also more responsible. As a presidential candidate, Romney picked his running mate the way he probably made hiring decisions as a businessman. Out of an array of qualified applicants, he picked the man who's done the most impressive and important work."

PAUL RYAN AT THE REPUBLICAN NATIONAL CONVENTION

Congressman Ryan's acceptance speech at the Republican National Convention was an articulation of the Romney campaign's strategy and reflected many of the reasons why Romney selected Ryan as his running mate. In the very first line of his speech, Ryan (2012) declared, "I accept the duty to help lead our nation out of a jobs crisis and back to prosperity." The entire address embodied the Romney campaign's desire to focus the election on jobs and the economy—topics Ryan was seemingly well equipped to address. While Ryan stressed the unity of the Romney-Ryan ticket, he also went to great lengths to demonstrate the complementary differences between himself and Governor Romney. A chief critique of Romney throughout the campaign cycle was his perceived inability to sympathize and empathize with the average American voter. The Romney campaign struggled to portray the wealthy Romney as an accessible candidate for the majority of Americans, and Ryan sought to fill this void in his acceptance speech. He described his life in a small town in Wisconsin, saying, "I live on the same block where I grew up. We belong to the same parish where I was baptized. Janesville is that kind of place" (Ryan 2012). Later in the speech he spoke of "waiting tables, washing dishes, or mowing lawns for money" in his pursuit of the American Dream as a young man (Ryan 2012). Ryan attempted to convey a down-to-earth persona that would appeal to the typical American struggling to scrape by in a difficult economy. The intended inference was that if he, as an average, middle-class American could embrace Romney's vision for America, so too could others in comparable situations.

Ryan also acknowledged the generational gap between himself and Romney and sought to use it to his advantage. He made light of the age difference when he discussed the discrepancy between their musical preferences, as he mentioned his affinity for rock bands AC/DC and Led Zeppelin. Furthermore, as a father of three young children, Ryan's concern for the fate of the younger generations was conveyed with immediacy. This was a fate he pledged to actively preserve in saying, "I accept the calling of my generation to give our children the America that was given to us" (Ryan 2012). Despite their generational differences, Ryan emphasized that he and Romney shared the same vision for placing America on a path to economic recovery. The Republican ticket was portrayed as a melding of various generations coming together for the common purpose of preserving America's future. This was a picture that Ryan repeatedly attempted to contrast against Obama's previous four years. In one of the most memorable lines of his address, he claimed, "College graduates should not have to live out their 20s in their childhood bedrooms, staring up at fading Obama posters and wondering when they can move out and get going with life" (Ryan 2012). Ryan's speech set out to articulate a vision starkly opposed to that of President Obama in order to give voters a clear ideological decision on Election Day.

Ultimately, however, the stark contrast Ryan offered in his speech was largely a rhetorical one, as it pitted the Obama administration against a rather vague Romney-Ryan vision. There seem to be several reasons why Ryan chose to avoid specific proposals. Most obviously, Ryan was speaking at his party's convention, a venue more comparable to a pep rally than a serious policy debate. A speech with many policy specifics would have been out of place in such a context. While Ryan's speech did include some specific statistics on Obama's performance and the economy under Obama's administration, there was little in the way of policy prescriptions that Romney would implement. As a politician, Ryan delivered a political speech, choosing to focus on the promise of the Romney campaign rather than a less appealing message of necessary spending cuts and fiscal austerity.

Ryan's discussion of the Medicare issue also provided insight into why his speech lacked detail. As chair of the House Budget Committee and architect of two budget plans, the restructuring of Medicare had become Ryan's calling card. No one dared go to the level of specificity that Ryan achieved with his budget plans, yet in his speech, his Medicare plan was noticeably neglected. Ryan asserted that he and Romney would preserve Medicare for future generations, but he gave no description of how this would be done. Although the absence of specifics was largely due to the context of the speech, Ryan also appeared to avoid any specificity that would upstage his running mate. At the time of Ryan's selection, Fred Barnes (2012b) of *The Washington Post* noted, "Never before has a vice presidential candidate become a central figure in a presidential race." Given the media's fascination with Sarah Palin in 2008, this may be a bit of an exaggeration by Barnes. Nevertheless, the announcement of Ryan proved to be a critical development within the campaign. Ryan's controversial record and popularity quickly made him the object of much of the nation's attention to the race. While this attention was initially somewhat beneficial, no campaign wishes the focus to shift away from its presidential candidate. If Ryan were to speak of his Medicare plan in detail, he would have bound the Romney campaign to his vision rather than that of Romney himself. By speaking in sweeping language without specifics, Ryan ensured that Romney would have room to articulate his own vision for the country. In spite of Ryan's limitation on this one critical issue, it appears that the Romney campaign chose Ryan based on the perception that Ryan had the ability to connect with Middle America, social conservatives, and voters in critical battleground states in the upper Midwest.

THE RENOMINATION OF JOE BIDEN

As the incumbent, President Obama's decision to nominate Joe Biden to be his vice presidential nominee came over four years ago. Just two days prior to the 2008 Democratic National Convention, presidential nominee-to-be Barack Obama announced (via a text message to supporters) that Senator Joe Biden, previously a critic of Obama's inexperience, would be his vice presidential nominee. At the time, Adam Nagourney and Jeff Zeleny (2008) of *The New York Times* suggested, "Mr. Obama's choice of Mr. Biden suggested some of the weaknesses the Obama campaign is trying to address at a time when national polls suggest that his race with Senator John McCain, the presumptive Republican nominee, is tightening." The article noted Biden's extensive experience on the Senate Foreign Relations Committee, his harsh criticism of the Bush administration's policies in Iraq, his working-class background, his Roman Catholic faith, and his familiarity with voters in Pennsylvania (where Biden had grown up). In addition, Biden provided the Obama campaign with a wealth of experience in Washington, D.C., something notably missing from candidate Obama's resume. David Axelrod (2009, 73) later argued that Biden "turned out to be a great pick for us" because voters wanted an experienced individual around Obama who could help Obama implement the change he had promised. Furthermore, Axelrod (2009, 73) explained that Biden "was someone from Scranton, Pennsylvania, who had a great profile with middle class voters and spoke to them in a compelling way."

As we look at the 2012 campaign, it should come as no surprise that the Obama campaign looked for Vice President Biden to fill the same roles, but there had been from time to time the question as to whether Biden should remain on the ticket. Former Democratic governor of Virginia Douglas Wilder argued on December 20, 2011, that Obama should drop Biden from the ticket. He suggested that Biden's original purposes for being on the ticket were his wealth of foreign policy experience and his ability to get things accomplished in the Senate, and neither of these had truly helped the Obama administration. Further, some observers considered Biden's continued gaffes too risky for President Obama as he geared up for reelection (Real Clear Politics 2011). There were also questions regarding Biden's future because of his disagreement with the president on the raid that led to the killing of Osama bin Laden. Still, while Internet rumors spread of a possible vice presidential nomination of either Hillary Clinton or Andrew Cuomo, there is no solid evidence to suggest President Obama came close to taking such action. The most likely time for such a break probably would have been in mid-August 2012, after Vice President Biden infamously said of the Republican ticket, "They gonna put y'all back in chains" (Halper 2012). According to CNN and *The Weekly Standard*, a senior advisor in the Obama campaign noted that Biden's comments were "not helpful" and "knocked them off track" (Halper 2012). But as Stephen Hess, a staffer in both the Eisenhower and Nixon administrations, told Elias Groll (2011) of *Politico*, by dropping a vice president from the ticket, a president admits that he made a major mistake. In particular, Hess explained how President Nixon would have preferred to drop Spiro Agnew from the ticket in 1972, but "He couldn't dump him because to dump shows that the president has made a mistake of such magnitude—that he couldn't even pick someone who could be president. . . . Really, it comes down to [the fact] that presidents are not about to admit an error—if indeed it is an error" (Groll 2011).

Consequently, even after Biden's mid-August gaffe, the White House quickly denounced calls by Republicans, including Senator McCain and Governor Palin, to remove Biden from the ticket. Rather than focus on the verbal mishaps of the vice president, the Obama campaign saw the continued strengths of keeping Biden on the ticket. He could continue to help in the Obama campaign's appeal to middle-class voters, especially in states like Iowa and Ohio. He could play the role of "attack dog" on President Obama's rival Mitt Romney. In fact, this can be linked to the first strategy, as Vice President Biden would be utilized to paint Governor Romney as an out-of-touch, wealthy businessman whose policies would hurt, rather than help, the middle class. Lastly, Biden had been a loyal vice president, and his experience could continue to give credibility to the Obama administration. Not surprisingly, Vice President Biden's acceptance speech zeroed in on these exact strategies. His speech emphasized President Obama's defense of the middle class by saving the auto industry, President Obama's steady leadership in foreign policy (which led to the killing of Osama bin Laden), and evidence of Governor Romney's anti-middle-class background from his days at Bain Capital.

JOE BIDEN AT THE DEMOCRATIC NATIONAL CONVENTION

Because the electorate was already familiar with Joe Biden, his acceptance speech focused much more on President Obama. In particular, the vice president delivered an acceptance speech that portrayed himself more as a privileged witness to the presidency of Barack Obama than a key player in the administration. His speech emphasized the courageous and responsible leadership of Barack Obama over the last four years, contrasting Obama's leadership with that of Mitt Romney. Biden depicted Obama as the people-oriented leader that America needed and characterized Romney as a dispassionate business executive. Biden's tale of the Obama presidency was told through two central events—the bailout of the automobile industry and the killing of Osama bin Laden—both of which illustrated (in Biden's telling) why America needed four more years of Barack Obama.

Biden's speech described Obama's handling of the automobile industry as a microcosm of the president's economic leadership. With much of America's automobile industry on the verge of collapse, the vice president explained how Obama stepped in to "rescue" the industry and "saved more than a million American jobs" in the process (Biden 2012a). Surprisingly, the vice president recounted Obama's presidential heroics from the perspective of a bystander in a "ringside seat." Biden spoke entirely to affirm Barack Obama's leadership and said little of his own role in leading America through its financial crisis. During his address, Biden existed only in the form of personal anecdotes to illustrate the wisdom of Obama's leadership. He described his own life in a blue-collar household with a father who worked as a manager in the automobile industry. Biden's mention of his father personalized President Obama's actions and highlighted their impact on the lives of many Americans. Despite pressure to abandon the automobile industry, Obama chose to "step up" and save the industry regardless of the risk involved (Biden 2012a).

Beyond affirming Obama's leadership, Biden's discussion of the automobile crisis also served as an indictment of Governor Romney's leadership. While Obama viewed the crisis in terms of helping people and preserving jobs, Romney "saw it in terms of balance sheets and write-offs" (Biden 2012a). This is an approach Biden deemed the "Bain way" (Biden 2012a). Throughout the election cycle, Romney took pride in his status as a businessman who understood how the economy functions. In his speech, Biden attempted to turn this image on its head. America did not need a business executive; it needed a devoted and concerned leader like Barack Obama. Biden asserted, "The Bain way may bring your firm the highest profits. But it's not the way to lead our country from the highest office" (Biden 2012a). Effective financial leadership in the private sector does not necessarily translate into strong presidential leadership, Biden contended. Governor Romney's primary concern was his own bottom line, but President Obama placed the greatest value on the welfare of the American people.

Biden's second example of the president's leadership was the U.S. military's success in killing Osama bin Laden during Obama's first term. He said, "Barack understood that the search for bin Laden was about a lot more than taking a monstrous leader off the battlefield.... It was about righting an unspeakable wrong. Literally, it was about healing...a nearly unbearable wound in America's heart" (Biden 2012a). While eliminating bin Laden was unlikely to make a tactical impact for the U.S. military, it made an immeasurable difference in remedying the wound that America had suffered. According to Biden, President Obama was not limited by cost-benefit analysis; he understood the need to uphold the American spirit by taking down bin Laden. Governor Romney, however, would be unable to see beyond the immediate logistical situation as president of the United States. Biden (2012a) derided him, saying, "When he was asked about bin Laden in 2007, here's what he said. He said it's not worth moving heaven and earth and spending billions of dollars just to catch one person." Biden depicted Romney as a pragmatic businessman who lacked Barack Obama's unique combination of courage, compassion, and resolve that make him such an ideal leader.

As might have been expected from the incumbent vice president, Joe Biden's role at the DNC was a distinctly supplementary one. He gave no reasons why he had been an effective vice president—only reasons why Barack Obama should remain president. He gave no specifics on the policies of a second Obama-Biden administration, only illustrations of Obama's capable leadership during his first term. He did not discuss the direction or destination of America's "journey of hope," only the contention that Barack Obama was the man who could bring that journey to its completion. Biden's speech portrayed Obama as an ideal leader whom he had been privileged to observe for the past four years and whose leadership America would be foolish to reject for the coming four years.

ASSESSMENT OF VP DEBATE

Following the two conventions, although the two vice presidential candidates campaigned furiously throughout the battleground states, it was not until October 11 that Ryan and Biden once again took center stage. Due to the perceived momentum shift (in favor of Romney) coming out of the first presidential debate held on October 3, the vice presidential debate on October 11 appeared to take on increased importance. Two days prior to the vice presidential debate, Dan Balz (2012a) of *The Washington Post* wrote, "Rarely has a vice presidential debate been as crucial as the one between Vice President Biden and Rep. Paul Ryan on Thursday night will be. After Mitt Romney's lopsided victory over President Obama in Denver last week, the exchange will arrive at a fluid and potentially pivotal moment in the campaign." *Politico*'s Mackenzie Weinger (2012) agreed. She noted, "Vice presidential debates are often seen as an October sideshow—an entertaining albeit mostly unimportant aspect of the presidential race—but it's now a different ballgame." Vice President Biden had the task of preventing further erosion of the Obama campaign's support. Jim Geraghty (2012) of *The National Review* explained, "While the Obama campaign can ride out a contentious, tied Biden-Ryan debate or a boring Biden-Ryan debate, a bad Biden-Ryan debate would reinforce the suddenly pervasive perception of an incumbent campaign in a tailspin." Representative Ryan, on the other hand, had the task of maintaining the support that the Romney campaign had gained since the first debate. Lastly, both candidates had the task of giving voters the confidence that they themselves could lead. Given Vice President Biden's history of gaffes and Representative Ryan's limited exposure on a national stage, there was a high level of unpredictability about the debate.

Maggie Haberman (2012) of *Politico* surmised that there were "7 Takeaways from the Danville Debate." She argued that "it was a brawl," "it was effectively a draw," there were misstatements of fact, jobs—surprisingly—were not the number one issue, Romney's 47 percent gaffe was highlighted, Martha Raddatz became part of the storyline, and the debate might have implications for the 2016 presidential race. The authors of this chapter believe the four most important developments from the debate were (1) Vice President Biden's demeanor, (2) the reenergizing of the Democratic base, (3) the lack of any overall momentum shift, and (4) Paul Ryan's ability to withstand the assault from Vice President Biden.

While not substantive, it seems that the biggest development coming out of the vice presidential debate was Vice President Biden's demeanor. In the immediate aftermath of the debate Jonathan Cohn (2012) of *The New Republic* aptly explained:

> Appearing in Danville, Kentucky on Thursday night, Vice President Biden gave one of the most aggressive, passionate, and substantive debate performances I can recall. I don't know how it played with the public as a whole and I don't imagine it influenced swing voters one way or another. If I had to bet, the media will spend at least as much time discussing Biden's facial expressions as they will dissecting the exchange over Iran.

Indeed, it seems the media and political pundits spent much more time on Biden's conduct than perhaps on all substantive issues combined. Byron York (2012) of *The Washington Examiner* stated, "Even though the 90-minute session covered Libya, Iran, Afghanistan, jobs, taxes, Social Security, Medicare, abortion, and several other issues, it was Biden's behavior that dominated the post-debate spin room." *Politico*'s Emily Schultheis (2012) authored an article entitled, "Is Joe Biden the New Al Gore?" In it, she chronicled the Romney's campaign's response that Biden was "unhinged," former Bush White House press secretary Ari Fleischer's comparison to Al Gore's "infamous sighs in the 2000 presidential debates against George W. Bush," Fox News's Brit Hume's reference to Biden as a "cranky old man," Representative Allen West's comment that Biden acted like a "rude curmudgeon," and CNN's Anderson Cooper's statement that Biden's facial expressions made it so viewers "could not turn away for a second."

Not surprisingly, the beauty of Vice President Biden's smile (and the nature of his behavior) was truly in the eye of the beholder. The critique from the political right was condemnatory. Barnes (2012b) argued, "You don't win a nationally televised debate by being rude and obnoxious. You don't win by interrupting your opponent time after time after time or by being a blowhard. You don't win with facial expressions, especially smirks or fake laughs, or by pretending to be utterly exasperated with what your opponent is saying." Similarly, former vice president Dick Cheney referred to Biden's display as "the most emotionally unstable debate performance in modern American politics" (Politi 2012).

But for every response like those from Barnes and Cheney, there was a response on the left like *The New Republic*'s "Biden Gave Democrats the Show They Wanted—and Needed" (Cohn 2012). That brings us to the second major development from the vice presidential debate—the reenergizing of the Democratic base. After President Obama's lackluster performance in the first presidential debate and the polls turning in the wrong direction for the Democratic ticket, Vice President Biden was tasked with securing the base. *Meet the Press* host David Gregory explained, "I think supporters of the president and Joe Biden will say, 'Hey, this was refreshing'" (Schultheis 2012). Perhaps more accurately, Gregory Krieg (2012) of ABC News observed, "Joe Biden drove a shot of adrenaline into the heart of the Democratic Party last night with the kind of persistent and colorful attack on the Romney ticket that President Obama had struggled to make just a week before," and E. J. Dionne (2012) of *The Washington Post* declared that Biden "May Have Saved [the] Obama Campaign."

Still, even with the reenergized base, the debate did not appear to cause any shift in the trajectory of the overall campaign. It seemed to have stopped the hemorrhaging for the Obama campaign, but Vice President Biden was not able to pull the momentum back into the Democrats' favor. Thus, we can conclude that the third important development of the vice presidential debate was the lack of a momentum shift. *The Washington Post* reported that in contrast to the first presidential debate, in the vice presidential debate there "was the absence of a clear winner," and thus, "With the race tighter than it was two weeks ago, Thursday's debate is not likely to result in a significant shift toward either Obama or Romney but is likely to raise the stakes when the two meet next week for their second forum" (Balz and Rucker 2012).

Lastly, while this was not a part of the major narrative found in the press, it is important to point out that Paul Ryan held steady as he faced a pugnacious and aggressive challenger. We should not lose sight of the fact that Congressman Ryan had never been in a situation like this. He was up against a sitting vice president and two-time presidential candidate, and—while this may set the bar low—Ryan at least proved he was not a potential liability like Dan Quayle or Sarah Palin. Instead, he stood (or sat) toe-to-toe with Vice President Biden, and with the exception of Vice President Biden's use of the terms "stuff" and "malarkey," arguably the most memorable line in the debate came from Congressman Ryan. When Biden attempted to utilize Mitt Romney's infamous "47 percent" line to prove the Romney-Ryan ticket did not care about average Americans, Ryan quickly countered, "Mitt Romney's a good man. He cares about 100 percent in this country, and with respect to that quote, I think the vice president very well knows that sometimes the words don't come out of your mouth the right way" (NPR 2012). In fact, in examining Representative Ryan's performance, it should be noted that had he performed poorly, the narrative of the campaign might have changed. Thus, while his performance did not give the Romney campaign additional momentum, he also performed at a high enough level that his performance was not savaged the way President Obama's was in the first presidential debate.

THE STRATEGIC USE OF RYAN AND BIDEN: TARGETED CONSTITUENCY GROUPS

The style of the two vice presidential candidates in the debate clearly showed the differences in their personalities. However, as much as Congressman Ryan and Vice President Biden would most likely point out the crucial differences between themselves, both in personality and ideology, the case can be made that the Obama and Romney campaigns largely used the same strategies for the two candidates. As previously indicated, Barack Obama chose Joe Biden in 2008 not only for his foreign policy experience and his longevity in Washington, D.C., but also because of his ability to appeal to blue-collar, rural, middle-class, white voters (and to some extent, Catholics). The same was true this time around with Paul Ryan. All of the targeted populations just mentioned were groups that the Romney campaign hoped that Congressman Ryan could bring over to its camp. Furthermore, the two campaigns specifically targeted the same states with their vice presidential candidates (mainly Ohio, Wisconsin, and Iowa).

Vice President Biden on the Campaign Trail

If the strategic use of Vice President Biden needed to be summed up in one line, it would simply be this: President Obama fights for the middle class and Governor Romney does not understand or care about the middle class. Biden's appeal was illustrated in early September, when over a two-day period he rubbed elbows with a group of bikers in an Ohio bar and a station full of firefighters in Pennsylvania (Lee 2012). For the Obama campaign, it was stops like these that contrasted Biden's small-town roots with Governor Romney's affluent lifestyle. In fact, this became a central theme in Vice President Biden's rhetoric throughout the campaign. At a September 17 rally in Iowa, Biden asserted that an individual with Swiss bank accounts and millions of dollars offshore in the Cayman Islands simply could not identify with average Americans (Bendery 2012). Days later in New Hampshire, Biden followed up on this theme, as he began his assault on Governor Romney for his infamous "47 percent" comment. Biden argued that Romney's words and demeanor in the video proved that Romney simply did not understand middle-class Americans (Travis 2012b). Then the vice president turned the argument toward Governor Romney's 2011 tax return, where Romney paid an effective 14 percent tax rate. Biden exclaimed, "He made over $13 million in income, almost all from investments which he paid in 17 percent or less....He got millions, he has millions stashed in tax havens like Bermuda and the Cayman Islands. The guy had a Swiss bank account. He refuses to release

10 years of his tax returns, which he demanded of his running mate?" (Travis 2012a).

Consequently, the Obama campaign was optimistic that Joe Biden could make the case that Governor Romney was simply out of touch and unconcerned with the middle class. Biden described how the middle class had been buried by the latest recession (Walshe 2012), that the middle class has "shouldered enough of the burden" (Korfhage 2012), and that President Obama's policies for a second term would provide the security that the middle class needed (Biden 2012b; Opoien and Bollier 2012). In fact, as the campaign dragged on, Biden eventually pinned the same "out-of-touch" label on Congressman Ryan (Saenz 2012).

Ultimately, Vice President Biden attacked Romney's aloofness to hammer home a key point—Governor Romney would not stand with American workers, especially those in the manufacturing sector. This could be seen in Biden's attacks on Romney for outsourcing, where he utilized a *Washington Post* article that described Mitt Romney, while at Bain Capital, as one of the pioneers of outsourcing, and Biden repeated his convention speech punch line that if Romney were elected and decided to take a "jobs tour, it's going to have to be a foreign trip" (Sweeny 2012). Throughout the campaign, this message from Biden focused particularly on the automobile industry (Noble 2012). His attacks sharpened in the waning days of the campaign, largely because of an ad by the Romney campaign in Ohio, where Romney tried to discredit the government auto bailout by claiming both Chrysler and General Motors planned to ship jobs overseas. Even in Congressman Ryan's own backyard, Biden emphasized the importance of the auto bailout by the Obama administration. Biden argued, "I know the guy next door doesn't recognize it, but we actually did rescue the automobile industry and saved a million jobs, a million jobs saved and 200,000 new jobs continuing to expand" (Saenz 2012). Two days later while at a campaign stop in Ohio, the vice president reiterated that not only did the Obama administration stand with the autoworkers, but Biden himself was a product of the auto industry. In particular, he argued, "I am the son of an automobile man—34 years my dad managed an automobile dealership.... Anybody in the automobile business whether they're on the line or in sales can tell you: if you're a child of an automobile man or woman, you're the first kid in the neighborhood to learn the definition of the word recession and then the last kid to understand what recovery means. We finally got some recovery going" (Lin 2012).

Congressman Ryan on the Campaign Trail

Interestingly, the strategies employed by the Romney campaign with regard to Representative Ryan largely paralleled the Obama campaign's utilization of Vice President Biden. Congressman Ryan continually emphasized how he was a product of the middle class and that he understood small-town America. This was illustrated by the places he visited. Not only did he go to battleground states where white, middle-class, blue-collar voters were critical, but he continually held events at locations that exemplified "small-town" America (Jacobs 2012). He visited places like Piedmont Precision Machine Company in Virginia (Dashiell 2012) and Lindsey's Bakery in Ohio (Ison 2012). He held an event with Kid Rock, where the Michigan rocker described Ryan as "a fellow hunter, a fellow fan of rock 'n' roll, a great Midwesterner who shares a vision not only with Mitt Romney, but also with myself, of what would be the best for our state and our country" (Gray and Zaniewski 2012). The message of Paul Ryan as a hunter, a fisherman, a product of a blue-collar town, and someone who would stand up for autoworkers, coal miners, and others in small-town and rural America became a central theme for the Romney campaign (Kelly 2012; Dashiell 2012). At a campaign stop in Youngstown, Ohio, Ryan explained, "Our part of Wisconsin is just like this part of Ohio. We need a strong manufacturing base in America if we want a strong middle class in America. We need to make more things in America and sell them overseas if we want to make sure we can keep good jobs and prosperity going in this country" (Grant 2012).

As the Romney campaign tried to establish Ryan's credibility with middle-class voters, this opened up the opportunity for the congressman to argue that this group of voters needed to change leadership in Washington, D.C., for their economic woes were the fault of the Obama administration. For instance, at a campaign event in Iowa, shortly after Vice President Biden's declaration that the middle class had been buried by the recession, Ryan remarked, "Of course the middle class has been buried. They are being buried by regulations, they are being buried by taxes…they are being buried by borrowing, they are being buried by the Obama administration's economic failures" (Walshe 2012). And according to Ryan, circumstances would only grow worse if Obama was reelected. Ryan lambasted the Obama administration for its assault on middle-class workers due to policies that Ryan argued hurt small businesses, as well as policies toward particular industries that affect blue-collar America, such as the increased taxes and regulations on the coal industry (Sincere 2012; Associated Press 2012).

But much of the final stretch of the campaign for Congressman Ryan once again paralleled that for Vice President Biden, as the auto bailout took center stage. At an October 28 event in Ohio, Ryan refined his critique of the Obama administration's bailout, asserting that as a result, certain groups received favoritism, while others suffered. Ryan argued, "You see the president likes to go around Ohio talking about how he saved the auto industry, how the auto bailout was such a success. Tell you what: He hasn't talked to these Oak Creek salaried employees, he hasn't talked to these Ohio Delphi salaried employees, because this is one of those examples of the government picking winners and losers" (Shepherd 2012). He continued with this same line of reasoning as he made his final stops in Wisconsin and Iowa (Beard 2012). And as Ryan made his closing argument in Ohio, he not only criticized the Obama administration's handling of the auto industry, but he returned full circle, as he reminded voters that he was "one of them." Ryan argued that what Ohioans had gone through was the same thing that his close friends went through in Wisconsin: "A lot of friends of mine from high school that I grew up with lost their jobs. It's not going the right way in some places in America, and you know what, it doesn't have to be like this. We don't have to settle for this. This may be the best that President Obama can do but it is not the best that America can do" (Lin 2012).

THE STRATEGIC USE OF RYAN AND BIDEN: BATTLEGROUND STATES

In addition to the similar messages and similar targeted groups, as the authors of this chapter assessed the role of the vice presidential candidates in the campaigns, we found additional similarities regarding where the campaigns sent their vice presidential candidates. Table 3.1

shows data compiled from *The Washington Post*'s tally of campaign visits by each candidate.[1] Based on the data provided, following the announcement of Paul Ryan as Governor Romney's vice presidential candidate on August 12, the presidential and vice presidential candidates made appearances at a total of 397 campaign-related events in 23 different states.[2] However, there were only seven states with over 25 events, which we report in Table 3.1.[3]

Table 3.1 Total Campaign Events by Candidates to Battleground States, August 12–November 6, 2012

State	Total Events	Ryan Events	Romney Events	Biden Events	Obama Events
Ohio	95	19	33	23	19
Florida	58	7	22	14	15
Virginia	51	12	22	8	9
Iowa	42	9	8	9	15
Wisconsin	28	10	3	9	6
Colorado	28	8	9	4	7
New Hampshire	25	2	4	12	7

Source: Presidential Campaign Stops: Who's Going Where, *The Washington Post* [Online]. Available at http://www.washingtonpost.com/wp-srv/special/politics/2012-presidential-campaign-visits/.

Naturally, these data only scratch the surface. What we found intriguing were the changes in campaign appearances throughout the 12 weeks from the Paul Ryan announcement until Election Day. Such differences (and potentially campaign strategies) emerge more starkly in Tables 3.2, 3.3, and 3.4.

Table 3.2 Total Campaign Events by Candidates to Battleground States, August 12–September 8, 2012

State	Total Events	Ryan Events	Romney Events	Biden Events	Obama Events
Ohio	15	4	4	5	2
Florida	11	3	4	1	3
Virginia	12	4	2	3	3
Iowa	18	3	2	1	12
Wisconsin	4	2	1	1	0
Colorado	3	2	0	0	1
New Hampshire	9	1	2	3	3

Source: Presidential Campaign Stops: Who's Going Where, *The Washington Post* [Online]. Available at http://www.washingtonpost.com/wp-srv/special/politics/2012-presidential-campaign-visits/.

Table 3.3 Total Campaign Events by Candidates to Battleground States,
September 9–October 6, 2012

State	Total Events	Ryan Events	Romney Events	Biden Events	Obama Events
Ohio	23	3	7	6	7
Florida	21	0	9	5	7
Virginia	14	4	6	1	3
Iowa	10	5	0	5	0
Wisconsin	5	1	0	1	3
Colorado	10	2	6	0	2
New Hampshire	8	1	0	7	0

Source: Presidential Campaign Stops: Who's Going Where, *The Washington Post* [Online]. Available at http://www.washingtonpost.com/wp-srv/special/politics/2012-presidential-campaign-visits/.

Table 3.4 Total Campaign Events by Candidates to Battleground States,
October 7–November 6, 2012

State	Total Events	Ryan Events	Romney Events	Biden Events	Obama Events
Ohio	57	12	22	13	10
Florida	26	4	9	8	5
Virginia	25	4	14	4	3
Iowa	14	2	6	3	3
Wisconsin	19	7	2	7	3
Colorado	15	4	3	4	4
New Hampshire	8	0	2	2	4

Source: Presidential Campaign Stops: Who's Going Where, *The Washington Post* [Online]. Available at http://www.washingtonpost.com/wp-srv/special/politics/2012-presidential-campaign-visits/.

In the first four weeks following the announcement of Ryan, the differences between the Romney and Ryan schedules appear negligible. Nevertheless, it is worth noting that following the announcement of Ryan as Romney's running mate, rather than making joint appearances, Ryan traveled to Iowa and Romney to Florida. The campaign suggested these were preplanned events and it was not because the campaign hoped to prevent a negative reaction to Ryan among Florida's high concentration of seniors due to his budget plan's cuts to Medicare. However, Ryan's first campaign event in Florida was a joint appearance with his mother at a senior community on August 18, and while he made two more appearances in Florida between August 18 and September 8, during the second four-week period reported in Table 3.3 he made no appearances in Florida. Regarding the Obama campaign, during this initial stage of the campaign there are two notable differences: President Obama made 12 appearances in Iowa, compared to only one by the vice president, while Vice President Biden made five appearances in Ohio, compared to two by the president.

The real differences in campaign travel are apparent in Tables 3.3 and 3.4. During this second four-week period, the two campaigns combined for a total of 21 trips to Florida, but Ryan was not involved in any appearances there. On the other hand, the campaigns made 10 trips to Iowa, but all 10 events were handled by the vice presidential candidates. In addition, the campaigns made six trips to Nevada, but all six events were handled by the presidential candidates. Finally, there were eight events in New Hampshire, but seven of these were lone appearances by Vice President Biden. Regarding the final four weeks, the only notable disparity in travel was in Wisconsin, where the two campaigns had a total of 19 events, but 14 were handled by the vice presidential candidates.

We must ask the simple question: Does any of this matter? We believe that it does. Before hypothesizing about the potential reasons for these travel patterns, we offer one additional table, Table 3.5.

Table 3.5 Total Events by Campaigns to Battleground States, August 12–November 6, 2012

State	Romney-Ryan Events	Obama-Biden Events
Ohio	52	42
Florida	29	29
Virginia	34	17
Iowa	17	24
Wisconsin	13	15
Colorado	17	11
New Hampshire	6	19
	Total = 168	Total = 157

Source: Presidential Campaign Stops: Who's Going Where, *The Washington Post* [Online]. Available at http://www.washingtonpost.com/wp-srv/special/politics/2012-presidential-campaign-visits/.

The figures in Table 3.5 are quite remarkable. In the final four weeks of the campaign, while Ryan, Biden, and Obama participated in 40, 44, and 41 events, respectively, Romney participated in 64. In spite of this disparity, the total number of events held by each campaign between August 12 and November 6 was 168 to 157, narrowly in favor of the Romney campaign. But the specific numbers begin to address the strategies of the two campaigns. While their total numbers of events in the battleground states parallel one another, the state-by-state comparison paints a different picture. Romney's increased travels in the final four weeks account for the difference in Ohio, Florida is identical, and Wisconsin would not be considered statistically significant. However, the Romney-Ryan ticket accounted for 67 percent of the events in Virginia and 60 percent of the events in Colorado, while the Obama-Biden ticket accounted for 76 percent of the events in New Hampshire and 59 percent of the events in Iowa.

Based on these initial figures, there are three brief takeaways. First, as we all expected, the two campaigns recognized the importance of both Ohio and Florida. Second, the Romney-Ryan campaign spent more resources trying to ensure victories in two states that account for 21 electoral votes (Virginia and Colorado), while the Obama-Biden campaign intriguingly spent a great deal of energy to win 10 electoral votes (New Hampshire and Iowa). Third, in the eyes of the two campaigns, Wisconsin truly was a battleground state. Although no Republican had won the state since President Reagan in 1984, both campaigns recognized its importance in 2012.

CONCLUSION

While we understand that voters traditionally do not determine their votes simply based on a presidential candidate's vice presidential selection, we can examine the strategies utilized by campaigns and assess their overall success. In analyzing the results of 2012, we have come to four conclusions.

First, while we cannot know for certain if President Obama gained votes because of his decision to keep Joe Biden on the ticket, given that in elections winning is the primary criterion, we conclude that Obama's inclusion of Biden on the ticket was a success. As explained in our analysis, Vice President Biden helped the president appeal to key constituency groups in Pennsylvania, Ohio, Michigan, Iowa, and Wisconsin, all states won by the Obama-Biden campaign.[4] Moreover, unlike the Romney campaign's decision to keep Ryan's visits to Florida to a minimum, there is no clear evidence that the Obama campaign felt the vice president was a liability in any of the swing states. Biden also was widely credited with reenergizing the Democratic base during the vice presidential debate, which was crucial after President Obama's lackluster performance in the first presidential debate. While conservatives disparaged Biden for his behavior and demeanor, polling data did not indicate a resulting negative shift in the electorate. Lastly, by keeping Biden on the ticket, President Obama illustrated steady resolve, the exact image he needed to convey to the electorate during the adverse circumstances the country had faced over the past four years. As outlined by Groll (2011), a decision to remove Biden would have been an admission to the public that President Obama's original choice was a mistake, and that would have undermined the central tenet of the reelection campaign—"Forward."

Second, if the reason why Governor Romney chose Representative Ryan was an effort to reach out to key constituency groups and win crucial battleground states, this strategy was a failure. This conclusion in no way diminishes Representative Ryan's political abilities or his supporters' recognition of his expertise in number crunching. However, the evidence does suggest that the strategies employed by the Romney campaign through its use of Paul Ryan were clearly not successful (assuming that winning is the goal). We believe there are two states worth examining in more detail: Wisconsin and Iowa. Given that both Governor Romney and Congressman Ryan campaigned extensively in Ohio and Virginia, and the fact that Governor Romney held more events in both of these states than Congressman Ryan, we should not view Congressman Ryan as the linchpin for the campaign's strategies in these two states. Wisconsin and Iowa are a different story. Not surprisingly, since Ryan is a native son of Wisconsin, he held 10 events there, compared to Romney's three, and although Romney eventually held eight events in Iowa, six of these came in the final four weeks of the campaign. Consequently, Wisconsin and Iowa appear to be the two states where the Romney campaign hoped to utilize Ryan to change the dynamics of the race.

On this point, however, the question remains, how do we gauge success? We can start by looking at the raw vote counts in each of these states. Table 3.6 begins to tell the story.

Table 3.6 Presidential Popular Vote Totals in Wisconsin and Iowa, 2004–2012

State	2004	2008	2012
Wisconsin	Kerry 1,489,504 Bush 1,478,020	Obama 1,677,211 McCain 1,262,393	Obama 1,613,950 Romney 1,408,745
Iowa	Kerry 741,898 Bush 751,957	Obama 828,940 McCain 682,379	Obama 816,429 Romney 727,928

Source: 2012 Presidential Election Results, *The Washington Post* [Online]. Available at http://www.washingtonpost.com/wp-srv/special/politics/election-map-2012/president/.

In examining this data, at first we recognized some evidence of success for the Romney-Ryan ticket. After all, while nationwide Mitt Romney received approximately the same total number of popular votes as John McCain in 2008, in Wisconsin and Iowa his vote count increased significantly. However, when we compare popular vote totals in these two states to 2004, in both cases the Romney-Ryan ticket received fewer votes. In other words, even in his native state, where the 2010 gubernatorial election seemed to energize Republicans, Paul Ryan could not deliver as many votes to the Republican ticket as George W. Bush received in 2004. Consequently, the decision to include Paul Ryan on the ticket and to focus his events in Wisconsin and Iowa must be considered a failure. The campaign lost both states and could not return the Republican vote count to where it had been in 2004.

Third, if the reason why Governor Romney chose Representative Ryan was for ideological purposes, that too was a failure. We deem this a failure for two reasons: Romney's late campaign strategy to deliver a more moderate message and the Romney campaign's strategy to minimize the "Ryan Effect" in Florida. In the final weeks of the campaign, Governor Romney clearly tried to pivot to the center. He seemed confident that he would hold the conservative base, so with such a close election both nationally and in the battleground states, he believed that he needed to pull moderates and independents into his coalition. Alana Semuels (2012) of *The Los Angeles Times* stated that as the campaign rolled on, "somewhere along the way, Ryan became less prominent as Romney's message shifted from conservatism to bipartisanship." Semuels discussed this very notion with vice presidential expert Joel Goldstein who noted, "There's sort of a dance that they have to play—Romney's moving in a direction towards moderation that's away from Ryan.... They're trying to appeal to demographics where Ryan's positions would hurt them, but by the same token, they can't bury him because he's on the ticket, and a big part of the base likes the fact that he's on the ticket." To put it more bluntly, Matt Taylor (2012) of *The Daily Beast* accurately observed that "in the campaign's final days, Ryan was absent from the national conversation, and his impact on the race proved to be something of a dud." As Governor Romney tried to appeal to middle-of-the-road voters, especially suburban women, the staunchly pro-life Catholic known for his willingness to axe entitlements no longer seemed like the best teammate.

Fourth, this brings us to Florida. Prior to his vice presidential nomination, Congressman Ryan's notoriety came largely because of his reputation for fiscal discipline, which brought with it the fear that a Romney-Ryan administration would precipitate severe cuts in entitlements, especially Medicare. It appears that even the Romney campaign recognized this. While Biden, Obama, and Romney held 14, 15, and 22 events in Florida, Ryan only held seven, and three of these came in a short period in late August. In fact, there was a nearly six-week period when Ryan did not hold any events in Florida. Given the razor-thin margin in Florida, and the evidence that both campaigns recognized Florida as probably the second-most important state (after Ohio), the hesitation of the Romney campaign to utilize Ryan in Florida is damning. Given Governor Romney's final moderate push for suburban voters in Virginia and Pennsylvania, along with his perceived acknowledgement that Florida was a "must-win" for his campaign, we believe that any ideological reasons for including Paul Ryan on the ticket should also be considered failures.

An examination of the 2012 presidential election seems to confirm Adkison's (1982, 334) finding that unless a presidential candidate can convince an "extremely popular" figure with a "loyal following" to join his ticket, there is a high risk that the vice presidential candidate can "hurt rather than help the ticket." With President Obama, the safe selection of keeping Biden on the ticket seems to have been a wise decision. A switch would have shown vulnerability and brought additional risks to a campaign, which, based on the outcome, would have been unwarranted. In contrast, Governor Romney's calculated risk backfired. Instead, a "safer" selection by the Romney campaign would have been wiser. While Republicans partially attributed their failures in 2008 to John McCain being a weak candidate, he nonetheless won more popular votes than Mitt Romney, in spite of the questions surrounding Sarah Palin. Ryan's budget expertise and Midwestern, blue-collar roots proved of negligible value. Though we have no ability to know the answers to the "what ifs," Republican insiders are no doubt wondering what would have happened if Romney had chosen another budget guru in former OMB director and current Ohio senator Rob Portman. Would Ohio have gone to Romney? Or what if Romney had chosen the longtime frontrunner Senator Marco Rubio? Would Florida have been in play? Would this have helped the campaign reach out to Hispanic voters? Or in spite of her limited experience, could New Mexico governor Susana Martinez have given Romney a bridge to both women and Hispanics?

We acknowledge that it is impossible to know how much of an impact any of these potential running mates would have had on the campaign, but the numbers must be troubling to Republican insiders. The simple fact is this: four million fewer Americans came out to support President Obama in 2012 than did in 2008, but Governor Romney only received approximately 890,000 more votes than Senator McCain in 2008. If Governor Romney could have simply added in crucial states a significant portion of those voters who dropped from the Obama ranks, the United States might have a different president today. Given the state of the economy, this should not have been a daunting task. Although vice presidential selection may not determine electoral outcomes, in elections resembling that of 2012, campaign strategies are critical. It appears in this case that Obama made the safe choice and won; Romney took a risk and lost.

REFERENCES

Adkison, D. 1982. "The Electoral Significance of the Vice Presidency." *Presidential Studies Quarterly* 12: 330–336.

Associated Press. 2012. "VP Nominee Ryan, in Va., Criticizes Obama on Coal." *Virginian Pilot,* October 26. Retrieved from http://hamptonroads.com/2012/10/vp-nominee-ryan-va-criticizes-obama-coal.

Axelrod, D. 2009. "Campaign Organization and Strategy." *Electing the President 2008: The Annenberg Election Debriefing*, edited by K. Jamieson, 55–83. Philadelphia: University of Pennsylvania.

Balz, D. 2012a. "Big Stakes for Biden and Ryan in VP Debate." *Washington Post,* October 9. Retrieved from http://www.washingtonpost.com/politics /decision2012/big-stakes-for-biden-and-ryan-in-vp-debate/2012/10/09 /b24d55de-1249-11e2-be82-c3411b7680a9_story.html.

Balz, D. 2012b. "How Mitt Romney's Choice of Paul Ryan Has Reshaped Presidential Campaign." *Washington Post*, August 13. Retrieved from http://www .washingtonpost.com/politics/how-mitt-romneys-choice-of-paul-ryan-has -reshaped-presidential-campaign/2012/08/12/27062ad6-e496-11e1-936a -b801f1abab19_story.html.

Balz, D., and P. Rucker. 2012. "Biden, Ryan Trade Sharp Words on Foreign Policy, Economy During Vice-Presidential Debate." *Washington Post,* October 11. Retrieved from http://www.washingtonpost.com/politics/decision2012 /biden-ryan-debate-features-two-washington-veterans-with-very-different -styles/2012/10/11/6f24b4fa-13d4-11e2-bf18-a8a596df4bee_story.html?.

Barnes, F. 2012a. "Biden Bombed." *Weekly Standard,* October 12. Retrieved from http://www.weeklystandard.com/blogs/biden-bombed_654263.html.

Barnes, F. 2012b. "How Ryan Recasts the Race." *Wall Street Journal,* August 20. Retrieved from http://online.wsj.com/article /SB10000872396390443989204577601254048147454.html.

Beard, S. 2012. "Ryan: 'As Wisconsin goes, so goes America.'" *Hill,* October 31. Retrieved from http://thehill.com/blogs/ballot-box/presidential-races /265183-ryan-as-wisconsin-goes-so-goes-america.

Bendery, J. 2012. "Joe Biden Mocks Mitt Romney for Using Same Definition of Middle Class as Democrats." *Huffington Post,* September 17. Retrieved from http://www.huffingtonpost.com/2012/09/17/joe-biden-mitt-romney_n _1891814.html.

Biden, J. 2012a. "Transcript: Joe Biden's Acceptance Speech at the Democratic National Convention." September 6. Retrieved from http://www .realclearpolitics.com/articles/2012/09/06/joe_bidens_acceptance_speech_at _the_democratic_national_convention_115377.html.

Biden, J. 2012b. "We'll Create Jobs, Restore Security." *USA Today,* October 25. Retrieved from http://www.usatoday.com/story/opinion/2012/10/25/joe -biden-obama-agenda/1659191/.

Cillizza, C. 2012. "Mitt Romney Goes Bold (and Risky) with Paul Ryan Vice Presidential Pick." *Washington Post,* August 11. Retrieved from http://www .washingtonpost.com/blogs/the-fix/post/mitt-romney-goes-bold-and-risky -with-paul-ryan-vice-presidential-pick/2012/08/11/7a6a04c2-e38d-11e1-a25e -15067bb31849_blog.html.

CNN. 2008. "Biden Attacks Cheney." *CNN,* October 2. Retrieved from http:// politicalticker.blogs.cnn.com/2008/10/02/biden-attacks-cheney/.

Cohn, J. 2012. "Biden Gave Democrats the Show They Wanted—and Needed." *New Republic,* October 11. Retrieved from http://www.tnr.com/blog/plank/108502 /biden-ryan-debate-instant-analysis-medicare-taxes-47-percent-policy.

Dashiell, J. 2012. "Paul Ryan Defends Mitt Romney, Dismisses Presidential Campaign of Virgil Goode." *WDBJ7.com,* September 19. Retrieved from http:// www.wdbj7.com/news/wdbj7-paul-ryan-defends-mitt-romney-dismisses -presidential-campaign-of-virgil-goode-20120919,0,4232900.story.

Dionne, E. J. 2012. "Energized VP May Have Saved Obama Campaign." *Columbus Dispatch,* October 14. Retrieved from http://www.dispatch.com/content /stories/editorials/2012/10/14/energized-vp-may-have-saved-obama- campaign.html.

Douthat, R. 2012. "Why Moderates Should Like Paul Ryan." *New York Times,* August 14. Retrieved from http://campaignstops.blogs.nytimes.com/2012 /08/14/why-moderates-should-like-paul-ryan/.

Geraghty, J. 2012. "The Task Before Joe Biden." *National Review,* October 9. Retrieved from http://www.nationalreview.com/campaign-spot/329787 /task-joe-biden#.

Grant, T. 2012. "Ohio Crowd Greets Paul Ryan Enthusiastically." *Pittsburgh Post-Gazette,* October 14. Retrieved from http://www.post-gazette.com /stories/news/politics-national/ohio-crowd-greets-paul-ryan- enthusiastically-657453/.

Gray, K., and A. Zaniewski. 2012. "Kid Rock, Crowd of 4,000 Cheer VP Candidate Ryan at Oakland University." *Detroit Free Press,* October 8. Retrieved from http://www.freep.com/article/20121008/NEWS15/121008087/paul-ryan -michigan-visit?odyssey=nav%7Chead.

Groll, E. 2011. "Could Barack Obama Drop Joe Biden?" *Politico,* July 6. Retrieved from http://www.politico.com/news/stories/0711/58441.html.

Haberman, M. 2012. "7 Takeaways from the Danville Debate." *Politico,* October 12. Retrieved from http://www.politico.com/news/stories/1012/82325.html.

Halper, D. 2012. "Obama Has Plenty of Time to Drop Biden." *Weekly Standard,* August 15. Retrieved from http://www.weeklystandard.com/blogs/obama -has-22-days-drop-biden_650014.html.

Ison, J. 2012. "Ryan Stirs Up Some Support." *Chillicothe Gazette,* October 28. Retrieved from http://www.chillicothegazette.com/article/20121028/NEWS01 /310280007/Ryan-stirs-up-some-support?.

Jacobs, J. 2012. "Ryan to Visit Cities on Mississippi." *Des Moines Register,* October 1. Retrieved from http://www.desmoinesregister.com/article/20121001/NEWS09 /310010013/Ryan-to-visit-cities-on-Mississippi?.

Kelly, A. 2012. "GOP VP Candidate Paul Ryan Buys Hunting Kit for His 10-Year- Old Daughter." *Irish Central,* September 28. Retrieved from http://www .irishcentral.com/news/-GOP-VP-candidate-Paul-Ryan-buys-hunting-kit-for -his-10-year-old-daughter-171772121.html#axzz2BsXdZlLS.

Korfhage, S. 2012. "Biden Courts Middle Class Voters in St. Augustine Appearance." *St. Augustine Record,* October 20. Retrieved from http://staugustine.com

/news/local-news/2012-10-21/biden-courts-middle-class-voters-st-augustine
-appearance#.UJ8aleRlHqI.

Krieg, G. 2012. "Democrats Delight in Joe Biden's Vice Presidential Debate
Performance." *ABC News,* October 12. Retrieved from http://abcnews.go.com
/Politics/OTUS/democrats-delight-joe-biden-vice-presidential-debate
-performance/story?id=17456093#.UIAwkW_A-XF.

Lee, K. 2012. "Joe Biden Gives Firefighter 'No Bullsh-t' Invite to White House." *New
York Daily News,* September 11. Retrieved from http://articles.nydailynews
.com/2012-09-11/news/33768862_1_vice-president-joe-biden-firefighters-
firehouse.

Lin, J. 2012. "Biden, Ryan Court Automobile Heart of Ohio." *Fox News,* November
4. Retrieved from http://politics.blogs.foxnews.com/2012/11/04/biden-ryan
-court-automobile-heart-ohio.

Nagourney, A., and J. Zeleny. 2008. "Obama Chooses Biden as Running Mate." *New
York Times,* August 23. Retrieved from http://www.nytimes.com/2008/08/24
/us/politics/24biden.html.

Natoli, M. 1985. *American Prince, American Pauper: The Contemporary Vice
Presidency in Perspective.* Westport, CT: Greenwood Press.

Nicholas, P., and M. Peters. 2012. "Ryan's Catholic Roots Reach Deep." *Wall Street
Journal,* August 18. Retrieved from http://online.wsj.com/article
/SB10000872396390444233104577595400789196454.html.

Noble, J. 2012. "Unions Love Vice President Joe Biden in Burlington." *Des Moines
Register,* September 17. Retrieved from http://blogs.desmoinesregister.com
/dmr/index.php/2012/09/17/unions-love-vice-president-joe-biden-in
-burlington.

NPR. 2012. "Transcript and Audio Vice Presidential Debate." *NPR,* October 11.
Retrieved from http://www.npr.org/2012/10/11/162754053/transcript
-biden-ryan-vice-presidential-debate.

Opoien, J., and J. Bollier. 2012. "Biden Focuses on Middle Class." *Post Crescent,*
October 26. Retrieved from http://www.postcrescent.com/article/20121027
/APC0101/310270309/Biden-focuses-middle-class-story-photos-?.

Politi, D. 2012. "Cheney 'Disturbed' by Biden's Debate Performance." *Slate,* October
13. Retrieved from http://www.slate.com/blogs/the_slatest/2012/10/13/dick
_cheney_disturbed_by_joe_biden_vice_president_debate_performance.html.

Polsby, N., and A. Wildavsky. 1991. *Presidential Elections: Contemporary Strategies
of American Electoral Politics,* 8th ed. New York: Free Press.

Real Clear Politics. 2011. "Fmr. Dem Gov. Doug Wilder to Obama: Drop Biden
from 2012 Ticket." December 20. Retrieved from http://www.realclearpolitics
.com/video/2011/12/20/fmr_dem_gov_doug_wilder_to_obama_drop_biden
_from_2012_ticket.html.

Ryan, P. 2012. "Transcript: Rep. Paul Ryan's Convention Speech." *NPR,* August 29.
Retrieved from http://www.npr.org/2012/08/29/160282031/transcript-rep
-paul-ryans-convention-speech.

Saenz, A. 2012. "Vice President Joe Biden Makes Final Wisconsin Push in Paul Ryan's Home State." *ABC News*, November 2. Retrieved from http://abcnews .go.com/blogs/politics/2012/11/vice-president-joe-biden-makes-final -wisconsin-push-in-paul-ryans-home-state/.

Schultheis, E. 2012. "Is Joe Biden the New Al Gore?" *Politico*, October 12. Retrieved from http://www.politico.com/news/stories/1012/82324_Page2.html.

Semuels, A. 2012. "As Romney Edges Toward Moderation, Ryan Takes a Lower Profile." *Los Angeles Times*, October 28. Retrieved from http://www.latimes .com/news/nationworld/nation/la-na-paul-ryan-20121029,0,312819.story.

Shepherd, S. 2012. "Ryan Hits Obama on Auto Bailout." *CNN*, October 28. Retrieved from http://politicalticker.blogs.cnn.com/2012/10/28/ryan-hits -obama-on-auto-bailout/.

Silver, N. 2012. "Will Ryan Pick Move the Polls?" *New York Times*, August 11. Retrieved from http://fivethirtyeight.blogs.nytimes.com/2012/08/11/aug-11 -will-ryan-pick-move-the-polls/.

Sincere, R. 2012. "Republican VP Nominee Paul Ryan Rallies Party Faithful in Charlottesville." *Examiner*, October 26. Retrieved from http://www.examiner .com/article/republican-vp-nominee-paul-ryan-rallies-party-faithful- charlottesville.

Sonmez, F., and A. Gardner. 2012. "Paul Ryan on Medicare: 'We Will Win This Debate.'" *Washington Post*, August 16. Retrieved from http://www .washingtonpost.com/blogs/election-2012/post/paul-ryan-on-medicare-we -will-win-this-debate/2012/08/16/2c764bc0-e740-11e1-a3d2-2a05679928ef _blog.html.

Sweeny, C. 2012. "Vice President Joe Biden Rips on Mitt Romney, Paul Ryan in Beloit." *Rockford Register Star*, November 2. Retrieved from http://www.rrstar .com/2012-elections/x565045632/Follow-our-tweets-from-Vice-President-Joe -Bidens-stop-in-Beloit.

Taylor, M. 2012. "Paul Ryan Was a Dud as Romney VP but Has a Bright Political Future." *Daily Beast*, November 7. Retrieved from http://www.thedailybeast .com/articles/2012/11/07/paul-ryan-was-a-dud-as-romney-vp-but-has-a -bright-political-future.html.

Travis, S. 2012a. "Biden Attacks Romney over 2011 Tax Return." *CNN*, September 25. Retrieved from http://politicalticker.blogs.cnn.com/2012/09/25/biden -attacks-romney-over-2011-tax-return/.

Travis, S. 2012b. "Biden: Romney Tape, Demeanor Shows He 'Does Not Under- stand' Middle Class." *CNN*, September 21. Retrieved from http://politicalticker .blogs.cnn.com/2012/09/21/biden-romney-tape-demeanor-shows-he-does -not-understand-middle-class/.

Walshe, S. 2012. "Ryan Backs Biden on 'Buried Middle Class.'" *ABC News*, October 2. Retrieved from http://abcnews.go.com/blogs/politics/2012/10/ryan-backs -biden-on-buried-middle-class/.

Weinger, M. 2012. "Media: Vice Presidential Debate Unlike Any Other." *Politico,* October 10. Retrieved from http://www.politico.com/news/stories/1012/82230 .html?.

York, B. 2012. "Dems: Biden Wasn't Rude, He Was Passionate." *Washington Examiner,* October 12. Retrieved from http://washingtonexaminer.com /dems-biden-wasnt-rude-he-was-passionate/article/2510558.

NOTES

1. *The Washington Post* tallied visits by the candidates (and their wives). We examined each date from August 12 (the day Paul Ryan's candidacy was announced) until November 6. We did not include fundraisers in our tally. We also did not include "non-campaign" related events. For example, the *Post's* data included the presidential and vice presidential debates. It also included speeches at non-campaign related events (i.e., former President Clinton's Global Initiative and the Al Smith charity dinner). We were only concerned with events focused on reaching voters and/or campaign workers.

2. Joint appearances count as two events because we were concerned with comparing how many events each candidate participated in, within each individual state.

3. The next two states in terms of number of events included Nevada with 19 and North Carolina with 12. All other states had 7 or fewer events.

4. The role of former president Bill Clinton in the Obama campaign further complicates the ability to accurately assess Joe Biden. In many ways, President Obama hoped that President Clinton would appeal to the same constituency groups (rural, white, blue collar, etc.) to which Biden was also supposed to appeal. Still, Clinton's appearances were heavily concentrated in Pennsylvania, Ohio, and Virginia. Thus, the strategy to utilize Biden in Iowa and Wisconsin appears to have been successful.

Chapter 4

The Political Geography of the 2012 Presidential Election

Chad Kinsella, Lander University

INTRODUCTION

Although the executive branch of the United States government is but one of three key branches, it is the most visible for many Americans. Therefore, for a large portion of the American electorate, the election of the president is the most familiar and meaningful office they will vote for. Presidential candidates are also viewed as the "standard bearers" of their respective parties and the party platforms. Candidates are often the personification of their parties. Presidential elections are closely and intensely followed by pundits, political scientists, the American electorate, and people around the world.

Given the level of interest in, and importance placed on, presidential elections, they are also heavily analyzed using a variety of methods. This chapter will focus specifically on the political geography of the 2012 presidential election. Given the focus of our federal system on states, and the unique features of the Electoral College, a geographical examination of presidential results is necessary. Not only will this chapter focus on states but also counties, which "are prime ingredients in the US presidential election system," making "an ecological analysis…therefore fully justified" (Lesthaeghe and Neidert 2009, 392). In light of the fact that counties serve as voting districts for states, thus ensuring the availability of election results for counties, along with the telling detail that county-level election data provide, this chapter will also analyze the 2012 presidential election by county.

THE ELECTORAL VOTE

Many scholars and pundits dubbed the 2008 presidential election as a major realignment ushering in a new Democratic majority. The 2012 presidential election left much of the electoral map from 2008 in place in a maintaining election (Campbell et al. 1966) in which the party in power maintains its coalition and advantage. From the perspective of the electoral map in Figure 4.1, not much changed between 2008 and 2012, creating the real possibility of an enduring winning electoral coalition for the Democratic Party.

Despite a weak economy, a well-funded Republican candidate, and a host of other disadvantages, President Obama was able to retain his 2008 state coalition with the exceptions of Indiana and North Carolina. With the exception of North Carolina, Obama was able to win every other battleground state. Although the margin of victory in many states, especially the battleground states, was much narrower in 2012, the results remained much the same. With 48 of 50 states relying on a winner-take-all system, even in states such as Florida, where the popular vote margin of victory was less than 1 percent, Obama maintained the necessary margin in key states, assuring a second term.

Perhaps more instructive of the current electoral trends is to examine the results in relation to the 2004 presidential election. In 2004, Republicans were at the pinnacle of their electoral strategy that counted on being able to win all western states, the South (minus Florida), and Indiana in the Midwest. Since 2004, Republicans have added no new states to that coalition but have lost many others. In the West, Democrats have been able to pick up New Mexico, Colorado, and Nevada. In the Midwest, the archetypal battleground states of Ohio and Iowa have now been retained by Democrats in two straight elections. Perhaps the biggest blow to the Republican coalition is the loss of Virginia. For generations,

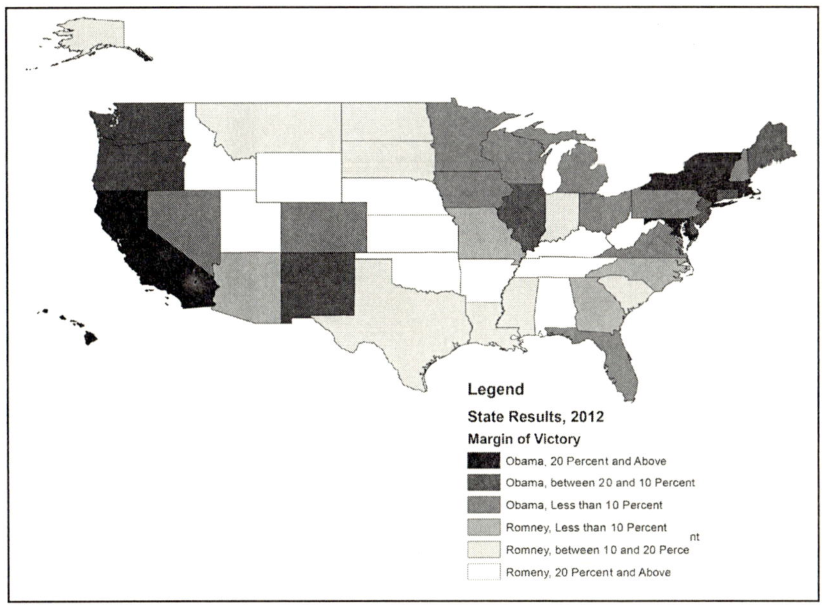

Figure 4.1 State Results of the 2012 Presidential Election

Sources: State secretaries of state and boards of elections and Dave Leip, *Atlas of Presidential Elections.*

first Democrats and later Republicans were able to count the South largely as a package deal. Since the 1980s, Republicans counted the South as a must-win, but Democrats now can create an electoral coalition without a single Southern state. With Virginia, Florida, and North Carolina assured battleground state status, the "Southern strategy" is in jeopardy and the southeast may cease to have as much political clout (Nossiter 2008). The 2008 and 2012 electoral results saw Democrats add to their coalition of West Coast, New England, and Midwestern states to create a large electoral advantage, grabbing over 60 percent of all electoral votes in 2012.

In examining the coalitions that did materialize for Obama and Romney, it becomes easy to see how the electoral vote was much more lopsided (332 for Obama versus 206 for Romney) than the popular vote, in which Romney came within five million votes or less than five percentage points of Obama. Obama was able to win five of the six states with the largest numbers of electoral votes including California, New York,

Florida, Illinois, and Pennsylvania, losing only the 38 electoral votes of Texas. Obama was also able to win several Midwestern states replete with large numbers of electoral votes. Romney's coalition, much like McCain's, was based completely in the Plains, Rocky Mountain West, and the South. Ultimately, the lion's share of electoral votes for Romney came out of the South from states including Texas, Georgia, and North Carolina. The rest of the Republican electoral vote haul came from smaller states in the South, Plains, and Rocky Mountain West, plus Indiana.

COUNTY-LEVEL ELECTION RESULTS

Although states are the building blocks of the Electoral College, there is still much to explore with county-level data. Counties are the main administrative units of their respective states. One administrative function counties perform that is pertinent to this analysis is that they are the voting districts of the states. Examining county-level data reveals key details helpful to understanding the political makeup of individual states and the country. Although counties do not provide the details that precincts provide, given that this analysis is examining presidential election results for the entire country, counties are the most appropriate units to provide visible detail and accompanying explanation of voting patterns within states.

There are several ways in which county-level election data may be analyzed. The most basic, and thus the starting place of this analysis is to examine who won and by what percentage. Figure 4.2 illustrates the county breakdown throughout the country. (It is important to note that because Alaska keeps its election results by state house districts and not boroughs (county equivalents), each analysis of Alaska is of its state house districts.) At first glance at the county map, if one were unaware of the population centers of the United States, it would be tempting to surmise that Romney had won the 2012 presidential election handily. The county map of the United States shows that the bulk of counties in the country were won by Romney by large margins. However, if one examines the findings of Tables 4.1 and 4.2, it becomes clearer as to why a simple glance at the county map can be deceiving.

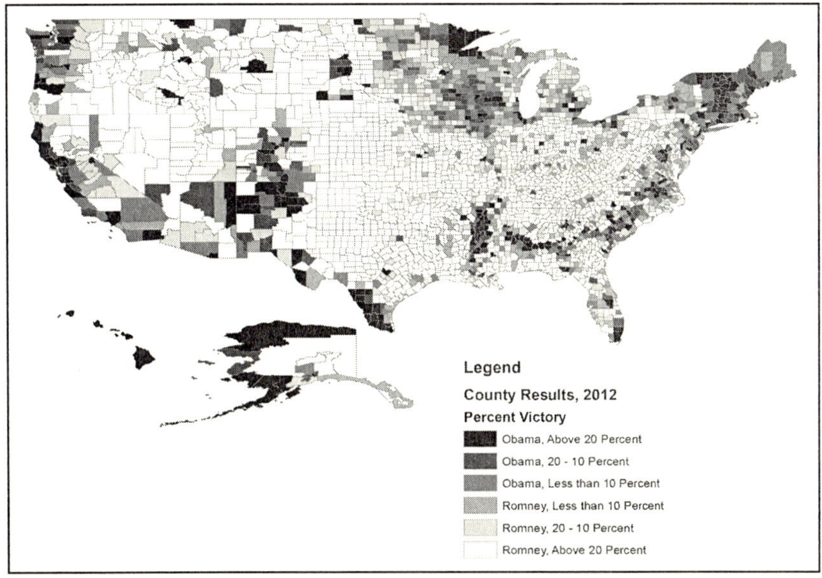

Figure 4.2 The 2012 Presidential Election Results by County

Sources: State secretaries of state and boards of elections and Dave Leip, *Atlas of Presidential Elections.*

Table 4.1 shows the counties won by Romney by the highest percentage. Overall, counties won overwhelmingly by Romney are characteristic of the bulk of counties throughout the United States, large in area but small in population. In contrast, Table 4.2 illustrates that the counties that gave the highest percentage of votes to Obama are typically one of two types of counties. Some are counties, particularly in the South, in which there are large minority populations yet they are still small-population, more rural counties. Obama also received high percentages of the vote from large, densely populated, urban counties that are home to large cities including Washington, D.C., Baltimore City, the Bronx, Philadelphia, and the like. Although Romney easily won the majority of counties, Obama performed well in highly populated areas that can be several times larger in population and number of votes than those counties won handily by Romney.

Table 4.1 Counties with Highest Percentage of Support for Romney

Rank	County	State	Votes	Percent
1	King	Texas	139	95.86
2	Madison	Idaho	13,445	93.29
3	Sterling	Texas	459	92.91
4	Franklin	Idaho	5,195	92.77
5	Roberts	Texas	408	92.73
6	Hansford	Texas	1,787	91.17
7	Glasscock	Texas	526	91.00
8	Oldham	Texas	786	90.87
9	Ochiltree	Texas	2,718	90.84
10	Rich	Utah	907	90.79
11	Cimarron	Oklahoma	1,082	90.39
12	Wallace	Kansas	702	90.23
13	Uintah	Utah	10,001	89.97
14	Leslie	Kentucky	4,439	89.68
15	Motley	Texas	538	89.67
16	Morgan	Utah	3,910	89.47
17	Sevier	Utah	6,961	89.46
18	Beaver	Oklahoma	2,062	89.42
19	Duchesne	Utah	5,608	89.40
20	Lipscomb	Texas	1,044	89.38

Table 4.2 Counties with Highest Percentage of Support for Obama

Rank	County	State	Votes	Percent
1	Shannon	South Dakota	2,922	93.35
2	Bronx	New York	288,378	91.25
3	District of Columbia	District of Columbia	222,332	91.12
4	Prince George's	Maryland	317,342	90.08
5	Petersburg	Virginia	14,377	89.95
6	Jefferson	Mississippi	3,508	88.74
7	Claiborne	Mississippi	4,633	88.11
8	Baltimore City	Maryland	202,327	87.45
9	Macon	Alabama	9,045	87.10
10	Menominee	Wisconsin	1,191	86.49
11	Starr	Texas	10,248	86.38
12	Philadelphia	Pennsylvania	558,158	85.25
13	Clayton	Georgia	81,479	84.81
14	Greene	Alabama	4,514	84.72

Rank	County	State	Votes	Percent
15	New York	New York	417,861	84.20
16	Holmes	Mississippi	6,775	83.89
17	San Francisco	California	234,076	83.28
18	Zavala	Texas	3,042	83.27
19	St. Louis	Missouri	116,654	82.65
20	Kings	New York	503,291	81.43

Change in County Vote, 2008–2012

Another critical aspect of the county analysis is to find if and where there was a change in voting behavior among the U.S. counties. Figure 4.3 shows the change in vote in counties between the 2008 and 2012 presidential elections, with darker-colored counties indicating an increase in the percentage of Democratic votes and lighter-colored counties indicating an increase in the percentage of Republican votes in a county. With a few exceptions, there were not many dramatic shifts, with most counties registering only small changes. Despite these small shifts in voting, there are some noticeable patterns. The strongest increase or at least maintenance of the Democratic percentage of the vote appears to be in New England, New York, central Ohio, Hispanic-populated counties in the Southwest, and, oddly enough, in many counties throughout the South.

There are some indications that Obama performed better in the South than any Democratic presidential candidate since Carter (Blackmon 2012), further indicating that the Republican Southern strategy may be increasingly vulnerable. This increase is not just explained by an increase in African American voters. There are indications that many white Southerners also may not have been enthusiastic about Romney. Romney consistently lost Republican primaries in the Deep South. Whether this is due to the perception that Romney is too moderate for more traditional conservative voters in the South, or perhaps a reaction to Romney's religious background, remains to be seen.

Republicans were able to increase their vote share in many places throughout the United States. Romney seems to have continued the trend started by McCain of increasing the number of votes in Appalachian

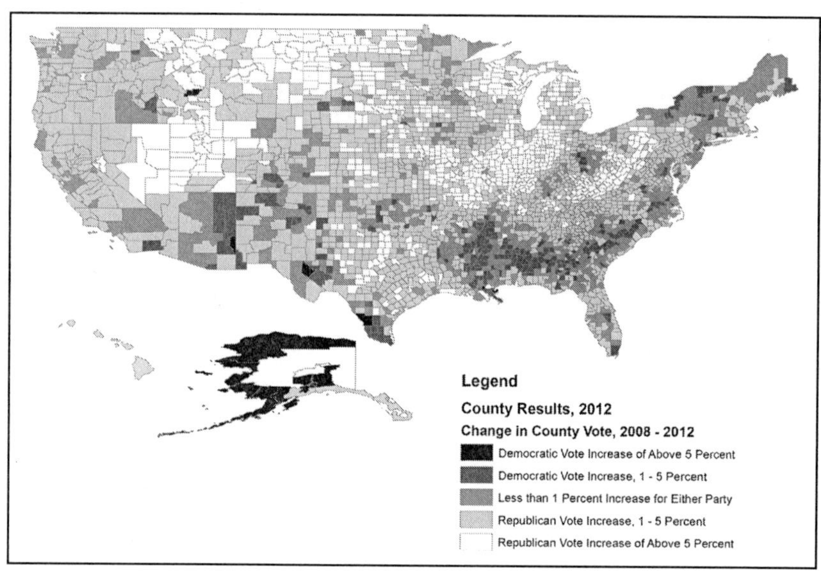

Figure 4.3 Percent Vote Change in Counties, 2008–2012

Sources: State secretaries of state and boards of elections and Dave Leip, *Atlas of Presidential Elections.*

regions from Kentucky through Pennsylvania, highlighting Obama's problem with voters who label their ethnic heritage as American or unhyphenated Americans (Arbour and Teigen 2011). There was also an increase in the Republican vote share in many counties throughout the Midwest from Indiana, Illinois, Michigan, and Wisconsin. Many of these areas are crucial for Republicans in their future presidential runs in order to try to pick up states in the Midwest to make up for losses elsewhere. Finally, Romney performed better in many counties in the western part of the United States including counties in Utah, Montana, Nevada, and the Dakotas.

Despite some indications that there were some shifts in voting behavior among voters in certain areas of the United States, it is important to keep the findings in perspective. As mentioned above, this election fits what Campbell et al. (1966) described as a "maintaining election" in which the party in control maintains control and partisan attachments remain stable. Not only does this appear to be correct when examining state-by-state results but county results as well. In a regression analysis,

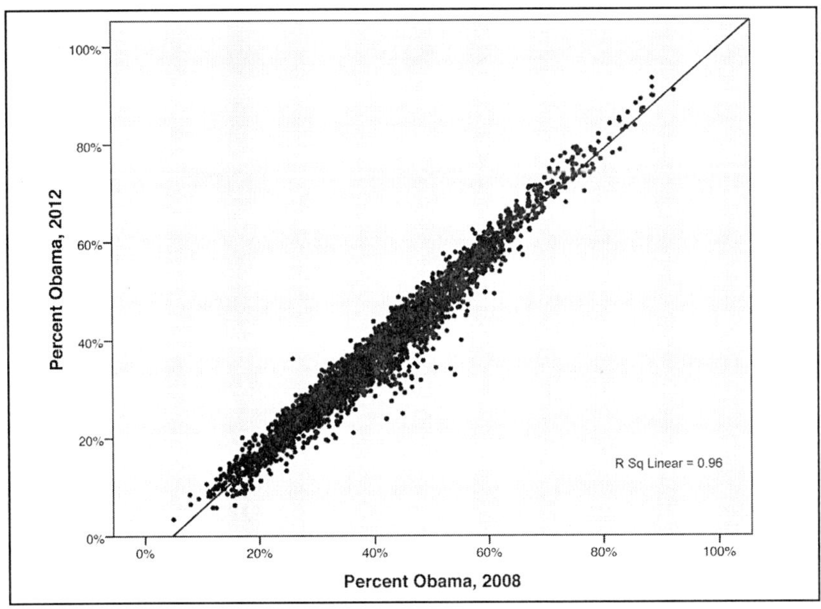

Figure 4.4 Regression of Percent Obama by County, 2008–2012

with the percent of a county voting Obama used as the dependent variable and the percent of the county vote in 2008 used as the independent variable, the 2008 results were able to explain 96 percent of the variance. This regression, performed in a scatterplot, demonstrates that much of the results at the county level in 2008 explain what happened in 2012 (see Figure 4.4).

WEIGHTING COUNTIES BY POPULATION

Examining counties by percent of the popular vote delivered to each presidential candidate gives us an excellent picture of the political culture within a county and surrounding counties. There are important conclusions that can be drawn from such an analysis; however, several recent analyses into state regional politics have pointed out that it is critical to examine vote share and where the bulk of vote share for a candidate comes from. In a critical article that examines David Duke's support in Louisiana, Voss (1996) dispels the idea that the bulk of Duke's votes came from rural Louisiana and found that they actually came from suburban areas.

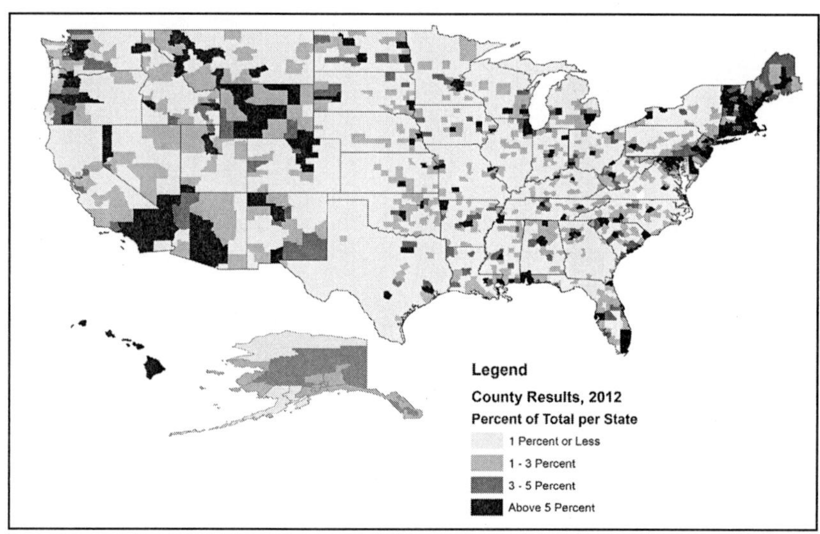

Figure 4.5 Percent of Romney's Total by State

Sources: State secretaries of state and boards of elections and Dave Leip, *Atlas of Presidential Elections.*

Perhaps the most critical analysis using this approach was accomplished by Gimpel and Schuknecht (2002) in their analysis of state regional voting behavior. Their research, which examined several states over a number of years, found that even urban counties that may vote overwhelmingly Democratic in terms of percentages may still deliver a large number of votes to the GOP candidate relative to sparsely populated rural counties that provide overwhelming support to the GOP but fewer actual votes.

Based on the findings of Voss, Gimpel, and Schuknecht, it is important to examine where the bulk of votes within each state came from for each presidential candidate. Figures 4.5 and 4.6 display all 50 states with counties labeled by the total percentage of votes they delivered to each candidate, with darker counties delivering higher percentages of votes than those with lighter colors. The findings reinforce the idea that examining the percentage each candidate receives in a county can be deceptive. The bulk of counties throughout the United States, particularly in areas of the country such as the Midwest and South that have a large number of counties, provide less than 1 percent of the total number of votes for either candidate. Ultimately, a handful of highly populated counties in many different states provide the largest share of votes.

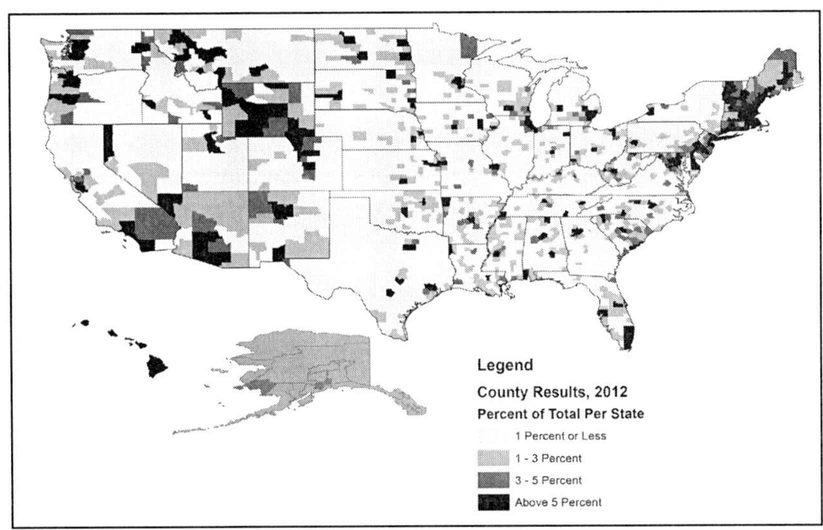

Figure 4.6 Percent of Obama's Total by State

Sources: State secretaries of state and boards of elections and Dave Leip, *Atlas of Presidential Elections.*

This vote share analysis, or weighting counties by number of votes cast by state, is helpful in several different capacities. It provides clarity to the county map because, as mentioned above, simply judging by which candidate won the most counties would make it look as if Republicans, including Romney, should have won by a landslide. As Gimpel and Schuknecht point out, it would appear that the bulk of Republican support comes from rural counties and that there are clear regional differences within states. In fact, Republicans and Democrats actually receive a large number of votes from essentially the same area. To point to a few examples, in Ohio, both Romney and Obama rely on the three large metropolitan areas of Cleveland (Cuyahoga County), Columbus (Franklin County), and Cincinnati (Hamilton County) for a large percentage of the votes needed in Ohio. Similarly, the largest percentage of votes in Georgia, for both candidates, comes from the Atlanta Metropolitan Area. In Nevada, Las Vegas (Clark County) provides over 60 percent of the total number of votes in the states to Republicans and over 70 percent of the votes for Democrats, making this one county critical to winning the entire state.

Overall, Figures 4.5 and 4.6 provide a couple of key conclusions. Democrats typically have a concentrated voting bloc in many states that rests primarily in and around densely populated urban centers and rural areas, particularly in the South, with large numbers of minorities. Republicans, on the other hand, typically must go "farther afield" (Gimpel and Schuknecht 2002, 349) to obtain votes, usually in the suburban areas around urban centers. Ultimately, both maps make it easy to see the major population centers throughout the country, particularly on the East and West coasts. There are instances where this analysis does not provide much detail, especially in states with few counties such as in some of the northeastern and western states as well as Hawaii. Finally, looking at Tables 4.3 and 4.4, which show the top counties for the popular vote, there are many counties that provide a large portion of the votes for both parties. It is interesting to note that even though Republicans lose large urban counties by large margins, such as Los Angeles County, they still receive the bulk of their votes from these counties and rely on these numbers in combination with other less populous counties. On the other hand, Democrats are able to rely on massive numbers of voters in these large counties and, in many states, receive enough votes in these populous counties to easily offset losses in other less populous counties.

Table 4.3 Highest Popular Vote Totals for Romney

Rank	County	State	Votes	Percent
1	Los Angeles	California	699,600	28.82
2	Maricopa	Arizona	628,327	55.04
3	Harris	Texas	584,866	49.33
4	Orange	California	526,976	53.27
5	Cook	Illinois	479,204	24.65
6	San Diego	California	404,182	46.70
7	Tarrant	Texas	348,686	57.13
8	Miami-Dade	Florida	332,602	37.91
9	Oakland	Michigan	296,531	45.60
10	Dallas	Texas	294,339	41.69
11	Riverside	California	290,227	49.21
12	Clark	Nevada	288,408	41.87
13	Middlesex	Massachusetts	266,307	35.66
14	Suffolk	New York	259,348	47.97
15	Hillsborough	Florida	248,746	46.22

Rank	County	State	Votes	Percent
16	Allegheny	Pennsylvania	246,540	42.00
17	King	Washington	246,360	28.99
18	Broward	Florida	243,675	32.28
19	Bexar	Texas	240,519	47.03
20	Hennepin	Minnesota	240,073	35.30

Table 4.4 Highest Popular Vote Totals for Obama

Rank	County	State	Votes	Percent
1	Los Angeles	California	1,672,164	68.87
2	Cook	Illinois	1,439,123	74.01
3	Wayne	Michigan	595,253	73.12
4	Harris	Texas	585,451	49.38
5	King	Washington	584,460	68.78
6	Philadelphia	Pennsylvania	558,158	85.25
7	Miami-Dade	Florida	540,776	61.64
8	Broward	Florida	507,285	67.19
9	Kings	New York	503,291	81.43
10	Maricopa	Arizona	490,393	42.96
11	Middlesex	Massachusetts	467,173	62.55
12	San Diego	California	444,110	51.32
13	Orange	California	440,527	44.53
14	Alameda	California	428,128	78.41
15	Hennepin	Minnesota	423,979	62.34
16	Cuyahoga	Ohio	420,953	68.90
17	New York	New York	417,861	84.20
18	Dallas	Texas	403,170	57.11
19	Queens	New York	399,970	78.78
20	Clark	Nevada	388,182	56.36

Landslide Counties

A final analysis of counties is to examine the partisanship of the 2012 presidential election. The method for accomplishing this is by examining landslide counties. In 2008, reporter Bill Bishop published his book, *The Big Sort*, which argues that Americans are moving to communities with politically like-minded individuals, or sorting themselves. Bishop argues that this sorting has increased dramatically since 1976, and he uses county-level data to demonstrate the political divisions within the United States. These findings are based on Bishop's analysis of the percent of voters who live in a landslide county during competitive (where the margin of victory in the popular vote was in single digits) and uncompetitive (where the margin of victory in the popular vote was in double digits) presidential elections since 1948. Bishop uses presidential elections as the measurement of geographic political sorting because it is the one common election among all counties, which avoids the effects of having different candidates and changing voting districts. According to Bishop's methodology, a landslide county is one in which there is a difference of 20 percentage points or more between the presidential candidates of the two major parties. Bishop excludes third parties to even out the comparison over time (Bishop 2008).

Like Bishop, the landslide analysis examines the percent difference between the two major parties, Democrats and Republicans, and excludes third parties because not all third parties have run in all states. Counties where Romney or Obama won by 20 percentage points or more are designated as landslide counties. Counties that are competitive, or where no candidate won over 20 percent of the vote in a county are designated as "No Landslide" counties. Much of the analysis within the field of political science examines the "who," or how different demographic and ideological groups vote. Over the last several decades there have emerged clear differences between Democratic and Republican voters. The idea of sorting and landslide counties argues that these groups not only vote similarly but also live in similar areas. Therefore, this analysis goes from the "who" to the "where."

Figure 4.7 displays the landslide counties in the 2012 presidential election. The pattern shows concentrations of Democratic landslide counties on the East and West coasts, in the Midwest, particularly the Great Lakes region, and in many large urban areas. Republican landslide counties are concentrated in the Midwest, particularly the Plains states, and in the South. Republican landslide counties tend to be rural and suburban counties, overall. There were 1,731 Republican landslide counties, 273 Democratic landslide counties, and 1,105 no landslide counties in the 2012 presidential election. There was a fairly significant change in landslide counties between 2008 and 2012. In 2012 there were 327 more Repub-

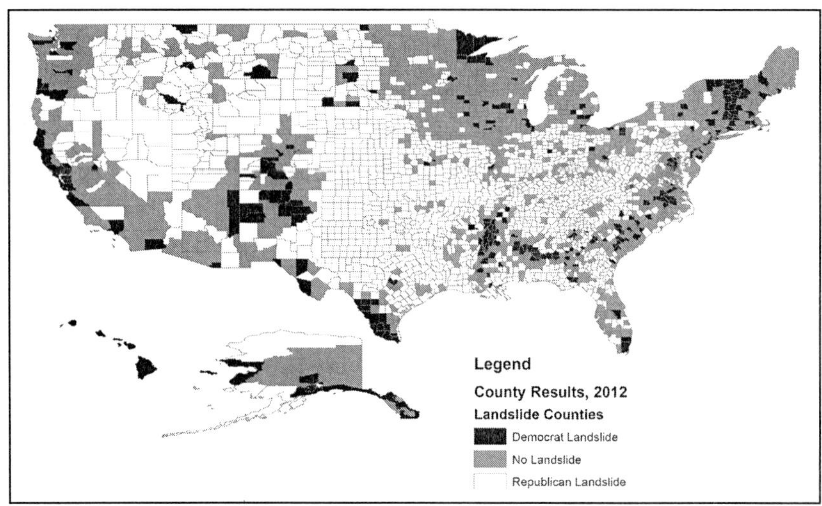

Figure 4.7 Landslide Counties

Sources: State secretaries of state and boards of elections and Dave Leip, *Atlas of Presidential Elections.*

lican landslide counties that came at the expense primarily of the 2008 no landslide counties. There also were 268 fewer no landslide counties in 2012 and 59 fewer Democratic landslide counties, which primarily moved into the no landslide county category. These figures that show the difference between 2012 and 2008 would seem to indicate a major shift in Republican fortunes. However, these likely indicate how well Obama performed in 2008, and the bulk of counties that shifted to the Republican landslide column are those with lower populations.

CONCLUSION

Presidential elections are the most popular and most followed elections in the United States. The results of the election have far-reaching repercussions for politics and policy in the country. Increasingly, presidential elections are indicative of the state of partisan affiliation in the country and, in many ways, are a way to gauge the ebb and flow of the major parties in the United States. Presidential candidates and their respective parties spent well over two billion dollars in the battle for the White House (Center for Responsive Politics 2012). Given this, it is critical to analyze the results of such a momentous social, political, and financial event.

The geographic findings may provide some predictive power for future presidential elections, especially in 2016. The state and county findings indicate a strong position for future Democratic candidates and an increasingly difficult electoral fight for Republicans. In the last two elections Obama has only lost one battleground state. To further complicate matters for Republicans, many states that they need in order to win the presidency have become battleground states. What makes this difficult for Republicans is they must win several battleground states whereas Democrats could lose several and still easily have a winning coalition. This is best highlighted in the South, where Republicans must win every southern state as part of their winning coalition whereas Democrats do not need any southern states in order to win (Schaller 2006). Campaign personnel working for the 2016 Republican candidate will have a much more difficult time putting together a coalition of states that add up to 270 electoral votes than their Democratic counterparts unless major electoral changes occur.

County results paint an equally difficult picture for Republicans. Democrats continue to win counties with high populations and high growth while Republicans overperform in counties that are sparsely populated and continue to lose population. Given that Democratic voters also tend to cluster in urban areas, it is easier for campaigns to find and turn out their voters whereas Republicans must go farther out to reach their perspective voters, representing a bigger commitment of time and money (Gimpel and Schuknecht 2002). Currently, the geography favors Democratic presidential candidates and will require considerable rebuilding for Republicans in order for them to win back the White House.

Finally, the analysis of landslide counties points to a public that is geographically polarized along partisan lines. Growing numbers of American voters live in counties that are filled with their fellow partisans. A recently analysis by Cho et al. (2012) finds that partisans increasingly choose to reside in counties where their fellow partisans also reside. Therefore, despite the discussion about the American electorate polarizing along ideological lines, they are also polarizing geographically.

The analysis presented here is descriptive in nature but still presents key findings through a diverse range of spatial analysis. Ultimately, the findings indicate that the 2012 presidential election represents the maintenance of a new political alignment in states and counties that favors the Democratic Party and led to the reelection of Barack Obama as president. Ultimately, a geographic analysis is an essential part of any presidential election study that provides critical details to understand what happened in a parsimonious manner—and a prism through which to gauge the probable fortunes of the two main political parties in future presidential contests.

REFERENCES

Arbour, B. K., and J. Teigen. 2011. "Barack Obama's 'American' Problem: Unhyphenated Americans in the 2008 Elections." *Social Science Quarterly* 92 (3): 563–587.

Bishop, B. 2008. *The Big Sort: Why the Clustering of Like-Minded America Is Tearing Us Apart*. New York: Houghton Mifflin.

Blackmon, D. A. 2012. "Republicans Face Unexpected Challenges in Coastal South amid Shrinking White Vote." *Washington Post,* December 15. Retrieved December 15, 2012 from http://www.washingtonpost.com/politics /republicans-face-unexpected-challenges-in-coastalsouth-amid-shrinking -white-vote/2012/11/23/02cbda58-336a-11e2bb9b288a310849ee_story.html.

Campbell, A., P. E. Converse, W. E. Miller, and D. E. Stokes. 1966. *Elections and the Political Order.* New York: John Wiley & Sons.

Center for Responsive Politics. 2012. "Overview." December 15. Retrieved December 15, 2012 from http://www.opensecrets.org/overview/index.php.

Cho, W. K. Tam, J. G. Gimpel, and I. S. Hui, I. S. 2012. "Voter Migration and Geographic Sorting of the American Electorate." *Annals of the Association of American Geographers* 103 (4): 856–870.

Gimpel, J. G., and J. E. Schuknecht. 2002. "Reconsidering Political Regionalism in the American States." *State Politics and Policy Quarterly* 2 (4): 325–352.

Lesthaeghe, R., and L. Neidert. 2009. "US Presidential Elections and the Spatial Pattern of the American Second Demographic Transition." *Population and Development Review* 35: 391–400.

Nossiter, A. 2008. "For South: A Waning Hold on National Politics." *New York Times,* October 23. Retrieved October 23, 2011 from http://www.nytimes .com/2008/11/11/us/politics/11south.html.

Schaller, T. 2006. *Whistling Past Dixie: How Democrats Can Win without the South.* New York: Simon and Schuster.

Voss, D. S. 1996. "Beyond Racial Threat: Failure of an Old Hypothesis in the New South." *Journal of Politics* 58 (1): 156–170.

Chapter 5

The Republican Advantage Continues
The 2012 Election in the South

Neal Allen, Wichita State University

The success of the Obama campaign justifiably dominates discussion of the 2012 elections. The president's success in holding enough of his 2008 coalition, and his success among growing portions of the electorate, support a narrative of continuing Democratic success. But returns from the South tell a different story, one of isolated Democratic opportunities amidst growing Republican dominance. The position of the Democratic Party in the South relative to the nation is the weakest in its history. The South, more specifically the white South, now forms the core of conservative and Republican opposition to President Obama in his second term.

The election of a president with a minority of Southern votes and little connection to the region is unique in modern American history. Since the 1920s America has elected presidents who were either from the South—Eisenhower (Texan by birth), Johnson, Carter, both Bushes, and Clinton—or who won large majorities of Southern popular and electoral votes—Roosevelt, Truman, Kennedy, Nixon, and Reagan. After two victories with a minority of support in the South and a life spent in Hawaii,

California, New York, Massachusetts, and Illinois, Barack Obama can be understood as the "least Southern" president since the 1920s. His narrow 2012 reelection wins in Virginia and Florida mask his larger weakness in the South. He won fewer Southern electoral votes than any candidate elected president since Calvin Coolidge in 1924. He could have won a clear Electoral College majority in both elections with no Southern states, and Florida and Virginia were his first and third narrowest victories, respectively, in 2012.

This chapter analyzes 2012 Southern election returns in the national and historical context. First it will review President Obama's vote in the region (defined as the former Confederate States plus Kentucky and Oklahoma), and how it compares with his vote in the Non-South and with other past major-party candidates. The chapter then will turn to the South as a collection of states and discuss how demographic shifts have led to competitive states within a strongly Republican region. The chapter also will discuss the continuing and growing weakness of Democrats in down-ballot Southern elections, as Republicans increased their share of U.S. House seats, governorships, and control of state legislatures in 2012. The chapter concludes by assessing the place of the South in national political institutions.

THE SOUTH AS A REGION IN 2012: CONTINUED DEMOCRATIC DECLINE

The 2012 presidential election in the South was a continuation of the long-term shift away from the Democratic Party in the region. Southern white voters, who make up the majority of the region's electorate, have moved in the last few decades from heavily Democratic to heavily Republican. Barack Obama, who had succeeding in winning three Southern states (Virginia, North Carolina, and Florida) where Al Gore in 2000 and John Kerry in 2004 had won none, faced a daunting challenge in the Republican Party's best region. None of his three statewide victories in 2008 were by large margins, and his party suffered massive losses in the 2010 midterm election in the South.

Mitt Romney also entered the contest for the region's electoral votes with clear weaknesses. His Mormon faith has relatively few adherents in the South and is seen negatively by many of the evangelicals that are concentrated in the region. The South was Romney's worst region in the nominating contests, with 6 of his 12 primary or caucus losses coming in the region. His loss to Newt Gingrich in South Carolina was particularly damaging, as it stopped his momentum after his apparent Iowa caucus victory and his strong win in the New Hampshire primary. The results of the general election, however, show the importance of partisanship in driving Southern election results. Romney took advantage of the long-term shift in regional voting, winning almost 55 percent of the region's votes and 74 percent of Southern electoral votes.

Romney's regional success came at the culmination of a shift lasting more than four decades, which is most clearly evident not merely in the long-term drop of Democratic support in the South from Truman's 63.8 percent in 1948 to Obama's 44.9 percent in 2012, but in the growing gap between how Democratic candidates for president perform in the South relative to how they perform in the rest of the country. Table 5.1 shows the Democratic candidate's percentage in the South, the Non-South, and the difference between them since the election of Harry Truman in 1948.

Table 5.1 Democratic Presidential Vote, 1948–2012

Year	South %	Non-South %	% Difference
1948	63.8	50.8	13.0
1952	51.9	43.3	8.6
1956	48.6	41.0	7.7
1960	50.9	49.9	1.0
1964	51.8	63.7	-11.9
1968	46.7	50.2	-3.6
1972	29.5	40.8	-11.3
1976	54.4	49.9	4.5
1980	46.1	44.2	1.9
1984	37.2	42.3	-5.1
1988	41.4	47.9	-6.6
1992	49.1	55.3	-6.3
1996	49.9	56.9	-7.0
2000	44.2	53.0	-8.8
2004	42.3	51.7	-9.4
2008	46.2	57.3	-11.1
2012	44.9	54.8	-9.8

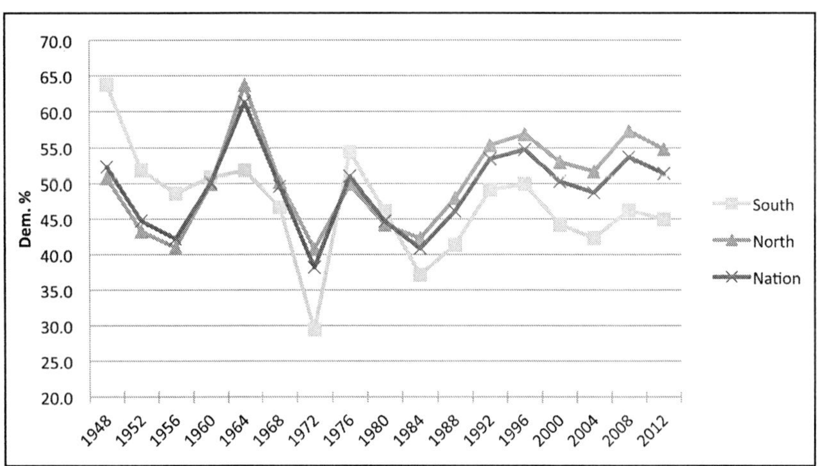

Figure 5.1 Democratic Presidential Vote by Region

Obama's 44.9 percent, down from 46.2 percent in 2008, is in the lower range for the period. No Democratic presidential candidate has won a majority of the two-party vote in the South since Jimmy Carter in 1976, which was itself a temporary recovery for his party amidst its long-term slide. Carter's appeal to white Southerners, combined with his near-unanimous support from the region's African Americans, also led to the last two elections (1976 and 1980) in which the Democratic candidate did better in the South than in the Non-South (see Figure 5.1). This group even included Arkansan Bill Clinton, who narrowly lost the total Southern vote in both 1992 and 1996 (although in 1996, Clinton actually won the South outside of Oklahoma).

The gap between the Southern and Non-Southern percentage for the Democratic Party has been increasing since 1980, as the party's position in the South relative to its position in the rest of the country has steadily deteriorated (see Figure 5.2).

The nomination of the Southerner Clinton, coming after the loss of Massachusetts Governor Michael Dukakis, only temporarily slowed the slide. Obama's South/Non-South gaps of negative 11.1 (2008) and negative 9.8 (2012) may indicate the region has reached a new partisan equilibrium. This equilibrium has two notable characteristics.

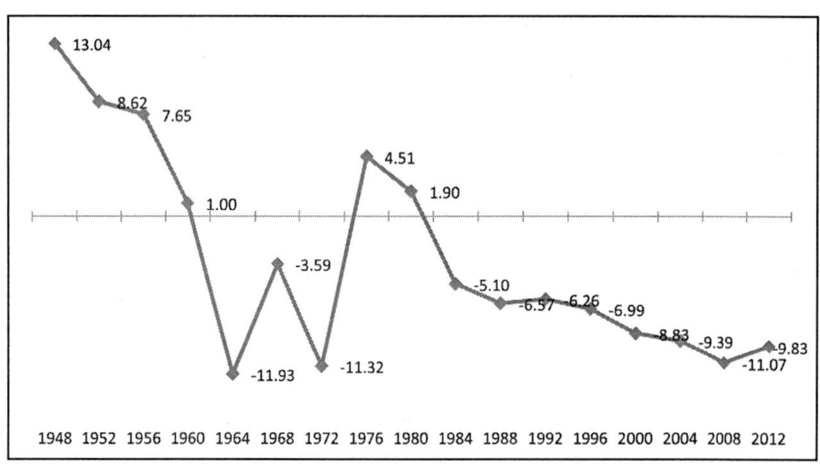

Figure 5.2 Democratic South and Non-South Percentages

First, the position of the Democratic Party in the South, relative to its position in the nation, is at present most similar to its position in the landslide elections of 1964 and 1972. The victories of Lyndon Johnson and Richard Nixon contained the only South/Non-South gaps larger than those present in the two Obama victories. In 1964, the Republican vote collapsed in the North in revulsion (at least temporarily) to the conservatism of Barry Goldwater. In 1972, the movement away from the dovish campaign of George McGovern led to an equivalent collapse of Democratic support in the South, with drops even more pronounced than the nationwide deterioration of the Democratic position. Demographic shifts in Virginia, Florida, and North Carolina have altered the distribution of partisanship in the region enough to make part of it competitive at the presidential level, but the long-term weakness of the party has become obvious.

This weakness is also likely to persist, at least in relation to the rest of the country. In previous election cycles, the Democratic decline among white Southern voters was amplified when the party was weak nationally. When the Democratic Party nationally got a cold, in the South it got the flu. But after previous regional drops in 1964, 1972, and 1980–1988, the Democratic Southern vote moved back toward the national median. The fact that the gap is increasing in years of Democratic victory may be evidence that a recovery to even the position of the 1990s in the South is exceedingly unlikely, even with a large shift to the Democrats nationwide.

The shrinking of the South/Non-South gap for Obama from -11.1 to -9.8 is notable and surprising. Three explanations for this seem possible. First, the Democratic vote might have, in effect, bottomed out in the South. Republicans might be approaching the point at which most of the remaining Democratic voters are minorities, or pockets of white liberals in places like Northern Virginia or Austin, Texas. The fact that Obama's two-party vote percentage held steady in the four Southern states with the largest African American populations—rising slightly in Louisiana and dropping slightly in Georgia, Mississippi, and South Carolina—supports this explanation. Also, the Obama campaign's focus on the battleground states of Virginia, Florida, and North Carolina may have slowed down his party's decline in the region. No Southern states moved from competitive in 2008 to mostly ignored in 2012, as was the case with Non-Southern states such as Indiana, Michigan, Minnesota, and Pennsylvania (until very late in the campaign). One final reason for the reversal of the Democratic slide in the South relative to the nation is the increasing minority population of the region that is at least partially counteracting the shift of whites to Republican voting.

A decline in Southern support like the Democrats have experienced since Jimmy Carter's elections would in past periods have damaged or even eliminated the Democratic nominee's chances of winning the presidency or either house of Congress. The effect of the Southern collapse has been mitigated, however, by the corresponding "counter-realignment" (see Reiter and Stonecash 2011) in the Northeast, with Democrats making similar gains there and on the West Coast. Obama's Non-Southern percentage of 57.3 percent in 2008 was the second-highest for a Democratic candidate since the New Deal, and his 54.8 percent in 2012 was higher than in the previous victories of Truman, Kennedy, and Carter. The contemporary Republican South is not as "solid" as the pre–civil rights movement Democratic South, but Obama's victories have not halted the larger regional decline.

VARIATIONS ACROSS SOUTHERN STATES:
COMPETITIVE MIXED WITH STRONGLY REPUBLICAN

The Republican advantage in the South at the presidential level is pronounced and growing, but is not uniform across states and subregions. Obama's wins in Virginia and Florida in 2012 and in North Carolina in 2008 show that Democrats have Southern opportunities in the contest for an Electoral College victory. The South is now a mix of closely competitive states—Virginia, Florida, and North Carolina—and strongly Republican states. This pattern has occurred in the last four presidential elections, as no Democratic candidate since Bill Clinton in 1996 has won more than 53 percent of the two-party vote in any Southern state (in that year he won convincingly in Arkansas and Louisiana).

A clear pro-Republican trend is evident in all 13 Southern states since 1948, but several have shifted their position in the period. Oklahoma and Kentucky, classified by some as Non-Southern border states, have shifted from being among the least Democratic of Southern states to Obama's worst and third-worst, respectively, in 2012. At the beginning of the period Virginia, with many of its votes controlled by the conservative Byrd machine that would not support Democrats for president, was often the least Democratic state. With growth in the Washington, D.C. suburbs, African American enfranchisement, and overall demographic diversification, it has now shifted to the most Democratic state in the region.

Table 5.2 Democratic Presidential Vote in Southern States

State	2012 %	Shift 2008–2012
VA	51.6	-1.22%
FL	50.4	-0.98%
NC	48.9	-1.2%
GA	46.0	-1.33%
SC	44.6	-0.76%
MS	44.0	-0.84%
TX	42.0	-2.07%
LA	41.2	+.71%
TN	39.6	-2.72%
AL	38.8	-0.33%
KY	38.5	-3.31%
AR	37.8	-0.98%
OK	33.2	-1.13%

Table 5.2 shows Obama's vote in the 13 Southern states and the shift from 2008 to 2012. Only in Virginia did Obama run better than he did nationally, and Virginia was not close to being the pivotal state that gave Obama the Electoral College victory (discussed below; see Table 5.3).

Table 5.3 Presidential Electoral Vote by Region

	Obama	Romney
South	42	120
Non-South	290	86
Total	332	206

Scholars of Southern politics have traditionally divided the region into the Deep South (Louisiana, Mississippi, Alabama, Georgia, and South Carolina) and the Peripheral South (Tennessee, Virginia, North Carolina, Texas, Arkansas, and possibly Oklahoma and Kentucky). The results of the 2012 presidential election suggest an altered tripartite distinction into competitive, high-minority noncompetitive, and low-minority noncompetitive.

The competitive South of Virginia, Florida, and North Carolina is characterized by growing minority populations, a large amount of migration from outside the region, and progressive-leaning metropolitan areas (Northern Virginia, Research Triangle, South and Central Florida). These groups and areas balance out the more traditionally Southern conservative areas such as Southside Virginia or Northern Florida. These states will remain battleground states in future campaigns.

The remaining peripheral Southern states and Alabama stand in contrast to the competitive South. Obama won less than 40 percent in all of them, as the white vote for the national Democratic Party has collapsed here. The nonwhite population is not large enough to provide a base for a Democratic resurgence, and Republican candidates are in a strong position in Senate and House elections. The larger black populations (and the Latino population in Texas) lead to a higher Democratic percentage in Georgia, South Carolina, Mississippi and Texas, but not greater statewide competitiveness. These states create a path for a Democrat to get to 40 percent and possibly even 45 percent, but not in 2012 a path to a plurality.

This pattern of clearly competitive Virginia, North Carolina, and Florida, and the rest of the region strongly Republican, will likely continue in competitive presidential elections in the near future. A Republican could certainly duplicate George W. Bush's sweep of the region's electoral votes, as looked quite possible for Mitt Romney until election night. A landslide victory by a Democrat might turn an additional state or two temporarily blue. The South will likely shift with the national partisan trends, remaining on the Republican end of the distribution of electoral votes.

The rapid shift of Virginia and North Carolina since 2004 raises the possibility of a similar shift by other states. The two clear possibilities are Georgia and Texas. Not only did Obama lose slightly less support in Georgia since 2008 than nationally, but it was his smallest state loss except for North Carolina. Any further movement toward the national median point for Georgia will depend on continued growth of the Latino population around Atlanta, coupled with a pro-Democratic shift of a sizable group of white voters. The first seems likely, the second less so. The much larger Latino population in Texas holds the possibility of a large pro-Democratic shift, but from a more Republican-dominant starting point. A study commissioned by the *Houston Chronicle* (Dunham 2012) finds that if white and Latino vote shares hold constant, Democrats will be a majority by 2024.

The possible movement of Georgia and Texas to competitive status, combined with continued movement of Virginia, North Carolina, and Florida to competitiveness or even Democratic advantage, raises the possibility of a competitive South like that of the 1950s–1990s. But placed in a national context, the effect of the declining white share of the Southern electorate is merely part of a national story of demography driving partisanship. If Republicans do so poorly among Latinos that Georgia and Texas are competitive, then every state Mitt Romney lost will also be out of reach. The continued movement of nonwhites into the suburbs of Atlanta, Dallas, and Houston will have implications for statewide elections and U.S. House elections, but will not shift the Republican Party from its advantageous position in Southern presidential elections. Republicans might also develop a more successful strategy for winning Latino votes, which could move their regional Electoral College position back to what they enjoyed in George W. Bush's elections.

THE 2012 ELECTIONS FOR CONGRESS: SOUTHERN EXCEPTIONALISM

President Obama began his second term at the head of a party with clear, but not overwhelming, strength outside of the South. Democrats have now held a majority of Non-Southern House seats since the 1996 elections, and a majority of Non-Southern Senate seats since 1992. In races for Congress in the South, the shallowness of the Obama victory is evident. He not only failed to provide coattails to gain back what the party had lost in 2010, but was unable to prevent further losses. The Republican Party's disappointing showing in 2012 nationally was partly mitigated by a strong showing in Southern elections to the House and Senate. The party gained House seats, held steady in Senate seats, and continued its momentum in statehouse races from 2010. Republicans have majorities in every Southern state legislative chamber except the Kentucky House, and hold all governorships in the region except in Kentucky and Arkansas.

In 2012, the Republicans, while their majority in the House slipped by 8 seats to 234 nationwide, actually gained seats in the South. Table 5.4 shows the regional distribution of House seats after the last three elections.

Table 5.4 House Seats by Region and Party, 2008–2012

Year	South	Non-South
2008	83R, 61D	196D, 112R
2010	102R, 37D	153D, 140R
2012	109R, 36D	163D, 125R

Republicans in the House have returned to their position after the elections of 1996–2004, with a majority in the chamber dependent on a Southern supermajority. The Republican caucus in the House is now 47 percent Southern, a percentage unmatched by either party since the Democrats of the 1950s.

The conservative white Democrat, who as recently as 1990 dominated Southern House elections, is nearly extinct. John Barrow (GA-12) is now the only white Democrat in the Deep South. He and Mike McIntyre (NC-7) are the only Democrats representing districts in the South outside of high-minority areas or pockets of white liberals. Republicans picked up an open seat previously held by Democrats in Oklahoma and gained newly created seats in South Carolina, Georgia, Florida, and Texas (2). Democratic gains were limited to new Latino-heavy districts in Florida and Texas (2), and two South Florida seats affected by redistricting and the Tea Party–backed candidacy of the controversial Allen West (FL-18).

House elections in the three Southern battleground states show the advantages the Republicans enjoy in the South and nationwide. Barack Obama won 50.3 percent of the combined votes in Virginia, Florida, and North Carolina, but Democrats hold only 31.4 (16/51) percent of House seats. The Obama campaign's turnout efforts could boost the Democratic vote in areas of Democratic concentration such as Northern Virginia, North Carolina's Research Triangle, Central Florida, and South Florida, but not overcome the gerrymanders of Republican legislators. The isolated Democratic gains in Florida came about because of the need to create a new Latino-majority district in the Orlando area to comply with the Voting Rights Act, and a reversal of the surprise 2010 victory of Tea Party–backed Allen West in the Democratic-leaning 22nd district.

In *The Rise of Southern Republicans* (2002), Earl and Merle Black attribute the Republican growth in House elections in the region to three factors: an increasingly conservative ideology by Southern whites beginning in the 1960s, the popularity of Ronald Reagan in the 1980s, and the destabilization caused by the race-conscious redistricting after the 1990 census. These factors combined to make Republicans the clear regional majority party in the House with the 1994 elections. The party's large gains in 2010 and smaller gains in 2012 show that the shift is durable and can withstand a Democratic presidential victory nationwide and demographic shifts that benefit Democrats.

The Democratic position in the Senate is weaker than in the House, mainly due to the fact that heavily African American or Latino seats allow them to salvage House seats in states that are uncompetitive statewide as in Texas or Mississippi. Democratic exposure was limited, since they only were defending two of the five Southern Senate seats, and these were in states where Obama won narrow victories. Democratic Virginia Governor Tim Kaine won the battle of the former governors over Republican George Allen 52.5 percent to 47.5 percent, and incumbent Democrat Bill Nelson handily defeated Congressman Connie Mack 55 percent to 42 percent. In 2014, however, Democrats Mary Landrieu of Louisiana and Mark Pryor of Arkansas faced reelection in states where their party has slipped to clear minority status. Just as in the House, the gains of Democrats in Non-Southern Senate races have produced an increasingly Southern Republican caucus.

Table 5.5 Senate Seats by Region, 2012

	Obama	Romney
South	6	20
Non-South	49*	25
Total	55	45

*Includes Independents Sanders and King

Table 5.5 shows the partisan and regional breakdown of the Senate after the 2012 elections. The Republican caucus is now 44 percent Southern, down from an all-time high of 48 percent in 2009–2010.

Southern Republicans, as part of the minority party, are in a weaker position in the Senate than in the House on votes to organize the chamber and to pass legislation. But the growing use of the filibuster, making 60 votes necessary to move most important legislation to a vote, puts Southern Senators in a similar position to their House colleagues. If the 109 Southern House Republicans stay united, the 109 make up half of the 218 votes needed to pass legislation. If Senate Republicans unite to oppose cloture on legislation favored by the Democratic majority, they make up nearly half of the 41 needed to filibuster.

CONCLUSION: THE SOUTH AND THE QUEST FOR A GOVERNING MAJORITY

Barack Obama began his second term at the head of a Democratic Party that has lost the Southern popular and electoral vote in nine consecutive elections. The party's share of Southern House seats is the lowest held by either party since the Republicans in 1968 (see McKee 2010). The Democrats are now in a position similar to that of the Republicans between Reconstruction and the New Deal, dependent on large majorities outside of the South to build a national governing majority. Such a result is possible, as shown by the results of 2006 and 2008. But Republicans, whether in a period of national strength or national weakness, are now the clear majority party in the South.

This concentration of Republican support in the most distinctive American region has significant consequences for how majorities are constructed in national governing institutions. Separation of powers, single-member district candidate-centered elections, bicameralism, and the Electoral College channel majority will lead to differing results. Republican domination of the South is a major contributor to the contemporary politics of divided government and constrained majorities.

Democrats won a majority of the total vote for the House of Representatives, but face a 34-vote deficit. If they could manage a mere 37 percent of Southern House seats, they would retake the majority with their 2012 strength in the Non-South. Such a result at this point seems impossible, and any effort to retake the House will concentrate on further gains in the Midwest and Northeast. Republican strength in the South, combined with the filibuster, makes building an effective governing majority in the Senate dependent on successive wave elections as occurred in 2006 and 2008.

The 2012 presidential election, in contrast to congressional results, reveals the weakness of the Republican position in the Electoral College. Black and Black in 1987 called the region the "Vital South," crucial to determining the winner of presidential elections. The shift of Southern whites into the Republican column moved the region from the Democratic "Solid South" to a position of competitiveness in the 1950s–1990s. Barack Obama's victories in 2008 and 2012 have shown that the South is no longer vital to both parties in the quest for the White House, but necessary only for a Republican victory. The "tipping point" state that pushed Obama past the 270-electoral vote milestone was Pennsylvania, and he won a total of 290 electoral votes outside of the South. He could have lost Virginia and Florida and still had several paths to reelection. In 2016, the Republican nominee will have to simultaneously engineer an incremental increase in the party's Southern support to regain those two states, while significantly improving on Mitt Romney's percentage in the Non-South. That is a formidable task.

REFERENCES

Black, E., and M. Black. 1987. *The Vital South.* Cambridge, MA: Harvard University Press.

Black, E., and M. Black. 2002. *The Rise of Southern Republicans.* Cambridge, MA: Harvard University Press.

Dunham, R. F. 2012. "Demographic Tides May Turn Texas Purple or Blue." *Houston Chronicle,* November 10. Retrieved December 21, 2012 from http://www.chron.com/news/article/Demographic-tides-may-turn-Texas-purple-or-blue-4026956.php.

McKee, S. C. 2010. *Republican Ascendancy in Southern U.S. House Elections.* Boulder, CO: Westview Press.

Reiter, H. L., and J. Stonecash. *Counter-Realignment: Political Change in the Northeastern United States.* New York: Cambridge University Press.

Chapter 6

The 2012 Presidential Race in Battleground Florida
Changing Demographics Challenge the Obama and Romney Campaigns

Susan A. MacManus and David J. Bonanza, University of South Florida

While many pundits long ago saw Florida as likely Romney country—after all, Democrats were virtually extinct in Tallahassee after 2012—the Obama campaign focused on demographics.
—Adam C. Smith, Tampa Bay Times, *November 7, 2012*

Palm Beach County Republican Chairman Sid Dinerstein said [the 2012 election] results were driven "almost totally" by demographics. The president, he said, effectively targeted groups that have eluded the GOP. The results have sparked a fresh round of Republican soul searching, with some leaders suggesting the party change its tone.
—Scott Powers and Jim Stratton, Orlando Sentinel, *November 7, 2012*

FLORIDA: THE BELLWETHER STATE

From beginning to end, Florida was seen as one of the nation's premier battleground states. Its 29 Electoral College votes (two more than in 2008) made it a bigger prize than any other swing state. Florida's size, diversity, and partisan competitiveness (see Figure 6.1) ensured that the

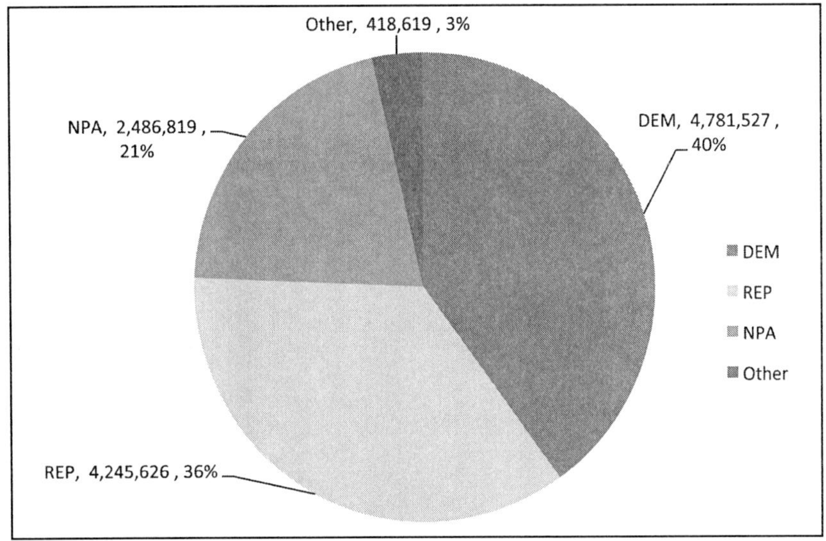

Figure 6.1 Florida's Registered Voters: The Partisan Divide

Source: Florida Division of Elections, book closing registration data, Fall 2012 election.

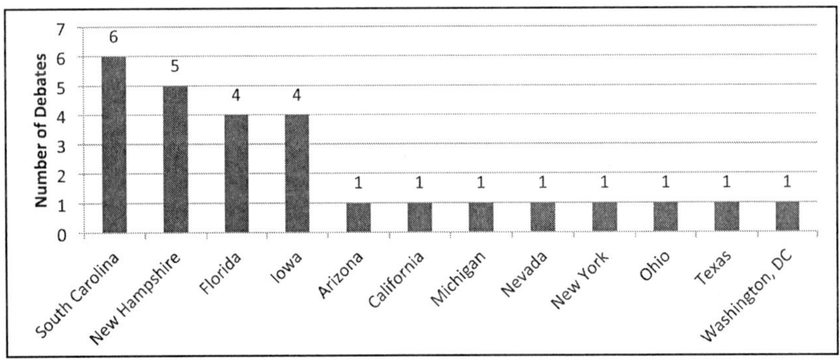

Figure 6.2 Florida Hosted Four GOP Primary Debates, 2011–2012

Note: Not every candidate participated in every debate and some debates were not televised.
Source: "2012 Primary Debate Schedule," 2012–2016 Election Central, accessed November 26, 2012. http://ww
w.2012presidentialelectionnews.com/2012-debate-schedule/2011-2012-primary-debate-schedule/.

state would be in the national spotlight (Goodman 2012; Curry 2012). Prior to Election Day, Florida was home to four televised GOP primary debates (see Figure 6.2), one nationally televised presidential debate (the last of three), and 40 visits from presidential/vice presidential candidates (see Figure 6.3). More money was spent on TV ads in Florida's 10 media

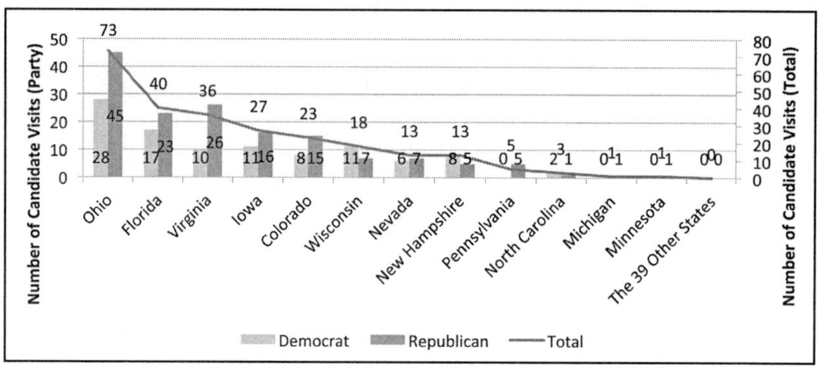

Figure 6.3 Presidential Candidates Visited Florida Often

Note: This chart shows the number of campaign events since the end of the Democratic National Convention. Source: "Presidential Tracker," The Center for Voting and Democracy, November 16, 2012. http://www.fairvote .org/presidential-tracker#.ULNroYbe-Sp.

markets than in any other state (Klas 2012b) (see Figure 6.4), and both parties engaged in highly targeted get out the vote (GOTV) mobilization efforts. At the outset, analysts agreed that without a win in Florida, Romney had little chance of capturing the presidency, while a victory by President Obama would virtually guarantee his reelection (Good 2012; Curry 2012; Campo-Flores 2012; Pace 2012).

Nearly everyone expected the race in Florida to be close. In 2008, Democrat Barack Obama defeated Republican John McCain by just 2.8 percentage points—the fifth closest popular vote margin in the nation. The state's 2010 gubernatorial race was the closest in modern history. Republican Rick Scott defeated Democrat Alex Sink by just 1.2 percentage points. And the results of most horse race polls (partisan and nonpartisan) pitting Barack Obama vs. Mitt Romney were within the margin of error for months, right up to Election Day.

Heading into the 2012 contest, many believed that another contested election was not out of the question (MacManus 2012). Early on, Bill Daley, Obama's former White House chief of staff and a key figure in the 2000 recount battle, warned the Obama campaign to prepare for a possible recount in Florida in 2012. Republican legal strategists issued similar warnings to their party and candidates. On Election Night, as the winner was called in every state but Florida, it looked as if the prediction might come true. Fortunately, it did not, but the race in Florida was so close that

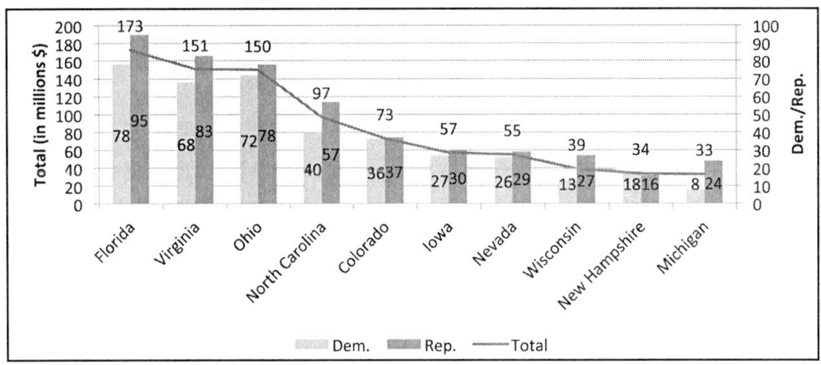

Figure 6.4 The Most Money Was Spent on TV Ads in Florida

Note: All data since April 11, 2012, the day after Rick Santorum dropped out of the Republican primaries. Source: "Mad Money: TV ads in the 2012 presidential campaign," *The Washington Post*, November 14, 2012. http://www.washingtonpost.com/wp-srv/special/politics/track-presidential-campaign-ads-2012/.

it took four days to officially declare the winner, although Romney conceded on Election Night.

Obama bested Romney by a mere 74,309 votes out of 8.5 million cast, once again affirming Florida's historical status as a bellwether state and the nation's most competitive. Nowhere was the highly sophisticated microtargeting of key constituencies more evident than in the Sunshine State with its racial/ethnic, age, gender, religious, and geographical diversity. In this chapter, we focus on how the two campaigns aimed their messages and outreach activities to various slices of the Florida electorate. We conclude with some thoughts about how Florida's experiences might affect the 2016 presidential campaign.

RACE/ETHNICITY

It is often said that Florida's racial/ethnic makeup mirrors the United States at large more so than any other swing state (see Table 6.1). Among Florida's registered voters, nearly one-third were nonwhite (see Figure 6.5). The two largest racial/ethnic groups were Hispanics (14 percent) and African Americans/Caribbean blacks (14 percent), followed by Asians (2 percent). Blacks are the most politically cohesive group, solidly Democratic both in registration (see Figure 6.6) and voting. Florida's Democrats and independents (No Party Affiliation, or NPAs) are more racially/ethnically diverse than the state's Republicans (see Figure 6.7).

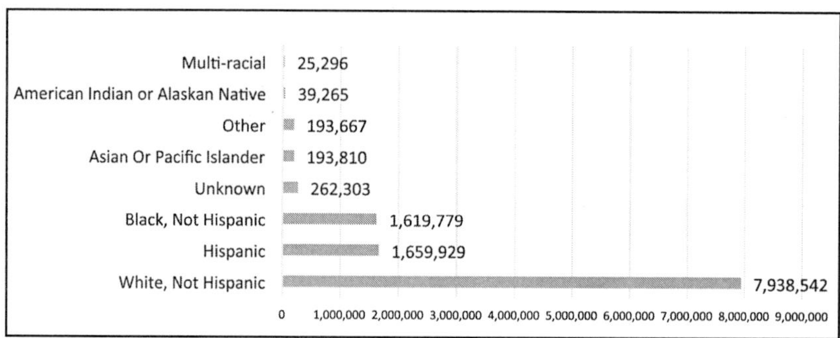

Figure 6.5 Nearly One-Third of Florida Registered Voters Were Nonwhite

Source: Florida Division of Elections, book closing registration data, Fall 2012 election.

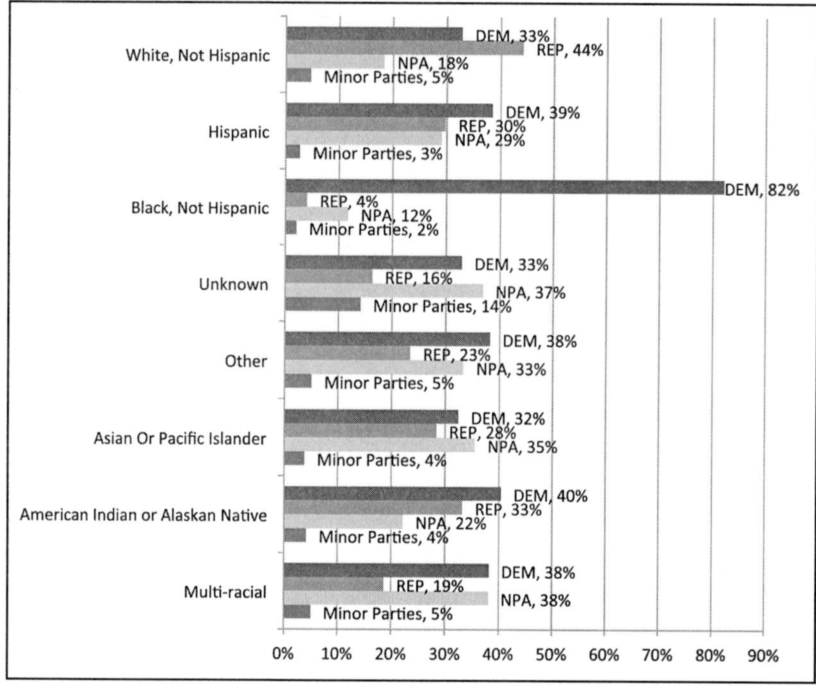

Figure 6.6 Florida Voter Registration by Race and Party

Source: Calculated from registration data provided by the Florida Division of Elections, book closing, August 12 primary.

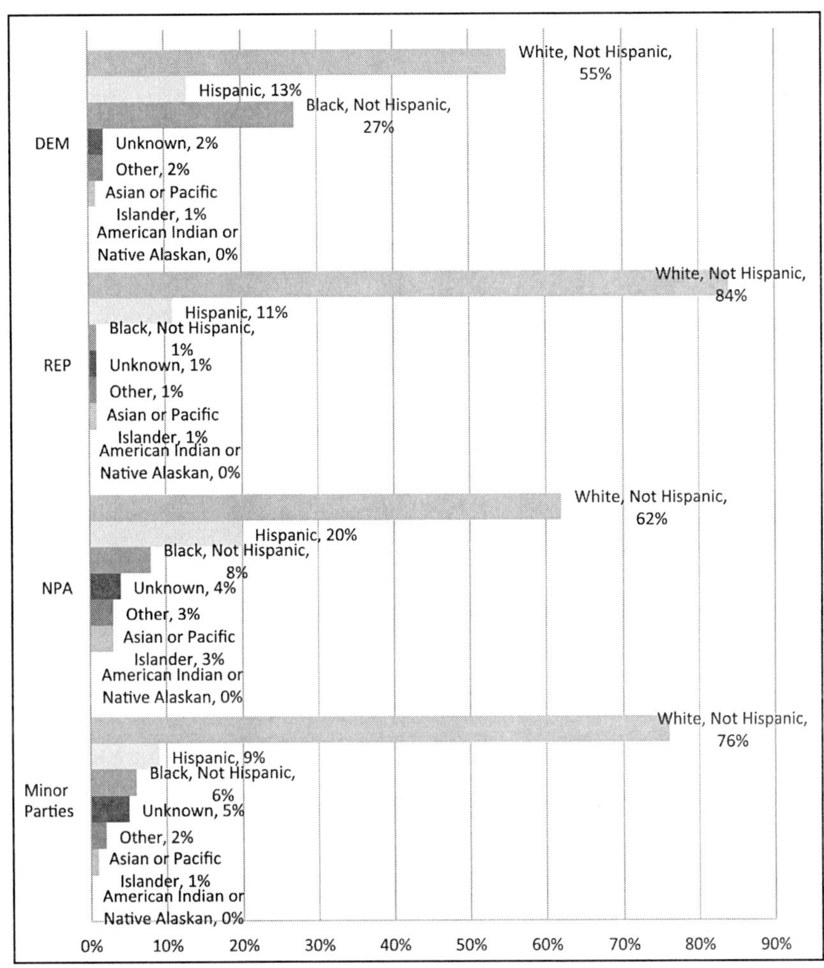

Figure 6.7 Democratic Party Registrants Most Racially Diverse

Source: Florida Division of Elections, book closing registration data, August 2012 primary election.

Table 6.1 Florida Racial and Ethnic Composition Mirrors United States

Race	Percentage of Population	
	Florida 2010 (%)	U.S. 2010 (%)
White	75.0	72.4
Non-Hispanic White	57.9	63.7
Hispanic/Latino	22.5	16.3
African American	16.0	12.6
Asian	2.4	4.8
Native American	0.4	0.9
Pacific Islander	0.1	0.2
Some other race	3.6	6.2
Two or more races	2.5	2.9

Source: U.S. Census Bureau, 2010 Census.

Hispanics

The 2010 U.S. Census results and the redistricting that followed heavily publicized the growth rate of Hispanics in Florida vis-à-vis other racial/ethnic groups (see Figure 6.8). The Hispanic population itself has become considerably more diverse in recent years, with non-Cuban Hispanics now outnumbering Cuban Hispanics (see Figure 6.9). One exit poll of Florida's Hispanic voters found that 34 percent were Cuban while 57 percent were non-Cuban (Lopez and Taylor 2012).

In 2012, both parties focused considerable attention on the burgeoning Puerto Rican community in the Orange and Osceola county areas (Schultz 2012; Buzzacco-Foerster and Carpenter 2012; Gibson 2012; Anderson 2012). In fact, President Obama's first post–Democratic National Convention stop in Florida was a rally at the Kissimmee Civic Center in Osceola County (Carpenter 2012). Democrats counted on the anti-immigration stances of Republicans to help them win the Puerto Rican vote (Babington 2012). Republicans were hopeful that they could make inroads by emphasizing higher-than-average unemployment rates among minorities since polls showed that Hispanics, like other Floridians, consistently ranked the economy as their top issue of concern (Henderson 2012; Bennett 2012c).

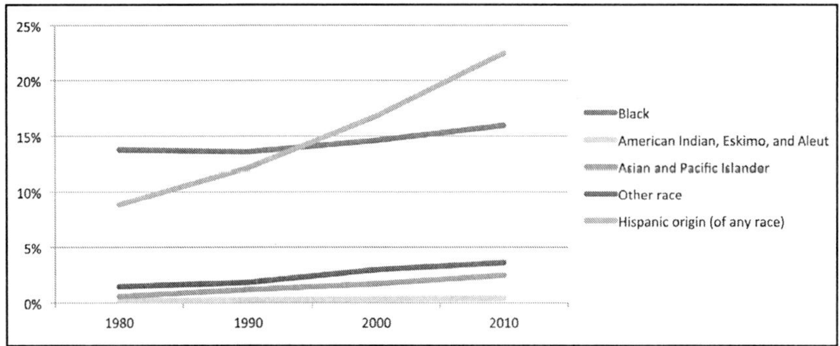

Figure 6.8 Hispanics Are Florida's Fastest Growing Racial/Ethnic Group

Source: U.S. Census Bureau.

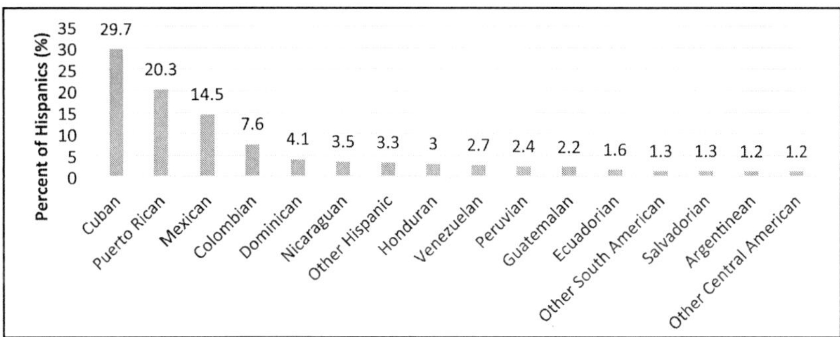

Figure 6.9 Non-Cubans Now Outnumber Cubans

Source: U.S. Census Bureau, American Community Survey, 2009.

As the election campaign progressed, national polls consistently showed heavy support for Obama among Hispanics (in the two-thirds range), but a much closer margin among Florida's Hispanic voters (Caputo and Mazzei 2012; Murray 2012). The narrower gap was attributed to the larger presence of Hispanic Republicans, namely Cubans, although their share of the Hispanic vote had been shrinking over the past few election cycles and trending a bit more Democratic (Man 2012a). There was considerable uncertainty as to the turnout rate of Puerto Ricans, a statistic that tends to be somewhat unpredictable. A Puerto Rican woman who was one of Obama's national cochairs acknowledged that the biggest challenge was with "first-generation voters who are just getting established and finding a good job and trying to send their kids to school" (Reinhard 2012).

Puerto Rican turnout is highest when there is a high-profile Puerto Rican candidate on the ballot, which was not the case in 2012 in the Puerto Rican–intensive Orlando area. To boost turnout, the Obama campaign brought in Bill Richardson, a Latino and former governor of New Mexico. Richardson helped organize a caravan to energize Hispanics in an Orlando area neighborhood to vote early (Babington 2012). (Caravans are a popular way of campaigning in Puerto Rican elections, featuring a parade of trucks with loudspeakers blaring candidate names and cars with windows decorated with slogans and GOTV information.)

The Florida exit poll showed that Hispanics increased their share of the electorate from 14 percent in 2008 to 17 percent in 2012; 60 percent voted for Obama—up 3 percent from 2008. The unexpectedly large vote for Obama was driven by a higher-than-expected vote for him among Cubans. Although there was some dispute about whether he won a majority of the Cuban vote, there was widespread agreement that he made major gains among that constituency, particularly among younger Cubans (Tamayo 2012; Bendixen and Amandi International 2012; Caputo 2012b; Faries and Nesmith 2012).

Generational replacement has made the Cuban vote less solidly Republican. Younger Cubans born in the United States are more interested in domestic than foreign policy and lean more Democratic than their parents or grandparents. Latinas made up a larger share of the Hispanic vote than their male counterparts for the second presidential election in a row, thanks to the heavy involvement of women in Obama's GOTV operation.

Spanish-language media (Univision, Telemundo) also played a big part in promoting cohesiveness among Hispanics in order to increase the political clout of Hispanics overall. Spanish-language TV and radio stations constantly pushed Hispanics to register and vote and down-played country-of-origin differences. There was evidence that Obama's Spanish-language campaign "Latinos pro Obama" was more extensive and effective in both message and reach than Romney's "Juntos con Romney" campaign (Powers 2012). The higher-than-anticipated cohesiveness among Hispanics prompted the chair of the Republican Party of Florida to proclaim: "We have some serious and significant work to do with Puerto Ricans and the younger generation of Cubans. Really, we need to become a more inclusive party" (Dixon 2012).

African American/Caribbean Blacks

There was never an expectation in the Romney camp that Republicans would make major inroads into the black vote. However, the Romney campaign was hoping to peel away some black support from Obama. Lieutenant Governor Jennifer Carroll, a native of Trinidad, and U.S. Congressman Allen West led the Romney minority outreach team in Florida. As with Hispanics, the strategy was to point to the economic failures of the Obama administration, emphasizing the high unemployment rate among African Americans, particularly youth (Turner 2012; Pounds 2012).

The major worry within the Obama campaign regarding black voters was a lower level of enthusiasm for the president than in 2008 when he made history by breaking the racial barrier. Specifically, there was some concern that enthusiasm for the president had fallen among African Americans because of the president's stance on gay marriage. A greater concern was that changes in Florida's election laws yielding new registration procedures and a reduction in the number of early voting days would result in fewer black voters. Civil rights groups' claims of voter suppression by the Republican-led legislature and the governor grew louder and ultimately worked to mobilize minority voters.

When voter suppression battles escalated, older African Americans quickly coalesced behind the president. These voters had fought long and hard for minority voting rights and were not about to see them taken away. Younger blacks were mobilized by Washington-based ministers brought into Florida to preach about the sacrifices of their elders on the Sunday of "souls to the polls" efforts, and by voter protection groups on college campuses. These efforts were quite effective. Exit polls showed that blacks as a share of all Florida voters were at the same level as in 2008 (13 percent) and solidly behind Obama (95 percent), with just a 1 percent slippage from 2008 (see Table 6.2).

Table 6.2 Minority Vote Solidly Behind Obama

Voter Characteristic	% of voters		2008		2012	
	2008	2012	Obama	McCain	Obama	Romney
Race						
White	71	67	42	56	37	61
Black	13	13	96	4	95	4
Hispanic/Latino	14	17	57	42	60	39
Asian	1	2	0	0	0	0
Other	1	2	0	0	59	39

Note: All figures from http://www.foxnews.com/politics/elections/2008-exit-poll; http://www.foxnews.com/politics/elections/2012-exit-poll/US/President.
Source: National Election Exit Poll, Edison Research.

AGE

The conventional wisdom among many outside of Florida was that the state's senior voters were the dominant cohort. By 2012, this was no longer true. Our preelection analyses of registered voters showed that 52 percent of Florida's registered voters were 50 years of age or older, but 48 percent were under age 50, with the largest cohort being 30–49-year-olds (see Figure 6.10).

The 2012 election cycle heightened awareness of generational political differences. Various polls and Census analyses established that younger voters are more diverse in their racial/ethnic makeup (Benac and Cass 2012) and more likely to be single (The Voter Participation Center and Lake Research Partners 2012), college-educated (CIRCLE 2012), secular (Goodstein 2012; Holt 2012), and residents of metropolitan areas (Hulse 2012) than older voters. Florida's older voters are trending more Republican, while its younger voters are increasingly registering as independents (NPAs) although voting Democratic (see Figure 6.11 and Table 6.3).

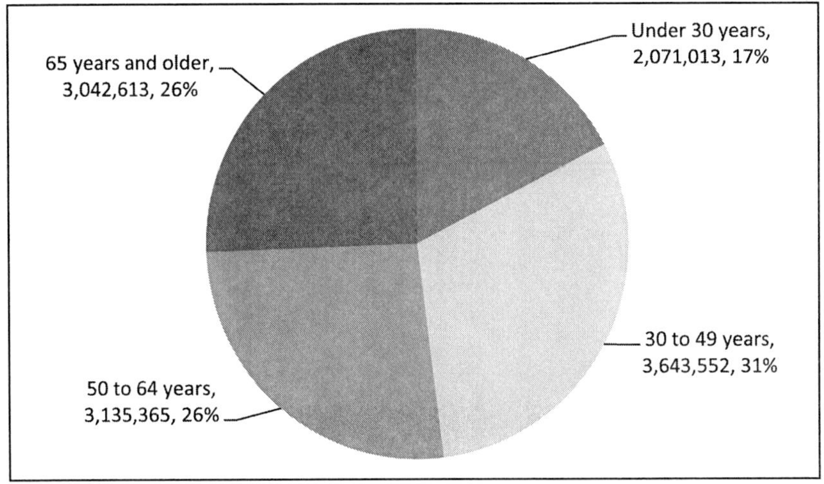

Figure 6.10 Florida's Electorate More Age-Diverse Than Commonly Thought

Source: Florida Division of Elections, book closing registration data, Fall 2012 election.

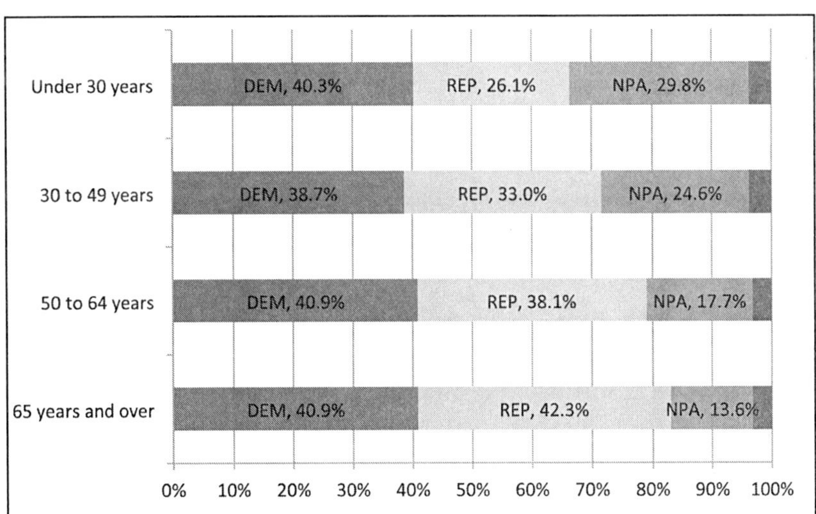

Figure 6.11 Older Floridians Leaning More Republican

Source: Florida Division of Elections, book closing registration data, Fall 2012 election.

Table 6.3 The Generational Divide: Young Voters for Obama, Older Voters for Romney

Voter Characteristic	% of voters		2008		2012	
	2008	2012	Obama	McCain	Obama	Romney
Age						
18–29	15	16	61	37	66	32
30–44	25	23	49	49	52	46
45–64	37	37	52	47	48	52
Other	22	24	45	53	41	58

Note: All figures from http://www.foxnews.com/politics/elections/2008-exit-poll; http://www.foxnews.com/politics/elections/2012-exit-poll/US/President.
Source: National Election Exit Poll, Edison Research.

Older Voters: Seniors and Baby Boomers

Florida's seniors are more divided from a partisan perspective. In 2012, among Florida's registered voters 65 and older, 42 percent were Republican, 41 percent Democratic. The rest were independents (NPAs) or affiliated with a minor party.

The Obama campaign initially believed that it could recapture some of the older vote lost to McCain in the 2008 campaign via the Medicare issue (Man and Wolford 2012; Smith 2012b; Sanders and Rossetter 2012). Millions of dollars were spent on TV ads focused on the Medicare issue by super PACs, the candidates, and the political parties, following Governor Romney's announcement that Paul Ryan would be his running mate (Klas 2012a). Newspaper headlines across the United States screamed "There goes Florida for the Republicans" since Ryan had expressed support for revamping popular senior-oriented entitlement programs. As it turned out, the issue was not the "slam dunk" for Obama that his campaign strategists had anticipated.

The media's and the Obama campaign's premature proclamations were based on antiquated notions of senior voters that presumed a heavy dependence on Social Security and Medicare among senior voters—a view that did not take into account generational replacement (Barrow 2012). Today's Florida seniors are somewhat younger, healthier, wealthier, and better educated than seniors in other regions of the country. Seniors in Florida also tend to be more informed about issues and were more likely to know that any plans to reform Medicare would not affect them (Bennett 2012d).

Young Voters

Could the Obama campaign mobilize Florida's younger voters as it had in 2008? Poll after poll showed lower levels of enthusiasm among younger voters. There was evidence that economic woes were taking their toll on college students (the high turnout portion of the youth vote). Many had seen their own parents suffer economically. Pressured to take more classes, they had less time to get engaged in campaign activities—a collective activity that spikes turnout. And some were disappointed with Obama's first four years in office on a number of fronts, ranging from gay rights to Guantanamo.

Still, Democrats had faith that the president *could* replicate his 2008 success with younger voters. In 2008, Obama won 61 percent of the 18–29-year-old vote—the most support he got from any age cohort. Democrats knew full well that the younger cohort (18–29) was the most solidly Democratic (and liberal) in its vote patterns and more progovernment than their elders. Obama's strategists understood viscerally that Obama's biggest challenge was getting younger voters to turn out, particularly young women and persons of color and those registered as independents. In 2012, 25 percent of those registering as NPAs were 18–29-year-olds; another 36 percent were 30–49-year-olds. Most of the slight shifts of the horse race polls in one direction or another throughout the campaign were attributable to young and independent voters (Caputo 2012a).

As with African Americans, the Romney campaign's goal was to erode Obama's support among young voters, rather than to capture a majority of that vote. Republicans believed they could do so by focusing on high unemployment rates, calling attention to the rapidly growing national debt, and then arguing that each problem had disproportionately landed on the shoulders of young voters.

The turnout and cohesion of younger voters was perhaps the biggest surprise of the 2012 election. No one had projected that the youth vote as a proportion of the Florida electorate would increase in 2012, but it did (from 15 percent in 2008 to 16 percent in 2012) (see Table 6.3). As in 2008, younger voters, especially young females and minorities, propelled Obama to victory in Florida. Many of these were late deciders. In Florida, exit polls showed that 3 percent of the voters made up their minds about voting on Election Day; another 5 percent did so just a few days in advance.

Postelection revelations showed Democrats had a much better plan for targeting young voters, often described as "low propensity" or "sporadic" voters and late deciders. The campaign heavily relied on embedded staff and a superior database that constantly informed volunteers and staff in the field as to who had not yet voted but had pledged to do so. The organizational superiority of Democrats was touted from the get-go, with countless articles detailing the Obama campaign's edge in the number of offices around the state (106 vs. 47) and paid staffers, with many having been left in place after the 2008 election (Avlon and Keller 2012; O'Toole 2012). President Clinton's visits to college campuses (Nicholas 2012), along with those by Obama in south Florida—and by Michelle Obama in Tallahassee, Orlando, Jacksonville, Gainesville, and Davie—also helped mobilize younger voters in the closing days of the election. The president and all his surrogates stressed Obama's college loan policies and his health care plan that allowed younger voters to remain on their parents' health insurance policies. Younger and single women were also pushed to vote by contraception and reproductive rights issues.

The 2012 election left many concluding that the 18–29-year-old cohort had become the state's most consistently solid Democratic voting bloc (age-wise), whereas in the past it was the senior vote, which is now almost evenly split between Democrats and Republicans. The younger cohort is increasingly described as the new entitlement generation, a marked change from the past when it was the senior cohort that was dominated by FDR-era voters who were more heavily dependent on Social Security and Medicare than are today's seniors.

GENDER

In Florida, as in the United States at large, women make up a majority of the voting-age population, registered voters (see Figure 6.12), and actual voters (see Table 6.4).

These facts explain why both major political parties (Democratic and Republican) and women's advocacy groups from across the ideological

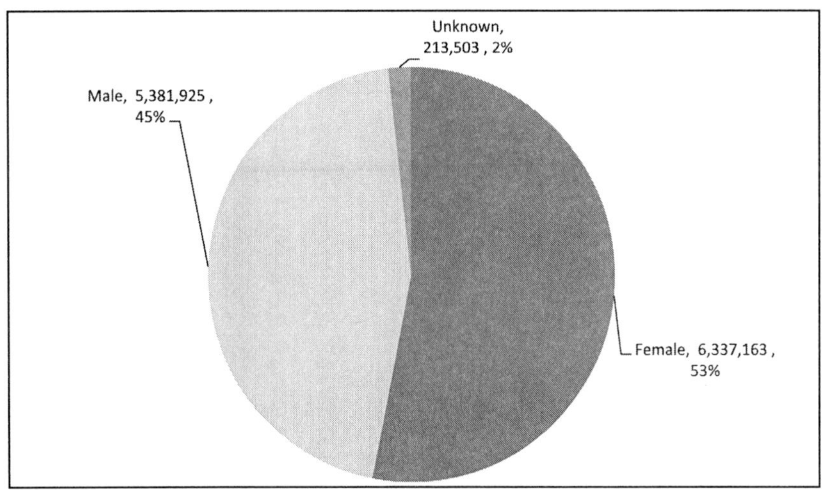

Figure 6.12 The Majority of Florida's Registered Voters Are Female

Source: Florida Division of Elections, book closing registration data, Fall 2012 election.

spectrum worked hard to mobilize women voters in 2012 (MacManus 2014). In fact, the competition for women's votes by both Obama and Romney was so intense that some characterized the 2012 campaign more as the "War *for* Women" than the "War *on* Women"—the latter being a label Democrats tried to hang on Republicans but Romney surrogates like Condoleezza Rice constantly refuted. In speaking at a GOP rally at Broward College, Rice counterattacked Democrats' comments: "All of this nonsense out there about the war on women—who are we kidding? I am a woman. I know that what we are getting from Mitt Romney and Paul Ryan is respect and understanding that women are single women and mothers and daughters and wives and that they too want an economy recovering where people can find jobs" (Bennett 2012g). Ann Romney took a similar message on the campaign trail.

The women's vote has never been a highly cohesive one at any level. Among Florida's female registered voters, 44 percent are Democrats, 34 percent Republicans, 19 percent NPAs, and 3 percent affiliated with a minor party (see Figure 6.13). Women make up a larger share of Florida Democrats than Republicans or NPAs (see Figure 6.14). Fifty-four percent of the state's female registrants are 50 or older, 46 percent are under age 50 (see Figure 6.15). Due to longer life expectancies, women make up a larger share of seniors (55 percent) than of 18–29-year-olds—the Millennials (51 percent) (see Figure 6.16). Black, Hispanic, and Asian women are a larger share of their racial/ethnic groups' registrants than are white or Native American women (see Figure 6.17). And larger shares of female than male registrants are minorities (see Figure 6.18).

Table 6.4 Gender Voting Patterns: Overall, by Race, and by Marital Status

Voter Characteristic	% of voters 2008	% of voters 2012	2008 Obama	2008 McCain	2012 Obama	2012 Romney
Sex						
Male	47	45	51	47	46	52
Female	53	55	52	47	53	46
Sex by race						
White men		30			33	65
White women		37			41	58
Black men		6			94	5
Black women		8			96	4
Latino men		7			58	40
Latino women		9			61	38
All other races		3			70	29
Sex by marital status						
Married men		28			41	58
Married women		30			45	54
Nonmarried men		16			57	41
Nonmarried women		26			63	36

Note: All figures from http://www.foxnews.com/politics/elections/2008-exit-poll; http://www.foxnews.com/politics/elections/2012-exit-poll/US/President.
Source: National Election Exit Poll, Edison Research.

In 2012, the two major political parties targeted women somewhat differently (Bowman and Marsico 2012; Meckler and Lippman 2012). The message and the messengers used to connect with younger and older women varied considerably, primarily because of the close connection between age and political party. For example, the Obama campaign heavily targeted younger, single women who tend to be more liberal, more secular, more racially diverse, and more Democratic than older women (Allison, 2012; Benac and Cass 2012; Ball 2012; The Voter Par-

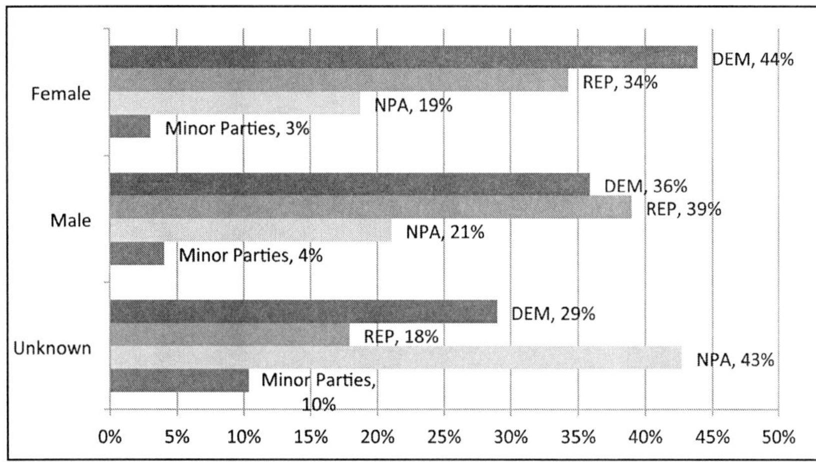

Figure 6.13 More Women Are Registered Democrats

Source: Florida Division of Elections, book closing registration data, August primary election.

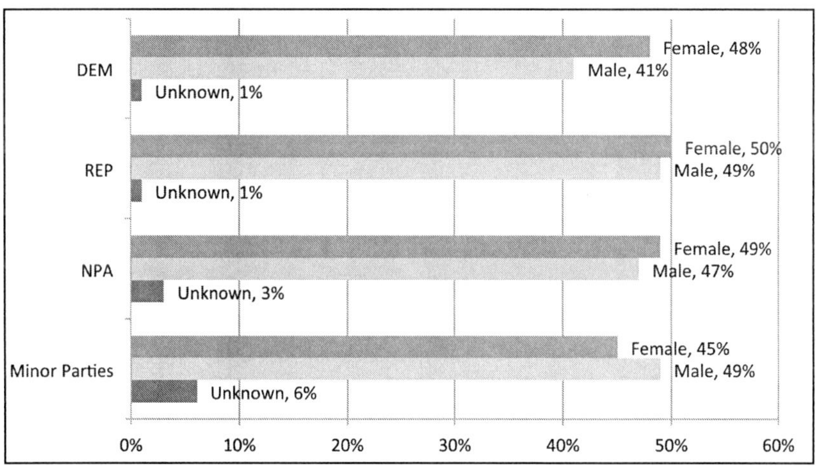

Figure 6.14 Females Are a Larger Share of Democrats Than Republicans

Source: Florida Division of Elections, book closing registration data, August 2012 primary election.

ticipation Center and Lake Research Partners 2012). The Romney camp focused more on older women—a higher proportion of whom are white, married, conservative, religious, and more likely to lean Republican. Both campaigns targeted suburban women, often the swing vote in presidential contests (Meckler and Lippman 2012).

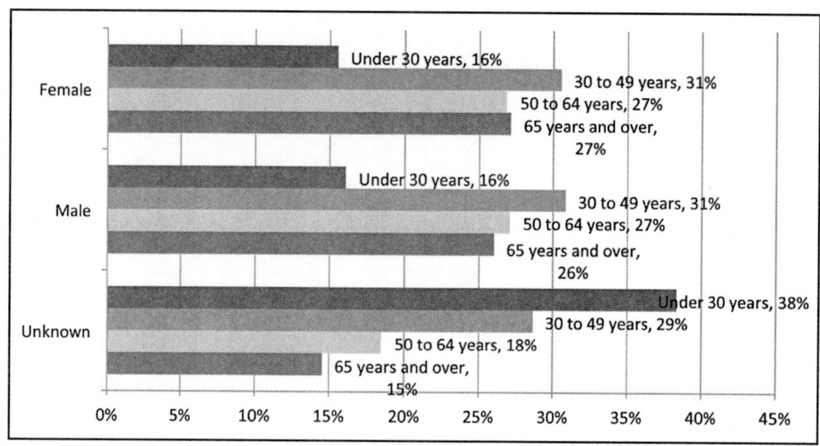

Figure 6.15 More Women Registrants Are Over 50 Than Under 50

Source: Florida Division of Elections, book closing registration data, August primary election.

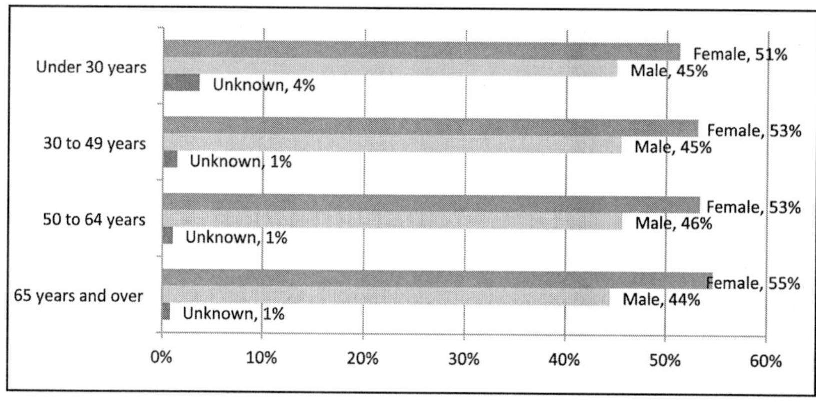

Figure 6.16 Women Are a Larger Share of Older Registered Voters

Source: Florida Division of Elections, book closing registration data, August 12 primary election.

Women's outreach efforts by both parties heavily relied on women-to-women networking (Sweet 2012) and surrogate visits by the candidates' wives and other popular female figures. The Women for Obama operation used phone banks (Women's Wednesdays), house parties, and Women Vote 2012 Summits featuring paycheck fairness, health care (including birth control), abortion rights, and education (Jackson 2012) to get out the women's vote in Florida. Similarly, the Romney campaign's

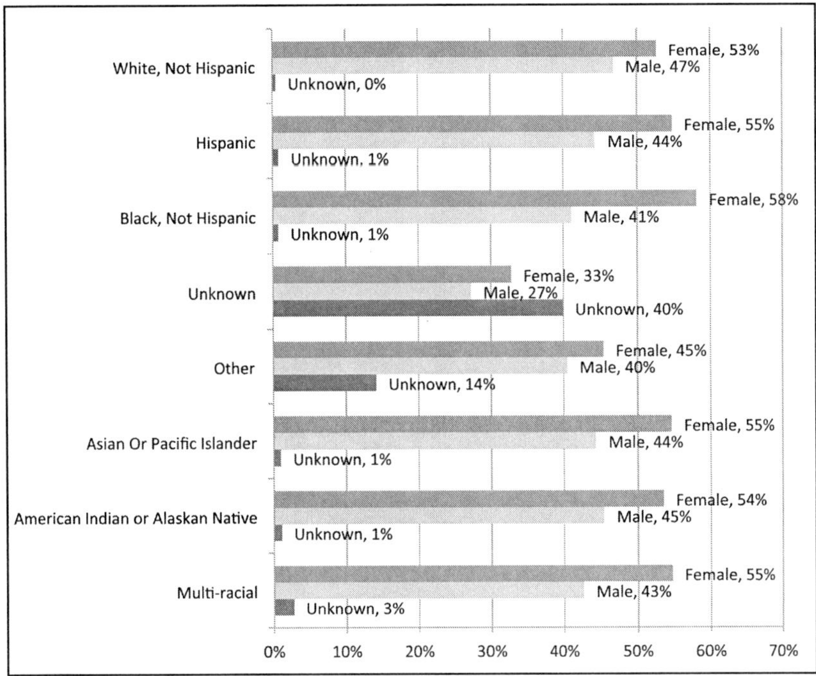

Figure 6.17 Women Are a Larger Share of Minority Group Registrants

Source: Florida Division of Elections, book closing registration data, August primary election.

Women for Mitt operation hosted roundtables, forums, and town hall meetings and conducted extensive phone-banking to get out the vote. At the heart of the Romney message was the sagging economy's impact on middle-class families. After all, Florida continued to lag behind the rest of the country in recovering from the recession, with higher than national average unemployment rates and home foreclosure rates.

Reflective of Florida's divided electorate, there was a lot more fluctuation in gender support patterns throughout the campaign than nationally. Several times, the divide among women voters narrowed considerably, giving hope to the Romney campaign. (It is often said that if the women's vote in Florida is split, Republicans will win the state.) Some analysts attributed the fluctuation to suburban women—who voted for Obama in 2008 but for Republicans in 2010, largely over economic issues. Democrats were optimistic these women could be drawn back to Obama

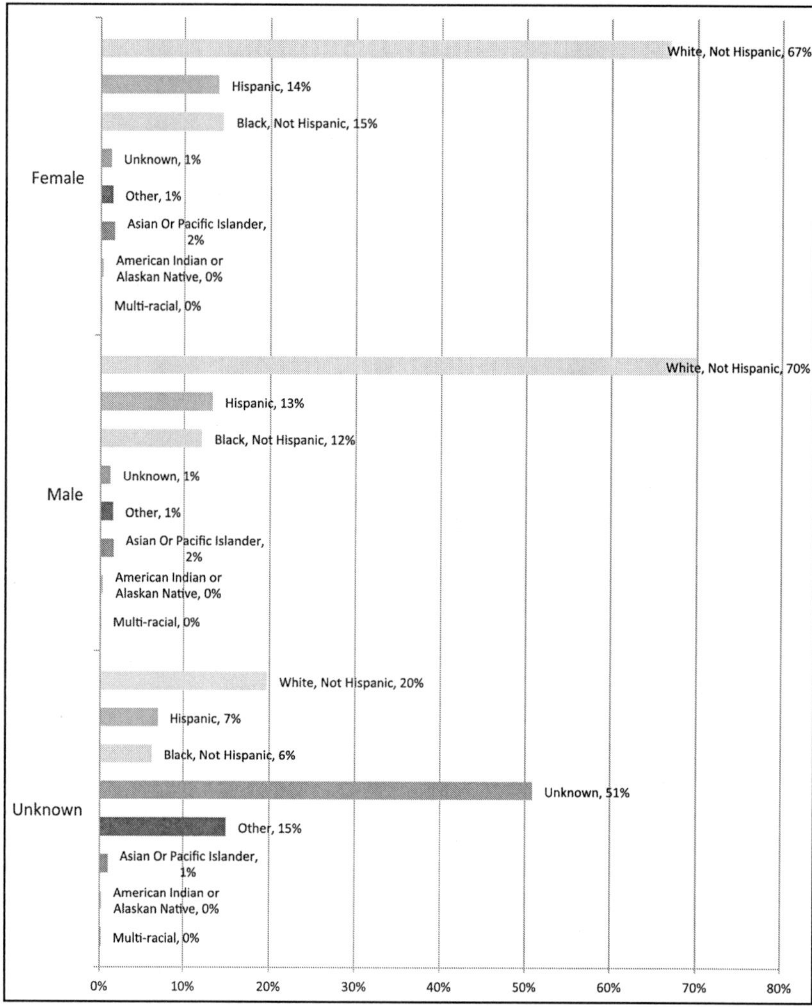

Figure 6.18 Larger Share of Female Registrants Are Minorities

Source: Florida Division of Elections, book closing registration data, August 12, 2012 primary election.

by reproductive rights issues and health care for themselves and their children. However, Democrats worried about turnout among younger minority women—a larger portion of Democratic-voting women—while Republicans were confident in their ability to turn out older and married women with historically higher turnout rates.

The women's vote in Florida expanded from 53 percent in 2008 to 55 percent in 2012 (see Table 6.4) and ended up more solidly behind Obama (53 percent) than polls taken earlier in the campaign had suggested. Just as they had done in 2008, Democrats were more successful at turning out younger women, women of color, and female late deciders. Postelection studies pointed to a surge in the younger women's vote near the end of the campaign, moved by powerful Amendment 6 (reproductive rights; abortion) ads on TV and by active women's groups on campus. Social issues like gay marriage and abortion ended up being more important than economic issues to younger single female voters. In fact, the gender gap between unmarried women and men was wider (6 percent) than between married women and men (4 percent). A majority of unmarrieds supported Obama, while marrieds preferred Romney (see Table 6.4).

Some suburban women who had initially favored Romney moved back to Obama at the campaign's end, pushed by concerns about pay equity and health care availability, and offended by highly publicized insensitive comments about rape by some male Republican office seekers in other states. Romney, too, had made some comments that did not sit well with some women voters. In the course of seeking the Republican nomination against a field of more conservative social-issue-focused competitors, he had taken stances on reproductive rights that clashed with his previous, more liberal actions as governor of Massachusetts.

RELIGION

Florida's religious makeup, like its racial and ethnic composition, is very close to the national average. According to Gallup surveys, Florida's religious identity composition is 54 percent Protestant, 24 percent Catholic, 3 percent Jewish, and 13 percent no religious identity or secular (Newport 2012).

There were uncertainties about the degree to which Romney's Mormon faith would cause some evangelical Christians to stay home (Pew Forum 2012), although that community is not as large in Florida as in other southern states. There were also questions about how much Jewish support for the president would fall based on some polls that had shown some slippage (Man 2012c). Democrats quickly brought in high-profile Jewish surrogates to Broward and Palm Beach counties to shore up support for the president (Man 2012c). The Catholic vote was also more unpredictable than usual because of the debate about whether the mandatory employer coverage of contraceptives was a violation of religious freedom (Associated Press 2012a).

As it turned out, there were few changes in religious voting patterns from the 2008 election, the biggest one being a decline in the Catholic share of the electorate (from 28 percent to 23 percent) and a switch in the Catholic vote choice from Obama in 2008 (50 percent) to Romney (52 percent) in 2012 (see Table 6.5).

Table 6.5 Religion Voting Patterns

Voter Characteristic	% of voters		2008		2012	
	2008	2012	Obama	McCain	Obama	Romney
Religion						
Protestant or other Christian	52	51	43	55	42	58
Catholic	28	23	50	49	47	52
Something else	6	6	80	18	68	28
Jewish	4	5	N.A.	N.A.	66	30
None	10	15	71	26	72	26
White evangelical						
White evangelical or white born-again Christian	24	24	21	77	21	79
All Others	76	76	61	37	62	37

Note: All figures from http://www.foxnews.com/politics/elections/2008-exit-poll; http://www.foxnews.com/politics/elections/2012-exit-poll/US/President.
Source: National Election Exit Poll, Edison Research.

There was no slippage in the white evangelical Christian share of the electorate (24 percent in both 2008 and 2012), who gave more support to Mormon Romney (79 percent) than to McCain (77 percent). Protestants and Catholics leaned toward Romney, while Jewish, Other, and Non-Religious (secular) voters favored Obama. The highest level of support (72 percent) for the president came from the seculars who are younger, more liberal voters.

Once again, Republican hopes for making major inroads into the Jewish vote were dashed, although by one estimate Jewish voters tilted slightly more Republican than in past elections. The American Jewish Committee reported that Obama won 76 percent of the Jewish vote in Florida in 2008 (Caputo and Sherman 2012). Exit polls in 2012 show it slipped to 66 percent. Nationally, Romney won about 5 percent more of the Jewish vote than McCain did in 2008 (Buzzacco-Foerster and Carpenter 2012). One of the reasons both campaigns fought hard to woo Florida's Jewish voters (Bennett 2012a, 2012e; Bolstad and Caputo 2012) is that they are high-turnout voters. One south Florida scholar estimates that 6 percent of Florida's voters are Jewish, compared to just 3.4 percent of the state's population (Man 2012c).

GEOGRAPHY

Florida's mix of urban, suburban, and rural voters closely parallels that of the nation at large. Historically, Democrats have done best in urban areas, Republicans in rural areas, and suburbs in large metropolitan areas have been the key swing vote. Many of these key suburban areas were in the powerful swing part of the state known as the I-4 corridor—a major thoroughfare cutting across the state from the Tampa–St. Petersburg area east to the Orlando-Daytona area.

Suburban Voters: Swing Voters

In 2008, suburban voters leaned toward Obama, but in 2010, they swung heavily Republican as the state's economy worsened. It was the suburban, or bedroom, areas that had been most negatively impacted by high unemployment and home foreclosure rates. Republicans calculated that suburban turnout and vote patterns in 2012 would be more like 2010 than 2008 due to slower-than-average economic recovery rates in many of these areas, especially those with larger concentrations of middle-class residents. Democrats counted on Obama's ability to attract support from suburban women and less affluent suburbanites. In the latter case, the Obama campaign bet that the president's proposals to more heavily tax the rich (redistribute wealth) would gain some support among lower- to middle-class suburbanites.

The Obama campaign's calculations were somewhat more accurate, although the president lost ground among Florida's suburban voters. Obama won 51 percent of the suburban vote, down slightly from 53 percent in 2008 (see Table 6.6).

Table 6.6 Geographic Location Voting Patterns

Voter Characteristic	% of voters 2008	2012	2008 Obama	McCain	2012 Obama	Romney
Geographic Location						
City over 50,000	25	27	52	47	56	44
Suburbs	62	60	53	45	51	48
Small city and rural	13	13	41	57	35	64

Note: All figures from http://www.foxnews.com/politics/elections/2008-exit-poll; http://www.foxnews.com/politics/elections/2012-exit-poll/US/President.
Source: National Election Exit Poll, Edison Research.

There is some anecdotal evidence suggesting that suburban women who had initially supported Romney, especially after the first debate, switched back to Obama, pushed toward the president by his strong stances on pay equity, health care, and reproductive rights. There is empirical evidence that turnout among white suburbanites fell in 2012.

Specifically, turnout was lower than expected in several key suburban counties along the I-4 corridor (the critical Tampa and Orlando media markets housing 44 percent of all Florida's registered voters), crushing the Romney campaign's hopes for big numbers there. Some have speculated that turnout among middle-class white suburbanites in highly TV-ad saturated areas (the I-4 Corridor) fell because neither candidate convinced these voters that they had a clear plan on how to fix the economy and fix it fast. Overall, Obama did better among voters with incomes under $50,000—a group that grew from 39 percent of the electorate in 2008 to 45 percent in 2012. A majority of those voters cast their ballots for Obama, while voters with incomes of $50,000 and up supported Romney.

The Famed I-4 Corridor

In 2012, 44 percent of all Florida registered voters lived in either the Tampa or Orlando media markets (see Figure 6.19).

The I-4 corridor is considered the swing part of the swing state, or "the highway to heaven" for candidates running statewide (McLaughlin 2011; Batten 2012). The area is nearly evenly divided between Democrats and Republicans. The Tampa end of the corridor houses one-fourth of

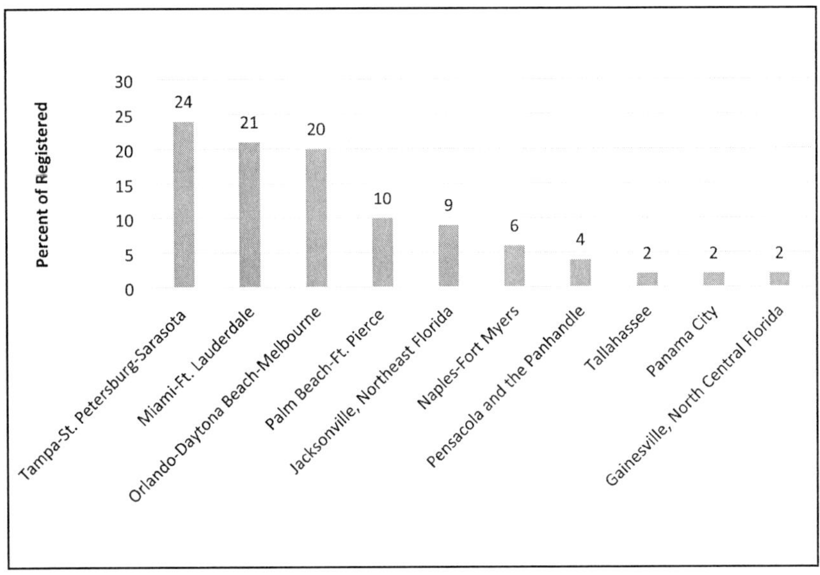

Figure 6.19 The Majority of Florida's Registered Voters Live Along the I-4 Corridor

Source: Florida Division of Elections, book closing registration data, Fall 2012 election.

Florida's registered voters. Hillsborough County, the market's largest, is considered the single best bellwether county of any in the state, having voted for the winning presidential candidate in every election since 1960, with the exception of 1992 (Smith 2012c). This record explains why both the Obama and Romney campaigns located their state headquarters in Tampa (the county seat), and why the candidates and their surrogates came to the area often (Wallace 2012a, 2012b). The Orlando media market (specifically Orange and Osceola counties) is home to the fast-growing Puerto Rican vote and was "ground zero" for GOTV efforts by Hispanic organizations such as La Raza, Mi Familia Vota, and the more conservative LIBRE Initiative (Powers and Stratton 2012a).

Candidate visits and TV ads flooded the Tampa and Orlando media markets, offering further proof that both parties saw the I-4 Corridor as critical to winning the state (Bender 2012; March 2012a, 2012b; Reston 2012; News Service of Florida 2012). The day before the election, both Governor Romney and First Lady Michelle Obama campaigned one last time in the

Sunshine State—in the I-4 corridor (Dunkelberger 2012; Powers and Jacobson 2012). At the Romney event, the Florida Republican Party chair shouted to the crowd: "I-4 corridor, baby. It's all about you now" (Leary 2012). Both markets ended up being the most evenly divided between Obama and Romney. For the seventh time since 1980, "the presidential election results out of Hillsborough County predicted the outcome of the 2012 presidential election—and which way Florida would swing" (Buzzacco-Foerster and Carpenter 2012). And, once again, the I-4 corridor vote mirrored the state-wide vote (see Figure 6.20), as the Orlando and Tampa media markets were the most closely contested (see Figure 6.21).

MAJOR GAINS FOR OBAMA IN SOUTH FLORIDA

By campaign's end, the Obama campaign recognized that South Florida was the most important territory in the state for the president (Smith, 2012a). "Without a high Democratic turnout in Broward, Palm Beach and Miami-Dade counties, Obama [had] no hope of overcoming Republican votes elsewhere in the state" (Man and Wallman 2012). High-profile surrogates repeatedly visited these areas (Man 2012b). As it turned out, the biggest gains for Obama were in Democratic vote–rich south Florida, with Miami-Dade giving President Obama a much larger margin of victory than in 2008 (Buzzacco-Foerster and Carpenter 2012) (see Figure 6.22).

"In a race won by razor-thin margins, nowhere mattered more than Miami-Dade, where Obama managed to increase his eye-popping 140,000-vote margin in 2008 to an unprecedented 204,000-vote margin this year. Miami-Dade by itself essentially delivered Florida to Obama," wrote one well-respected Florida reporter (Smith 2012d).

The Obama turnout machine was in full force here, yielding much-needed support from African Americans, older Jewish voters, and young voters (minorities, including Cubans, and single females) (Kam 2012). Late visits to the area by President Obama, President Clinton, Michelle Obama, and Vice President Biden were quite effective in ramping up turnout among some wavering Democrats and tentative young voters (Bustos and Sherman 2012; Man and Wallman 2012; Sedensky and Lush 2012a, 2012b). So, too, was having the third presidential debate, with its emphasis on foreign policy, in Palm Beach County at Lynn University.

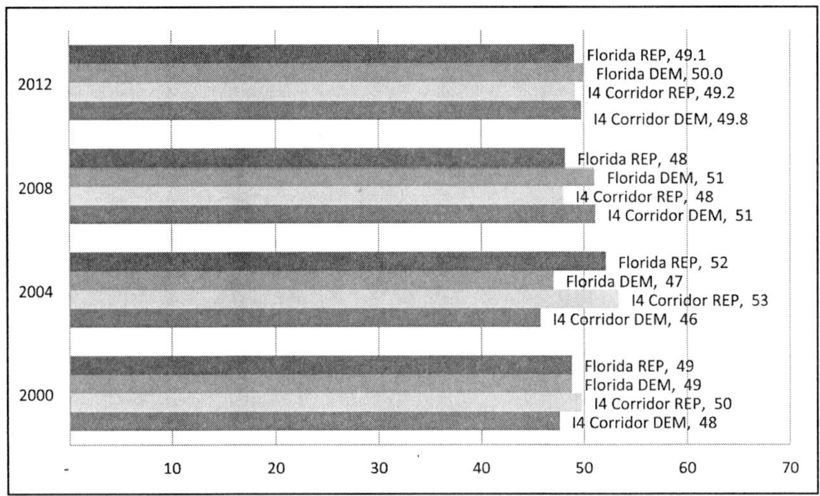

Figure 6.20 I-4 Corridor Vote Consistently Mirrors Statewide Vote

Source: Calculated from data available from the Florida Division of Elections website.

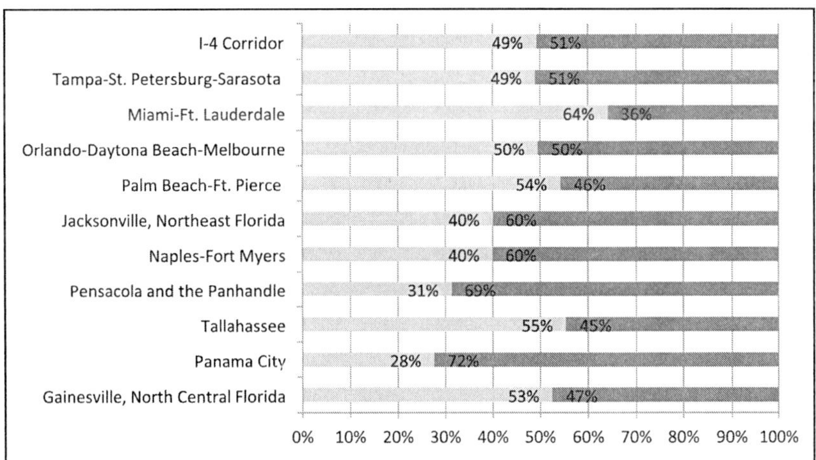

Figure 6.21 Orlando and Tampa Media Markets (I-4) Were the Most Closely Contested

Note: Light Grey: Obama; Dark Grey: Romney.
Source: Calculated from election return data reported by the Florida Division of Elections.

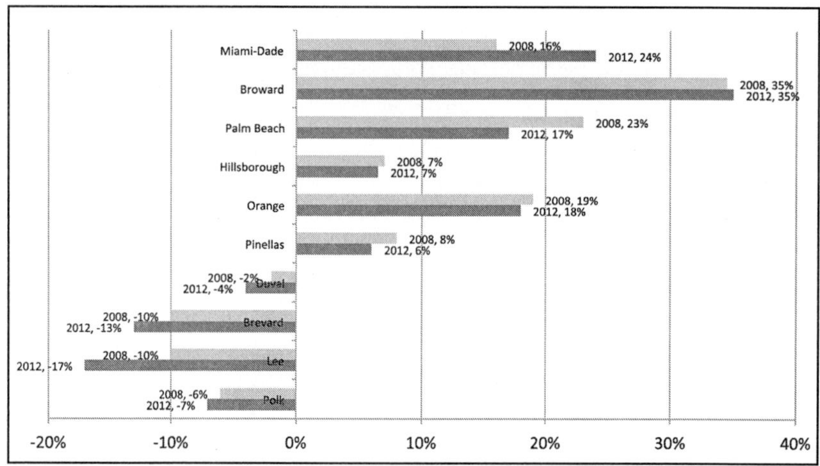

Figure 6.22 Obama's Significantly Larger Margin of Victory in Miami-Dade County Was Key to Winning Florida

Source: Calculated from election return data reported by the Florida Division of Elections.

PROJECTING AHEAD TO 2016

Florida's experiences in presidential election 2012 have generated considerable debate over how future campaigns should/will be conducted in an era of constantly changing technology and in a state (and country) experiencing major demographic shifts that are yielding a deepening generational political divide: young (Democratic) vs. old (Republican) (MacManus 2013).

Fewer Televised Presidential-Primary-Stage Debates?

What was perhaps the most unexpected dimension of the GOP primaries was the record number of high-profile TV debates featuring GOP candidates, the first of which occurred on May 5, 2011! Florida hosted four of these contentious events. Proponents of multiple TV debates at the primary stage argue that it helps the eventual nominee to hone his or her debating skills and positions the candidate to be better prepared for the general election debates. As proof positive, they point to Romney's superior performance at the first debate against Obama, prematurely labeled a "game changer" by many analysts. But opponents of a seemingly endless number of intraparty debates strung out for months on end complain that these forums aid the opposition party's nominee by supplying that candidate with all the ammunition he or she needs to craft effective negative ads against the debate survivor. Certainly Obama was given general election ammunition to use against Romney by the governor's fellow Republicans on a wide range of issues, ranging from immigration, taxes, energy, and health care to women's issues such as pay equity and reproductive rights. In 2016, both parties may have contested primaries, probably reducing the likelihood of numerous cable TV debates.

Iowa and New Hampshire First?

In an election that proved that population composition (demographics) matters, the parties, especially the Republicans, are questioning the wisdom of leading off with these two unrepresentative states. In both 2008 and 2012, Florida's party leaders chose to ignore the national party's primary calendar, in each instance leapfrogging ahead of the state's assigned date in spite of losing delegates to the national convention. The Florida rationale for ignoring national party dictates was/is that winning primaries in diverse, large, critical swing states is vital to determining whether a nominee can successfully appeal to younger, more racially/ethnically and ideologically diverse electorates (*Miami Herald* 2011). In 2012, Romney fared poorly in those types of states because of having to move further right on *social* issues in the smaller, more rural, Anglo-dominated states. And moving to the right in those states to try to win them ultimately damaged his ability to win the large, diverse swing states.

Shorter National Party Conventions?

Florida Republicans' worst fears seemed likely to come true—an August hurricane headed toward the Tampa area. However, Tropical Storm Isaac never really hit the area, although rain and winds forced the party to cancel the first day of the Republican National Convention, leaving the host city, the delegates, and hundreds of vendors holding their breath that the storm would veer away from the area by the next day. It did. But the cancellation of events and the successful readjustment of the schedule raised anew questions of whether four-day conventions are really necessary any more or even desirable with networks offering fewer hours of prime-time coverage (King 2012).

Scheduling National Party Conventions in Mid- Rather Than Late Summer?

Floridians were bombarded early with attack ads launched by the Obama campaign against Governor Romney in the summer before the GOP convention held in late August. These ads effectively branded Romney as wealthy and out-of-touch with average Americans. Romney was unable to instantly respond with counter ads because under federal campaign finance rules, a candidate cannot receive federal funds to be used in the general election phase of a presidential campaign until he or she is officially nominated by the party. Romney was not officially nominated until the late August GOP convention. Looking ahead to 2016, it is doubtful that either party will be anxious to hold its convention in late summer.

Campaign Spending Priorities: TV Ads v. Major Databases?

Postelection analyses left Republicans in Florida (and nationally) asking whether the Romney campaign had spent too much on TV ads and too little on extensive databases that enabled better microtargeting and last-minute GOTV efforts. The closest thing the Romney camp had to the Obama database (nicknamed Narwhal) was Project Orca—a new software program designed to keep track of who had already voted on Election Day, leaving volunteers to target those who had not yet gone to the polls. It never worked as planned (Robertson 2012) and even got tagged as "Failed Whale" by the popular website Politico.com.

ONWARD TO 2016

As both parties hustle to keep up with Florida's rapidly changing politics, the state's status as the most important swing state is sure to remain unchanged through the next election cycle. The 2012 election results demonstrate that, even in a state hit particularly hard by economic downturn, parties cannot rely on circumstances (the economy) to deliver votes, especially when neither candidate emerges with what is perceived by undecided voters to be a superior plan. In 2016, Republicans hope to turn the tide, which will likely require a more innovative approach, both in crafting a more strategic message that appeals to an increasingly diverse electorate and in carefully structuring a campaign, beginning with the primary debates, that best communicates that message to registrants. But even more importantly, they must be much more attentive to the nation's changing demographics in crafting their messaging and get out the vote efforts. Florida, like the nation, is becoming much more racially/ethnically diverse and the generational political divide is widening.

REFERENCES

Allison, M. 2012. "Why the Young Women's Vote Will Matter in 2012." *Mirror,* April 28. Retrieved January 6, 2013 from www.erskinemirror.com/why-the-young -women-s-vote-will-matter-in-2012.

Anderson, Z. 2012. "Obama Reaches Out to Florida Minorities." *Ocala Star Banner,* September 8. Retrieved September 8, 2012 from http://www.ocala.com /article/20120908/ARTICLES/120909779.

Associated Press. 2012a. "Ryan Blasts Contraception Requirement in Orlando." *TBO.com,* September 22. Retrieved September 22, 2012 from http://www2.tbo .com/news/politics/2012/sep/22/1/ryan-courts-cuban-american-voters-in -miami-ar-509776/.

Associated Press. 2012b. "Four Days Later: Obama Declared Winner of Florida's 29 Electoral Votes." *Naples Daily News,* November 10. Retrieved November 10, 2012 from http://www.naplesnews.com/news/2012/nov/10/presidential-race -florida-declared-obama-win-29/.

Avlon, J., and M. Keller. 2012. "Ground Game: Obama Campaign Opens Up a Big Lead in Field Offices." *Daily Beast,* October 19. Retrieved October 19, 2012 from http://www.thedailybeast.com/articles/2012/10/19/ground-game -obama-campaign-opens-up-a-big-lead-in-field-offices.html.

Babington, C. 2012. "Puerto Ricans Are Key in Florida Presidential Vote." *Associated Press,* November 4. Retrieved November 4, 2012 on http://news.yahoo .com/puerto-ricans-key-florida-presidential-vote-095301711--election.html.

Ball, M. 2012. "This Election Will Be All About Women." *Atlantic,* April 2. Retrieved April 3, 2012 from http://www.theatlantic.com/politics /archive/2012/04/this-election-will-be-all-about-women/255355/.

Barrow, B. 2012. "In Florida, Medicare Is Not a Senior-Only Issue." *Miami Herald,* September 2. Retrieved September 2, 2012 from http://www.theledger.com /article/20120902/POLITICS/120909919.

Batten, B. 2012. "State Democrats' Mantra: Winner of I-4 Corridor Wins the White House." *Naples Daily News,* September 5. Retrieved September 5, 2012 from http://www.naplesnews.com/news/2012/sep/05/state-democrats-mantra -winner-of-i-4-corridor/.

Benac, N., and C. Cass. 2012. "Face of US Changing; Elections to Look Different." *Associated Press,* November 15. Retrieved November 15, 2012 from http:// bigstory.ap.org/article/face-us-changing-elections-look-different.

Bender, M. C. 2012. "Orlando Draws Political Tourists in Tight Florida Contest." In *Bloomberg Businessweek,* November 1. Retrieved November 1, 2012 from http://www.bloomberg.com/news/2012-11-01/orlando-draws-political -tourists-in-tight-florida-contest.html.

Bendixen & Amandi International. 2012. "Exit Poll of Hispanic Voters in Florida." November 8. Retrieved November 8, 2012 from http://bendixenandamandi .com/wp-content/uploads/2011/05/ElectionResults-ExitPoll.pdf.

Bennett, G. 2012a. "Democratic Platform Flap on Jerusalem Signals Battle for Sliver of Jewish Vote in Florida." *Palm Beach Post,* September 8. Retrieved September 8, 2012 from http://www.palmbeachpost.com/news/news/state-regional -govt-politics/democratic-platform-flap-on-jerusalem-signals-batt/nR6FH/.

Bennett, G. 2012b. "Romney Comment about 'Dependent' 47 Percent Not His First Misfire in Palm Beach County." *Palm Beach Post,* September 19. Retrieved September 20, 2012 from http://www. palmbeachpost.com/news/news /state-regional-govt-politics/romney-comment-about-dependent-47-percent -not-his-/nSFDc/.

Bennett, G. 2012c. "Jeb Bush Joins Ryan to Court Latinos in Miami." *Palm Beach Post,* September 22. Retrieved September 22, 2012 from http://www .palmbeachpost.com/staff/george-bennett/stories/?page=4.

Bennett, G. 2012d. "Florida Ground Game: Paul Ryan's Mom Helps Out." *Palm Beach Post,* October 9. Retrieved October 10, 2012 from http://www .palmbeachpost.com/news/news/state-regional-govt-politics/florida-ground -game-a-potential-vps-mom-helps-out/nSYgx/.

Bennett, G. 2012e. "Conservative Israeli Legislator Criticizes Obama to Century Village Audience." *Palm Beach Post,* October 10. Retrieved October 11, 2012 from http://www.palmbeachpost.com/news/news/state-regional-govt -politics/conservative-israeli-legislator-criticizes-obama-t/nSZWp/.

Bennett, G. 2012f. "In Final Florida Campaign Appearance, Obama Invokes Spirit of Change Again." *Palm Beach Post,* November 4. Retrieved November 4, 2012 from http://www.palmbeachpost.com/news/news/state-regional-govt -politics/in-final-florida-campaign-appearance-obama-invokve/nSxLL/.

Bennett, G. 2012g. "'Rock Stars' for Romney: Jeb and Condi Campaign in Broward County." In *Palm Beach Post,* November 5. Retrieved November 7, 2012 from http://www.postonpolitics.com/2012/11/rock-stars-for-romney-jeb-and -condi-campaign-in-broward-county/.

Bolstad, E., and M. Caputo. 2012. "Obama, Democrats on Defense over Party Platform Language on Jerusalem." *Miami Herald,* September 5. Retrieved September 5, 2012 from http://www.miamiherald.com/2012/09/05/2986500 /democrats-on-defense-over-party.html.

Bowman, K., and J. Marsico. 2012. "The Past, Present, and Future of the Women's Vote." *The American,* October 4. Retrieved October 4, 2012 from http://www. american.com/archive/2012/october/the-past-present-and-future-of-the -womens-vote.

Bustos, S. R., and A. Sherman. 2012. "President Barack Obama Rallies 23,000
    Supporters in Broward County." *Miami Herald,* November 4. Retrieved
    November 5, 2012 from http://www.miamiherald.com/2012/11/04/v-print
    /3081521/obama-romney-surrogates-to-stump.html.
Buzzacco-Foerster, J., and J. Carpenter. 2012. "Swing State: Razor-Thin Margin in
    Presidential Race Proves Florida Still Divided." *Naples Daily News,* November
    11. Retrieved November 11, 2012 from http://www. naplesnews.com/news/2012
    /nov/11/swing-state-razor-thin-margin-presidential/.
Campo-Flores, A. 2012. "Candidates Flock to Florida, Coveting Electoral Votes."
    Wall Street Journal, October 18. Retrieved October 19, 2012 from http://
    professional.wsj.com/article
    /SB10000872396390444 592704578064910572038882.html?.
Caputo, M. 2012a. "Swing Voters Decide Fate of Presidential Race in Fla." *Miami
    Herald,* November 3. Retrieved November 3, 2012 from http://www
    .miamiherald.com/2012/11/03/3081215/swing-voters-decide-fate-of
    -presidential.html.
Caputo, M. 2012b. "Poll: Obama Got Big Share of Cuban-American Vote, Won
    Among Other Florida Hispanics." *Miami Herald,* November 8. Retrieved
    November 8, 2012 from http://www.miamiherald.com/2012/11/08/3087889
    /poll-obama-got-big-share-of-cuban.html.
Caputo, M., and P. Mazzei. 2012. "Poll: Obama Holds Big Lead over Romney among
    Hispanic Voters Nationwide; Margin Much Smaller in Florida." *Miami Herald,*
    October 14. Retrieved October 14, 2012 from http://www.miamiherald
    .com/2012/10/14/3049990/poll-president-barack-obama-holds.html.
Caputo, M., and A. Sherman. 2012. "Vice President Joe Biden Seeks Seniors' Votes
    in Florida Stops." *Miami Herald,* September 28. Retrieved September 29, 2012
    from http://www.tampabay.com/news/politics/national/article1253834.ece.
Carpenter, J. 2012. "Swing State: Heavy Population of Puerto Rican Residents Could
    Tip Vote in I-4 Corridor." *Naples Daily News,* October 13. Retrieved October
    13, 2012 from http://www.naplesnews.com/news/2012/oct/13/florida-swing
    -state-obama-romney-kissimmee-I4/.
CIRCLE. 2012. "Young Voters in the 2012 Presidential Election: The Educational
    Gap Remains." November 15. Retrieved November 15, 2012 http://www
    .civicyouth.org/wp-content/uploads/2012/11/2012-Exit-Poll-by-Ed-
    Attainment-Final.pdf.
Curry, T. 2012. "As Hours Tick Down to Election Day, Florida Looms Large." *NBC
    News,* October 21. Retrieved from http://nbcpolitics.nbcnews.com/
    _news/2012/10/21/14586245-as-hours-tick-down-to-election-day-florida
    -looms-large?lite.
Dixon, M. 2012. "Lenny Curry Says GOP Needs to Be 'More Inclusive,' He's Going
    to 'Study' Obama's Ground Game." *Florida Times-Union,* November 7.
    Retrieved from http://jacksonville.com/opinion/blog/403455/matt
    -dixon/2012-11-07/lenny-curry-says-gop-needs-be-more-inclusive-hes-going.

Dunkelberger, L. 2012. "Campaign Schedules Show Last-Minute Strategies." *Sarasota Herald-Tribune,* November 2. Retrieved from http://politics.heraldtribune.com/2012/11/02/campaign-schedules-show-last-minute-strategies/.

Faries, B., and S. Nesmith. 2012. "Obama Won Record Share of Florida's Cuban-Americans: Poll." *Bloomberg,* November 8. Retrieved from http://www.bloomberg.com/news/2012-11-08/obama-won-record-share-of-florida-s-cuban-american-poll.html.

Gibson, W. E. 2012. "Obama, Romney Immigration Clash Gives Voters Distinctive Options." *South Florida Sun-Sentinel,* September 9. Retrieved from http://articles.sun-sentinel.com/2012-09-09/news/fl-immigration-presidential-issues-20120909_1_hispanic-voters-immigration-reform-overhaul-immigration-law.

Good, Chris. 2012. "Get to Know a Battleground State." *ABC News,* November 5. Retrieved from http://abcnews.go.com/Politics/OTUS/battleground-florida/story?id=17639540.

Goodman, L-A. 2012. "Florida's Diversity Makes Key Swing State a Tough Nut to Crack for Obama, Romney." *Canadian Press,* October 24. Retrieved from http://www. winnipegfreepress .com/world/floridas-diversity-makes-key-swing-state-a-tough-nut-to-crack-for-obama-romney-175682501.html.

Goodstein, L. 2012. "Christian Right Failed to Sway Voters on Issues." *New York Times,* November 9. Retrieved from http://www.nytimes.com/2012/11/10/us/politics/christian-conservatives-failed-to-sway-voters.html?.

Henderson, N-M. 2012. "Ahead of Final Debate, Campaigns Converge on Florida." *Washington Post,* October 19. Retrieved from http://articles.washingtonpost.com/2012-10-19/politics/35498424_1_presidential-debate-orc-international-poll-mitt-romney.

Holt, M. 2012. "With Young Voters, Republicans Must Give Up on Social Issues or Give Up Altogether, Poll Data Suggests." *Blaze,* December 5. Retrieved from http://www.theblaze.com/stories/with-young-voters-republicans-must-give-up-on-social-issues-or-give-up-altogether-poll-data-suggests/.

Hulse, C. 2012. "Republicans Face Struggle over Party's Direction." *New York Times,* November 7. Retrieved from http://www.nytimes.com/2012/11/07/us/politics/after-loss-gop-faces-struggle-over-partys-direction.html?pagewanted=all.

Jackson, D. 2012. "Obama '12 Targets Women Where They Live." *USA Today,* June 27. Retrieved from http://usatoday30.usatoday.com/NEWS/usaedition/2012-06-27-Women-summits_ST_U.htm.

Kam, D. 2012. "Will 'Anybody-but-Obama' Strategy Work for Romney?" *Palm Beach Post,* September 23. Retrieved from http://www.palmbeachpost.com/news/news/national-govt-politics/will-anybody-but-obama-strategy-work-for-romney/nSH3w/.

King, N., Jr. 2012. "Parties Weigh Convention Revamp." *Wall Street Journal,* September 7. Retrieved from http://online.wsj.com/article/SB10000872396390443589304577637793947006780 .html.

Klas, M. E. 2012a. "Medicare Messaging Wars Target Florida Seniors." *Miami Herald,* October 16. Retrieved from http://www.miamiherald.com /2012/10/16/3052889/medicare-messaging-wars-target.html.

Klas, M. E. 2012b. "Political Ad War in Florida Is Breaking Records." *Miami Herald,* October 31. http://www.miamiherald.com/2012/10/31/3076533/political-ad -war-in-florida-is.html

Leary, A. 2012. "Mitt Romney in Sanford: 'I'll Deliver the Change Obama Promised but I Need Your Vote.'" *Tampa Bay Times,* November 5. Retrieved from http:// www.tampabay.com/blogs/the-buzz-florida-politics/content/romney-sanford -ill-deliver-change-obama-promised-i-need-your-vote.

Lopez, M. H., and P. Taylor. 2012. "Latino Voters in the 2012 Election." *Pew Hispanic Center,* November 7. Retrieved from http://www.pewhispanic.org/2012/11/07 /latino-voters-in-the-2012-election/.

MacManus, S. A. 2012. "The Battle over Election Reform in the Swing State of Florida." *New England Journal of Political Science,* November. Retrieved from http://nepsanet.org/wp-content/uploads/2013/01/The_Battle_Over_Electin _Reform_in_the_Swing_State_of_Florid.pdf.

MacManus, S. A. 2013. "From 2012 to 2016: Concluding Thoughts on the Permanent Campaign." In *Barack Obama and the New America,* edited by L. Sabato, 195–226. Lanham, MD: Rowman & Littlefield.

MacManus, S. A. 2014. "Voter Participation and Turnout: The Political Generational Divide among Women Voters." In *Gender and Elections,* 3rd ed., edited by S. J. Carroll and R. L. Fox, 80–118. New York: Cambridge University Press.

Man, A. 2012a. "Paul Ryan Courts Cuban-Americans on South Florida Campaign Swing." *South Florida Sun-Sentinel,* September 22. Retrieved from http:// articles.sun-sentinel.com/2012-09-22/news/fl-paul-ryan-florida-campaign -20120922_1_congressman-ryan-ros-lehtinen-romney-ryan.

Man, A. 2012b. "Biden Here Again? Surrogates Come to Pitch Presidential Messages." *South Florida Sun-Sentinel,* September 27. Retrieved from http:// articles.sun-sentinel.com/2012-09-27/news/fl-joe-biden-florida-again -20120927_1_vice-president-joe-biden-court-cuban-american-voters-obama -campaign.

Man, A. 2012c. "South Florida Jewish Voters Key in Obama-Romney Contest." *South Florida Sun-Sentinel,* October 16. Retrieved from http://articles .sun-sentinel.com/2012-10-18/news/fl-jjbs-vote-1018-20121018_1_south -florida-jewish-voters-obama-or-romney-obama-romney-contest.

Man, A., and Wallman, B. 2012. "Obama Makes Final Florida Push in Broward." *South Florida Sun-Sentinel,* November 5. Retrieved from http://articles .sun-sentinel.com/2012-11-05/news/fl-obama-last-florida-stop-20121104_1 _romney-surrogates-mitt-romney-fire-obama.

Man, A., and Wolford, B. 2012. "Biden Tells South Florida Retirees Romney Doesn't Care about Older Americans." *South Florida Sun-Sentinel,* September 28. Retrieved from http://articles.sun-sentinel.com/2012-09-28/news/fl-joe -biden-condos-20120928_1_vice-president-joe-biden-romney-campaign -lucy-faires.

March, W. 2012a. "The Battle Is Joined: Tampa Is Election's Frontline." *Tampa Tribune,* September 4. Retrieved from http://www2.tbo.com/news/politics /2012/sep/04/tampa-is-elections-frontline-ar-482303/.

March, W. 2012b. "Biden, Ryan Battle for Voters in Tampa Bay Area." *Tampa Tribune,* October 19. Retrieved from http://www2.tbo.com/news/politics/2012 /oct/19/8/biden-supporters-pack-sun-city-center-hall-ar-538294/.

McLaughlin, S. 2011. "Interstate 4 Corridor Drives Florida Politics." *Washington Times,* October 3. Retrieved from http://www.washingtontimes.com /news/2011/oct/3/interstate-4-corridor-drives-florida-politics/?page=all.

Meckler, L., and D. Lippman. 2012. "Campaigns Put Focus on Suburban Women." *Wall Street Journal,* August 8. Retrieved from http://professional.wsj.com /article/SB10000872396390443517104577571300017481434.html?.

Miami Herald. 2012. "Editorial: An Absurd Primary System." October 4. Retrieved from http://www.nytimes.com/2012/02/21/opinion/an-absurd-vote-counting -system.html.

Murray, S. 2012. "Cuban-Americans Give Romney Opening in Florida." *Wall Street Journal* November 3. Retrieved from http://professional.wsj.com/article /SB10001424052970204846304578095151624194978.html?mg=reno64-wsj.

Newport, F. 2012. "Religion, Santorum and Romney, New Hampshire and South Carolina." *Polling Matters,* January 6. Retrieved from http://pollingmatters .gallup,com/2012/001/religion.

News Service of Florida. 2012. "John McCain Tours Florida by Bus for Mitt Romney." September 17. Retrieved from http://politics.nsfblogs.com/2012 /09/17/john-mccain-bus-tour-mitt-romney/.

Nicholas, P. 2012. "Bill Clinton Rallies Young Voters in Florida." *Wall Street Journal* September 11. Retrieved from http://online.wsj.com/article/ SB10000872396390443 841045776 46311918135178.html.

O'Toole, J. 2012. "Florida Looming Larger as Presidential Race Tightens, Final Debate Nears." *Pittsburgh Post-Gazette,* October 21. Retrieved from http:// www.post-gazette.com/stories/news/politics-national/florida-looming-larger -as-presidential-race-tightens-final-debate-nears-658486/.

Pace, J. 2012. "Obama, Romney Both See Reasons to Worry in Florida." *Associated Press,* September 14. http://rhodeisland.onpolitix.com/news/156873/obama -romney-both-see-reasons-to-worry-in-florida.

Pew Forum. 2012. "Religion and the 2012 Florida Republican Primary." February 1. Retrieved from http://www.pewforum.org/Politics-and-Elections/Religion -and-the-2012-Florida-Republican-Primary.aspx.

Pounds, M. H. 2012. "Minorities Not Recovering from Recession, FIU Report Says." *South Florida Sun-Sentinel,* September 3. Retrieved from http://articles. sun-sentinel.com/2012-09-03/business/fl-florida-recovery-inequality -20120903_1_unemployment-rate-workforce-one-recession.

Powers, S. 2012. "Romney, Obama Run Aggressive Spanish-Language Campaigns." *Orlando Sentinel,* October 14. Retrieved from http://articles.orlandosentinel

.com/2012-10-14/news/os-spanish-campaigns-20121014_1_lynnette-acosta
-obama-campaign-obama-ad.

Powers, S., and S. Jacobson. 2012. "Romney, Michelle Obama Plan Rallies in Central Florida Monday." *Orlando Sentinel,* November 3. Retrieved from http://orlandosentinel.com/news/local/breakingnews/os-romney-in-sanford -20121102,0,4072574.story.

Powers, S., and J. Stratton. 2012. "Campaigns Field Thousands to Get Out the Vote." *Orlando Sentinel,* November 2. Retrieved from http://articles.orlandosentinel. com/2012-11-02/news/os-get-out-vote-20121103_1_romney-and-obama -campaigns-smart-phones-republican-mitt-romney.

Powers, S., and J. Stratton. "Hispanics, Women, Young Voters Boosted Obama in Florida." *Orlando Sentinel*, November 7. Retrieved from http://articles. orlandosentinel.com/2012-11-07/news/os-florida-statewide-vote-20121107_1 _mitt-romney-young-voters-president-barack-obama.

Reinhard, B. 2012. "The Story of the Hispanic Vote Is the Story of the 2012 Campaign." *National Journal,* November 1. Retrieved from http://www .nationaljournal.com/magazine/the-story-of-the-hispanic-vote-is-the-story -of-the-2012-campaign-20121101.

Reston, M. 2012. "With Florida Race Tight, Romney Rallies Bikers in Daytona Beach." *Los Angeles Times,* October 19. Retrieved from http://articles.latimes .com/2012/oct/19/news/la-pn-romney-daytona-beach-florida-020121019.

Robertson, Adi. 2012. "Killer Fail: How Romney's Broken Orca App Cost Him Thousands of Votes." *The Verge,* November 9. Retrieved from http://www .theverge.com/2012/11/9/3624636/killer-fail-how-romneys-broken-orca-app -cost-him-thousands-of-votes.

Sanders, K., and S. Rossetter. 2012. "Biden Talks Medicare, Women's Issues at Sun City Center Rally." *Tampa Bay Times,* October 19. Retrieved from http://www .tampabay.com/news/politics/elections/biden-talks-medicare-womens -issues-at-sun-city-center-rally/1257291.

Schultz, R. 2012. "Schultz Commentary: Republicans in Florida Ignoring the New Majority." *Palm Beach Post,* November 11. Retrieved from http://www .palmbeachpost.com/news/news/opinion/schultz-commentary-republicans -in-florida-ignoring/nS3C2/.

Sedensky, M., and T. Lush. 2012a. "Ryan, Biden Court Fla. Voters before Final Debate." *Associated Press,* October 19. Retrieved from http://www.floridatoday .com/viewart/20121020/NEWS05/310200019/Ryan-Biden-court-Fla-voters -before-final-debate.

Sedensky, M., and T. Lush. 2012b. "Bill Clinton Pushes Obama's Case in Florida Tour." *Associated Press,* November 2. Retrieved from http://www.ocala.com /article/20121102/WIRE/121109925 (accessed November 2, 2012).

Smith, A. C. 2012a. "Inside Complex, Colorful Miami-Dade, Florida's Largest County Where Every Vote Is Critical for Obama." *Tampa Bay Times,* October 8. Retrieved from http://www.tampabay.com/news/politics/stateroundup /article1255344.ece.

Smith, A. C. 2012b. "Obama Adviser David Plouffe Says Campaign in Good Shape in Florida." *Tampa Bay Times,* October 14. Retrieved from http://www.tampabay.com/news/politics/stateroundup/obama-adviser-david-plouffe-says-campaign-in-good-shape-in-florida/1256355.

Smith, A. C. 2012c. "Hillsborough County: Florida's True Presidential Bellwether." *Tampa Bay Times,* November 1. Retrieved from http://www.tampabay.com/news/politics/local/article 1259455.ece.

Smith, A. C. 2012d. "Strong Turnout for Barack Obama Tilts Florida His Way." *Tampa Bay Times,* November 7. Retrieved from http://www.tampabay.com/news/politics/national/article1260500.ece.

Sweet, L. 2012. "Election Could Come Down to What Women Want." *Chicago Sun-Times,* October 13. Retrieved from http://www.suntimes.com/news/sweet/15721901-452/election-could-come-down-to-what-women-want.html.

Tamayo, J. O. 2012. "Did Obama or Romney Win the Cuban-American Vote?" *Miami Herald,* November 12. Retrieved from http://www.miamiherald.com/2012/11/12/3094299/winner-of-cuban-american-vote.html.

Turner, J. 2012. "Allen West, Jennifer Carroll to Lead Charge for Mitt Romney with Black Voters." *Sunshine State News,* September 5. Retrieved from http://www.sunshinestatenews.com/story/allen-west-jennifer-carroll-lead-charge-mitt-romney-black-voters.

Voter Participation Center and Lake Research Partners. 2012. *The Rising American Electorate.* The Voter Participation Center Virtual Summit. Retrieved from http://www.voterparticipation.org/wp-content/uploads/2012/07/The-Rising-American-Electorate-An-Examination-of-Growth-in-a-Presidential-Year.pdf.

Wallace, J. 2012a. "Clinton Could Hold Obama's Key to Florida." *Sarasota Herald-Tribune,* September 5. Retrieved from http://politics.heraldtribune.com/2012/09/05/clinton-could-hold-obamas-key-to-florida/.

Wallace, J. 2012b. "Both Obamas in Florida Next Week." *Sarasota Herald-Tribune,* September 13. Retrieved from http://politics.heraldtribune.com/2012/09/13/both-obamas-in-florida-next-week/.

II. Domestic and Economic Policy

Chapter 7

"Let Detroit Go Bankrupt"
Using the Past to Win the Present

Steve A. Stuglin, Georgia Highlands College

INTRODUCTION

The 2008–2009 global financial crisis is a well-known feature of our recent history. During that time, the domestic auto industry, like many other industries in the United States, suffered greatly. The economic crisis could very well have taken the auto industry beyond recovery, with General Motors and Chrysler potentially disappearing altogether. Scholars have covered the multiple economic crises in the auto industry well (Reich & Donahue 1985; Rubenstein 1992; Vlasic 2001; Ritholtz 2009; Ingrassia 2010; Rattner 2010; Taylor III 2010; Vlasic 2001, 2011). These works have generally focused on a retelling of the events that led up to the crisis, the government intervention, and at times, on the implications of that intervention for the industry or the relationship between government and private enterprise.

Once George W. Bush and later Barack Obama decided to intervene on behalf of the industry, each president spoke to the nation justifying the use of taxpayer funds to aid the automakers. Some recent scholarship has begun to investigate how the justification for intervention can teach us something about how presidential rhetoric works and what that might mean for understanding presidential speech about economic issues (Stuglin 2012). This chapter builds on that area of inquiry with a close analysis of how the auto industry intervention issue was handled by the 2012 presidential campaigns.

The chapter begins by situating the present analysis in a broader discussion about whether and how political speech about economic issues matters. Next, each mention of the intervention during the Republican primary debates, the Republican and Democratic national conventions, the vice presidential debate, and the three presidential debates is analyzed. The analysis supports the claim that Romney's tactics, while effective at one point, were years behind popular opinion by the time of the election. In addition, Romney's tactics were effectively countered by Obama's tactics and those of his campaign. The two presidential candidates appropriated the real past events of the intervention differently: Romney used the issue as a warning about a failed choice while Obama shaped the past into a success story. Obama's narrative more closely matched public opinion at the time of the election, and in the battleground state of Ohio, it may have been a contributing factor in his victory. The chapter concludes with a discussion of the implications for our understanding of how politicians draw on the past to construct narratives and the real dangers of such rhetorical tactics used with large government interventions.

THE POLITICAL UTILITY OF THE PAST

Scholars of political rhetoric can hardly debate that presidents *attempt* to influence the public and win votes through speech. Some scholars acknowledge the attempts but question whether they are effective (Corrigan 2000; Edwards III 2003; Gabrielson 2005). Still, other scholars are confident that presidential speech can accomplish things, including signaling constituencies (Bose 1998; Eshbaugh-Soha 2006), setting an agenda (Cohen 1963; Cohen 1995), persuading other elites (Neustadt 1960), framing events or issues (Koch 1998; Maslin-Wicks 1998), gaining support for an action (Kernell 1997; Powell 1999), constructing national identities (Beasley 2004; Stuckey 2004), and defining or redefining terms (Zarefsky 2004). Although some scholars have noted that presidents may be more effective than other politicians in certain areas of influence (Fridkin and Kenney 2005; Schnell and Callaghan 2005), others, including presidential candidates, certainly still try and may have similar efficacy.

When we consider economic issues the potential influence of presidential speech is a little easier to see. B. Dan Wood (2004) argued that presidential economic speech affects the tone under which business leaders and consumers make decisions. According to David Rankin (2006), the presidential voice is the most powerful contributor to national conversations about economic issues, perhaps because of the complexities involved. Presidents are judged for macroeconomic performance (Monroe 1978; Clark & Stewart 1994; Edwards III et al. 1995) even though it is often outside of administration control. Thus, the way that a president chooses to talk about the economy may be especially important during periods of economic hardship. As M. Stephen Weatherford (2012) demonstrated, the losses for Democrats in the 2010 midterm elections were a result not of poor economic policy but of poor economic messaging.

Often, due to issue complexity, economic policy is recast as a story. It is no stretch of the imagination to think of politicians as storytellers. Political figures, including presidents, construct narratives with heroes, villains, plot lines, and lessons (Lewis 1987; Stuckey 1991; Goodnight 1996; Ivie 1996; Dorsey 2007). These narratives are often a strategic construction used to accomplish political goals (Bose and Greenstein 2002; Stuckey 2008, 2013). Many of these constructed narratives rely on the past as an inventional source; politicians draw on, shape, and deploy history to accomplish goals in the present. According to Clark and McKerrow, "history is … an argument—a selective remembering to validate thought and action" (1998, 35). Bruce Gronbeck argued that "the past is not so much constructed—though of course it really is—as it is appropriated, made into something useful for today" (1998, 56). We look to our past and write stories about it, highlighting some features and omitting others. Often, these stories "constitute a warning. The analogy works to identify a moment in time where choice failed and to remind the audience that such a decision is looming again" (Goodnight 1996, 134). History has the power to teach us lessons, connect to audiences, increase support, and win votes.

To win elections, presidential candidates engage in zero-sum electoral math. Candidates view the electoral playing field and make informed guesses on whether a county or a state is safe, a lost cause, or a battleground. In closely contested areas, we expect to see more campaigning from candidates. We expect to see stump speeches redirected to local needs and specialty speeches crafted for local pet issues. To win, presidents must forge coalitions of constituency groups, often with wildly different concerns (Seligman and Covington 1989). The keystone group may be one that demands special outreach—to add these to the coalition presidents may engage in what Jeffrey Cohen (2010) called "going narrow," focusing a message on a local representation of a highly differentiated interest group.

In 2012, Ohio was a battleground state. Both candidates needed to win Ohio, in most scenarios, to win the election. To win Ohio, Romney's and Obama's coalitions needed the support of a relatively local group of constituencies united by a common industry: those connected to the Big Three automakers in the region. If either candidate could successfully connect to the workers, the union, the owners, the dealers, and all the small business owners nearby that depended on the auto industry to provide customers, that candidate would win Ohio. To connect to each of these different groups demanded a retelling of history: a story about the intervention in the industry and its aftermath. Both Romney and Obama attempted to tell such a story in 2012. Next, this chapter moves to an analysis of each.

THE AUTO INDUSTRY ISSUE IN THE 2012 CAMPAIGN

This section presents a detailed account of the auto industry issue during the 2012 presidential election. Based on an analysis of the tactics for addressing the issue, countertactics, and overall narratives, this section presents an explanation for the success of the Obama narrative. The section begins with the GOP primaries, then moves to the national conventions, the national debates, and the last week of Ohio election ads. Each of these events, excluding the last, was televised and widely viewed, presenting a good indicator of Romney's and Obama's national message on the auto industry.

The Auto Industry Issue in the Primaries

During the GOP primary debates, a host of issues gained occasional prominence and propelled candidates to surprise wins in straw polls. Of these, the auto industry bailout was not a major concern. In fact, in the entire primary season, the candidates only discussed the issue at any length in two debates: in November 2011 in Michigan and four months later in February 2012 in Arizona. The general agreement between the candidates on the issue may have been a factor in its surprising absence from the GOP discussion, although some differences arose between candidates when it did come up. It is useful to examine the sparse references in the primary debates because during this time Romney established his tactics for handling the issue, tactics later employed against Obama in the general election campaign.

In Michigan, historically the heartland of American automobile production, the GOP candidates likely expected to answer questions about the auto industry bailout. At a debate held November 9, 2011, moderator John Harwood delivered on that expectation: "No state understands…the bailout drama…better than the state of Michigan," Harwood began. Addressing Mitt Romney, he continued: "You said, no, let Detroit go bankrupt. Now that the companies are profitable again…you said…President Obama implemented my plan all along—or he gravitated to my plan…[your record] seems to be on all sides of the issue" (CNBC 2011, 51–53). "No, let Detroit go bankrupt" referred to the title of a 2008 op-ed piece that Romney wrote for the *New York Times*. In it he argued that the government should not intervene in the auto industry. If it *did* intervene, such action would ensure the industry's demise (Romney 2008). Romney, after smiling at the audience and reminding them that he, too, was a Michigander, attempted to explain the position he had presented in that 2008 op-ed piece: "I said from the very beginning they should go through a managed bankruptcy process, a private bankruptcy process. The idea of billions of dollars being wasted initially then finally they adopted the managed bankruptcy, I was among others that said we ought to do that" (CNBC 2011, 56–57). Here Romney established the first of multiple rhetorical tactics on the issue: he claimed that the government ultimately did what he would have done all along.

This approach employs a form of strategic ambiguity, whereby the speaker is intentionally vague about a policy position (Bose and Greenstein 2002; Lucas 2002) in the service of a political or policy agenda (Stuckey 2008, xvi). Romney seemed to clearly state his position here, but ambiguity came from an unstated awareness that the general voting public is not well versed in the complexities of bankruptcy law. His original op-ed piece suggested a managed bankruptcy and federal guarantees for postbankruptcy financing. After the bailout and the auto industry turnaround, Romney reminded viewers that he had originally suggested "a managed bankruptcy, a private bankruptcy" all along.

As always, the devil is in the details. There are three terms for bankruptcy deployed by this point: "private," "managed," and the implied "government-managed." Simply put, a private bankruptcy would be the everyday corporate bankruptcy, with no third-party interference, whereas managed would have some third-party intervening. During the debate in Michigan, Romney equated "private" with "managed." In this usage, an outside institution from the *private sector only* would step in and help automakers through the bankruptcy process. Yet, the Bush-Obama intervention was a government-managed bankruptcy, with management supplied by the Obama administration through the Team Auto task force. When Romney reminded viewers that the Bush-Obama intervention was in line with what he had suggested all along, as he continued to do in the Arizona debate (CNN 2012, 182–188), he counted on the ambiguity between private, managed, and government-managed bankruptcy. For this to work, private- and government-managed bankruptcy would need to appear equivalent.

If successful, if voters believed Romney when he said "Then they finally realized I was right" (CNN 2012, 189), if voters missed the subtle difference between forms of bankruptcy, then Romney might have been able to claim for himself some credit for the success of the bailout and the resurgence of the industry. Yet in the Michigan debate and in the Arizona debate Romney employed a second tactic that ultimately undermined the first: he claimed that the government-managed bankruptcy was done incorrectly. It involved too much "government playing its heavy hand" (CNBC 2011, 58) and too much wasted money (CNBC 2011, 57; CNN 2012, 189). So, although Romney had suggested something like this since his original op-ed piece, his contention now was that the government had botched the job by involving itself too much, and for too long, in the wrong ways. If voters accepted this position it would make accepting the first position more difficult: how could one take positive credit for something done poorly and even counterproductively? Is the idea somehow to be considered worth more than the execution and tangible effects?

The third tactic Romney employed had the most staying power. Romney argued that bailouts themselves were just *wrong*. "My view with regards to the bailout was that whether it was by President Bush or by President Obama, it was the wrong way to go" (CNBC 2011, 56). This last tactic required clarity between a government-managed bankruptcy and a "bailout." While it would be useful to align his stance with the former and take some credit for it, Romney's GOP opponents and large sections of his base were opposed to bailouts. For Romney, a managed bankruptcy would be right, a bailout was wrong.

This third tactic came under fire four months later in Arizona, when Rick Santorum accused Romney of inconsistency. Santorum said he had opposed the Wall Street bailout and maintained a "consistent position when it came to the auto bailouts…with respect to Governor Romney, that was not the case. He…bailed out Wall Street, was all for it. And then when it came to the auto workers, the folks in Detroit, he said no. That to me is not a consistent, principled position" (CNN 2012, 181). Ron Paul agreed that consistency was important: "I don't like the idea that you have good bailouts and bad bailouts. If bailouts are bad, they're bad, and we shouldn't be doing it" (CNN 2012, 198). Romney explained that he supported Wall Street because it was "the right thing to do. It was an emergency" (CNN 2012, 186). In what Joshua Hanan (2011) argued was a common approach to defending the intervention, Romney contended that the "emergency" constituted an exception that rendered all prior moral and ethical positions moot. So while Romney could be opposed to bailouts on principle, the Wall Street collapse was an exception that demanded the temporary sacrifice of principle on the altar of necessity.

For those in attendance the exception argument may have seemed more practical than Santorum's or Paul's adamant opposition to all bailouts always. For independents and Democrats that worked in the auto industry, this claim amounted to Romney not taking the crisis in the auto industry seriously. If extreme emergencies allow for exceptions to principled opposition, and Wall Street was one such emergency, then the auto industry *must not have been* in so bad a shape. Suggesting, even subtly, that the auto industry crisis was not an emergency and was thus undeserving of anything but normal procedures could prove troublesome with voting constituencies in auto-industry strongholds.

Throughout the primary debate cycle Romney established three tactics for handling the auto industry bailout issue. First, Romney intentionally blurred the lines between forms of bankruptcy in his retelling of the events, positing that he deserved credit for the managed bankruptcy idea. Second, he argued that the government had intervened too much, botching the rescue. Finally, Romney argued that bailouts in general were wrong, although exceptions could be made. These tactics were well suited to the situation: his GOP opponents largely agreed with him. The auto issue did not play a large enough role in the primaries for Romney's approach to it to become much of a deciding factor between him and other candidates, and there is little reason to suspect it hurt him or helped him in the primaries.

The Auto Industry Issue at the Conventions

By the time of the national conventions, Romney's nomination was all but assured. These conventions are important objects for analysis because, as Rachel Holloway has argued, they are "highly scripted political rituals, part political rally and part infomercial" (2008, 18). Most of what viewers see and hear of the conventions is what they were meant to see and hear. Given this, the 2012 conventions explain how each party approached the auto industry issue going into the fall presidential campaign.

The Republican National Committee ignored the issue entirely. Not a single speaker in the entire convention program mentioned it. Of course, as Brandon Rottinghaus noted (2012), the entire convention seemed "vague" and bereft of policy discussion. We learned about Romney's and Ryan's families, and that they "tell hard truths," but not much else. The RNC was selling people, not policy. In stark contrast, the Democratic National Convention *featured* the issue. Four videos and eight speakers addressed the auto industry success story, countering the tactics employed by Romney during the primary.

Romney's first tactic was to argue that the managed bankruptcy was his original idea—leaving unspecified whether government or a private entity would do the managing. Speakers at the DNC chose to roll over this ambiguity and hammer home, again and again, Romney's 2008 op-ed piece. Particularly important were speakers from auto strongholds Ohio and Michigan. Ted Strickland, former governor of Ohio, said, "Mitt Romney proudly wrote an op-ed titled, 'Let Detroit Go Bankrupt.' If he had had his way, devastation would have cascaded from Michigan to Ohio and across the nation" (2012, 11). Jennifer Granholm, former two-term governor of Michigan, continued: "Mitt Romney saw the crisis and you know what he said? 'Let Detroit go bankrupt'" (2012, 5). Acknowledging that Romney had close ties to Michigan made it worse, according to Joe Biden: "Mitt Romney grew up in Detroit. His father ran American Motors. Yet he was willing to let Detroit go bankrupt" (2012, 20).

Each of these speakers used the words of the op-ed title as an attack against Romney's claim that his idea was similar to the plan executed by the administration. This relied on the assumption that voters would equate an op-ed title with its author. The phrase "Let Detroit Go Bankrupt" is almost offensive in its uncaring simplicity. By attributing it to Romney, the speakers attempted to continue the Bain Capital narrative: Romney was a cold and calculating financier, unafraid to eviscerate organizations and throw workers out of their jobs in pursuit of profits. The speakers all knew that Romney had never actually uttered these words in quite this way, making them completely out of context with his plan. According to Mark Halperin (2012, 27–28) the Romney campaign maintained that the newspaper had created the op-ed headline "Let Detroit Go Bankrupt" in the first place, not Romney. And yet, when paired with Romney's statements about managed bankruptcy being advisable, the phrase seemed to be something Romney *could have* said. So speakers at the DNC said that he had, and the uncaring and simplistic phrase stuck.

Bill Clinton's marathon convention speech did not make use of the op-ed title as other speakers had. Clinton attacked Romney's first tactic on another, broader note. Simply put, according to Clinton, "Governor Romney opposed the plan to save GM and Chrysler" (2012, 56). Notice that "the plan" is singular, final. There were not multiple options or forms of bankruptcy. There was one plan—*the* plan—and Romney had opposed it. The speakers would not allow Romney to lay claim to partial credit for the success of the intervention. He wanted to "Let Detroit Go Bankrupt," which sounded substantially different from a government-managed bankruptcy, and though he had an idea, he did not support *the* plan.

The speakers at the convention were also determined to counter Romney's second tactic from the primaries—his contention that the government had executed the intervention poorly. It may well have been that speakers agreed that the intervention process could have been done better, but rather than publicly concede the point, speakers chose to shift the focus to product: intervention had worked. Granholm cheered because "all across America, autos are back! Manufacturing is rebounding!" (2012, 8). The auto industry, according to Strickland, was now "alive and growing in America again" (2012, 5). Clinton explained it simply: "The auto industry restructuring worked. It saved more than a million jobs" (2012, 55). And this restructuring had a single person in charge. Deval Patrick thus referred to Obama as "the president who saved the American auto industry from extinction" (2012, 10), while Jim Clyburn claimed "President Obama's actions saved our beloved automobile industry" (2012, 7). When Obama took the stage on the final night of the convention, he said: "We're making things again. I've met workers in Detroit and Toledo who feared they'd never build another American car. Today, they can't build them fast enough, because we reinvented a dying auto industry that's back on top of the world" (2012, 20–21).

All of these speakers focused on product while avoiding process—it did not matter whether the intervention could have been done better because the intervention had worked. Throughout, archetypal metaphors of life and rejuvenation dominated: "rebounding," "alive and growing again," "saved," "saved from extinction," and "reinvented the dying industry." Not only did this usage reinforce the seriousness of the situation—after all, death and extinction are final—but it emphasized the rescue from that danger, via the preservation and resurrection of life. The two uses of life worked in tandem to suggest that the intervention not only protected that which was worth protecting from ruin but also improved upon it in the process, creating something new and better. The idea of resurrection involves sacrifice, loss, and pain. Whereas Romney's second tactic focused on the problems with the process, DNC speakers' usage of resurrection implied that the process was painful but necessarily so—and that the product was worth it.

The speakers also addressed Romney's third tactic: his contention that bailouts are just *wrong*. Speakers countered in three ways. First, they claimed that it was just *right*; second, that it was the right thing to do because it was *necessary*; and third, that it was right because of the *people* involved.

Harry Reid began by acknowledging that it was not an easy decision, but in this first form of rebuttal, Reid claimed that it was actually right: "Some said he shouldn't save Detroit, but President Obama made the tough and right call to save more than a million American jobs in an important, iconic industry" (2012, 2). The "some" identified here went unnamed by Reid, but thanks to other speakers reminding the audience over and over again that Romney would "Let Detroit Go Bankrupt," Reid did not need to identify him. Obama further argued that "we don't want handouts for people who refuse to help themselves, and we don't want bailouts for banks that break the rules" (2012, 51), because those things would be wrong. Obama implied that the people in the auto industry were willing to help themselves, and that automakers were not "breaking rules." Thus, the auto industry intervention was the right thing to do.

The second rebuttal to Romney's "bailouts are wrong" tactic was to flip the script on his emergency claim from the primaries. Romney had defended himself against claims of inconsistency by relying on a definition of emergency that precluded inclusion of the auto crisis in that category. Speakers at the convention made the case that the auto industry *was* in a truly precarious position, and that it was the blue-collar workers at the bottom that would feel the most pain from a collapse. For Granholm, "the entire auto industry, and the lives of over one million hard-working Americans, teetered on the edge of collapse; and with it, the whole manufacturing sector" (2012, 4). As demonstrated previously, the industry was threatened with "extinction," and here it "teetered on the edge of collapse." By Romney's own logic, the only thing one could do was to act—even if that meant temporarily sacrificing one's free market principles. Yet Romney had not been willing to take the kind of action required.

Finally, speakers at the DNC argued that the intervention was right because of those that it saved—individual blue-collar workers. Biden explained that Obama "knew what it would mean to leave one million people without hope or work if we didn't act" (2012, 23). Whereas Romney would only step in to save the financiers, Strickland argued that "Obama is betting on the American worker" (2012, 12). Obama "understood that it wasn't just about cars," according to Biden, "it was about the Americans who built those cars" (2012, 18). These appeals called on the mythos of the American worker: hard-working, honest, loyal, and independent. In contemporary American politics, the middle class and the worker are golden identities, to which we pay the kind of reverence once paid to Thomas Jefferson's yeoman farmer. Anything done to help the worker is a thing done *right*, so the usage here effectively countered opposition to bailouts, whomever the ultimate beneficiaries of the auto industry bailout were.

By the end of the two national conventions, each party had demonstrated an approach to the auto industry issue. The Romney-Ryan campaign chose to ignore it. The Obama-Biden campaign featured it prominently. Prepared video packages and speakers focused on the issue, in the process rebutting the three tactics Romney developed on the issue during the primaries. The relative unimportance of the issue during the primaries worked against Romney during the conventions. He was either unaware of or unwilling to highlight the issue and his stance on it, thereby leaving himself open to intense criticism on the matter from Democrats. The DNC, televised to a wide audience, was able to write the narrative on the auto industry issue because nothing had been said about it at the RNC. Given that, a nuanced explanation that could have awarded Romney some credit for the idea was never made. Instead the image of a Romney that wanted to "Let Detroit Go Bankrupt" stuck.

The Auto Industry Issue in the Presidential Debates

Since the DNC followed the RNC, Romney and his team likely realized that Obama and Biden were prepared to bring up the auto industry issue frequently in the debates, so it is safe to assume that Romney considered his tactical approach on the issue going forward. Coming into the debates, Romney had three tactics on the issue: ambiguity on bankruptcy that allowed him to suggest the intervention was his idea, a critique of the administration for handling the intervention poorly, and a principled stance against bailouts, except in cases of emergencies. Obama had counters to these tactics: Romney had an idea but would have "Let Detroit Go Bankrupt," a focus on product rather than process, and multiple reasons for saying that the intervention was the right thing to do in the auto industry case.

During the first presidential debate, in response to the first question about the economy, Obama began by referencing the auto industry issue in his opening statement: "Four years ago we went through the worst financial crisis since the Great Depression…the auto industry was on the brink of collapse.…And because of the resilience and the determination of the American people, we've begun to fight our way back.…The auto industry has come roaring back" (Politico 2012a, 66). The situation was an emergency, so intervention was justified, and the auto industry had recovered.

Unfortunately, there are a few problems with the way the narrative was being told this time. The most obvious problem was that the intervention was missing from the story. The narrative went from crisis to recovery with no modifier. Nothing had exerted the effect of changing the situation. "The resilience and the determination of the American people" was provided as an explanation for the recovery. During the convention, Obama and other speakers clearly identified the Obama administration as integral. It had *done* something—intervened, rescued, or saved the industry—and that *action* was responsible for the resurrection and recovery. But one could conceivably read Obama's statement as suggesting that the crisis had somehow righted itself—that no action of the administration was necessary because the workers were so resilient and determined—which would confirm Romney's critique.

The serious problem with this version of the auto industry success story went unnoticed by Romney. He chose not to respond to the point on the auto industry, and the issue was not mentioned during the rest of the debate. As most are aware, Obama delivered a weak performance in a number of other areas in the first debate. Had the auto industry issue been brought up again and Romney engaged, it might have been possible to for Romney to win points there as well. As it was, the flawed narrative made barely a ripple in what was otherwise a great night for Romney and a tough one for Obama.

Joe Biden, famous for saying "Bin Laden is dead and General Motors is alive" on the campaign trail, gave the auto industry issue much more attention in the vice presidential debate. In Biden's version of the narrative, there was again an emergency situation that demanded government action: "The economy was in freefall…we knew we had to act for the middle class" (Politico 2012b, 77–78). Biden remembered to give the administration credit for the turnaround in the auto industry. The first thing the administration did for the economy was to "immediately [go] out and rescue General Motors.…Romney said, No, let Detroit go bankrupt" (Politico 2012b, 78). By foregrounding the administration action as the cause, Biden argued that credit for the new success of the auto industry should go to the administration.

Ryan, in responding to Biden, attempted to paint Romney as a good and charitable man that cared about workers. "They keep misquoting him," Ryan began, "but let me tell you about the Mitt Romney I know" (Politico 2012b, 85). Romney "cares about 100 percent of Americans in this country" (Politico 2012b, 88), Ryan continued. While this passage was a play on Romney's infamous "47 percent" statement, it was also a response to claims that Romney did not care about workers. Biden knew the administration "had to act for the middle class." Here, Ryan said Romney cared about those workers, too.

Biden replied, "Look, I don't doubt his personal generosity.…I don't doubt his personal commitment to individuals. But you know what? I know he had no commitment to the automobile industry. He said, let it go bankrupt, period. Let it drop out" (Politico 2012b, 90). As argued previously, this statement is a distortion of the truth. Romney never really said such a thing quite that way—but the phrase had stuck since the convention. Although the conversation on the economy continued for a considerable length after this exchange, Ryan chose not to address the auto industry issue again, perhaps conceding the point or hoping to move to stronger ground.

In the third debate, which was the second presidential debate and in a town hall format, the first question was from a college student asking about his future under each potential administration. Romney chose to answer the question by focusing on education policy. Obama answered by focusing on the economy and on jobs. In his answer, Obama brought up the op-ed title: "I want to build manufacturing jobs in this country again. Now when Governor Romney said we should let Detroit go bankrupt, I said we're going to bet on American workers and the American auto industry and it's come surging back. I want to do that in industries, not just in Detroit, but all across the country" (Politico 2012c, 23). Unlike in the first debate, Obama was able to fully lay out the success story narrative, including the crucial role that the government intervention played in the result. We "saved an auto industry that was on the brink of collapse" (Politico 2012c, 32), meaning that the emergency was real. Additionally, Obama extended that success story, in a rare case (at least throughout the debates) of discussing his second term.

After having been critiqued for the op-ed title on the campaign trail, throughout the convention season, and during the early debates, Romney finally responded to it clearly: "My plan was to have the company go through bankruptcy…and come out stronger…he keeps saying, you want to take Detroit bankrupt. Well, the president took Detroit bankrupt. You took General Motors bankrupt. You took Chrysler bankrupt. So when you say that I wanted to take the auto industry bankrupt, you actually did.… That was precisely what I recommended and ultimately what happened" (Politico 2012c, 25–27). Romney aides and supporters who understood the semantics of the auto industry issue must surely have clapped at Romney finally having a chance to get this counterargument out. It was true: Romney had advocated bankruptcy in his 2008 op-ed, and the Auto Task Force ultimately took both GM and Chrysler through bankruptcy. Had Romney been able to phrase the point this way earlier in the year he might have come into the second presidential debate on better footing for the issue.

Just as it had in the primaries, this tactic of attempting to take some credit for the idea relied on the general public not really understanding bankruptcy in a nuanced way. Moderator Candy Crowley gave the president a chance to respond to the point directly. Unfortunately for Romney, Obama's answer began to educate the audience on bankruptcy, rather than relying on a lack of understanding about it: "What Governor Romney said just isn't true. He wanted to take them into bankruptcy without providing them any way to stay open" (Politico 2012c, 29). What Obama's answer hinted at, but did not fully explain, was the difference between bankruptcy as proposed by Romney and the intervention as executed. As Chris Isidore (2012, 5) explained, an immediate bankruptcy such as Romney suggested in 2008 would not have worked. For it to function would have required private banks to have lending power and the will to lend to an industry in mortal peril. These things would have had to exist at the worst possible time—in the middle of the global financial meltdown of 2008–2009. In truth, banks did not have the money or will to lend on the scale necessary, so the newly bankrupt automakers would not have been able to survive through restructuring, leaving them to disappear entirely.

Had Romney's statement gone unanswered, he would have succeeded in disarming Obama on the op-ed, removing a major critique levied against Romney countless times up to that point. As it happened, Obama's clarification derailed that attempt, although it did not go far enough in fully explaining exactly what would have been wrong with a no-safety-net bankruptcy process for the automakers.

During the final presidential debate, the foreign policy debate, the auto industry issue came up again. In the second to last issue discussion of the evening, before the final statements, the candidates were discussing the global economy. Obama, aware that time was short, used his time to again plug the auto industry success story: "You are familiar with jobs being shipped overseas.... I've made a different bet on American workers. If we had taken your advice about our auto industry, we'd be buying cars from China instead of selling cars to China" (Politico 2012d, 349–351).

Romney's response employed the same tactics he had used since the GOP primaries. He reiterated that a "managed bankruptcy" was his idea. He was also still opposed to a bailout for the industry, as he disagreed with "writing checks." All of this was couched in an attempt to identify with auto workers and Detroit: "I'm a son of Detroit. I was born in Detroit. My dad was head of a car company. I like American cars. And I would do nothing to hurt the U.S. auto industry" (Politico 2012d, 360). Romney's response was a continuation of his message on the auto industry rescue that had remained strikingly consistent in the year since the Michigan primary debate, and indeed since the 2008 op-ed piece. Yet this time Romney also said: "These companies need to go through a managed bankruptcy. And in that process, they can get government help and government guarantees" (Politico 2012d, 360). The phrase "government help and government guarantees" led to one of the most heated exchanges of the entire debate cycle.

> Obama: That's not what you said…you did not…
> Romney: You can take a look at the op ed.…
> Obama: You did not say that you would provide government help.
> Romney: I said that we would provide guarantees and that was what was able to allow these companies to go through bankruptcy.…
> Obama: Let's check the record.
> Romney: That's the height of silliness.…(Politico 2012d, 361–368)[1]

The crosstalk continued. Obama said Romney never mentioned government help. Romney said he did. Obama said he did not, and that "the people in Detroit don't forget" (Politico 2012d, 374). Obama interjected after a while, arguing that "anybody out there can check the record. You keep trying to, you know, airbrush history here. You were very clear that you would not provide government assistance to the U.S. auto companies" (Politico 2012, 390). Romney replied with "you're wrong" multiple times (Politico 2012, 391, 393). Finally, both men agreed that "people can look it up" (Politico 2012, 396).

As it turned out, people *did* look it up. According to Google metrics (Google 2012), the most searched term during and directly following the debate was "Romney and auto bailout," with a top result pointing to the 2008 op-ed. In it, Romney only suggested that "government should provide guarantees for post-bankruptcy financing" (2008, 5). However, as Bob Lutz, the chair of GM at the time, explained: "Loan guarantees don't do any good if the banks don't have any money" (Isidore 2012, 11). Romney was correct in the debate in saying that he had originally offered government guarantees in his op-ed—but those guarantees would have kicked in *after* bankruptcy, and given the lack of lending power by banks, it likely would not have done any good. Aside from assuring "car buyers that their warranties are not at risk" (2008, 5), Romney did not, as he claimed in the debate, offer other government help for the bankruptcy process.

Although the auto industry issue did not play a major role in the first two debates, it received quite a bit of attention in the last two—and was the subject of some memorable exchanges. Romney stuck to his original tactics from the primaries with two notable exceptions. First, he attempted to directly counter the force of the op-ed title as a weapon against him. Second, he attempted to add the phrase "government help" to a four-year-old article, making him appear more in line with the intervention as executed. Both of these tactics had less positive impact than Romney surely hoped; the former was countered by clarification of the timing of the bankruptcy process and the latter by viewers at home live-fact-checking the debate.

The Auto Industry Issue in Last-Minute Campaigning

Following the debates and the level of attention that Obama gave to the auto industry issue, it became increasingly possible that this issue could play a role in deciding certain closely contested states. As has been argued here, Obama was largely winning the issue. If the battleground state of Ohio was truly a tossup, its large automaking sector might prove the deciding factor in winning the state and the election. Romney and Ryan spoke about the auto issue in the area (Shepherd 2012), and since Romney could not afford to lose Ohio, the campaign began running specialized auto ads during the final weeks.

The first counterattack ad, designed to soften the blows Romney took on the auto industry issue during the convention and the debates, claimed that "Obama took GM and Chrysler into bankruptcy, and sold Chrysler to Italians who are going to build Jeeps in China" (Streitfeld and Liptak 2012, 4). This new tactic went straight into the untested waters at the heart of the success story. The ad claimed that the intervention had actually failed, or more specifically, that the success was an illusion. Obama and his supporters had been claiming that the intervention had worked and saved jobs at home. The new ad claimed that any jobs saved were temporary and ultimately more jobs would be lost to China.

This jobs-to-China claim was false, at least according to Chrysler's senior vice president of corporate communications, Gualberto Ranieri, who said that "Jeep has no intention of shifting production of its Jeep models out of North America to China" (Streitfeld and Liptak 2012, 10). Joe Klein, writing for *Time*, called the ad "insultingly false" (2012, 33). Yet its potential power in the final week of the campaign was not worth leaving unchallenged. The Obama campaign responded to the ad with one of its own, opening with the "Let Detroit Go Bankrupt" op-ed and highlighting Ranieri's response to the Romney ad. "After Romney's false claim of Jeep outsourcing to China, Chrysler itself has refuted Romney's lie," the narrator explained (Wallace, Bohn, and Liptak 2012, 4). On the campaign trail, Biden condemned the Romney ad, accusing Romney of pushing an "outrageous lie" (Travis 2012, 2). "The ad was very misleading, to be kind," according to Dave Green, president of a United Auto Workers local (Flesher 2012, 19).

The day after the new Obama ad, Greg Martin, a spokesman for General Motors, called Romney's ad "cynical campaign politics at its worst.... [Romney] is bereft of any fundamental understanding of the global automotive industry" (Killough 2012a, 3, 13). Martin was referring to the common industry practice of making parts in many places around the world and assembling the vast majority of completed vehicles near the point of sale. It would not make financial sense to assemble cars in China to be shipped and sold in the United States or to assemble cars in the United States to be shipped to and sold in China. The accusation of jobs lost because of foreign expansion obscured this basic tenet of large durable goods manufacturing while appealing to American fears of outsourcing.

On the campaign trail in Ohio, Obama defended his actions during the rescue, using the tried and true tactics levied against Romney in the convention and the debates. He retold the success story narrative and defended the action that was "the right thing to do" (Schwarz 2012, 7). At the same time, he critiqued the Romney campaign for the China ad and trying to "scare hard-working Americans just to scare up some votes" (Schwarz 2012, 2). The campaign released a second ad attacking Romney on the auto industry issue. This ad, titled "Cynical," began with a narrator saying, "We know the truth, Mitt" (Wallace 2012, 4). Ohio senator Rob Portman appeared on CNN's *State of the Union* and defended the Romney auto ad. Portman claimed that the ad simply said new production in China would cost jobs through lost exports in Ohio (Killough 2012b, 1). Radio ads supporting Romney airing at the time continued the claim that GM and Chrysler would cut jobs in the United States to expand production in China, ads that the fact-checking group Politifact rated a "pants on fire" lie (Killough 2012b, 15).

Romney's original three tactics on the issue, established during the primaries, were countered quite effectively during the Democratic

National Convention and the debates. Left untested on the main stage was the claim that the auto industry intervention had actually failed. Of course, Romney could not easily make this claim because signs of recovery in the industry were too well documented. Instead, the Romney campaign chose to suggest that the recovery was illusory and would not last. Jobs that had returned to the Midwest would soon go to workers in China. This last tactic was effective; the mere fact that Obama, Biden, automakers, and others responded so quickly and loudly meant that the tactic struck close to a nerve. Unfortunately for Romney, the responses universally condemned the ads featuring the new tactic. The misleading implications of the ads were labeled hyperbolically as "insultingly false," "outrageous lies," and so on. The response to the ads was stronger than the ads themselves, meaning that the last tactic, while fleetingly effective, was almost certainly a net negative for the Romney campaign.

LESSONS FROM 2012

The analysis in the preceding section presents enough of a picture of how the auto industry issue was deployed in 2011–2012 to offer some tentative lessons. This chapter now turns to discussing the auto industry narratives in context with shifting popular opinion, which helps to explain why Obama's narrative connected in the way that it did. The chapter concludes by considering the implications of the 2012 auto industry rescue for our understanding of government interventions in theory and in practice.

As noted at the beginning of this chapter, Weatherford (2012) argued that a failure of messaging contributed to the lack of electoral gains in 2010 following the success of economic programs Obama initiated in 2009. In this line of thinking, had the administration changed some aspects of economic programs to be more visible, and had the administration more clearly told the story of those economic programs, 2010 might not have been the drubbing for the Democrats that it was. The election of 2012 should serve as confirmation of Weatherford's argument. One of the chief economic programs of Obama's first term was the auto industry rescue. In 2012, the Obama campaign delivered a much tighter and more aggressive message on the issue, with a well-defined success story and a harsh attack program against Romney. This ensured that

Romney could not take partial credit. In 2010 and in 2012, the deciding factors on the economy may have been less about actual economic performance and more about the way candidates explained that performance to the people.

This is in line with Bruce Gronbeck's claim that "the past can be hammered into stories that promise glory or shame, ease or difficulty, glorification or eternal damnation" (1998, 56). For Romney, the intervention in the industry was something he had suggested all along, although he would have handled it differently, and he was opposed to bailouts on principle. The auto industry crisis did not constitute an emergency of the scale necessary for him to compromise those principles. Romney also claimed late in the campaign that the intervention had actually failed— that the apparent success would prove short-lived and illusory. For Obama, the intervention in the industry was the right thing to do at the time. It was importantly *not* the same thing as Romney would have done. It was necessary precisely because the auto industry crisis *was* an emergency and the workers' jobs were important. Finally, for Obama, the auto industry intervention was a remarkable success story—it worked and it worked well. Both Romney and Obama appropriated the past: Romney hammered home a story of blame, Obama one of glory. Whatever part the competing auto industry narratives played in the election results, particularly in Ohio, Obama's narrative won. Given the ubiquity of the auto industry in the region, the way each candidate retold the story of 2008–2009 would surely have had consequences for the vote. Bob Bennett, chair of the Ohio Republican Party, confirmed this when he said, after the results were in, "The biggest determining factor was that we couldn't handle the automobile bailout issue" (Flesher 2012, 4).

Some of the success Obama had on the auto issue can be attributed to shifting popular opinion. Back in 2008 and 2009, the public was strongly opposed to the auto bailout and any intervention in the industry. A Gallup poll in February 2009 reported that 72 percent of Americans did not want the government to expand its aid to the industry (Saad 2009), and a second poll in March 2009 reported that 59 percent of Americans disapproved of "the federal loans given to General Motors and Chrysler last year to help them avoid bankruptcy" (Jones 2009, 2). A poll conducted by the Pew Research Center around the same time found that

54 percent of Americans considered the intervention bad for the economy (Pew Research Center 2012, 2). This remarkably negative view of the intervention, which also extended to the bailout of Wall Street, was the environment in which Romney had penned his "Let Detroit Go Bankrupt" op-ed. His solution, to have government stand aside and let the automakers go through natural private bankruptcies, with the promise of postbankruptcy loan guarantees on the other side, was actually well in line with public opinion—*then.*

At that point, however, the intervention had not yet had time to work. Years later, in March 2012, during the GOP primaries, the public opinion tide had shifted in favor of the bailouts. A February poll by the Pew Research Center found that the public thought the government loans "mostly good for economy, 56 percent to 38 percent" (Pew Research Center 2012, 1). Gallup reported a near-tie in public opinion, with 51 percent still opposed to the auto intervention and 44 percent in support, although the party divide was telling: 63 percent of Democrats approved in February 2012 while 73 percent of Republicans disapproved (Jacobe 2012). Views of the auto industry improved as well. Fifty-five percent of Americans said the auto industry "has a positive effect on the way things are going in the country," as opposed to 29 percent who viewed the industry as having a negative effect (Pew Research Center 2012, 3).

Some of the shift in popular opinion may be due to the fact that the intervention worked—at least in terms of stabilizing the automakers so that they could return to profitability and resume hiring. The industry had added roughly 200,000 jobs by the time of the election, according to Federal Reserve Economic Data (FRED 2012). Additionally, public opinion about the intervention may have shifted in response to a continually falling estimate of its final costs to taxpayers. What was originally marketed as an $80–$100 billion rescue of automakers has gradually, and loudly, been revised downward. Estimates prior to the election of the final cost range from $14 billion (Gardner 2011) to $25 billion (Reuters 2012). The lower apparent cost to taxpayers of the intervention may have also shifted public opinion in favor of the automakers and the intervention that saved them. A study released in December 2013 by the independent Center for Automotive Research concluded that the intervention ultimately cost taxpayers $13.7 billion, but in intervening saved or avoided the loss of roughly eight times that amount, while preserving 2.6 million jobs (McAlinden and Menk 2013). Although this report was released well after Obama's reelection, it demonstrates that the success narrative more accurately reflected the reality of the intervention than the failure narrative.

Unfortunately for Romney, the tactics he employed during the GOP primaries, which later served as a structure for his approach in debates against Obama, were still in line with popular opinion from four years prior. The intervention had improved things, popular opinion had changed in response, and yet Romney held the ground he staked out in his 2008 op-ed. Much of the reason why Romney's tactics and narrative failed to resonate as Obama's did can be explained by these polls: the public had changed its mind. That shift would translate into votes; a number of studies have documented the link between perceptions of macroeconomic performance and views of the president (Monroe 1978; Clark and Stewart 1994; Edwards III et al. 1995). If voters in Ohio perceived the intervention a success, the costs of intervention shrinking, and the economy improving, that would lead to more votes in the key state.

Given the increasing role that the auto industry issue played in the election as it was trumpeted at the Democratic convention and became a flashpoint in the debates, rhetoricians and political scientists could continue to heed Paul Quirk's call. "The economy will be an even larger preoccupation for presidents in the foreseeable future than it has been in the relatively recent past.... [We] need to give far more attention to presidential economic governance than [we] have in the past" (Quirk 2012, 1). We need more research on how presidents negotiate economic agendas with Congress, justify economic policies to the public, and retell the lessons of economic policies in the past.

None of this speaks to the actual morality of bailouts—which in many ways *do* contribute to moral hazard. However, there are three lessons related to government interventions that are worth reporting here. First, success story narratives invite replication. Second, the time to debate intervention is not during economic crises. Third, there is an electoral moral hazard that comes with intervention.

First, as Weatherford has argued and as has been shown here, the retelling of the events plays an important role in the electoral outcomes following the events. Yet that retelling, the shaping of the past for use in the present, can invite imitation in a dangerous way. As Barry Ritholtz argued in *Bailout Nation*, successive bailouts have had negative consequences and "the repercussions have often led to the next bailout. Each negative impact seems to have the perverse effect of making future bailouts less surprising and more tolerable" (2009, 12). Ritholtz described an economic danger—the fact that bailouts shore up industries and companies, allowing them to continue without changing in meaningful ways. In the long run, this creates entities that are inherently weak and will need further assistance. Is this true in the auto case? Possibly. The industry may be internally weakened by government attempts to protect it from collapse. More important, in this case, the power and popularity of the success story conceals internal weaknesses and invites other companies or industries to follow in those same footsteps. The appearance of successful government intervention could be more dangerous than a visible failure.

Second, we need to realize that the time to debate intervention is not during a crisis. As Ritholtz remarked about the financial crisis of 2008–2009, "just as there are no atheists in foxholes, there were no free market capitalists in the face of the financial system collapse" (2009, 176). People from practically every shade of the political and philosophical spectrum conceded that 2008–2009 was different. The political figures discussed in this chapter disagreed during the primary debates, conventions, and presidential debates on whether a philosophically consistent approach or a situational approach was the better answer for determining when and whether to intervene in private companies, industries, or banks. A consistent approach may never work because there will always come an emergency of unexpected proportions that threatens our resolve.

Instead, we should adopt a situational standard for determining when government intervention is called for. This standard should have an agreeable balance of economic indicators that determines the necessity for government intervention. This might sound like an unnecessary and problematic constraint. Unnecessary—maybe. Problematic—certainly. Yet the alternative is to continue employing an ad hoc approach to interventions during crises. The alternative is to continue facing new crises and having too little time to debate intervention; someone chooses to act and others can demonize the decision maker for it forever. Also, importantly, the alternative leaves open the possibility of using other justifications for intervention. Presidents have used multiple, competing justifications for intervention in the auto industry in the past (Stuglin 2012). Some of these justifications have been more symbolic than economic—intervening, for example, to save "iconic industries" that "restore American pride" (Halperin 2012, 27–28). While the symbolic is certainly important, the economic should hold more weight in determining government intervention, else we begin on a path toward largely symbolic but economically unimportant industries receiving government aid. Periods of economic stability are the time for a reasonable discussion about government intervention and what constitutes a case worthy of it.

Finally, there is an electoral moral hazard that is demonstrated in the auto industry case and the 2012 election. Moral hazard is the decision making that leads an entity to take on increased risk because of an assumption of aid in the case of failure. Electoral moral hazard, as used here, refers to the electoral capital gained by successful interventions in private enterprise. If bailing out a bank or an automaker appears to have won Obama even a few votes, whether it actually did or not, then we have electoral moral hazard. Bailouts may become more common, or easier to digest when the situation might call for one, not because they appear to work for the industry or because they appear to work for the economy, but because they appear to work for the politician.

REFERENCES

Beasley, V. 2004. *You, the People: American National Identity in Presidential Rhetoric*. College Station: Texas A&M University Press.

Biden, J. 2012. "DNC Speech." *Politico*, September 6. Retrieved from http://www.politico.com/news/stories/0912/80885.html.

Bose, M. 1998. "Words as Signals: Drafting Cold War Rhetoric in the Eisenhower and Kennedy Administrations." *Congress and the Presidency* 25: 25–41.

Bose, M., and F. I. Greenstein. 2002. "The Hidden Hand vs. The Bully Pulpit: The Layered Political Rhetoric of President Eisenhower." In *The Presidency and Rhetorical Leadership*, edited by Leroy Dorsey, 184–199. College Station: Texas A&M University Press.

Clark, H., and M. Stewart. 1994. "Prospections, Retrospections, and Rationality: The "Bankers" Model of Presidential Approval Considered." *American Journal of Political Science* 38: 1104–1123.

Clark, E., and R. McKerrow. 1998. "The Rhetorical Construction of History." In *Doing Rhetorical History: Concepts and Cases*, edited by K. Turner, 33–46. Tuscaloosa: University of Alabama Press.

Clinton, W. 2012. "DNC Speech." *Politico,* September 5. Retrieved from http://www.politico.com/news/stories/0912/80808.html.

Clyburn, J. 2012. "DNC Speech." *Politico,* September 6. Retrieved from http://www.politico.com/news/stories/0912/80867.html.

CNBC. 2011. "Transcript of GOP Primary Debate in Michigan." November 10. Retrieved from http://www.cnbc.com/id/45074943/.

CNN. 2012. "Arizona GOP Primary Debate Transcript." February 22. Retrieved from http://archives.cnn.com/TRANSCRIPTS/1202/22/se.05.html.

Cohen, B. C. 1963. *The Press and Foreign Policy.* Princeton: Princeton University Press.

Cohen, J. E. 1995. "Presidential Rhetoric and the Public Agenda." *American Journal of Political Science* 39: 87–107.

Cohen, J. E. 2010. *Going Local: Presidential Leadership in the Post-Broadcast Age.* Cambridge: Cambridge University Press.

Corrigan, M. 2000. "The Transformation of Going Public: President Clinton, the First Lady, and Health Care Reform." *Political Communication* 17: 149–168.

Dorsey, L. 2007. *We Are All Americans, Pure and Simple: Theodore Roosevelt and the Myth of Americanism.* Tuscaloosa: University of Alabama Press.

Edwards III, G. C., W. Mitchell, and R. Welch. 1995. "Explaining Presidential Approval: The Significance of Issue Salience." *American Journal of Political Science* 39: 108–134.

Edwards III, G. C. 2003. *On Deaf Ears: The Limits of the Bully Pulpit.* New Haven: Yale University Press.

Eshbaugh-Soha, M. 2006. *The President's Speeches: Beyond Going Public.* Boulder: Lynne Rienner Press.

Flesher, J. 2012. "Romney Never Overcame Bailout Opposition in Ohio." *Mercury News,* November 11. Retrieved from http://www.mercurynews.com/presidentelect/ci_21976324/romney-never-overcame-bailout-opposition-ohio.

FRED/Federal Reserve Economic Data. 2012. "All Employees: Durable Goods: Motor Vehicles and Parts." *Federal Reserve Economic Data,* November 18. Retrieved from http://research.stlouisfed.org/fred2/series/CES3133600101.

Fridkin, K. L., and P. J. Kenney. 2005. "Campaign Frames: Can Candidates Influence Media Coverage?" In *Framing American Politics,* edited by K. Callaghan and F. Schnell. Pittsburgh: University of Pittsburgh Press.

Gabrielson, T. 2005. "Obstacles and Opportunities: Factors That Constrain Elected Officials' Ability to Frame Political Issues." In *Framing American Politics,* edited by K. Callaghan and F. Schnell. Pittsburgh: University of Pittsburgh Press.

Gardner, G. 2011. "Ex-Auto Czar: Auto Bailout Will Cost Taxpayers $14 Billion." *USA Today,* December 18. Retrieved from http://content.usatoday.com

/communities/driveon/post/2011/12/gm-general-motors-chrysler-auto
-bailout-loss-obama/1#.UNItonco-Os.

Goodnight, G. T. 1996. "Reagan, Vietnam, and Central America." In *Beyond the Rhetorical Presidency*, edited by M. J. Medhurst, 122–151. College Station: Texas A&M University Press.

Google. 2012. "Google Trends." October 22. Retrieved from http://www.google.com/trends/

Granholm, J. 2012. "DNC Speech." *Politico,* September 6. Retrieved from http://www.politico.com/news/stories/0912/80875.html.

Gronbeck, B. E. 1998. "The Rhetorics of the Past." In *Doing Rhetorical History: Concepts and Cases,* edited by K. Turner, 47–60. Tuscaloosa: University of Alabama Press.

Halperin, M. 2012. "All the Right Moves…and Some Wrong Ones." *Time,* November 19, 27–28.

Hanan, J. S. 2011. "Stating the Exception: (Ir)rationalizing Interventionism During the Creation and Passage of EESA." Presented at the National Communication Association Annual Conference, New Orleans.

Holloway, R. 2009. "The 2008 Presidential Nominating Conventions: Fighting for Change." In *The 2008 Political Campaign,* edited by Robert Denton. New York: Rowman and Littlefield.

Ingrassia, P. 2010. *Crash Course: The American Automobile Industry's Road from Glory to Disaster*. New York: Random House.

Isidore, C. 2012. "Auto Bailout: If Romney Had His Way." *CNN Money,* October 23. Retrieved from http://money.cnn.com/2012/10/23/news/companies/romney-auto-bailout/index.html.

Ivie, R. L. 1996. "Tragic Fear and the Rhetorical Presidency: Combatting Evil in the Persian Gulf." In *Beyond the Rhetorical Presidency,* edited by M. Medhurst. College Station: Texas A&M University Press.

Jacobe, D. 2012. "Republicans, Democrats Differ over U.S. Automaker Bailout." *Gallup Economy,* February 23. Retrieved from http://www.gallup.com/poll/152936/Republicans-Democrats-Differ-Automaker-Bailout.aspx.

Jones, J. M. 2009. "Americans Continue to Oppose GM, Chrysler Loans." *Gallup Economy,* March 31. Retrieved from http://www.gallup.com/poll/117211/Americans-Continue-Oppose-Chrysler-Loans.aspx.

Kernell, S. 1997. *Going Public: New Strategies of Presidential Leadership.* Washington, D.C.: CQ Press.

Killough, A. 2012a. "Auto Companies Hit Back against Romney Ads." *CNN,* October 30. Retrieved from http://politicalticker.blogs.cnn.com/2012/10/30/auto-companies-hit-back-against-romney-ads/.

Killough, A. 2012b. "Portman Stands by Romney Auto Ads." *CNN,* November 4. Retrieved from http://politicalticker.blogs.cnn.com/2012/11/04/portman-stands-by-romney-auto-ads/.

Klein, J. 2012. "Closing Arguments." *Time,* November 12, 33.

Koch, J. W. 1998. "Political Rhetoric and Political Persuasion: The Changing Structure of Citizens' Preferences on Health Insurance During Policy Debate." *Public Opinion Quarterly* 62: 209–229.

Lewis, W. F. 1987. "Telling America's Story: Narrative Form and the Reagan Presidency." In *Readings in Rhetorical Criticism*, 2nd ed., edited by C. R. Burgchardt. State College, PA: Strata Publishing.

Lucas, S. E. 2002. "George Washington and the Rhetoric of Presidential Leadership." In *The Presidency and Rhetorical Leadership*, edited by L. Dorsey, 42–72. College Station: Texas A&M University Press.

Maslin-Wicks, K. 1998. "Two Types of Presidential Influence in Congress." *Presidential Studies Quarterly* 28: 108–126.

McAlinden, S. P., and D. M. Menk. 2013. "The Effect on the U.S. Economy of the Successful Restructuring of General Motors." *Center for Automotive Research*, December 5. Retrieved from http://www.cargroup.org/?module =Publicationsandevent=ViewandpubID=102.

Monroe, K. R. 1978. "Economic Influences on Presidential Popularity." *Public Opinion Quarterly* 42: 360–369.

Neustadt, R. 1960. *Presidential Power*. New York: Wiley.

Obama, B. 2012. "DNC Speech." *Politico*, September 6. Retrieved from http://www .politico.com/news/stories/0912/80890.html.

Patrick, D. 2012. "DNC Speech." *Politico*, September 4. Retrieved from http://www .politico.com/news/stories/0912/80701.html.

Pew Research Center. 2012. "Growing Support for Auto Industry Bailout." *Pew Research Center for the People and the Press*, March 7. Retrieved from http:// www.pewresearch.org/daily-number/growing-support-for-auto-industry -bailout/.

Politico. 2012a. "Transcript of First Presidential Debate." *Politico*, October 3. Retrieved from http://www.politico.com/news/stories/1012/81994.html.

Politico. 2012b. "Transcript of Vice Presidential Debate." *Politico*, October 3. Retrieved from http://www.politico.com/news/stories/1012/82310.html.

Politico. 2012c. "Transcript of Second Presidential Debate." *Politico*, October 3. Retrieved from http://www.politico.com/news/stories/1012/82484.html.

Politico. 2012d. "Transcript of Third Presidential Debate." *Politico*, October 3. Retrieved from http://www.politico.com/news/stories/1012/82712.html.

Powell, R. J. 1999. "'Going Public' Revisited: Presidential Speechmaking and the Bargaining Setting in Congress." *Congress and the Presidency* 26 (2): 153–170.

Quirk, P. J. 2012. "Editor's Introduction." *Presidential Studies Quarterly* 42 (1): 1–7.

Rankin, D. M. 2006. "Featuring the President as Free Trader: Television News Coverage of U.S. Trade Policies." *Presidential Studies Quarterly* 36: 633–659.

Rattner, S. 2010. *Overhaul: An Insider's Account of the Obama Administration's Emergency Rescue of the Auto Industry*. Boston: Houghton Mifflin Harcourt.

Reich, R. B., and J. D. Donahue. 1985. *New Deals: The Chrysler Revival and the American System*. New York: Penguin.

Reid, Harry. 2012. "DNC Speech." *Politico,* September 4. Retrieved from http://www.politico.com/news/stories/0912/80688.html.

Reuters. 2012. "U.S. Auto Bailout Will Cost Billions More Than Previously Thought: Treasury." *Huffington Post,* August 13. Retrieved from http://www.huffingtonpost.com/2012/08/13/us-auto-bailout-treasury_n_1773811.html.

Ritholtz, B. 2009. *Bailout Nation: How Greed and Easy Money Corrupted Wall Street and Shook the World Economy.* Hoboken, NJ: Wiley.

Romney, M. 2008. "Let Detroit Go Bankrupt." *New York Times,* November 18. Retrieved from http://www.nytimes.com/2008/11/19/opinion/19romney.html.

Rottinghaus, B. 2012. "Convention Speeches Too Vague on Policy to Help Romney." *U.S. News,* August 31. Retrieved from http://www.usnews.com/debate-club/was-the-republican-national-convention-a-success-for-mitt-romney/convention-speeches-too-vague-on-policy-to-help-romney-2.

Rubenstein, J. 1992. *The Changing US Auto Industry: A Geographical Analysis.* New York: Routledge.

Saad, L. 2009. "Americans Reject Sequel to Auto Bailout." *Gallup Economy,* February 26. Retrieved from http://www.gallup.com/poll/116107/Americans-Reject-Sequel-Auto-Bailout.aspx.

Schnell, F., and K. Callaghan. 2005. "Terrorism, Media Frames, and Framing Effects: A Macro- and Microlevel Analysis." In *Framing American Politics,* edited by K. Callaghan and F. Schnell. Pittsburgh: University of Pittsburgh Press.

Schwarz, G. 2012. "Obama Tries to Run Over Romney's Auto Claims." *CNN,* November 2. Retrieved from politicalticker.blogs.cnn.com/2012/11/02/obama-tries-to-run-over-romneys-auto-claims/.

Seligman, L. G., and C. R. Covington. 1989. *The Coalitional Presidency.* Chicago: Dorsey Press.

Shepherd, S. 2012. "Ryan Hits Obama on Auto Bailout." *CNN,* October 28. Retrieved from http://politicalticker.blogs.cnn.com/2012/10/28/ryan-hits-obama-on-auto-bailout/.

Streitfeld, R., and K. Liptak. 2012. "Romney Ad Pushes Back on Auto Bailout Attacks." *CNN,* October 28. Retrieved from http://politicalticker.blogs.cnn.com/2012/10/28/romney-ad-pushes-back-on-auto-bailout-attacks/.

Strickland, T. 2012. "DNC Speech." *Politico,* September 4. Retrieved from http://www.politico.com/news/stories/0912/80699.html.

Stuckey, M. E. 1991. *The President as Interpreter-in-Chief.* Chatham, NJ: Chatham House Publishers.

Stuckey, M. E. 2004. *Defining Americans: The Presidency and National Identity.* Lawrence: University Press of Kansas.

Stuckey, M. E. 2008. *Jimmy Carter, Human Rights, and the National Agenda.* College Station: Texas A&M University Press.

Stuckey, M. E. 2013. *The Good Neighbor: Franklin D. Roosevelt and the Rhetoric of American Power.* East Lansing: Michigan State University Press.

Stuglin, S. A. 2012. "U.S. Auto Industry Rescue." In *The Obama Presidency: A Preliminary Assessment*, edited by R. P. Watson, J. Covarrubias, T. Lansford, and D. M. Brattebo, 145–160. New York: SUNY.

Taylor III, A. 2010. *Sixty to Zero: An Inside Look at the Collapse of General Motors and the Detroit Auto Industry*. New Haven: Yale University Press.

Travis, S. 2012. "Biden Accuses Romney Camp of 'Outrageous Lie.'" *CNN*, October 31. Retrieved from http://politicalticker.blogs.cnn.com/2012/10/31/biden -accuses-romney-camp-of-outrageous-lie/.

Vlasic, B. 2001. *Taken for a Ride: How Daimler-Benz Drove Off with Chrysler*. New York: HarperCollins.

Vlasic, B. 2011. *Once Upon a Car: The Fall and Resurrection of America's Big Three Automakers—GM, Ford, and Chrysler*. New York: HarperCollins.

Wallace, G. 2012. "Second Obama Ad Responds to Romney Auto Charge." *CNN*, November 1. Retrieved from http://politicalticker.blogs.cnn.com/2012/11/01 /second-obama-ad-responds-to-romney-auto-charge/.

Wallace, G., K. Bohn, and K. Liptak. 2012. "Obama Campaign Unveils Response to Romney Auto Ad." *CNN*, October 29. Retrieved from http://politicalticker. blogs.cnn.com/2012/10/29/obama-campaign-unveils-response-to-romney -auto-ad/.

Weatherford, M. S. 2012. "The Wages of Competence: Obama, the Economy, and the 2010 Midterm Elections." *Presidential Studies Quarterly* 42 (1): 8–39.

Wood, B. D. 2004. "Presidential Rhetoric and Economic Leadership." *Presidential Studies Quarterly* 34 (3): 573–606.

Zarefsky, D. 2004. "Presidential Rhetoric and the Power of Definition." *Presidential Studies Quarterly* 34 (3): 607–619.

NOTES

1. The full-text version of the much more extended exchange intersperses "crosstalk" between every statement, and often between individual words, as the two candidates both spoke at once. The "crosstalk" notes have been removed and the speaker statements reduced to complete utterances, while not adding or deleting words, for clarity.

Chapter 8

Health Care in the 2012 Election

Michael K. Gusmano, New York Medical College

INTRODUCTION

The Patient Protection and Affordable Care Act (ACA) was the signature domestic policy achievement of President Obama's first term in office. Ironically, the ACA was based on the Massachusetts health reform signed into law in 2006 by Obama's opponent in the 2012 presidential election, former governor Mitt Romney. While the adoption of the ACA made it likely that health policy would play a prominent role in the 2012 election, the results of the 2010 midterm elections and Governor Romney's selection of Representative Paul Ryan (R-WI) as his running mate made it a certainty. Unlike Governor Romney, Congressman Ryan's health policy positions offered a stark contrast to the approach favored by Democrats. Congressman Ryan, after all, has called for fundamentally altering the structure of Medicare and turning it into a voucher system that would cap the federal government's financial obligations to beneficiaries.

This chapter reviews how the presidential candidates framed their health policy platforms for the American public. Efforts by Governor Romney and Representative Ryan to raise fears about the consequences of the ACA built on the successful efforts by the so-called Tea Party during the 2010 congressional elections and tapped into much older rhetoric used by previous opponents of government-sponsored health insurance. The language Romney and Ryan used in describing the law known as "Obamacare" echoed themes that have appeared in debates about government health insurance in the United States during the past century. Unlike the 2010 midterm elections, however, the attacks on the ACA did not translate into electoral gains for the Romney-Ryan ticket. The Ryan plan for Medicare, embraced during the campaign by Governor Romney, was problematic for the Republican ticket because although this may have resonated with some older voters, most of the electorate rejected the claim that the Republican Party is more likely than the Democratic Party to protect the Medicare program. Furthermore, the similarities between the Massachusetts law enacted with the support of Governor Romney and the ACA put the Romney-Ryan ticket in a contradictory position.

THE ACA'S IMPLEMENTATION TIMELINE AND ELECTORAL POLITICS

To understand the debate about health reform during the 2012 presidential election, it is important to appreciate a key feature of the ACA. The law was signed into law in early 2010, but most of its major provisions, particularly its expansion of public and publicly subsidized private insurance, were not scheduled to go into effect until 2014. The law delayed implementation of insurance expansion because President Obama and the Democratic leadership in Congress wanted to achieve a favorable scoring for the bill by the Congressional Budget Office (CBO), which is charged with producing a formal cost estimate for almost every bill approved by a full committee of either house of Congress. The Democrats managed to achieve a favorable score from the CBO without building serious cost controls into the law (Gusmano 2011). Obama enjoyed significant Democratic majorities in both houses of Congress, but a complete lack of support by Republicans along with divisions within the Democratic Party meant that the success of health reform in 2010 was far from inevitable. Powerful interests—including organized medicine, the pharmaceutical industry, and the private health insurance industry— that had taken advantage of our fragmented political institutions to block change in the past may well have succeeded in doing so this time around (Peterson 1992; Steinmo and Watts 1995). The adoption of the ACA was due in large part to the administration's efforts to "work around" these veto points (Brown 2008; Starr 2011).

Obama worked hard to co opt stakeholders, particularly those who had worked against reform in the past, and was successful because he placed much less emphasis on cost control than the Clinton administration in 1993. Because the ACA does not include significant efforts to curb the price of health care, Democrats needed another mechanism to achieve a favorable CBO score. Delaying implementation of insurance expansion until 2014 made this possible. The CBO projected that over its first 10 years (the period of time required for CBO projections) the law would decrease, rather than increase, the federal budget deficit even though it included large new expenditures for health insurance.

In contrast to the ACA's timeline, President Johnson signed Medicare and Medicaid into law in 1965 and by the start of 1966, these programs started enrolling beneficiaries. The fast implementation and early success of these programs led the public to embrace them and led to "sustained electoral benefits for Democrats" (Kersh 2011). The ACA's long implementation delay had the potential of undermining the political gains for the Democrats and public support for the law because the potential benefits of the law were not yet experienced by most voters in 2010 or 2012. As a result, "the fate of this elongated implementation phase is uncertain" (Marmor 2011). The delayed implementation gave opponents a great deal of time to raise concerns about the law, and they began an effort to repeal it within days of its enactment (Kersh 2011).

The Tea Party, which emerged as a new force in American politics in 2009, pointed to the ACA as an example of what was wrong with government and used anger about the law to increase turnout among conservative activists in the 2010 midterm elections. The success of the Tea Party in the 2010 midterms, its members' intense dislike of the law referred to derisively as "Obamacare," the perception that attacks on the ACA helped produce the 2010 Republican electoral victories, and the need for Romney to shore up his conservative base (especially during the primaries) all contributed to the rhetoric he adopted with regard to health reform during the 2012 campaign.

THE 2010 ELECTIONS AND TEA PARTY ATTACKS ON THE ACA

The Tea Party had emerged in 2009 following CNBC commentator Rick Santelli's on-air complaints against President Obama's plan to address the mortgage crisis. Santelli claimed that "the government is rewarding bad behavior!" and argued that the administration's policies would "subsidize the losers' mortgages." He called for a "Chicago Tea Party" to protest the administration's housing policy. Santelli's language was picked up by conservative activists around the country. By the summer of 2009, fueled by money from business conservatives and promoted by the Fox News Channel, the movement grew into a significant force. Its members, who represent only a small portion of the American public, waged an effective grassroots campaign aimed at defeating the Democrats and repealing President Obama's policies, including the ACA.

The Tea Party movement is a new iteration of longstanding conservative ideas in U.S. politics (Williams et al. 2011). While polls found that the vast majority of people affiliated with the Tea Party are motivated by anger "with Washington as a whole," rather than with a particular law or policy, the ACA is extraordinarily unpopular with this group (Henry J. Kaiser Family Foundation 2010). In the months leading up to the 2010 midterm elections, a Kaiser Family Foundation tracking poll found that 63 percent of Tea Party supporters claimed to be angry about health reform and 68 percent viewed it as either "somewhat" or "very" unfavorable (Henry J. Kaiser Family Foundation 2010). In the summer of 2009, the St. Louis Tea Party website claimed that "the legislation pending in Congress regarding socialized medicine incorporates the institution of eugenics, forced abortions, euthanasia, and geriatricide. In other words, Barack Obama and the Congressional majority party want the United States to promote evil through selective murder of undesirables." The website urged people to attend a town hall meeting with Senator Claire McCaskill's regional director to "fight like hell" against this "evil."[1]

Why are those associated with the Tea Party hostile toward the ACA despite substantial and durable public support for large government programs such as Social Security and Medicare? Interviews with the movement's activists in Massachusetts suggest that the Tea Party believes that the ACA, like the mortgage policies that upset Santelli, provides government support to an "undeserving" poor (Williams et al. 2011). This perspective reflects a longstanding split in the American welfare state. Social insurance programs such as Medicare provide benefits to what many see as the "deserving" poor. Social welfare programs such as Medicaid allegedly support the "undeserving" poor that have not earned these benefits (Weir et al. 1988).

Was the Tea Party campaign against the ACA effective? During the 2010 election, three states amended their constitutions to overturn the ACA's individual mandate to purchase insurance (Kersh 2011). In addition, Republicans focused on 20 Democratic House members in Republican-leaning districts who had voted for the ACA (targeted, infamously, by Sarah Palin with gunsight images superimposed on a U.S. map), and 18 either retired or lost their seats (Kersh 2011). Several analyses of the 2010 midterm elections suggest that many Democrats who lost in the 2010 midterm elections were harmed by their support for health care reform (Aldrich et al. 2012; Kersh 2011; Konisky and Richardson 2012; Nyhan et al. 2012).

The apparent success of this strategy encouraged Republican candidates to highlight health reform as an issue in the 2012 election. At the same time, it created a potential problem for Governor Romney because ACA was modeled on the 2006 Massachusetts health reform that he signed into law and championed as a "conservative" approach to reform because it encouraged personal responsibility (Starr 2011). Governor Romney felt compelled to attack the ACA in order to bolster his support among conservatives, but often tried to do so while defending the Massachusetts health reform law. These efforts seemed to convince few people, but they did raise further suspicions about the governor among conservatives and reinforced the perception that, rather than adopting policy positions on the basis of principle, he was willing to say anything to get elected. During the Republican primaries and the general election, Romney did as much as possible to distance himself from the ACA and convince voters that the law he had signed in Massachusetts and the ACA were fundamentally different. To do so, he tapped into a set of conservative arguments about government health insurance that originated a century ago, as well as arguments about the deserving and undeserving poor that are reflected in the distinction between social insurance and social welfare programs (Weir et al. 1988).

POLITICS OF FEAR REDUX

The rhetoric of the attacks against the ACA by the Tea Party in 2010 and by the Romney campaign during the 2012 campaign was not new. Some of the specific language, as well as the overall tenor of the campaign against the ACA, echoed previous campaigns by opponents of government health insurance proposals in the United States. This section offers a brief historical overview of campaigns against government health insurance in the United States and illustrates the similarity between these previous efforts to discredit national health insurance and Medicare and Governor Romney's criticism of the ACA.

The first campaign to adopt national health insurance in the United States took place during the Progressive Era. Between 1910 and 1920, reformers attempted to pass legislation at the state level to establish programs of compulsory government health insurance. These efforts were damaged, however, by the U.S. involvement in World War I and the subsequent burst of anti-German rhetoric throughout the country. Because the idea of compulsory health insurance was so closely linked to Germany, physicians were able to associate it with totalitarianism. Beginning in 1917, a number of articles appearing in the *Journal of the American Medical Association* denounced compulsory health insurance as "Un-American" and warned against allowing the "evils of foreign systems" to ruin the medical system in the United States (Gusmano 1995). The AMA was also able to convince the federal government's Creel Committee on Public Information to attack German social insurance as a sham that had been used to placate German workers (Numbers 1978, 78). The federal government, consumed by its effort to discredit Germany, gladly complied with the request.

During the California campaign, launched on the eve of American involvement in the First World War, opponents often used anti-German rhetoric in their attacks on the bill. One pamphlet pictured a German soldier under the inscription, *Compulsory health insurance made in Germany!* (Viseltear 1969, 177–178). Another, put out by the California League for the Conservation of Public Health (CLCPH), a group of paid lobbyists and physicians, stated: "*What is compulsory health insurance? It is a dangerous device invented in Germany, announced by the German Emperor from the throne the same year he started plotting to conquer* the world" (as cited in Viseltear 1969, 178). Even Samuel Gompers, the president of the American Federation of Labor, adopted this language when he claimed that the concept was "at variance with our concepts of voluntary institutions and of freedom for individuals" (Mandel 1963, 184). Tapping into wartime hysteria regarding Germany and the kaiser, such attacks were quite effective (Starr 1982, 253).

In every attempt to adopt national health insurance since the Progressive campaign, opponents have tried to characterize the idea as "Un-American," "Foreign," or "Socialist." During the Truman presidency, Republicans, working with the AMA, tried to claim that national health insurance was part of a larger Socialist scheme. They accused the Truman administration of spending federal funds on behalf of "socialized medicine" and "in furtherance of the Moscow party line" (Starr 1982, 284). In 1948, Truman decided to counter this effort during the presidential campaign by arguing that national health insurance was "100 percent American" (Poen 1979, 130). Truman's surprise victory over Dewey gave reformers new hope, but it also mobilized the AMA like never before.

After Truman's victory, the AMA began a nearly $5 million campaign to defeat national health insurance (Kelly 1956, 106). The public relations firm of Whitaker and Baxter made effective use of the special social role played by doctors and the emotional ties that they had with their patients (Kelly 1956). In their now famous poster, Whitaker and Baxter displayed a reproduction of Sir Luke Fildes's painting of a doctor at the bedside of a sick child. Underneath the picture the poster read "KEEP POLITICS OUT OF THIS PICTURE!" It claimed that "compulsory health insurance is political medicine. It will bring a third party—a politician—between you and your doctor. It would bind your family's health up in red tape. It would result in heavy payroll taxes—and inferior medical care for you and your family. Don't let this happen here!"

Whitaker and Baxter also evoked the familiar theme of socialized medicine in their pamphlets, falsely claiming that Lenin had declared socialized medicine to be the keystone of the socialist state (Starr 1982, 285). This campaign was wildly successful. By the end of the year they had been able to get 1,829 organizations on record opposing compulsory health insurance (Kelly 1956, 81). Support in public opinion polls also evaporated and the measure remained deadlocked in Congress (Starr

1982, 285). The Whitaker and Baxter campaign, in addition to being a great success, sounded several themes that continue to shape our debates about national health insurance. In addition to "socialism," they evoked the specters of bureaucracy, red tape, high taxes, and a government-imposed restriction of choice. Many of the claims made against the Truman plan in 1949 were repeated by the opponents of subsequent efforts to pass national health insurance.

When the Democrats, after the election of President Kennedy in 1960, decided to change tactics and focus on health insurance for older people based on Social Security, the American Medical Association (AMA) and other opponents used the same arguments. In 1961, the AMA launched "operation coffee cup," which involved enlisting doctors' wives to convince friends and neighbors to write letters to Congress opposing the "King bill," a later version of which became Medicare. As part of this effort, the AMA hired Ronald Reagan to record an album that would be played during these coffee meetings. Reagan explained that the King bill was a call for socialized medicine and one part of a broader effort to create a system of socialism in America. Toward the end of the record, Reagan warned that if the King bill were adopted, "you and I are going to spend our sunset years telling our children and our children's children what it was like in America when men were free" (Reagan 1961).

All of these themes—and even much of the exact language—were adopted by Governor Romney during the 2012 presidential election. He described the ACA as a government takeover of health care that would undermine quality, raise taxes, and interfere with liberty. In an essay published in the *New England Journal of Medicine*, he declared that "President Obama believes the answer lies in a bigger government that decides what care Americans should receive and how much providers should be paid for it.... My plan tackles our health care challenges without a federal takeover of the entire system" (Romney 2012).

Similarly, during an August 23, 2012, interview with a CBS affiliate in Denver, Colorado, Governor Romney said, "My health care plan I put in place in my state has everyone insured, but we didn't go out and raise taxes on people and have an unelected board tell people what kind of health care they can have" (Associated Press 2012). His reference to an "unelected board," which was repeated throughout the campaign, was a reference to the Independent Payment Advisory Board (IPAB), a 15-member agency created by the ACA that has responsibility for finding savings in the Medicare program without reducing quality or coverage. Congress can only change the agency's decisions by offering a plan that results in comparable reductions in Medicare spending or if both houses of Congress, including a three-fifths majority in the Senate, vote to do so (Haberkorn 2011). Although IPAB is explicitly prohibited from including "any recommendation to ration health care, raise revenues or Medicare beneficiary premiums…increase Medicare beneficiary cost sharing (including deductibles, coinsurance, and co-payments), or otherwise restrict benefits or modify eligibility criteria," Governor Romney continued to suggest that this would lead to "rationing" by "uncontrollable" bureaucrats.

Following the decision by the Supreme Court in *National Federation of Independent Business v. Sebelius*, in which the U.S. Supreme Court upheld most provisions of the ACA, Governor Romney issued a statement in which he promised to repeal the law. His statement about the ACA combined many of the classic themes from previous arguments against government health insurance. According to Governor Romney, "Obamacare raises taxes on the American people by approximately $500 billion. Obamacare cuts Medicare, *cuts Medicare*, by approximately $500 billion. And even with those cuts, and tax increases, Obamacare adds trillions to our deficits and to our national debt and pushes those obligations on to coming generations.… And perhaps most troubling of all, Obamacare puts the federal government between you and your doctor."[2]

DEFENDING MEDICARE?

Along with the familiar complaints that expanding government health insurance would restrict choice, undermine quality, and raise taxes, Governor Romney and Congressman Ryan also focused on the degree to which the ACA would undermine the popular Medicare program. The governor argued that "His $700 billion in Medicare cuts 'will not be viable,' according to the program's trustees, jeopardizing access to care for senior citizens and throwing millions of beneficiaries off the coverage they rely on" (Romney 2012). In his first solo interview as a vice presidential candidate on Fox News, Congressman Ryan echoed this language, saying, "We are the ones who are not raiding Medicare to pay for 'Obamacare.' President Obama is actually damaging Medicare for current seniors. It's irrefutable."[3] Later, Ryan made an appearance with his 78-year-old mother at a retirement community in Florida and said, "When I think of Medicare, it's not just a program, it's what my mom relies on, it's what my grandma had" (Tanne 2012).

President Obama rejected the claim that the ACA would harm the Medicare program. In the first presidential debate, which most observers believe was won by Governor Romney, Obama defended his Medicare policy. Responding to Governor Romney's claim that the ACA included cuts to Medicare, the president argued that "$716 billion we were able to save from the Medicare program by no longer overpaying insurance companies by making sure that we weren't overpaying providers. And using that money, we were actually able to lower prescription drug costs for seniors by an average of $600, and we were also able to make a—make a significant dent in providing them the kind of preventive care that will ultimately save money throughout the system."[4]

The president did more than defend the ACA. He also went on the attack and released television ads explaining that the Romney-Ryan plan for Medicare would threaten the program and raise costs for beneficiaries. An ad released in September 2012 claimed that "Mitt Romney would replace Medicare's guaranteed benefits with a voucher system.... The Romney-Ryan plan could raise seniors' costs up to $6,400 a year" (Siddiqui 2012). A spokesperson for the Romney campaign shot back that the ad was "an attempt to cover up the fact that President Obama is the only candidate who has robbed $716 billion from Medicare to pay for Obamacare" (Siddiqui 2012). Nonpartisan critics of the ad suggested that it was based on outdated analysis because the Romney-Ryan plan was more generous than the one originally offered by Congressman Ryan.[5]

There are two explanations for the intensity of the battle over which party was more likely to protect Medicare. First, this was a clear effort to capture the support of older people. Most evidence from previous elections indicates that older people do not vote as a self-interested block that punishes candidates who threaten to cut Social Security, Medicare, and other programs that benefit older people (Campbell 2005). Nevertheless, there is some evidence that Republican arguments about the negative impact of the ACA on Medicare may have worked in 2010, so the candidates were anxious to either exploit or allay these concerns (Binstock 2010). Second, by contrasting their opposition to the ACA with their support for the Medicare program, Romney and Ryan were attempting to tap into Tea Party fears about the (allegedly) undeserving poor. In contrast to the deserving beneficiaries of the Medicare program, who paid into the system during their working lives, many Tea Party activists view Medicaid recipients, and those who would benefit from the ACA's subsidies for the purchase of private health insurance, as undeserving.

Again, this strategy had its roots in the 2010 midterm election. Republican National Committee chair Michael Steele opposed the 2010 health care reform proposal, claiming it would harm Medicare (Bartlett 2009). In August 2009, the Republican National Committee proposed a "Health Care Bill of Rights for Seniors" to protect Medicare from cuts and outlaw medical care rationing on the basis of age (Kenny 2009). Even conservative radio talk show host Rush Limbaugh joined the defense of Medicare, arguing that any cuts in Medicare would violate the existing social contract (Limbaugh 2009). In the fight against expanding government involvement in health care, the rhetoric shifted dramatically. Rather than presenting Medicare as an unaffordable and unfair transfer of resources from the young to the old, the conservative critics characterized the program as a key feature of the existing social contract—one that should be defended against cuts proposed by the Obama administration. Interestingly, the Republican opposition depicted older people as vulnerable victims of a callous abandonment of a longstanding promise, rather than "greedy geezers" consuming a disproportionate share of society's resources. The rhetorical shift by the Republican establishment, picked up by Romney and Ryan, attempted to describe Medicare as a program for a deserving "us" that was under threat from an irresponsible government program designed to benefit an undeserving "them" (Morone 1997). As one Republican campaign ad during the 2012 presidential campaign asserted, "So now the money you paid for your guaranteed health care is going to a massive new government program that's not for you" (*New York Times* 2012). By taking this approach, the Republican attacks on the ACA, coupled with an ironic defense of the Medicare program, fit with a longstanding effort to embed social welfare programs "in a cultural construction of 'us'" (Morone 1997).

DID THE ATTACKS ON "OBAMACARE" AND MEDICARE INFLUENCE THE 2012 PRESIDENTIAL ELECTION?

Unlike in the 2010 midterm elections, the attacks on the ACA do not appear to have shaped the outcome of the 2012 presidential race. On one hand, the public remained evenly divided over the ACA and the law (Blendon et al. 2012), and debate over the ACA did not provide President Obama or other Democrats with the sort of electoral gains associated with Medicare. On the other hand, the efforts by Governor Romney and Congressman Ryan to gain support beyond the Republican base did not appear to work either. The fact that the basic structure of the ACA was modeled on the 2006 Massachusetts health reform muddled Romney's message and led to suspicion among Republican conservatives. Romney and Ryan simply could not speak unambiguously regarding health care reform.

During the first presidential debate, Romney attacked "Obamacare," but he upset conservatives by defending "Romneycare." Romney claimed, "What we did in Massachusetts is a model for the nation, state by state." Although Romney emphasized that he favored a state by state rather than a federal government solution, Fox News commentator Juan Williams claimed that this was evidence that Romney would implement policies "to the left of George W. Bush and Barack Obama" (Williams 2012). Columnist Jonah Goldberg dismissed Romney's claim that the Massachusetts law was fundamentally different from the ACA. In a caricature of Romney's argument, Goldberg wrote, "I stand by my successful healthcare plan in Massachusetts, but ObamaCare is a disaster because it does all of the things that RomneyCare does, just on a national level," and he concluded, "I don't think it will work" (Goldberg 2012). As one commentator put it, "When it comes to inspiring Tea Party support, Mitt Romney often seems more burdened by his record than helped by it" (Stevenson 2012).

Similarly, while the Republican efforts to portray the ACA as a threat to Medicare may have resonated with leaders in the Tea Party movement and other social conservatives, the evidence suggests it did not resonate with the general public. The defense of Medicare by the Republican ticket was harmed not only by the party's historic opposition to the program but also by Congressman Ryan's proposal to reform Medicare by turning it into a voucher program. In earlier decades, conservative Republicans opposed Social Security (1935) and Medicare (1965). Although many conservative Republicans never accepted the premise of social insurance, after it was adopted, Medicare's popularity, coupled with Democratic control of the U.S. House of Representatives, meant that most Republicans came to accept it. Since the Republican victories in the 1994 midterm elections, the bipartisan consensus around Medicare that existed between 1965 and 1994 (Oberlander 2003) has disintegrated and calls for privatizing Medicare have become frequent among Republican members of Congress. In 1996, Republican presidential candidate Senator Robert Dole boasted of his opposition to the original Medicare bill. During a speech to the American Conservative Union he said, "I was there, fighting the fight, voting against Medicare…because we knew it wouldn't work in 1965" (Tribune News Services 1996). In early 2009, Republicans proposed replacing Medicare with fiscal subsidies that would allow older people to purchase private health insurance (Benen 2009).

The Republican majority in the House passed Congressman Paul Ryan's proposal to replace Medicare with vouchers for older people to buy private health insurance (while realizing that the proposal had little or no chance to pass the Congress). In fact, that experience was similar to proposals to dismantle Social Security in 1996 by Republican leader Newt Gingrich. Predictably, Democrats tried to exploit fears about this proposal for gain in the 2012 election. Medicare, Medicaid, and Social Security became daily topics in the media and in policy debates about public deficits and debt, and clear targets for spending cuts. There is some evidence that the Democratic arguments influenced public perception. Polls found that likely voters believed that President Obama and the Democrats were more likely to protect Medicare than Governor Romney and the Republicans (Dinan 2012). Similarly, among the 20 percent of voters who listed health care as "the most important issue" in the 2012 election, only 14 percent indicated that calling for the repeal of the ACA would make them more likely to support the candidate, and 40 percent indicated that this position would make them less likely to support the candidate. Similarly, only 11 percent of these voters indicated that they would be more likely to support a candidate that favored turning Medicare into a voucher program, but 39 percent indicated it would make them less likely to support such a candidate (Blendon et al. 2012).

WHAT ARE THE IMPLICATIONS OF THE 2012 ELECTION FOR THE FUTURE OF HEALTH POLICY IN THE UNITED STATES?

Many viewed 2012 as a "watershed" election that would determine whether health reform was implemented or repealed (Blumenthal 2011). Immediately following the 2012 election, many argued that the Affordable Care Act was no longer in danger. CNN, for example, published an online article declaring that "Obama's re-election secures health care reform."[6] While it would have been nearly impossible for Governor Romney to "repeal" the ACA, as he frequently promised on the campaign trail, he might have been able to kill the health reform law through a combination of executive orders that delayed implementation of key provisions and budget decisions that deprived the Department of Health and Human Services of the funds necessary to carry out the law's requirements. Even the possibility that Governor Romney might be elected was sufficient to encourage many states to delay their efforts to create health insurance exchanges necessary to implement the law (Thompson and Gusmano 2013). In that sense, the reelection of President Obama did dramatically increase the probability that the ACA would be fully implemented. There is little doubt that the 2012 presidential election was crucial to the direction of federal and state health insurance policy in the subsequent years.

It is not at all clear, however, that the heated debates about the ACA and Medicare had a great deal of influence on the outcome of the 2012 election. Unlike the 2010 midterm elections, in which a number of key races were influenced by the candidates' positions on health care, this was not the case in 2012. Furthermore, the 2012 election did not lead to a strong public consensus about the ACA or its future. Polls suggest that the public remains deeply divided about the law and confused about its content (Blendon et al. 2012). Likewise, as demonstrated by the 2013 government shutdown, the president's victory over Governor Romney did nothing to temper the Tea Party efforts to abolish the ACA. The 2012 presidential election did not resolve the political future of the ACA; it was merely a recent skirmish in the long and continuing battle over national health insurance in the United States. The Republican Party has made opposition to "Obamacare" a central component of its electoral strategy in 2014 and they are likely to continue attacking the law during the 2016 presidential election (Nicks 2014). Democrats, in contrast, are torn between defending the law and running away from it (Todd, Murray, and Dann 2014).

Between the late 19th and early 20th centuries, most of the other countries in the developed world decided that essential health care services should be financed by the public and that access to care should be based on need rather than ability to pay. After a century of debate, the adoption of the ACA was an effort to move the United States closer to this international standard. The fights over its implementation reflect continued disagreement over whether such a system is fair and affordable.

REFERENCES

Aldrich, J. H., B. H. Bishop, R. S. Hatch, D. Sunshine Hillygus, and D. W. Rohde. 2012. "Blame, Responsibility, and the Tea Party in the 2010 Midterm Elections." Paper presented at the Annual Meeting of the Midwest Political Science Association, Chicago, IL.

Associated Press. 2012. "Romney: Massachusetts Health Plan Superior: The GOP Presidential Hopeful Argues That Health Care Reform Should Be a State Prerogative." *Portland Press Herald,* August 21, A1.

Bartlett, B. 2009. "The Party of Medicare: That's the GOP, in Case You Hadn't Noticed." *Forbes,* August 28. Retrieved from http://www.forbes.com /2009/08/27/medicare-republicans-george-w-bush-opinions-columnists -bruce-barlett.html.

Benen, S. 2009. "Did Republicans Really Vote to 'Kill' Medicare?" *Washington Monthly*, September 5. Retrieved from http://www.washingtonmonthly.com/ archives/individual/2009_09/01976.php.

Binstock, R. 2010. "Older Voters: Myths and Realities." Presentation to Atlantic Philanthropies, New York City.

Blendon, R., J. M. Benson, and A. Brulé. 2012. "Understanding Health Care in the 2012 Election." *NEJM Special Report,* August 25, 1658–1661.

Blumenthal, D. 2011. "2012—A Watershed Election for Health Care." *New England Journal of Medicine* 365: 2047–2049.

Brown, L. D. 2008. "The Amazing Noncollapsing U.S. Health Care System—Is Reform Finally at Hand?" *New England Journal of Medicine* 358 (4): 325.

Campbell, A. L. 2005. "The Non-Distinctiveness of Senior Voters in the 2004 Election." *Public Policy and Aging Report* 15 (1): 3–6.

Dinan, S. 2012. "Seniors Boost Obama over Fears of GOP Medicare Cuts." *Washington Times*, August 26. Retrieved from http://www.washingtontimes.com /news/2012/aug/26/seniors-boost-obama-over-fears-of-gop-medicare- cut/?page=all.

Goldberg, J. 2012. "Romney: ObamaCare Is Nationalized...RomneyCare." *American Enterprise Institute,* May 12. Retrieved from http://www.aei-ideas .org/2011/05/romney-obamacare-is-nationalized-romneycare/.

Gusmano, M. K. 2011. "Do We Want to Control Health Costs?" *Journal of Health Politics, Policy and Law* 36 (3): 495–500.

Gusmano, M. K. 1995. "Stability and Change in Health Care Politics." PhD diss., University of Maryland College Park.

Haberkorn, J. 2011. "GOP Dilemma: How to Oppose IPAB." *Politico Pro* (July 13). Retrieved from http://www.politico.com/news/stories/0711/58930.html.

Henry J. Kaiser Family Foundation. 2010. "Health Reform and the Tea Party Movement." Retrieved from http://www.kff.org/health-reform/poll-finding /health-reform-and-the-tea-party-movement/.

Kelly, S. 1956. *Professional Public Relations and Political Power.* Baltimore: Johns Hopkins University Press.

Kenny, H. 2009. "Should the Republicans Save Medicare?" *NewAmerican,* August 26. Retrieved from http://www.thenewamerican.com/index.php/usnews /health-care/1741.

Kersh, R. 2011. "Health Reform: The Politics of Implementation." *Journal of Health Politics, Policy and Law* 36 (3): 613–623.

Konisky, D. M., and L. E. Richardson, Jr. 2012. "Penalizing the Party: Health Care Reform Issue Voting in the 2010 Election." *American Politics Research.*

Limbaugh, R. 2009. "Democrats, Not Republicans, Are the Hypocrites on Medicare Cuts." *Rush Limbaugh Show.* Retrieved from http://www.rushlimbaugh.com /home/daily/site_121709/content/01125113.guest.html.

Mandel, B. 1963. *Samuel Gompers: A Biography.* Yellow Springs, OH: Antioch Press.

Marmor, T. R. 2011. "Health Reform 2010: The Missing Philosophical Premises in the Long-Running Health Care Debate." *Journal of Health Politics, Policy and Law* 36 (3): 567–570.

Morone, J. 1997. "Enemies of the People: The Moral Dimension to Public Health." *Journal of Health Politics, Policy and Law* 22 (4): 993–1020.

New York Times. 2012. "Editorial: Truth and Lies About Medicare." *New York Times,* August 19, SR10.

Nicks, D. 2014. "Republicans Double Down on Obamacare for 2014." *Time,* March 21. Retrieved from http://time.com/33880/obamacare-2014-midterm-elections -democrats-republicans/.

Numbers, R. 1978. *Almost Persuaded: American Physicians and Compulsory Health Insurance, 1912–1920.* Baltimore: Johns Hopkins University Press.

Nyhan, B., E. McGhee, J. Sides, S. Masket, and S. Greene. 2012. "One Vote out of Step? The Effects of Salient Roll Call Votes in the 2010 Election." *American Politics Research* 40 (5): 844–879.

Oberlander, J. 2003. *The Political Life of Medicare.* Chicago: University of Chicago Press.

Peterson, M. A. 1992. *National Health Care Reform in the 1990s: Politics, Structure, and Change from Iron Triangles to Policy Networks.* Center for American Political Studies, Harvard University. Occasional Papers 92.

Poen, M. M. 1979. *Harry Truman versus the Medical Lobby: The Genesis of Medicare.* Columbia, MO: University of Missouri.

Reagan, R. 1961. "Ronald Reagan Speaks Out about Socialized Medicine." Retrieved from http://www.youtube.com/watch?v=z43NCL6Fxug.

Romney, M. 2012. "Replacing Obamacare with Real Health Care Reform." *New England Journal of Medicine* 367 (15): 1377–1381. Retrieved from http://www.nejm.org/doi/full/10.1056/NEJMp1211516?.

Siddiqui, S. 2012. "Obama Medicare Ad Praises His Plan, Knocks Paul Ryan's." *Huffington Post,* September 20. Retrieved from http://www.huffingtonpost.com/2012/09/20/obama-medicare_n_1901997.html.

Starr, P. 1982. *The Social Transformation of American Medicine: The Rise of a Sovereign Profession and the Making of a Vast Industry.* New York: Basic Books.

Starr, P. 2011. *Remedy and Reaction: The Peculiar American Struggle over Health Care Reform.* New Haven, CT: Yale University Press.

Steinmo, S., and J. Watts. 1995. "It's the Institutions, Stupid." *Journal of Health Politics, Policy and Law* 20 (2): 395–438.

Stevenson, R. W. 2012. "Tea Party Movement Takes the Long View." *New York Times, The Caucus: The Politics and Government Blog of The Times,* March 9. Retrieved from http://thecaucus.blogs.nytimes.com/2012/03/09/tea-party-movement-takes-the-long-view/?_r=0&pagewanted=print.

Tanne, J. H. 2012. "Romney's Running Mate Backtracks on Plans to Slash Health Insurance Cover for Older People." *BMJ* 345: e5634.

Thompson, F. J., and M. K. Gusmano. 2013. "The Administrative Presidency and Fractious Federalism: The Case of Obamacare." Presented at the 2013 American Political Science Association Annual Meeting, Chicago, Illinois.

Todd, C., M. Murray, and C. Dann. 2014. "Democrats Weigh Embracing Obamacare in Midterm Campaign." *NBC News, Politics, First Read.* Retrieved from http://www.nbcnews.com/politics/first-read/democrats-weigh-embracing-obamacare-midterm-campaign-n85606.

Tribune News Services. 1996. "Bush Promises Full Support for Dole: GOP Candidate Defends Molinari on Marijuana." *Chicago Tribune,* July 27, A1.

Viseltear, A. J. 1969. "Compulsory Health Insurance in California, 1915–18." *Journal of the History of Medicine and Allied Sciences* 24 (2): 151–182.

Weir, M. T., A. S. Orloff, and T. Skocpol. 1988. *The Politics of Social Policy in the United States.* Princeton, NJ: Princeton University Press.

Williams, J. 2012. "Conservatives, Be Careful What You Wish For with Mitt Romney." *Fox News,* November 2. Retrieved from http://www.foxnews.com/opinion/2012/11/02/conservatives-be-careful-what-wish-for-with-mitt-romney/.

Williams, V., T. Skocpol, and J. Coggin. 2011. "The Tea Party and the Remaking of Republican Conservatism." *Perspectives on Politics* 9 (1): 25–43.

NOTES

1. http://stlouisteaparty.com/2009/07/obamacare-not-just-bad-policy-but-evil/; accessed September 15, 2013.

2. http://blogs.wsj.com/washwire/2012/06/28/transcript-of-romneys-remarks-on-the-supreme-court-ruling/; accessed September 1, 2013.

3. http://www.cnn.com/2012/08/15/politics/romney-medicare-counteroffensive/index.html; accessed October 2, 2013.

4. http://elections.nytimes.com/2008/president/debates/transcripts/first-presidential-debate.html; accessed July 30, 2013.

5. http://www.factcheck.org/2012/08/a-campaign-full-of-mediscare/; accessed October 1, 2013.

6. http://money.cnn.com/2012/11/07/pf/health-care-reform-obama/index.html; accessed October 5, 2013.

Chapter 9

The Obama Regulatory Record
Partisanship, Perception, and the
2012 Election
Richard S. Conley, University of Florida

INTRODUCTION

In most presidential elections federal rulemaking processes and regulatory outcomes are typically not regarded by candidates or their campaigns as themes likely to capture the attention of voters, let alone their hearts and minds. The 2012 contest between incumbent Democratic president Barack Obama and Republican standard-bearer Mitt Romney proved an exception. The economy's lackluster standing throughout Obama's first term—with unemployment consistently above 8 percent, stagnant or negative growth as measured by gross domestic product, and a particularly noteworthy decline in consumer and small business owner confidence—raised the critical question of how Obama-era regulations may or may not have contributed to the economy's torpid performance following the financial crisis of 2008.

The president's detractors in the Grand Old Party (GOP) and in the private sector posited unrelentingly that the Obama administration's new regulations of business and industry—from oil and gas exploration to health care, financial institutions, and small businesses—were destabilizing and detrimental to economic growth and recovery. A Romney campaign advertisement in Colorado, similar to ones unleashed in seven other "swing" states in early September 2012, contended that "excessive government regulations are crushing job creation…thousands of jobs lost…the Romney Plan? Repeal Obama's excessive regulations, foster innovation" (9news.com). In a scathing critique of Obama's regulatory "czar" Cass Sunstein, who headed the administration's Office of Information and Regulatory Affairs (OIRA) in the Office of Management and Budget (OMB), *Forbes Magazine* argued that "government regulation has been one of the nation's few growth industries" under Sunstein's watch: "stultifying, job-killing regulation has been a hallmark of the Obama administration" (Miller 2012).

President Obama expressed no regrets about his administration's regulatory record. In an interview with CBS's Steve Croft on *60 Minutes* in late September 2012, the chief executive asserted confidently that:

> When it comes to regulations, I've issued fewer regulations than my predecessor, George Bush, did during that same period in office. So it's kind of hard to argue that we've overregulated. Now, I don't make any apologies for putting in place regulations to make sure banks don't make reckless bets and then expect taxpayers to bail them out. I don't make any apologies for regulating insurance companies, so that they can't drop a family's coverage, just when somebody in their family needs it most. And, you know, the problem that Governor Romney has is that he seems to only have one note: tax cuts for the wealthy and rolling back regulations as a recipe for success. Well, we tried that vigorously between 2001 and 2008 and it didn't work out so well. (*60 Minutes* 2012)

Moreover, in an expressive and rather artful op-ed in the *Chicago Tribune* Sunstein (2012) defended the regulatory record of the Obama presidency by focusing on alleged cost savings. He asserted that "Over the Obama administration's first three years, the net benefits of regulations reviewed by OIRA and issued by executive agencies exceeded $91 billion—25 times the corresponding number in the Bush administration and more than eight times the corresponding number in the Clinton administration." Sunstein was careful to underscore the utilization of cost-benefit analysis—his forté—to justify new regulations that putatively have constructive, long-term societal impacts—from food and automobile safety to health care. His operationalization of the Obama administration's regulatory methodology matched the *National Journal's* (2012) contention that "Obama approaches regulation as a pragmatist. He wants 'basic rules of the road' to make the economy more fair."

So which side—Romney's or the president's—do the facts support relative to the Obama regulatory record and the impact on the national economy? It is a significant methodological challenge for any objective researcher to determine the merits of such vastly contradictory accounts of rulemaking from 2009 to 2012 and the potential economic effects. Simply tallying the raw number of regulations passed in one presidency or another, as the president suggested—or adding up the pages of regulations in the Federal Register across time to compare records, as some pundits have done—conveys little about the relative significance of any given regulation. Calculating relative benefits to costs across presidencies is even more problematic, whether the claims are from the president's supporters or rivals.

As the OMB noted in a 2011 report to Congress, agencies often cannot quantify the cost-benefit ratio of regulations due to an absence of information, as "prospective estimates may contain erroneous assumptions, producing inaccurate predictions" (OMB 2011, 4). In other cases it is impossible to monetize societal benefits that *prevent* actions such as discrimination or crimes. Moreover, a draft report by the OMB (2012, 11) underscored "the difficulty of estimating and aggregating the benefits and costs of different regulations over long time periods and across many agencies using different methodologies. Any aggregation involves the assemblage of benefit and cost estimates that are not strictly comparable." For example, when the Environmental Protection Agency (EPA) issues new Corporate Average Fuel Efficiency (CAFE) standards for automobile emissions every five or 10 years, the estimated future benefits of hundreds of billions of dollars in savings compared to annual costs potentially can skew any White House administration's record depending on the timing of the new regulations. According to the *Washington Post*, Sunstein's analysis "drew the exact type of comparisons that the budget office has cautioned against" (Hicks 2012). In a like fashion, a *Heritage Foundation* report highly critical of Obama-era regulations engaged in a similarly dubious comparison to the Bush years to lambaste White House rule-making (Gattuso and Katz 2012).

This research does not purport to reconcile the debate about cost-benefit analyses of federal regulations. Alas, sizing up the relative benefits of regulations, monetary or otherwise, in any presidential administration is a *subjective endeavor better left to voters*. On the other hand, an objective analysis of the *costs* of regulations during the Obama presidency is possible. Indeed, such an examination is critical to understanding the role the federal regulatory environment played in the 2012 presidential campaign and how voters perceived the Obama economic record.

The Congressional Review Act (5 U.S.C. § 802(a)), passed in 1996, mandates that an agency promulgating a rule submit it to Congress and the Government Accountability Office (GAO) before the rule can take effect. GAO has tracked rules since 1997 and made available a searchable database on the Internet.[1] The vast majority of agency submissions include prospective costs, however imperfectly derived, to implement the rule.

This research focuses on rules implemented by the Obama administration and classified by OIRA and the GAO as "significant." Significant rules are defined as those that are expected to have an annual effect on the economy of $100 million or more; involve a major increase in costs or prices for consumers, individual industries, federal, state, or local government agencies, or geographic regions; or may have significant adverse effects on competition, employment, investment, productivity, or innovation, or on the ability of U.S.-based enterprises to compete with foreign-based enterprises in domestic and export markets (GAO). From 2009 to August 2012 there were 302 new significant regulations promulgated by the White House, 233 of which had detailed cost estimates. The cost of new regulations is analyzed by department and agency to pinpoint the regulatory focus of Obama's first term.

In assessing the number and cost of significant new regulations by policy area, this chapter juxtaposes the regulatory record of the Obama administration with public opinion data leading up to the 2012 presidential election. The central objective is to place into context the ways in which the debate about Obama-era regulation added to the essential economic narratives of the Democratic and Republican presidential campaigns. The analysis underscores how regulatory issues became subsumed into the larger, partisan divide about the state of the economy and perceptions of Obama's record of economic management. The evidence suggests that as the election neared, Republican voters became increasingly discontented with alleged "overregulation." By contrast, Democratic voters approved of greater regulation of the environment, business, and health care—all central tenets of Obama's policy agenda. Independents remained largely divided on the president's regulatory strategy. In sum, assessments of the Obama regulatory record were notably—if not unexpectedly—connected to perceptions of the economy and filtered through partisan lenses as the 2012 election approached.

This chapter unfolds in four parts. The first section provides a very brief discussion of presidential power and innovations in regulatory control since Nixon to situate Obama's presidency in "political time." The second section analyzes the number and costs of new regulations by department and agency to underscore the regulatory focus of the Obama administration. The third section assesses public opinion data, limited as they are, in the lead-up to the 2012 election in order to emphasize how regulatory issues were absorbed into the economic narratives of the Obama and Romney campaigns. The concluding section discusses the implications of regulatory policies moving beyond the 2012 race for the White House.

PRESIDENTIAL POWER, AGENCY RULEMAKING, AND REGULATORY REVIEW

Presidents' use of "unilateral administrative tools as a mechanism for policy change" (Rudalevige 2009, 11) has captured the increased attention of scholars of the "institutional" or "administrative" presidency in the last 30 years (Burke 2000; Hart 1995; Howell 2003; Moe and Howell 1999; Nathan 1983; Waterman 1989). In their attempt to control policy implementation, presidents have engaged in strategic efforts to politicize the bureaucracy through their appointment power and to centralize decision making by shaping organizational structures (see *inter alia*, Heclo 1975; Lewis 2008; Moe and Wilson 1994; Rudalevige 2005). Presidents execute control in a top-down fashion through institutional structures and processes they can craft autonomously (Moe 1985), avoiding the well-documented collective action problems of Congress (Cox and McCubbins 1993; Mayhew 1974; Weingast and Marshall 1988).

The quest to understand the parameters of presidential influence over agency rulemaking is a prime example of scholars' renewed focus on the *formal,* institutional powers of the American executive rather than the *informal* bargaining powers championed by Neustadt (1960). On this account the OMB and OIRA stand out as the most important structures in the executive establishment. Scholars generally concur that regulatory review by the White House fundamentally shapes the institutional balance of power between the presidency and Congress vis-à-vis policy implementation. Writing several decades ago, Moe and Wilson (1994, 37) posited that "Presidents have imposed new procedures on regulatory agencies in a sustained attempt, stretching over twenty years, to gain control over agency rulemaking and assert presidential priorities." The evolution of centralized regulatory review has indeed been bipartisan. Attempts to scale back regulation have been an article of faith among Republicans who have occupied the White House since 1972. But Presidents Carter and Clinton made their own contributions to greater presidential control of rulemaking to fit their own agendas. A brief inventory of presidential innovations in rulemaking since Nixon places the Obama administration into a comparative, historical frame of reference and underscores the institutionalization of regulatory review.

President Nixon's "plot" to restrain the bureaucracy through super-secretaries and administrative means may have failed in his abbreviated second term (Nathan 1975). Nonetheless, it is critical to note that his "Quality of Life" interagency review of proposed rules represented the first White House effort to come to terms with regulatory costs and alternatives, particularly with respect to the Environmental Protection Agency. One impact was to delay the rulemaking process, and consequently, implementation of regulations (Bruff 1988–1989, 546–547; Quarles 1976).

Nixon's successor, Gerald Ford, used his discretion via Executive Order (E.O.) 11821 to empower the OMB to develop criteria to be utilized by federal agencies to assess the economic costs of regulations. The strategy was part of Ford's anti-inflation strategy, dubbed WIN ("Whip Inflation Now"). Agency cost-benefit analyses, or "inflation impact statements," had to be submitted and approved by the OMB (Fuchs and Anderson 1987, 27). Critics charged, however, that the process was too decentralized and that agency estimates had little consequence in halting the regulatory onslaught of the 1970s (see O'Reilly and Brown 1987).

President Carter's primary innovation in regulatory matters consisted of establishing a Regulatory Council in the White House. Comprised of the heads of regulatory agencies, the council developed and published a "Calendar of Federal Regulations" in an effort to take a longer term view of rules in the pipeline and coordinate streamlined implementation. The calendar identified rules with "significant" economic impacts and sought to assess relative benefits to costs. The council paid particularly close attention to potential interjurisdictional disputes in implementation (Bruff 1988–1989, 548–549).

The Reagan–H. W. Bush era represented nothing less than a major assault by the two Republican presidents on new regulations. At the outset of his first term Reagan established a Task Force on Regulatory Relief, headed by Vice President Bush, to undertake cost-benefit analyses of existing regulations. Further, in February 1981, Reagan signed E.O. 12291, which *mandated* that agencies submit economic impact analyses of proposed regulations deemed "significant" (exceeding costs of $100 million). E.O. 12291 significantly enhanced presidential control of the bureaucracy. As Cooper and West (1988, 870–871) note, OMB was "empowered to stay the publication of notice of proposed rulemaking or the promulgation of a final regulation by requiring that agencies respond to its criticisms" and OMB could "recommend the withdrawal of regulations which cannot be reformulated to meet its objections." Finally, early in his second term Reagan again took aim at halting an expansion of federal regulations. E.O. 12498 required OMB review of proposed agency rules to ensure consistency with the president's agenda and policies (Hahn 1998, 202)—a new form of "central clearance" that had been previously reserved for legislation (see Neustadt 1974).

Reagan's two executive orders remained in effect during George H. W. Bush's term. Bush replaced the Task Force on Regulatory Relief with the Council on Competitiveness, chaired by Vice President Quayle, which was charged with undertaking broad cost-benefit analyses of regulations. The Council on Competitiveness was notable for rather spectacular battles between the White House and the Democratic-controlled Congress over implementation of regulations connected to the 1990 Clean Air Act Amendments (see Duffy 1996).

Cost-benefit analyses of proposed regulations continued as the norm during the presidency of Bill Clinton. E.O. 12886, which Clinton signed in December 1993 and which superseded Reagan's E.O. 12291, mandated a "National Performance Review" (NPR), affectionately nicknamed "reinventing government." Headed by Vice President Al Gore, the objective of the NPR was to cut red tape and render government programs more efficient and performance-based (Kamensky 1996). The Republican-led 104th Congress also played a role in attempting to curtail the thrust of new regulations, and Clinton did not mount significant opposition. The Unfunded Mandates Reform Act (1995) and the Small Business Regulatory Enforcement Fairness Act (1996) were examples of congressional efforts to reestablish greater levels of regulatory oversight on Capitol Hill (Hahn 1998, 203).

Regulatory review under President George W. Bush, as William West (2005, 79) contends, was "reenergized" and in large measure further politicized. Shapiro (2007, 271) argues that reforms undertaken in Bush's first term by OIRA director John Graham resulted in the potential concentration of rulemaking power "in a small group of interests with more established access, influence, and power." Further, E.O. 13422 (2007) mandated that federal agencies designate a "regulatory review officer," appointed by the president, with the ability to decide whether new rules were warranted. The order also provided for enhanced executive review of "guidance documents" issued by regulatory agencies for the implementation of rules (Copeland 2007). Finally, upon Graham's departure from OIRA in 2006, Bush was "sufficiently concerned with installing his preferred head of OIRA in April 2007 that he did so by recess appointment, evading Senate scrutiny, at some political cost" (Rudalevige 2009, 15). Bush's appointee, Susan Dudley, stirred significant controversy when OIRA opposed proposed Environmental Protection Agency (EPA) rules on greenhouse gases in 2008 (Eilperin 2008).

The Obama Presidency and Regulation: Angst, Perception, and Republican Contretemps

The preceding examination of White House regulatory review, albeit cursory, emphasizes the degree to which President Obama clearly inherited an "institutionalized" and significantly more centralized White

House configuration for rulemaking than existed four decades earlier. Whether the politicization of the Bush years would follow in OIRA remained an open question in 2009. There is little doubt, though, that the structure enhanced not only the Obama administration's early quest to repeal a host of Bush-era rules but also facilitated the focus on financial market reform, climate change, and health care—among the most controversial elements of the Obama agenda.

Some in the private sector were alarmed by Obama's appointment of Cass Sunstein as OIRA director in mid-2009. Others quietly welcomed his selection, as they viewed his "academic" approach to regulatory affairs as a potential hedge against expansive regulation championed by more liberal elements in the administration and the Democratic Congress. Indeed, one observer suggested the degree to which OIRA under Sunstein was "wonky." [2] "OIRA," according to David Brooks (2011), was "composed of career number-crunchers of no known ideological bent who try to measure the trade-offs inherent in regulatory action.... This office has tried to elevate the role of data so that every close call is not just a matter of pleasing the right ideological army." Sunstein's scholarship on transcending traditional partisan debates over regulation and his abiding faith in cost-benefit analysis suggested, to the discreet delight of many industry officials and to the nascent chagrin of progressive Democrats, that he might oppose expensive new regulations and moderate the thrust of administration rulemaking by prioritizing economic growth (Layton 2009; Skrzycki 2009).

Not surprisingly, positive perceptions of Sunstein and the regulatory thrust of the Obama White House were neither universal nor enduring. "Republicans," Peter Baker and John Broder (2012) contend, "saw what they considered a liberal Harvard professor and Obama pal and were deeply skeptical." The pace of criticism of regulation in the Obama presidency hastened as the economic recovery stalled, especially after the $789 billion stimulus package, passed in 2009, seemingly did little to spur private sector growth. The GOP alleged that regulatory profligacy emanating from the White House was the proximate cause of continuing levels of high unemployment. Environmental regulation became the focal point of contention.

Obama faced a growing onslaught of condemnation—particularly by Republicans in Congress following the mid-term elections of 2010—

that regulations aimed at addressing climate change, in particular, were devastating jobs in the manufacturing and energy sectors. At the very outset of the new legislative session in 2011, House Republicans introduced a number of bills to preclude implementation of proposed EPA regulations targeting greenhouse gases (Cappiello 2011). The strategy was part of a larger GOP campaign promise to block or defund the administration's efforts to combat "global warming." Republicans cried foul and contended that the Obama White House was trying to carry out an unprecedented and extensive environmental agenda *administratively* following the failure of "cap-and-trade" legislation in Congress (*Orange County Register* 2011).

Generalized Republican critiques of the president's regulatory record were bolstered by a bevy of reports undertaken by conservative think tanks, some of which the chair of the House Oversight and Government Reform Committee, Darryl Issa (R-CA), sought to exploit skillfully in hearings and reports. Such studies posited that Obama-era regulations, environmental or otherwise, were the primary impediment to an economic rebound. For instance, the Mercatus Institute asserted that the president's policies had increased federal employment by 3.5 percent while the private sector continued to lose jobs (de Rugy 2010). As another example, the Competitive Enterprise Institute accentuated the putatively deleterious impact of regulatory burdens on small business job creation (Crews 2011).

In an effort to stem the tide of criticism that his administration's regulatory policies were repressing an economic resurgence, Obama signed E.O. 13563, entitled "Improving Regulation and Regulatory Review," in January 2011. The order mandated a government-wide review of existing regulations. The nominal objective, akin to Clinton's NPR, was to streamline rulemaking processes and dismantle "overlapping, inconsistent, or redundant" rules. The order also focused on cost-benefit analyses to justify new regulations and championed greater transparency and public involvement in rulemaking processes (Hemphill 2012).

But the order arguably had more symbolic than substantive value. The review effort, with an emphasis on Sunstein's approach to cost-benefit analysis, was not historically novel. Rather, presidential action was aimed at assuaging anxiety in the private sector over the financial impact of regulations in the pipeline that might dissuade new hiring. Further, the executive order was an attempt to soften the image of the Obama White House as hostile to business concerns. Obama took the extraordinary step of writing an op-ed in the *Wall Street Journal* to explicate his rationale to business and industry. The review constituted part of a broad effort by the administration to prompt business leaders to identify regulations they believed posed obstacles to "job-creating private investment" (Williamson 2011). Trade associations such as the U.S. Chamber of Commerce and the National Federation of Independent Business (NFIB) applauded the effort, particularly given Obama's explicit acknowledgment that many regulations negatively affected small businesses, which were the presumed backbone of any economic recovery (Bogardus and Viebeck 2011).

The war of words between House Republicans and the White House over regulation escalated in the 112th Congress nonetheless. In August 2011 House Republicans drafted a list of "the 10 most harmful job-destroying regulations" of the Obama presidency. The lion's share involved environmental rules (particularly emissions standards), which Eric Cantor (R-VA) suggested were "reflective of the types of costly bureaucratic handcuffs that Washington has forced upon business people who want to create jobs" (quoted in Stiles 2011).

House Republicans' efforts to expose the Obama White House's alleged "overregulation" of business and industry on Capitol Hill complemented Mitt Romney's indefatigable—if sometimes factually questionable—critiques of Obama's economic record on the campaign trail in advance of the 2012 election. At the first presidential debate in Denver, Colorado, in early October, Romney criticized the Dodd-Frank banking bill regulation as exemplary of an Obama-era regulation he would repeal. The Massachusetts governor emphasized that "regulation can become excessive, it can become out of date. And what's happened with some of the legislation that's been passed under President Obama's first term is you've seen some of the regulation become excessive and it has hurt the economy" (quoted in Mutikani 2012). In the second presidential debate in Hempstead, New York, the GOP standard-bearer contended that regulations had quadrupled under Obama. Fact-checkers such as "OMB Watch" found that the total number of regulations was about average under Obama, although "significant" regulations ($100 million or more in impact) had increased by about 24 percent over the first four years of George W. Bush's presidency (Bruner 2012). And finally, less than a week before the election, Romney campaign spokesman Ryan Williams reiterated Republicans' aggravation with Obama's regulatory record, underscoring that "We need a new president who actually understands businesses and won't punish them with higher taxes, more regulations, and job-destroying energy policies" (Jackson 2012).

In light of the vastly different competing claims of the Obama White House and Romney campaign, the contours of the Obama regulatory record are best assessed by an objective review of the number, cost, and policy focus of rulemaking from 2009 to August 2012. The following section takes up these questions in close detail. The analysis elucidates several key points. The total *number* of significant and nonsignificant regulations in Obama's first term was *not* appreciably different compared to George W. Bush or Bill Clinton (second term). The costs of significant rules were, however, greatest with respect to health and environmental policies. And therein lay key similarities and profound differences between the regulatory records of Obama and his predecessor that figured prominently into the Romney campaign's regulatory rhetoric. In both administrations the cost of regulations emanating from Health and Human Services was comparable. But the estimated costs of environmental rules in the first three and three-quarter years of Obama's presidency were more than 15 times the new regulations adopted over the entirety of Bush's *two terms*.

THE OBAMA REGULATORY RECORD: UNRESTRAINED OR UNREMARKABLE?

GAO data on the number, cost, and policy focus of regulations provide a substantial basis on which to analyze rulemaking during the Obama presidency and make some basic comparisons across time since 1997. Figures 9.1 and 9.2 show the number of nonsignificant and significant rules adopted from 1997 to August 2012, respectively. Nonsignificant rules are classified as those that have economic impacts of less than $100,000; the economic impact of significant rules exceeds $100,000.

Figure 9.1 shows that the pace of nonsignificant regulations was slightly higher during the second term of Bill Clinton (1997–2000) com-

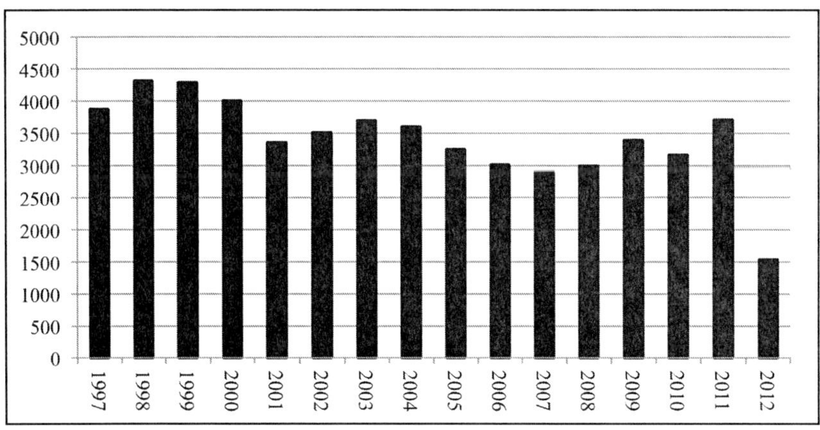

Figure 9.1 Nonsignificant Regulations, 1997–2012*

*Data for 2012 through August. Nonsignificant regulations < $100,0000 million.
Source: U.S. Government Accountability Office, Legal Decisions & Bid Protests. http://www.gao.gov/legal/
congressact/fedrule.html.

pared to his two immediate successors. The rate of nonsignificant rules was lowest in the last three years of George W. Bush's second term (2006–2008). There was only a slight uptick during Obama's first term, most notably in 2011. The increase, however, is not statistically significant.

Figure 9.2 focuses on significant regulations. From 1997 to August 2012, the pinnacle came during Obama's second year in office, in 2010, at 100. The number is perhaps not extraordinary considering the swift passage of important elements of the president's agenda a year earlier. Nonetheless, the rhythm of the most costly regulations was considerably higher in the first three years of Obama's first term compared to the entirety of George W. Bush's two terms. From 2001 to 2008 the annual average was 62. From 2009 to 2011 under Obama the average was 88. A simple means test shows that the difference is statistically significant at $p < .02$. Taken together, the data in Figures 9.1 and 9.2 suggest a misrepresentation in President Obama's contention in September 2012 during the televised *60 Minutes* interview that he issued fewer regulations than his predecessor. While there was little change in the number of minor rules, those with the greatest economic and social impact according to GAO *did mount appreciably*. But it is also imperative to note that significant regulations did *not* increase fourfold as Romney claimed during the presidential debates.

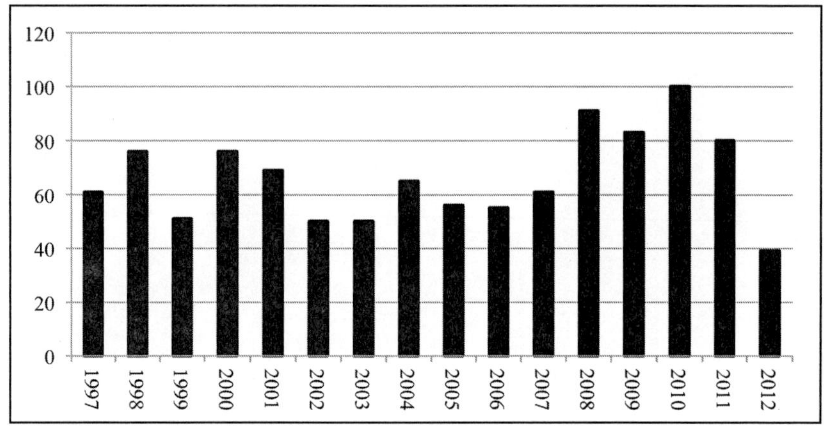

Figure 9.2 Significant Regulations, 1997–2012*

*Data for 2012 through August. Significant regulations > $100,000 million.
Source: U.S. Government Accountability Office, Legal Decisions & Bid Protests. http://www.gao.gov/legal/
congressact/fedrule.html.

Figure 9.3 provides some indication of which policy areas drew the greatest focus during Obama's first term. The data underscore that the number of regulations under the Department of Health and Human Services (HHS) was roughly *four times greater* than for any other single agency, including the EPA and the Department of Agriculture. Of the 78 new HHS regulations promulgated between 2009 and August 2012, 60 (77 percent) concerned the Centers for Medicare and Medicaid Services. While some of the new rules were connected to the controversial Affordable Care Act (ACA or "Obamacare"), others represented ongoing efforts to streamline these entitlement programs. Examples of new regulations span Medicare prescription drug plans to hospital, surgery, and physician fee schedules.

Just how costly were regulations in Obama's first term? As noted earlier, the overwhelming share of department and agency reports to the GAO on new regulations include cost estimates (and sometimes benefit estimates). These data on costs extend back to 1997. In most cases a *range* of estimated costs for implementing the new rule is included in the departmental or agency report. Critics make the valid charge that government forecasts may be inaccurate or "low-ball" actual costs (Gattuso and Katz 2012), and OMB (2011, 2012) does not dispute methodological

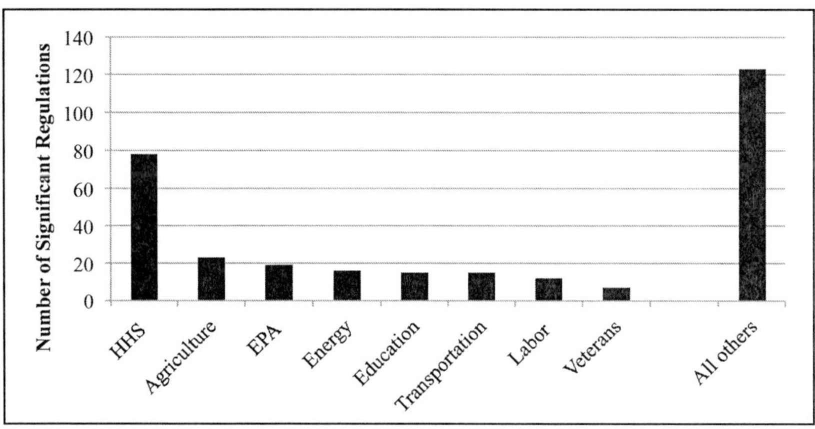

Figure 9.3 Number of Significant Regulations by Department/Agency, 2009–2012*

*Data for 2012 through August. Significant regulations > $100,000 million.

difficulties in both cost estimates and longitudinal comparisons. Nonetheless, these official data—which represent the only systematic effort to assess future economic costs—are the sole metric available to researchers. At a minimum the data represent a baseline estimate. In aggregating overall anticipated costs of new regulations, as well as those by department and agency, this analysis is admittedly conservative in its findings by consistently employing the *lowest possible cost* estimated in the report for each new regulation when an upper and lower range is provided. As such, the analysis gives the "benefit of the doubt" to the White House in terms of negative economic impact.

Indubitably the debate between Republicans and Democrats about Obama-era regulations has much more to do with costs than the simple number of new rules. Figure 9.4 shows the aggregate costs by year from 2009 to August 2012. The data suggest why House Republicans, such as Daryl Issa, took aim at the president's regulatory record following the mid-term elections and why the Romney campaign sought to seize the issue of government regulation in the 2012 campaign. Between 2009 and 2010 the aggregate estimated cost of new regulations grew from $35 billion to a high water mark of approximately $63 billion, or by a factor of 75 percent. Obviously rulemaking during these two years corre-

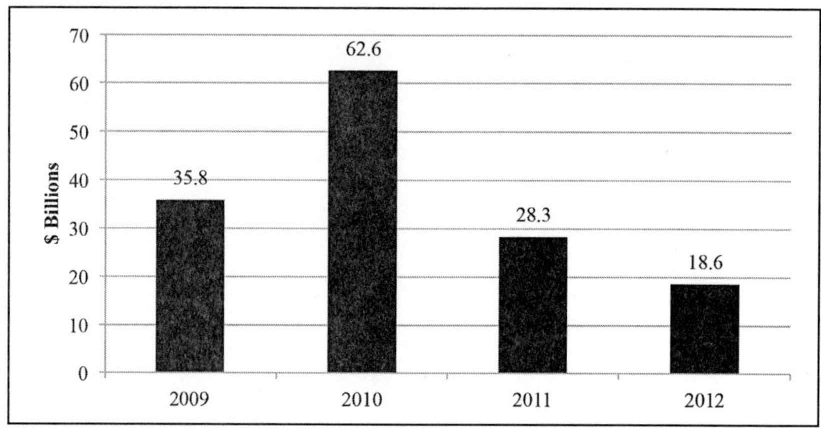

Figure 9.4 Total Costs ($ Billions) of New Regulations, Significant Rules, 2009–2012*

*Data for 2012 through August.
Source: U.S. Government Accountability Office, Legal Decisions & Bid Protests. http://www.gao.gov/legal/congressact/fedrule.html. Costs calculated by author; see text for details.

sponded to the large Democratic majorities on Capitol Hill that were swept into office with the president in 2008. Regulatory costs dropped considerably in 2011 and for the partial year of data included in 2012 (through August). The data point to the relative importance of legislative cycles. Scholars and pundits typically recommend that presidents (and the Congresses they control) "hit the ground running" in their first two years before their popularity wanes and they face almost inevitable seat losses in the mid-term elections. During Obama's first term the costs paralleled the growth in the number of new significant rules in his first two years, many of which were linked to legislation that emerged from the Democratic-controlled Congress, from health care and banking to the stimulus package (American Reinvestment and Recovery Act).

Figure 9.5 details the departments and agencies promulgating the most costly regulations in the aggregate from 2009 to August 2012. HHS led the charge at $43.1 billion, with most of the costs relating to the Centers for Medicare and Medicaid Services (CMS). Notably, Republican opposition in Congress after the mid-term elections, and from the Romney campaign in 2012, focused far more on either defunding the ACA or on repealing the law in its entirety rather than on the steady, if piecemeal regulations

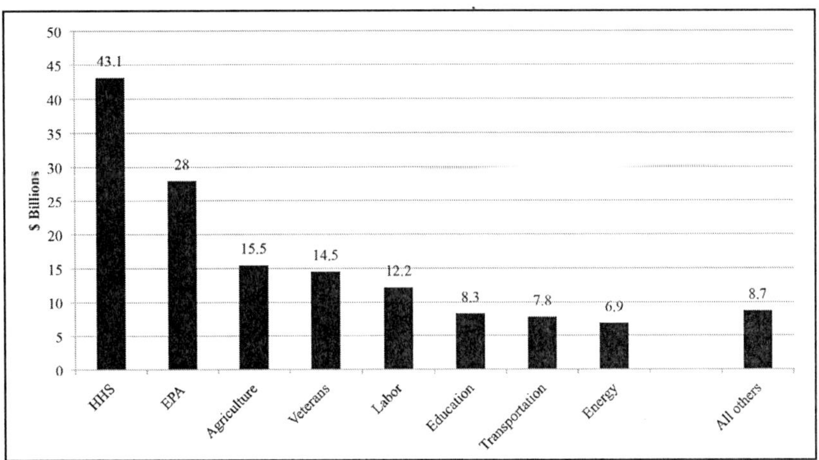

Figure 9.5 Aggregate Costs ($ Billions) of Significant Regulations by Department/Agency, 2009–2012*

*Data for 2012 through August.
Source: U.S. Government Accountability Office, Legal Decisions & Bid Protests. http://www.gao.gov/legal/congressact/fedrule.html. Calculated by author; see text for details.

the new CMS director, Dr. Donald Berwick, sought to implement and which arguably had a greater financial impact (*New York Times* 2011; Pear 2010). Regardless, the $43 billion figure for new regulations is not comparatively unreasonable for the entitlement programs in HHS that were responsible for 36 percent of federal outlays in fiscal year 2010. During the first four years of George W. Bush's presidency, quantifiable costs of new regulations (n = 54) for HHS were estimated by the author at $59.5 billion, which translates to about $63.1 billion in inflation-adjusted 2010 dollars. While critics of the ACA would certainly contend that the full impact of regulatory (and other) costs of the legislation are unlikely to be borne until after 2014, new HHS regulations during Bush's first term *were* somewhat higher compared to Obama's. At a minimum, the data suggest the extent to which both administrations struggled to gain control of and streamline seemingly intractable entitlement spending through new regulations that had profound and uneven costs to health care facilities, providers, subscribers, and the federal government.

New environmental and energy regulations in Obama's presidency, however, do stand in stark contrast to his predecessor's first term, not in quantity but most particularly in economic impacts. Across Bush's first term new EPA regulations totaled only \$2.3 billion (approximately \$2.7 billion in inflation-adjusted 2010 dollars); the aggregate cost of \$28 billion to consumers and industry for Obama's first term (\$35 billion if Department of Energy rules are included) was 9 to 11 times greater. As Figure 9.5 indicates, the \$28 billion figure for EPA was nearly twice as much for any other single agency from 2009 to August 2012, including Agriculture, Veterans Administration, and Labor. The most costly EPA rule (2010) mandated new greenhouse gas emission standards for automobiles and set new CAFE standards at an annualized cost of \$10.5 billion.[3] The regulation prompted a legislative proposal by GOP senator Lisa Murkowski (AK) in June 2011 to preclude the EPA from regulating greenhouse gases under the Clean Air Act. The bill failed 47–53, but placed the Obama administration's energy policy and attempts to pass a comprehensive energy bill in the media spotlight (see Geman 2011; Dinan 2010). A follow-up EPA regulation in 2012 on air pollutants from coal- and oil-fired electric utility steam-generating units was estimated to cost \$9.6 billion.[4] These two regulations represented aggressive EPA action that had been put on hold by the Bush Administration, which worried about the relative economic strength of the automobile and coal industries (Lipton 2010). Finally, a single 2010 DOE regulation mandating "weatherization" assistance to low-income persons accounted for another \$5 billion in new costs and was part of the American Recovery and Reinvestment Act or 2009 stimulus bill.[5]

Although environmental regulations galvanized Republican opposition to the administration's climate change agenda, many costly "big ticket" regulations in other policy areas drew little or no attention from GOP members in Congress or the Romney campaign. For example, a \$13.6 billion regulation in August 2010 from Veterans Affairs (VA) mandating an expansion of health care benefits to Vietnam veterans exposed to Agent Orange proved noncontroversial (*US Federal News* 2010a). This single regulation accounted for more than 90 percent of all costs of new VA rules in Obama's first term. Similarly, a \$2.5 billion regulation promulgated by the Federal Aviation Administration, which added performance standards to aircraft transmitters for air traffic control monitoring and safety, spurred little disagreement (*US Federal News* 2010b).

Finally, a \$4 billion regulation by the Department of Education in late fall 2009 outlining criteria for federal grants to the states for the "race to the top" program as part of the economic stimulus bill garnered more criticism from education groups, which denounced a "a one-size-fits-all approach to improving education" (McNeil 2009), than from Republicans in Congress who by then had accepted the American Recovery and Reinvestment Act spending as a fait accompli.

Cost Estimates, Cassandra, and Regulatory Reckoning: Implications for the 2012 Campaigns

Incredulity at agency cost estimates of regulations has become nothing less than dogmatic among many conservative watchdog organizations and think-tanks. For groups like the Heritage Foundation, Melanie Klein's (1975, 293) use of the Cassandra metaphor seems most apropos, as government agencies putatively engage in "a refusal to believe what at the same time they know to be true" and a "universal tendency toward denial." A Competitive Research Institute working paper titled "Tip of the Costberg: On the Invalidity of All Cost of Regulation Estimates and the Need to Compile Them Anyway" sums up the disbelief that the ultimate price tag of aggregate regulations for the U.S. economy can ever be accurately measured. As Gattuso and Katz (2012) assert:

> the agencies that perform the analyses have a natural incentive to minimize or obfuscate the costs of their own regulations. For some, costs are only partially quantified; for others, not quantified at all. But even quantified costs may often fail to capture the true impacts, as regulators cannot estimate intangibles, the costs of which could dwarf the direct compliance burden.

The consequence is that portrayals of the regulatory costs mandated by the federal government are subject to vastly differing estimates from nongovernmental entities. The Competitive Research Institute forecasts the annual costs of all regulations at \$1.8 trillion, or half of the federal budget, and suggests that Congress's delegation of rulemaking processes to unelected representatives in the executive branch is as undemocratic as the estimates are unrealistic (Crews and Young 2012).

The argument about "unquantified" costs of new regulations *is* perhaps the most persuasive and troubling for any administration

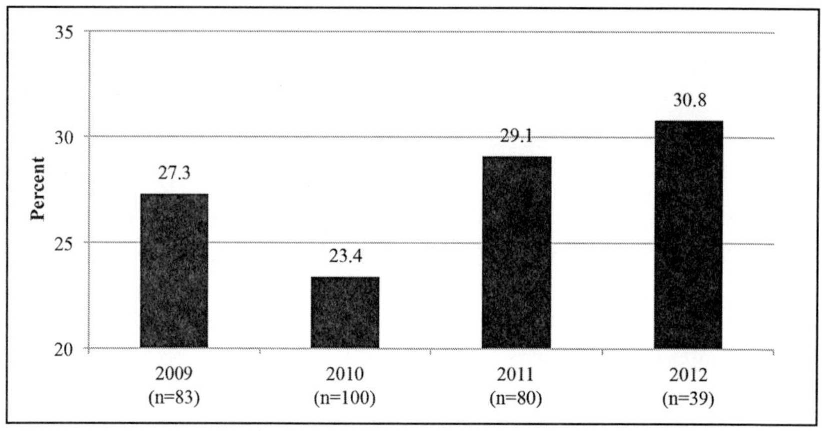

Figure 9.6 Significant Regulations without Cost Estimates (Percent), 2009–2012*

*Data for 2012 through August.
Source: U.S. Government Accountability Office, Legal Decisions & Bid Protests. http://www.gao.gov/legal/congressact/fedrule.html. Calculated by author; see text for details.

seeking to defend its regulatory record. Figure 9.6 shows the annual percentage of new rules for which departments and agencies were unable to arrive at a methodology to forecast future economic impacts during Obama's first term. The percentage of annual regulations without cost estimates ranges from just under a quarter to nearly a third from 2009 to August 2012. The most that can be said about these significant rules is that they were expected to impose costs of at least $100,000,000 or more according to the GAO. But in actuality the costs for new Agriculture and Energy regulations on wetlands and environmental protection, Department of Defense stop-loss and homeowner assistance rules, and a whole host of Federal Reserve regulations on truth-in-lending compliance that fell into this category may far exceed the minimum figure.

How did such critiques affect the 2012 presidential race? The lack of empirical data on costs of many regulations, as well as challenges to the veracity of agency estimates, would seemingly facilitate the challenger's (Romney's) ability to make reasonable if not easily verifiable arguments about alleged regulatory profligacy of an incumbent administration. At the same time, the competing claims about the benefits and drawbacks of new regulations test the electorate's ability to discern the truth, leaving

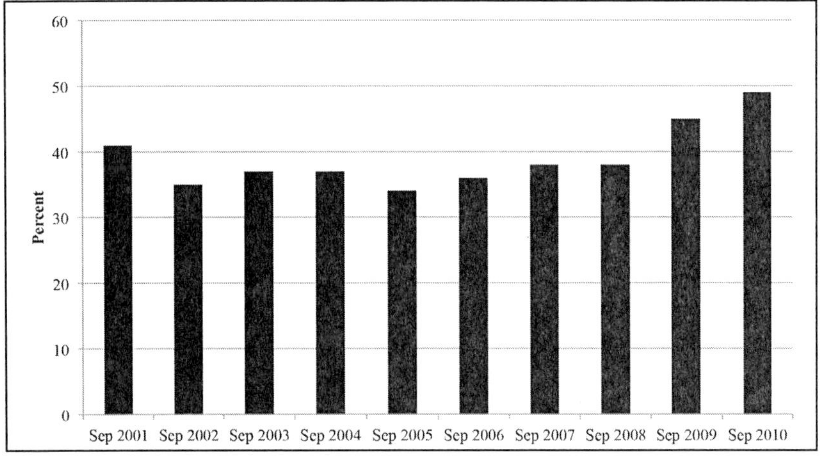

Figure 9.7 Public Opinion: "Too Much Government Regulation of Business and Industry," 2001–2010

Source: Karlyn Bowman, "The Public View of Regulation, Revisited," American Enterprise Institute for Public Policy Research, No.1 (January 2011): p. 4.

many voters to rely on perceptions that are almost naturally filtered through partisan lenses and reinforce their own predilections. Evidence of this phenomenon is apparent in public opinion data on regulation prior to the 2012 presidential election.

REINFORCING PARTISAN CLEAVAGES: PUBLIC OPINION ON REGULATIONS

Public opinion polls do not regularly include specific questions on federal regulations. However, a limited number of polls, both longitudinal and in the last two years of Obama's first term, cast some light on how the economic narratives of the president's and Romney's campaign reinforced traditional partisan divides about the role of the federal government generally, and some key regulations in detail.

Taking a longer view since the new millennium, polling data suggest that Americans became more skeptical of the regulatory thrust of the Obama term. Figure 9.7 shows that throughout George W. Bush's two terms, approximately 40 percent or fewer of respondents believed that there was "too much government regulation of business and industry." The American Enterprise Institute for Public Policy Research data show

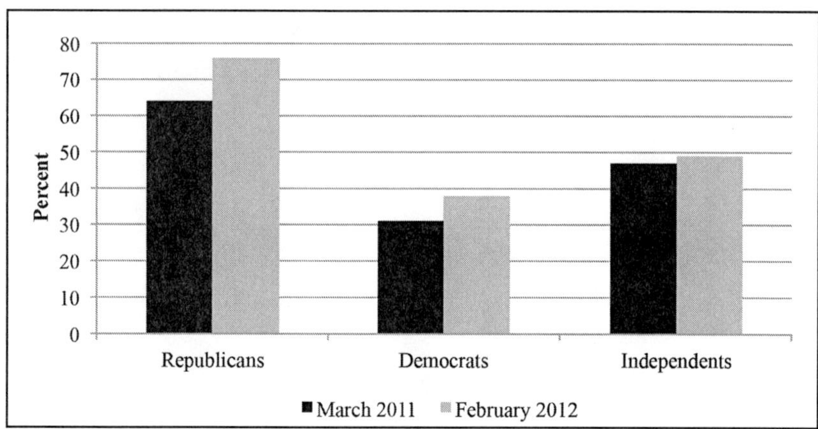

Figure 9.8 Public Opinion: "Government Regulation Does More Harm Than Good"

Source: Pew Research Center, February 2012. http://www.people-press.org/2012/02/23/section-2-views-of-government-regulation/.

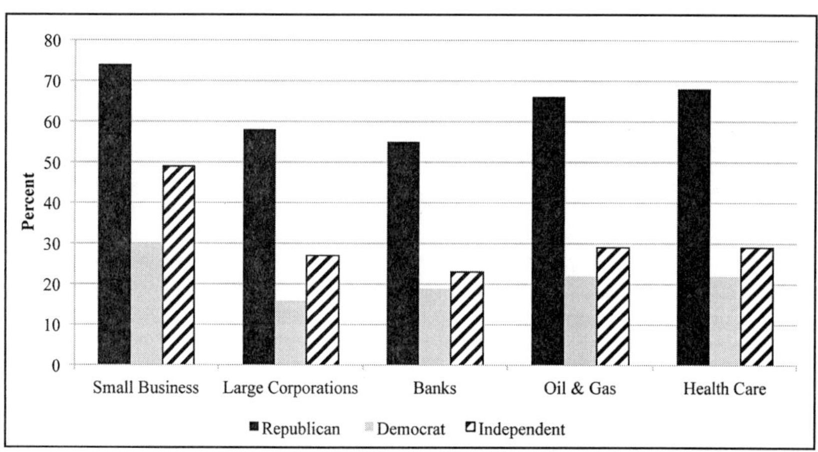

Figure 9.9 Public Opinion: "Too Much Regulation of ____?"

Source: Pew Research Center, February 2012. http://www.people-press.org/2012/02/23/section-2-views-of-government-regulation/.

a significant rise in the figures for 2009 and 2010 to just under 50 percent in the last year in the time series. As noted earlier, 2010 was the high water mark for "significant" regulations, both in terms of number and cost, in Obama's two years. The evidence suggests that congressional enactment

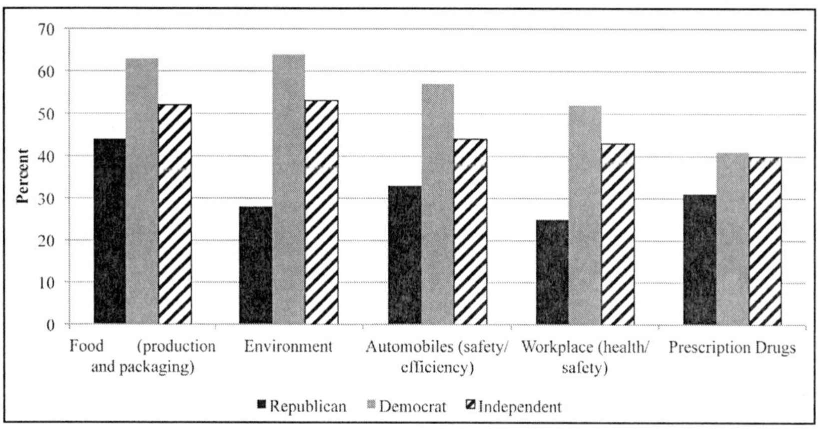

Figure 9.10 Public Opinion: "Should the Federal Government Strengthen Regulations for _____?"

Source: Pew Research Center, February 2012. http://www.people-press.org/2012/02/23/section-2-views-of-government-regulation/.

of Wall Street reform legislation (Dodd-Frank) and the ACA in the first two years of Obama's presidency raised concerns about overregulation.

Pew Research Center polling data in the latter two years of the Obama term buttress the assertion that partisan cleavages deepened over regulatory issues. Figure 9.8 shows opinions by party affiliation in March 2011 and February 2012 as Romney's path to the GOP nomination became clearer. Republican views that "government regulation does more harm than good" grew by approximately 12 points in the span of the two surveys. Democrats' skepticism grew only slightly and remained below 40 percent. Independents' views changed little across time, as they were virtually split at 49 percent by 2012.

The partisan gap on regulatory issues is elucidated in Figures 9.9 and 9.10. Figure 9.9 underscores Republican antipathy toward regulation generally. The percentage of GOP supporters contending there was "too much regulation" of everything from small businesses to health care never fell below 50 percent as of the 2012 survey. Indeed, Republican distaste for small business regulation was the highest in the five categories and suggests that the Romney campaign's steadfast focus on the alleged harm of Obama-era regulations on this front reinforced GOP voters' predispositions. It is critical to note, however, how *few* Democrats surveyed agreed with the statement—particularly with respect to large corporations and banks. Less than 20 percent of self-identified Democrats had negative views of the regulatory environment in the private sector. Finally, Independents were most skeptical about small business regulation but split at 49 percent. On regulation of large corporations, banks, the oil industry, and on health care Independents were more closely aligned with Democrats.

Finally, Figure 9.10 presents polling data by party affiliation on whether federal regulations on several categories should be strengthened. Apart from food production and packaging, less than 30 percent of Republicans consistently supported strengthening environmental, automobile efficiency, workplace health and safety, or prescription drug regulations. Notwithstanding prescription drugs, significant majorities of Democrats endorsed stronger regulations on all other categories. Independents were most divided on food and environmental regulations, and considerably less enthusiastic than Democrats on bolstering automobile efficiency, workplace, and prescription drug regulations.

REPRISE AND CONCLUSIONS: THE REGULATORY TABLEAU OF THE 2012 ELECTION

Unsurprisingly, postelection surveys following the November 6, 2012, presidential election did not come close to placing regulatory issues specifically front and center in most voters' minds. Rather, poll after poll leading up to Election Day demonstrated consistently that the overall state of the economy, more than any other single issue, dominated the concerns of voters. A margin of more than four million voters nationally apparently accepted the Obama campaign's arguments that the economy was improving, or would improve, if the president were reelected. Whether Obama-era regulations helped or hindered the economic recovery remains an open question, and the path forward in federal rulemaking is uncertain in the second Obama term.

The argument of this chapter has been that the controversies over the scope and cost of new regulations in Obama's presidency were part and parcel of the larger economic narratives of the two campaigns. For Romney and the GOP, the regulatory glass was half empty: Costly, job-killing regulations impeded an economic recovery and stifled private sector innovation. For Obama and the Democrats the glass was half full: Swift new regulatory frameworks put in place by the administration after the housing and financial crisis of 2008 may not have brought about a full recovery, but they wrenched the economy back from the brink of imminent collapse. The most that can be said following the November 6, 2012, results is that voters were willing to stay with Obama's regulatory course. The data used to measure costs (and benefits) by government agencies are imperfect, sometimes skewed by both sides of the debate, and remain controversial.

The limited opinion data available on the public's views of Obama-era regulations buttress the contention that Republicans were predisposed to oppose the hallmark private sector, health, and environmental regulations that the administration aggressively pursued. Democrats, on the other hand, were not only content with new rules but most also preferred *more* regulation. The Obama and Romney campaigns reinforced these partisan predilections in the 2012 race, while Independents (as on many other issues) were divided on regulatory questions and both campaigns pursued their support determinedly. Romney's argument fell short.

No sooner had the 2012 election ended than pundits, editorialists, and future presidential challengers in the GOP began to call into question the regulatory policies of the second Obama term. *Reste à voir* how the Affordable Care Act (Obamacare), which went into full effect in 2014—not to mention the administration's dogged pursuit of policies to combat "global warming"—will impact the economy in the immediate future. But what is certain is that the lack of consensus on the ways to measure empirically the costs and benefits of federal regulations will provide fodder to those who contend that the Obama presidency, now in its second term, will be remembered for excessive red tape in Washington. Peter Lewin (2009) sums up the essential debate that will likely play out between Democrats and Republicans in the next presidential election cycle:

> Regulators are fallible human beings whose knowledge of the present and ability to predict the future—including the future consequences of their actions—are seriously limited. The future is and will always be unpredictable. One might wonder whence even dedicated public servants are to come up with such "accurate assessments" when such assess-

ments depend on events beyond their ability to foresee. Why should they do better than the market in this respect? After all, it is not even their own money they are regulating.

Obama's reelection—especially with the GOP firmly in control of the House of Representatives—scarcely ended the debate. The topic of regulatory policy will likely emerge as a major factor in 2016 as the Obama administration pursues the implementation of some fraction of the more than 6,000 new regulations under review at the close of 2012, according to Regulation.gov.

REFERENCES

Baker, P. and Broder, J. M. 2012. "Top Regulatory Adviser to Depart White House." *New York Times Blog,* August 3. Retrieved from http://thecaucus.blogs. nytimes.com/2012/08/03/top-regulatory-adviser-to-depart-white-house/.

Bogardus, K., and E. Viebeck, E. 2011. "Business Lauds Obama's Call for Review of 'Excessive' Regs." *Hill,* January 19, 6.

Brooks, D. 2011. "The Wonky Liberal." *New York Times,* December 6, 29.

Bruff, H. 1988–1989. "Presidential Management of Agency Rulemaking." *George Washington Law Review* 57: 533–595.

Bruner, J. 2012. "Fact Check: Regulations under Obama." *The Tennessean,* October 20. Retrieved from http://www.tennessean.com/article/20121020/NEWS08 /310200057/FACT-CHECK-Regulations-under-Obama.

Burke, J. 2000. *The Institutional Presidency: Organizing and Managing the White House from FDR to Clinton,* 2nd ed. Baltimore: Johns Hopkins University Press.

Cappiello, D. 2011. "GOP Strikes Early in Global Warming Battle." *Associated Press Financial Wire,* January 6.

Cooper, J., and W. West. 1988. "Presidential Power and Republican Government: The Theory and Practice of OMB Review of Agency Rules." *Journal of Politics* 50: 864–895.

Copeland, C. 2007. "The Law: Executive Order 13422: An Expansion of Presidential Influence in the Rulemaking Process." *Presidential Studies Quarterly* 37: 531–544.

Cox, G., and M. McCubbins. 1993. *Legislative Leviathan.* Berkeley, CA: University of California Press.

Crews, C. 2011. *Ten Thousand Commandments: An Annual Snapshot of the Federal Regulatory State.* Washington, DC: Competitive Enterprise Institute. Retrieved from http://cei.org/sites/default/files/Wayne%20Crews%20-%2010,000 %20Commandments%202011.pdf.

Crews, Jr., C., and R. Young. 2012. "Regulations and Rules Equal Broken Government; Equivalent to Half the Federal Budget." *Washington Times,* October 3, B1.

De Rugy, V. 2010. "Has Government Grown Since the Recession Started?" *National Review,* December 28. Retrieved from http://www.nationalreview.com /corner/255951/has-government-grown-recession-startedveronique-de-rugy.

Dinan, S. 2010. "Senate Hands Climate Backers 1st Win; Vote Allows EPA to Act on Greenhouse Gases." *Washington Times,* June 11, A1.

Duffy, R. 1996. "Divided Government and Institutional Combat: The Case of the Quayle Council on Competitiveness." *Polity* 28: 379–399.

Eilperin, J. 2008. "EPA Seeks Comment on Emissions Rules, Then Discredits Effort." *Washington Post,* July 1, A4.

Fuchs, E., and J. Anderson. 1987. "The Institutionalization of Cost-Benefit Analysis." *Public Productivity Review* 10: 25–33.

Gattuso, J., and D. Katz. 2012. "Red Tape Rising: Obama-Era Regulation at the Three-Year Mark." *Heritage Foundation,* March 13. Retrieved from http://www .heritage.org/research/reports/2012/03/red-tape-rising-obama-era-regulation -at-the-three-year-mark.

Geman, B. 2011. "Senate Turns Down Resolution to Block EPA Gas Regulations." *Hill,* June 11, 3.

Hahn, R. 1998. "Policy Watch: Government Analysis of the Benefits and Costs of Regulation." *Journal of Economic Perspectives* 12: 201–210.

Hart, J. 1995. *The Presidential Branch: From Washington to Clinton,* 2nd ed. Chatham, NJ: Chatham House.

Heclo, H. 1975. "The OMB and the Presidency—The Problem of 'Neutral Competence.'" *Public Interest* 38: 80–98.

Hemphill, T. 2012. "The Obama Administration's Regulatory Review Initiative: A 21st Century Federal Regulatory Initiative?" *Business and Society Review* 117: 185–195.

Hicks, J. 2012. "Who Has the Better Regulatory Record—Obama or Bush?" *Washington Post,* March 27. Retrieved from http://www.washingtonpost.com /blogs/fact-checker/post/who-issued-more-regulations--obama-or-bush /2012/03/22/gIQAVvGYWS_blog.html.

Howell, W. 2003. *Power without Persuasion: The Politics of Direct Presidential Action.* Princeton, NJ: Princeton University Press.

Jackson, D. 2012. "Obama Lauds Bipartisanship, Attacks Romney." *USA Today,* November 1. Retrieved from http://www.usatoday.com/story/news/politics /2012/11/01/obama-campaign-sandy-green-bay/1674039/.

Kamensky, J. 1996. "Role of the 'Reinventing Government' Movement in Federal Management Reform." *Public Administration Review* 56: 247–255.

Klein, M. 1975. *Envy and Gratitude, and Other Works 1946–1963.* New York: Delacorte Press/S. Lawrence.

Layton, L. 2009. "A Vigorous Push from Federal Regulators; Consumer, Workplace Agencies More Active." *Washington Post,* October 13, A1.

Lewin, P. 2009. "Free-Marketeers Should Welcome Regulation?" *Freeman* 59 (October).

Lewis, D. 2008. *The Politics of Political Appointments: Political Control and Bureaucratic Performance.* Princeton, NJ: Princeton University Press.

Lipton, E. 2010. "With Obama, Regulations Are Back in Fashion." *Washington Post,* May 13. A15.

Mayhew, D. 1974. *Congress: The Electoral Connection.* New Haven, CT: Yale University Press.

McNeil, M. 2009. "Rules Set for $4 Billion Race to Top Contest; Final Rules Give States Detailed Map in Quest for $4 Billion in Education Stimulus Aid." *Education Week* 29: 1.

Miller, H. 2012. "Regulation, the Democrats, and the Parallel Universe." *Forbes*, September 26. Retrieved from http://www.forbes.com/sites/henrymiller /2012/09/26/regulation-the-democrats-and-the-parallel-universe/.

Moe, T. 1985. "The Politicized Presidency." In *The New Direction in American Politics*, edited by John Chubb and Paul E. Peterson, 235–271. Washington, DC: Brookings Institution.

Moe, T., and W. Howell. 1999. "Unilateral Action and Presidential Power: A Theory." *Presidential Studies Quarterly* 29: 850–873.

Moe, T., and S. Wilson. 1994. "Presidents and the Politics of Structure." *Law and Contemporary Problems* 57: 1–44.

Mutikani, L. 2012. "Romney Stresses He Wants Bank Regulation, but Slams Obama Reforms." *Reuters,* October 4. Retrieved from http://www.reuters.com /article/2012/10/04/us-usa-campaign-economy-idUSBRE8930A020121004.

Nathan, R. 1975. *The Plot That Failed: Nixon and the Administrative Presidency.* New York: Wiley & Sons.

Nathan, R. 1983. *The Administrative Presidency.* New York: Wiley.

National Journal. 2012. "How Obama, Romney Positions on Government Regulation Differ." *National Journal*, June 15. Retrieved from http://www .nationaljournal.com/pictures-video/how-obama-romney-positions-on -government-regulation-differ-pictures-20120615.

Neustadt, R. 1960. *Presidential Power and the Modern Presidents.* New York: Free Press.

Neustadt, R. 1974. "The Presidency and Legislation: The Growth of Central Clearance." *American Political Science Review* 48: 641–671.

New York Times (Editorial). 2011. "Reform Moves Ahead." July 19, 20A.

9News.com. 2012. "Truth Test: Mitt Romney's New Ad on President Barack Obama's Over-Regulation." Retrieved from http://www.9news.com/news /article/289050/339/TRUTH-TEST-Romneys-ad-on-over-regulation.

Office of Management and Budget (OMB). 2011. "2011 Report to Congress on the Benefits and Costs of Federal Regulations and Unfunded Mandates on State, Local, and Tribal Entities." Retrieved from http://www.whitehouse.gov/sites /default/files/omb/inforeg/2011_cb/2011_cba_report.pdf.

Office of Management and Budget (OMB). 2012. "Draft 2012 Report to Congress on the Benefits and Costs of Federal Regulations and Unfunded Mandates on State, Local, and Tribal Entities." Retrieved from http://www.whitehouse.gov /sites/default/files/omb/oira/draft_2012_cost_benefit_report.pdf.

Orange County Register (Commentary). 2011. "GOP Ready to Battle EPA." December 3, H.

O'Reilly, J., and P. Brown. 1987. "In Search of Excellence: A Prescription for the Future of OMB Oversight of Rule." *Administrative Law Review* 39.

Pear, R. 2010. "Short of Repeal, G.O.P. Will Chip at Health Law." *New York Times,* September 21, A1.

Quarles, J. 1976. *Cleaning Up America: An Insider's View of the Environmental Protection Agency.* Boston: Houghton Mifflin.

Rudalevige, A. 2005. "The Structure of Leadership: Presidents, Hierarchies, and Information Flow." *Presidential Studies Quarterly* 35: 333–360.

Research Agenda." *Presidential Studies Quarterly* 39: 10–24.

Shapiro, S. 2007. "An Evaluation of the Bush Administration Reforms to the Regulatory Process." *Presidential Studies Quarterly* 37: 270–290.

60 Minutes (CBS). 2012. "Transcript of Obama on *60 Minutes*." September 24. Retrieved from http://www.foxnews.com/politics/2012/09/24/transcript -obama-on-60-minutes/.

Skrzycki, C. 2009. "The Rule Czar's Balancing Act." *Washington Post,* January 13, D2.

Stiles, A. 2011. "Ten Job Destroying Regulations." *National Review,* August 11. Retrieved from http://www.nationalreview.com/articles/275797/ten-job -destroying-regulations-andrew-stiles#.

Sunstein, C. 2012. "Why Regulations Are Good—Again." *Chicago Tribune,* March 12. Retrieved from http://articles.chicagotribune.com/2012-03-19/news /ct-oped-0319-regs-20120319_1_regulation-baseball-scouts-requirements.

US Federal News. 2010a. "Rep. Hill: New VA Regulation Vastly Expands Care for Agent Orange Exposure." August 31.

US Federal News. 2010b. "FAA Issues Final Rule about Automatic Dependent Surveillance." May 29.

Waterman, R. 1989. *Presidential Influence and the Administrative State.* Knoxville: University of Tennessee Press.

Weingast, B., and W. Marshall. 1988. "The Industrial Organization of Congress; or, Why Legislatures, Like Firms, Are Not Organized as Markets." *Journal of Political Economy* 96: 132.

West, W. 2005. "The Institutionalization of Regulatory Review: Organizational Stability and Responsive Competence at OIRA." *Presidential Studies Quarterly* 35: 76–93.

Williamson, E. 2011. "Obama Launches Rule Review, Pledging to Spur Jobs, Growth." *Wall Street Journal,* January 18. Retrieved from http://online.wsj .com/article/SB10001424052748703396604576088634252904032.html.

NOTES

1. http://www.gao.gov/legal/congressact/fedrule.html.

2. Sunstein left OIRA in August 2012.

3. The rule was promulgated simultaneously by the EPA, Department of Transportation, and National Highway Transportation Safety Administration. See http://www.gao.gov/products/GAO-10-739R#mt=e-report.

4. The EPA estimated the net benefits of the regulation at $33 to $90 billion. See http://www.gao.gov/products/GAO-12-489R#mt=e-report.

5. As the DOE report notes, the regulation was technically "cost-neutral" because funds for the weatherization grants were already appropriated by Congress in the stimulus bill. See the full report at http://www.gao.gov/products/GAO-10-409R#mt=e-report.

Chapter 10

Conspicuous Silence
Global Climate Change and the 2012 Presidential Election

Byron W. Daynes, Brigham Young University

A VEXING PROBLEM

Global climate change is without question a distressing global threat. It affects the United States and other developed and developing nations throughout the world. It is potentially one of the most perilous situations the human race has ever faced. It was the United Nations International Panel on Climate Change (IPCC) that stated in its Fourth Report published in 2007: "Climate change will affect national security…potentially affecting everything from economic growth to social stability" and thus may require "military and other government responses" (Center for New American Security 2012).

The possibility that global climate change can have such serious social and political consequences in the United States and in the world at large is reason enough to be concerned. Several years before this report, Lynton Caldwell and Michael Kraft examined environmental problems including climate change at the international level. Caldwell expressed his concern about how acute our global environmental problems have become over the last few years (Caldwell and Weiland 1996, 5–10). As he stated, "By early 1990, global climate change could be regarded as the single greatest international environmental policy issue" (Caldwell and Weiland 1996, 212). Agricultural economists Bruce A. McCarl, Richard M. Adams, and Brian H. Hurd, in their study several years ago, added their concerns regarding the agricultural consequences of climate change. As they indicated: "Temperature, precipitation, atmospheric carbon dioxide content, the incidence of extreme events and sea level rise" are the primary climate change attributes that have agricultural consequences (2001, 1).

2012: AN ELECTION YEAR

Yes, 2012 was a presidential election year, yet global climate change never made it as an election issue of consequence. At first appearance, this seems odd given its importance and also that it had been mentioned in previous years. In the 1988 vice presidential debate between Lloyd Bentsen and Dan Quayle, for example, it was Quayle who mentioned that the drought suffered during the summer of 1988 "highlighted the problem that we have." He then went on to suggest that "The greenhouse effect is an important environmental issue. . . . it's important for us to get the data in to see what alternatives we might have to fossil fuels." Quayle then indicated that "we need to get on with it" (Henneberger 2012).

Yet hardly a word was spoken in 2012 by either President Obama or Governor Romney during the campaign despite efforts by several environmental interest groups to insist that this issue be addressed by the candidates. The League of Conservation Voters, for example, launched an online petition to that effect, while 160,000 solicited requests to talk about climate change came from the Environmental Defense Action Fund (EDF) urging PBS's Jim Lehrer, moderator of the first presidential debate devoted to domestic affairs, to ask President Obama and Governor Romney about the climate crisis (Shelby 2012). Despite this being one of the greatest challenges of this generation, Lehrer ignored all of the requests and petitions as did the other three moderators for the remaining debates. Thus, climate change was never mentioned even as an aside.

*Reasons That May Explain Why Climate Change Was Not a 2012
Election Issue*

Giving the candidates their due, there may have been good reasons for them to ignore this crisis. Possibly, the potential voters were not really interested in climate change. If this were the case, there would be every reason why the candidates would not press the issue.

Evidence for the 2012 failure to discuss climate change, however, appears mixed. According to Table 10.1, based on a Gallup survey, there is a real question as to how concerned voters actually were. When asked to prioritize a select number of issues about which the candidates should be concerned, environmental concerns, including global warming, rank next to last in this July Gallup poll. Yet in March 2012 Connie Roser-Renouf, Anthony Leiserowitz, and Edward Maibach reminded us that when individuals are asked specifically about the importance of global warming, "A majority of all registered voters (55%) say they will consider candidates' views on global warming when deciding how to vote." They further suggest, "Among these climate change issue voters, large majorities believe global warming is happening and support action by the U.S. to reduce global warming even if it has economic costs" (2012, 1). The results of this data would seem to suggest that the way the question is asked to the voters becomes all-important as to whether their interest is piqued.

Table 10.1 How Important a Priority Should Each of the Following Issues Be for the Next President?

	Extremely Important	Extremely/ Very Important
	%	%
Creating good jobs	48	92
Reducing corruption in the federal government	45	87
Reducing the federal budget deficit	44	86
Dealing with terrorism and other international threats	42	86
Ensuring the long-term stability of Social Security & Medicare	40	85
Improving the nation's public schools	38	83
Setting high moral standards for the nation	36	76
Making healthcare available and affordable	36	74
Overcoming political gridlock in Washington	35	76

	Extremely Important	Extremely/ Very Important
	%	%
Making <u>college education</u> available and affordable	30	69
Dealing with <u>environmental</u> concerns, such as global warming	21	52
Increasing <u>taxes on wealthy</u> Americans	21	49

Source: *USA Today*/Gallup poll, July 19–22, 2012.[1]

A second reason that climate change was not on the electoral agenda may be tied to the position for which each was campaigning—namely, the presidency—since, over time, few presidents have ever been concerned about it. Jimmy Carter was an exception as the first president to appreciate climate change's seriousness, and the first to have laid the groundwork for Americans' awareness of global warming and climate change. His concern led him to become the first president to think in terms of interconnected climate systems.

When Carter assumed the presidency, he was ready to initiate measures to protect both the domestic and global environment. During his first year in office, Carter announced to the Congress in an Environmental Message that it was his intention to organize the first comprehensive study of the global environment. As the president indicated: "Environmental problems do not stop at national boundaries. In the past decade, we and other nations have come to recognize the urgency of international efforts to protect our common environment" (Carter 1980, Preface). He then asked the Council on Environmental Quality, the Department of State, the Environmental Protection Agency, the National Science Foundation, and the National Oceanic and Atmospheric Administration to create a yea-by-year projected study, to extend through the year 2000, taking account of the changes in the world's population, in its natural resources, and in the environment (Carter 1980, Preface).

Among the issues involved in this study—*The Global 2000 Report*—there was an entire chapter devoted to climate change (Carter 1980, 51). The study went on to warn readers, "Some human activities, especially those resulting in releases of carbon dioxide into the atmosphere, are known to have the potential to affect the world's climate." Further, the report concluded, "Many experts…feel that changes on a scale likely to affect the environment and the economy of large regions of the world are not only possible but probable in the next 25–50 years" (Carter 1980, 52–53, 257, 259).

President Carter also was the first president to mention climate change in any presidential speech. In his "Science and Technology Message to the Congress," for example, he indicated, "Advances that can be made in understanding climate change, in predicting it—and perhaps in influencing it beneficially—will be of enormous help to us and the rest of the world" (Carter 1979).

Based on this foundation of climate change inquiry and discovery, Bill Clinton became the first president to encourage U.S. and world leaders to come to an agreement as to how to respond to the crisis of climate change. President Clinton, Vice President Gore, and others in the administration put a great deal of effort into recruiting and encouraging nations to give support to the Kyoto Protocol. U.S. leadership was important in soliciting this support. Clinton sent Al Gore to the Kyoto negotiations with the primary mission of encouraging European countries, energy producers, and coal users to accept a "workable middle ground" (*New York Times* 1997).

The Kyoto Protocol was intended to bring stability to greenhouse gas emissions in the atmosphere by setting firm limits on these emissions. It was the first effort to bind nations in agreement to reduce greenhouse gases. Methane (CH_4), nitrous oxide (N_2O), hydrofluorocarbons (HFCs), perfluorocarbons (PFCs), sulphur hexafluoride (SF_6), and carbon dioxide (CO_2) were included as a focus for the Kyoto Protocol and the Environmental Protection Agency (EPA), but the primary target for the reductions was carbon dioxide (CO_2), which produced the largest share of the emissions. Major developed nations were to reduce their combined emissions by 5.2 percent compared to their 1990 level.

Clinton did recognize that the Protocol was "not a perfect agreement, and there were criticisms of it at the time" (Clinton 2005). The Senate more than agreed with him, sternly notifying him in a 1997 vote on the Byrd-Hagel Resolution (S. Res. 98) that it opposed ratification of the Protocol by a 95–0 vote unless developing countries such as India and China—two major polluters—were also included and restricted in their emissions. The Senate then added that "the exemption for Developing Country Parties is inconsistent with the need for global action on climate change and is environmentally flawed" (U.S. Congress, *Cong. Rec.*, 1997, 143, pt. 11: 15808). Thus, even though Clinton signed the Protocol, he never submitted it to the Senate for ratification.

Despite this setback, Clinton made references to climate change in every State of the Union Address from 1997 to 2000, with each of his addresses drawing increasing attention to climate change. In his last State of the Union Address for 2000, the president stated:

> The greatest environmental challenge of the new century is global warming. The scientists tell us the 1990s were the hottest decade of the entire millennium. If we fail to reduce the emission of greenhouse gases, deadly heat waves and droughts will become more frequent, coastal areas will flood, and economies will be disrupted. That is going to happen, unless we act. (Clinton 2000)

Clinton's influence on the Democratic Party Platform regarding climate change was evident when one compares the 1992 and 1996 party platforms. The former merely stated that "The United States must become a leader, not an impediment, in the fight against global warming. We should join our European allies in agreeing to limit carbon dioxide emissions to 1990 levels by the year 2000" (Democratic Party 1992). The 1996 platform, in contrast, was more detailed, focusing more on the particular efforts of the Clinton-Gore administration's actions regarding global climate change:

> After years in which Republicans neglected the global environment, the Clinton Administration has made America a leader in the fight to meet environmental challenges that transcend national borders and require global cooperation.... We will seek a strong international agreement to further reduce greenhouse gas emissions worldwide and protect our global climate. (Democratic Party 1996)

While Congress prevented the Clinton administration from becoming an effective world leader against climate change, there was real promise in the election of Barack Obama in 2008. In the 2008 presidential campaign, for example, there was no one who was more supportive of doing something about climate change than was Obama. In a speech he gave in Portsmouth, New Hampshire, Obama indicated that the president's politics must not be "timid politics when the future of our planet is at stake." He asserted, "Global warming is not a someday problem, it is now." And he concluded by stating how severe conditions were becoming:

> We are already breaking records with the intensity of our storms, the number of forest fires, the periods of drought. By 2050 famine could force more than 250 million from their homes.... The polar ice caps are now melting faster than science had ever predicted.... It's not the future any of us want for our children. And if we act now and we act boldly, it doesn't have to be. (Obama 2007)

After his election to the presidency in November 2008, Obama stated, "Once I take office, you can be sure that the United States will once again engage vigorously in these negotiations and help lead the world toward a new era of global cooperation on climate change. Now is the time to confront this challenge once and for all. Delay is no longer an option. Denial is no longer an acceptable response. The stakes are too high" (McKibben 2009).

Yet the longer Obama was in office, the more opposition he confronted from Congress for his stance on climate change and the less he said about it. While the president continued to encourage Congress to support his efforts to mitigate global climate change, he made a number of concessions on his original strong statements against climate change. Confronting such opposition in Congress, for example, led Obama to begin stressing other policy options related to climate change domestically, such as clean energy, to avoid further confrontations with lawmakers. But this time he chose to rely on his own presidential authority. In 2010, for example, the president signed a memorandum for the improvement of fuel economy standards that represented a positive step forward in reducing greenhouse gas emissions (Obama 2010).

While the president recognized the limitations resulting from congressional opposition, in his 2010 State of the Union message Obama again urged the Congress to pass a "comprehensive energy and climate bill with incentives that will finally make clean energy the profitable kind of energy in America" (Williamson 2010). Yet the month following this address, he was willing to divide the climate bill, separating the popular request for "green jobs" from a bill to control greenhouse gases. As he stated: "The only thing I would say about it is this: We may be able to separate these things out. And it's possible that that's where the Senate ends up" (Williamson 2010).

Interior Secretary Ken Salazar did indicate that the Obama administration had had some major accomplishments during its time in office, pointing to its instigation of "more utility-scale renewable projects on public lands than in the past two decades combined" (Associated Press 2012). But it was Amy Harder who downplayed the accomplishments of the president when compared to his promises. She asserted: "Obama has managed to make progress around the edges—tougher fuel-economy standards that cut emissions from cars, for instance—but as a result of congressional gridlock, he has been unable to fulfill his 2008 campaign promise to fight climate change by putting a price on carbon emissions. Having failed on that front, the president still faces attacks from fossil-fuel interests for having tried" (Harder 2012).

Mitt Romney was also critical of President Obama for even suggesting climate change as an issue of importance. Romney actually belittled the president, in his acceptance speech at the Republican National Convention, for promising to do anything related to the global environment. As Romney made plain: "President Obama promised to begin to slow the rise of the oceans and heal the planet. My promise…is to help you and your family" (Romney 2012). Although Democrats were offended by this allegation, Gabriel Malor put this into context when he suggested that Democrats should be more offended by the fact that "the President has been AWOL on the issue of climate change since about 2009. Taking a shot at him now for his old campaign promises seems like shooting fish in a barrel. Romney's joke hits environmentally-conscious Democrats who actually believed the President's 2008 promises right where they live" (Malor 2012).

A more severe criticism of Obama's lack of assertiveness regarding climate change came from Al Gore—longtime environmentalist, vice president, and presidential candidate—who strongly disapproved of Obama's lack of political leadership on climate change since his 2008 election. As he indicated in *Rolling Stone*, on June 11, 2012:

without presidential leadership that focuses intensely on making the public aware of the reality we face, nothing will change. The real power of any president, as Richard Neustadt wrote, is "the power to persuade." Yet President Obama has never presented to the American people the magnitude of the climate crisis. He has simply not made the case for action. He has not defended the science against the ongoing, withering and dishonest attacks. Nor has he provided a presidential venue for the scientific community—including our own National Academy—to bring the reality of the science before the public.

John M. Broder agreed with Gore, suggesting, "Many scientists and policy experts say the lack of a serious discussion of climate change in the presidential contest represents a lost opportunity to engage the public and to signal to the rest of the world American intentions for dealing with what is, by definition, a global problem that requires global cooperation" (2012a).

The Reluctant Candidates Themselves

Neither of the candidates in 2012 saw it as politically expedient to raise this issue in the campaign even though both recognized the effect it has had in warming the planet. "Throughout the campaign," observed John M. Broder, "Obama and Romney have seemed most intent on trying to outdo each other as lovers of coal, oil and natural gas—the very fuels most responsible for rising levels of carbon dioxide in the atmosphere" (2012a).

Neither Obama nor Romney really wanted to have climate change as an agenda item since it is a "social issue" that can always be guaranteed to create controversy. A social issue is by definition "a public policy that possesses legal authority having the potential of influencing or changing moral practices, including individual standards of behavior as well as community values" (Daynes and Sussman 2001, 1). Environmental policies possess the same characteristics as any social issue, as George McKenna recognized, since the "political dynamics of environmental issues also evoke 'moral questions' as well as directing our thoughts to 'social concerns'" (1997, 435).

Another reason neither candidate was eager to see climate change as an agenda issue dealt with the disadvantages that the cost of responding to climate change would entail. The candidates anticipated that this would be unpopular with the voters. For Governor Romney, this was reason enough to do nothing about it. Romney reasoned that "achieving the Kyoto objectives would cost $150 billion a year and only delay the global temperature that would otherwise have been reached in the year 2100 by six years" (Romney 2010, 228–229). President Obama, on the other hand, actually thought that the cost would make this an election issue. As he stated in April 2012, the "amount of money poured into fighting the scientific consensus on climate change will push the issue into the presidential campaign" (Berman 2012). Furthermore, neither candidate wanted to see this issue as an agenda item since the most important concerns raised in the 2012 election were not related to climate change. These included creating jobs, reducing government corruption, and reducing the federal deficit as Table 10.1 makes clear (Jones 2012).

Additionally, neither candidate really wanted to have climate change as an agenda item given that both felt there was only limited encouragement from both parties to raise the issue. While the Democratic Platform certainly was more encouraging to party leaders to do something of consequence to regulate climate change, and mentions climate change some 18 times, it was not persuasive enough to convince the president that this was the right time to direct his focus to the issue. The 2012 Democratic Platform makes clear that:

> We know that global climate change is one of the biggest threats of this generation—an economic, environmental, and national security catastrophe in the making. We affirm the science of climate change, commit to significantly reducing the pollution that causes climate change, and know we have to meet this challenge by driving smart policies that lead to greater growth in clean energy generation and result in a range of economic and social benefits. (Democratic Party 2012)

As a final point, the platform remarkably considers the seriousness of climate change in the same category as terrorism, nuclear proliferation, cyber and biological attacks, and transnational crime as being among "the greatest dangers we face" (Democratic Party 2012).

The Republican Party Platform was quite another story. It had no section on climate change but under a section on "Our Nation's Energy

Abundance," it opposed "any and all cap-and-trade legislation." Republicans assured themselves that the status quo showed, "The environment is getting cleaner and healthier. The nation's air and waterways, as a whole, are much healthier than they were just a few decades ago. Efforts to reduce pollution, encourage recycling, educate the public, and avoid ecological degradation have been a success" (Republican Party 2012). In Broder's words, "the Republican Party has essentially declared climate change a nonproblem" (2012). And finally, the Republican Party Platform strongly criticized the Democratic Platform for elevating "'climate change' to the level of a 'severe threat' in the same category as 'foreign aggression.'" The Republican Platform went on to assert that the Democrats overemphasized climate change at the expense of other things. As it states: "The word 'climate,' in fact, appears in the current President's strategy more often than Al Qaeda, nuclear proliferation, radical Islam or weapons of mass destruction. The phrase 'global war on terror' does not appear at all, and has been purposely avoided and changed by his Administration to 'overseas contingency operations'" (Republican Party 2012). Candidate Romney seemed quite satisfied with this criticism and this platform.

WILL GLOBAL CLIMATE CHANGE BECOME A PRIORITY IN THE FUTURE?

While neither candidate in this election said anything about this critical issue during the 2012 presidential campaign, Nicholas D. Kristof suggested that Hurricane Sandy made climate change quite noticeable: "President Obama and Mitt Romney seemed determined not to discuss climate change in this campaign. So thanks to Hurricane Sandy for forcing the issue: Isn't it time to talk not only about weather, but also about climate?" (2012). The most important concern, of course, would be whether climate change would become for President Obama an issue on which he would be willing to use his political capital to respond to this pressing global crisis. Can we expect the president to include it as a priority agenda item during this next term? Will the president agree with Andrew Street, the former envoy for climate change at the World Bank and president of the World Resources Institute, that as far as climate change is concerned, "the political discourse here is massively out of step with the rest of the world" (Broder 2012)?

Taking into account the record of both the president and Mitt Romney, how far would the president be willing to go in responding to climate change in the future? And how far would Mitt Romney have been willing to go had he been elected? As Amy Harder indicated: "Even though neither candidate wants to talk about climate, the *winner of the election will have to address it regardless of what he or his supporters might prefer*" (2012) [italics added by the author].

ScienceDebate.org, a nonprofit 501(c)(3) interest group "dedicated to elevating science and engineering policy issues in the national dialogue of the United States," asked both candidates in writing the following question:

> The Earth's climate is changing and there is concern about the potentially adverse effects of these changes on life on the planet. What is your position on cap-and-trade, carbon taxes, and other policies proposed to address global climate change—and what steps can we take to improve our ability to tackle challenges like climate change that cross national boundaries? (2012)

Mitt Romney responded:

> I am not a scientist myself but my best assessment of the data is that the world is getting warmer, that human activity contributes to that warming, and that policymakers should therefore consider the risk of negative consequences. However, there remains a lack of scientific consensus on the issue—on the extent of the warming, the extent of the human contribution, and the severity of the risk—and I believe we must support continued debate and investigation within the scientific community. (Science Debate 2012)

To understand this response from Governor Romney, one must take this statement in context with his other pledges against the environment—namely, his desire to make major revisions in the Clean Air Act and oppose significant steps to combat climate change. He also has said he would revisit a recently announced fuel economy standard for cars and light trucks that would double fuel efficiency to an average of 54.5 miles per gallon for the 2025 model year while markedly reducing greenhouse gas emissions (Broder 2012). In doing this, Romney would be setting aside what John M. Broder pointed to as a fuel efficiency agreement that was "the result of years of negotiation among automakers, the Department of Transportation, the E.P.A. and regulators in a number of states, led by California" (2012).

Obama's answer to the ScienceDebate.org inquiry was somewhat different. He indicated:

> Climate change is one of the biggest issues of this generation.... Since taking office I have established historic standards limiting greenhouse gas emissions from our vehicles for the first time in history.... We are also showing international leadership on climate change, reaching historic agreements to set emission limits in unison with all major developed and developing nations. There is still more to be done to address this global problem. I will continue efforts to reduce our dependence on oil and lower our greenhouse gas emissions while creating an economy built to last. (Science Debate 2012)

One must read both of these responses to the ScienceDebate.org questions, of course, in the context of the party platforms, on which this chapter previously focused, in order to assess how bound these candidates are to the interests of their parties. Certainly, as previously stated, the Democratic Party Platform is far more encouraging to the president to respond positively to climate change than is the Republican Party Platform. And based on this, it seems probable that President Obama would do more in response to climate change than candidate Romney would have done. But as to what Obama will actually accomplish, one must take into account future climatic disasters that may occur in the United States and around the world, as well as public demands made of the president. And most important, for Obama, it will depend on the politics and the political environment that would exist during his second term. If the new Congress were to continue to resist presidential efforts creating political gridlock, as it did during Obama's first term, then certainly he would be held back from making major responses to climate change. Table 10.2 summarizes the dilemma that may well be faced by the president or would have been faced by Romney had he been elected.

Table 10.2 The Political Future for Presidential Leadership Against Climate Change: Summary

2012 Situation	Obama	Romney
Candidate Rhetoric	More supportive	Less supportive
Party Platform	More supportive	Not supportive
Party Support	More supportive than not	Not supportive with Tea Party strong
Persuasiveness of President	Not persuasive	Not persuasive
Relationship with Congress	Possible continued gridlock of Republican-controlled House	Possible gridlock with slight Democratic majority

Source: Author.

In reflecting on his frustration over the lack of progress he has been able to make internationally because of the strong resistance he has confronted from Congress, Obama admitted:

> Frankly, I'm deeply concerned that internationally, we have not made as much progress as we need to make. Within the constraints of this Congress, we've tried to do a whole range of things, administratively, that make a difference—doubling fuel-efficiency standards on cars is going to take a whole lot of carbon out of our atmosphere. We're going to continue to push on energy efficiency and renewable energy standards, and the promotion of green energy. But there is no doubt that we have a lot more work to do. (Wenner 2012)

The president did make an allusion to some of that work left to do in his acceptance speech on November 7, 2012, when he indicated, "We want our children to live in an America that isn't burdened by debt, that isn't weakened by inequality, that isn't threatened by the destructive power of a warming planet" (*Washington Post* 2012). But, again, we must take into account Al Gore's assessment of Obama's first-term efforts that Gore considered a failure—namely, that if the president is unwilling to exert "presidential leadership that focuses intensely on making the public aware of this reality we face, *nothing will change*" (Gore 2012) [italics added by the author]. Certainly environmentalists sensitive to the gravity of the climate crisis hope this will not be the case. And there is reason to believe that the president will make a major effort to more clearly explain the gravity of the climate situation to the public as he indicated in his Second Inaugural Address given January 21, 2013. As he stated:

> We the people still believe that our obligations as Americans are not just to ourselves, but to all posterity. We will respond to the threat of climate change, knowing that the failure to do so would betray our children and future generations. Some may still deny the overwhelming judgment of science, but none can avoid the devastating impact of raging fires and crippling drought and more powerful storms. (The White House, Second Inaugural Address by President Barack Obama, January 21, 2013)

In addition to what he said here regarding climate change, he put these concerns into a broader context when he talked about finding sustainable energy sources to "maintain our vitality and national treasures—our forests and waterways, our crop lands and snow-capped peaks. That is how we will preserve our planet, commanded to our care by God. That's what will lend meaning to the creed our fathers once declared" (The White House, Second Inaugural Address by President Barack Obama, January 21, 2013).

REFERENCES

Associated Press. 2012. "Climate Change Not a Presidential Election Issue Yet." *CBS News,* August 8. Retrieved from http://www.cbsnews.com/2102-250_162 -57489676.html?tag=conten.

Berman, D. 2012. "President Obama: Climate Change Will Be a Campaign Issue." *Politico,* April 25. Retrieved from http://www.politico.com/news/stories /0412/75590.html.

Broder, J. M. 2012a. "Both Romney and Obama Avoid Talk of Climate Change." *New York Times,* October 25. Retrieved from http://www.nytimes.com /2012/10/26/us/politics/climate-change-nearly-absent-in-the-campaign.html.

Broder, J. M. 2012b. "Romney's Goals on Environmental Regulation Would Face Difficult Path." *New York Times,* October 7.

Caldwell, L. K., and P. S. Weiland. 1996. *International Environmental Policy: From the Twentieth Century to the Twenty-First Century*, 3rd ed. Durham: Duke University Press.

Carter, J. 1979. "Science and Technology Message to Congress." *The American Presidency Project,* March 27. Retrieved from http://www.presidency.ucsb.edu /ws/print.php?pid=32109.

Carter, J. 1980. *The Global 2000 Report to the President.* New York: Penguin Books.

Center for New American Security. 2012. "'Climate Change' Natural Security: Climate Change." Retrieved from http://www.cnas.org/naturalsecurity /consequences/climate-change.

Clinton, W. J. 2000. "Address Before a Joint Session of the Congress on the State of the Union." *The American Presidency Project,* January 27. Retrieved from http://www.presidency.ucsb.edu/ws/index.php?pid=58708.

Clinton, W. J. 2005. "Remarks by President William J. Clinton." December 8. Sierra Club Canada. Retrieved from http://www.sierraclub.ca/national/postings /clinton-speech-12-2005.html.

Daynes, B. W., and Sussman, G. 2001. *The American Presidency and the Social Agenda.* Upper Saddle River, New Jersey: Prentice Hall.

Democratic Party. 1992. Democratic Party Platform of 1992 *The American Presidency Project,* July 13. Retrieved from http://www.presidency.ucsb.edu/ws /index.php?pid=29610.

Democratic Party. 1996. "Democratic Party Platform of 1996." *The American Presidency Project,* August 26. Retrieved from http://www.presidency.ucsb.edu /ws/index.php?pid=29611.

Democratic Party. 2012. "Moving America Forward: 2012 Democratic Party Platform." *The American Presidency Project*, September 3. Retrieved from http://www.presidency.ucsb.edu/ws/index.php ?pid=101962.

Gore, A. 2012. "Climate of Denial: Can Science and the Truth Withstand the Merchants of Poison?" *Rolling Stone,* June 11. Retrieved from http://www .rollingstone.com/politics/news/climate-of-denial-20110622?print=true.

Harder, A. 2012. "On Climate, It's Not the Heat, It's the Timidity." *National Journal*, August 26. Retrieved from http://www.nationaljournal.com/daily/on-climate -it-s-not-the-heat-it-s-the-timidity-20120826.

Henneberger, M. 2012. "Sandy Puts Climate Change Back in the Conversation." *Washington Post,* November 1. Retrieved from http://www.washingtonpost .com/politics/decision2012/sandy-puts-climate-change-back-in-the -conversation/2012/11/01/685da046-2487-11e2-9313-3c7f59038d93print.html.

Jones, J. M. 2012. "Americans Want Next President to Prioritize Jobs, Corruption: Lowest Priorities Are Taxing Wealthy and Environmental Problems." *Gallup Politics*, July 30. Retrieved from http://www.gallup.com/poll/156347/americans -next-president-prioritize-jobs-corruption.aspx.

Kristof, N. D. 2012. "Will Climate Get Some Respect Now?" *New York Times,* October 31.

Malor, G. 2012. "Obama's Empty Climate Change Promises." *New York Daily News,* August 31. Retrieved from http://www.nydailynews.com/blogs/the_rumble /2012/08/obamas-empty-climate-change-promises.

McCarl, B. A., R. M. Adams, and B. H. Hurd. 2001. "Global Climate Change and Its Impact on Agriculture." February 6. Retrieved from http://agecon2.tamu.edu /people/faculty/mccarl-bruce/papers/879.pdf.

McKenna, G. 1997. *The Drama of Democracy: American Government and Politics,* 3rd ed. Guildford, CT: Dushkin.

McKibben, B. 2009. "Obama Should Act Urgently on Climate Change." *Washington Post,* November 22. Retrieved from http://www.washingtonpost.com/wp-dyn /content/article/2009/11/20/AR2009112002894.html.

New York Times. 1997. "Mr. Gore's Mission in Kyoto." December 4.

Obama, B. 2007. "Promoting a Healthy Environment." Portsmouth, NH. October 8. Retrieved from https://inlportal.inl.gov/portal/server.pt/document/71678/tab _7,_barack_obama_and_joe_biden_promoting_a_healthy_environment_pdf.

Obama, B. 2010. "Remarks on Signing a Memorandum Improving Energy Security, American Competitiveness and Job Creation, and Environmental Protection Through a Transformation of Our Nation's Fleet of Cars and Trucks." *The American Presidency Project,* May 21. Retrieved from http://www.presidency .ucsb.edu/ws/index.php?pid=87932.

Republican Party. 2012. "We Believe in America 2012: Republican Platform 2012." *GOP.com.* Retrieved from http://www.gop.com/wp-content/uploads /2012/08/2012GOPPlatform.pdf.

Romney, M. 2010. *No Apology: A Case for American Greatness.* New York: St. Martin's Press.

Romney, M. 2012. "Transcript: Mitt Romney's Acceptance Speech." *NPR,* August 30. Retrieved from http://www.npr.org/2012/08/30/160357612/transcript-mitt -romneys-acceptance-speech.

Roser-Renour, C., A. Leiserowitz, and E. Maibach. 2012. "The Political Benefits of Taking a Pro-Climate Stand in 2012." *Yale Project on Climate Change Communication.* George Mason University Center for Climate Change Communication. Retrieved from http://environment. yale.edu/climate/files/Political-Benefits-Pro-Climate-Stand.pdf.

Science Debate. 2012. "The Top American Science Questions: 2012. Candidates' Answers, a Side by Side Comparison." September 4. Retrieved from http:// www.sciencedebate.org/debate12/.

Shelby, H. 2012. "Is the Climate Crisis Up for Debate?" *Environmental Defense Fund.* Retrieved from http://support.edf.org/site/MessageViewer?em _id=23321.0

U.S. Congress. *Congressional Record.* 1997. 105th Cong., 1st sess. Vol. 143, pt. 11.

Washington Post. 2012. "President Obama's Acceptance Speech (Full Transcript)." November 7. Retrieved from http://www.washingtonpost.com/politics /decision2012/president-obamas-acceptance-speech-full-transcript /2012/11/07/ae133e44-28a5-11e2-96b6-8e6a7524553f_story.html.

Wenner, J. S. 2012. "Ready for the Fight: Rolling Stone Interview with Barack Obama: The President, in the Oval Office, Discusses His Job, the Position and the Coming Campaign." *Rolling Stone,* April 25. Retrieved from http://www .rollingstone.com/politics/news/ready-for-the-fight-rolling-stone-interview -with-barack-obama-20120425.

The White House, Office of the Press Secretary. "2013 Inaugural Address by President Barack Obama." January 21. Retrieved from http://www.whitehouse .gov/the-press-office/2013/01/21/inaugural-address-president-barack-obama.

Williamson, E. 2010. "Obama Retreats from Goal of Cap-Trade Bill." *Wall Street Journal,* February 3. Retrieved from http://online.wsj.com/article /SB10001424052748704022804575041632860721438.html.

NOTES

1. Jeffrey M. Jones, "Americans Want Next President to Prioritize Jobs, Corruption," Gallup, http://www.gallup.com/poll/156347/americans-next-president-prioritize -jobs-corruption.aspx (accessed September 24, 2012).

III. Foreign Policy

Chapter 11

American Exceptionalism and the Elections of 1976, 1980, and 2012

Stephen D. Wrage, United States Naval Academy

INTRODUCTION

A number of indicators suggested that the concept of American exceptionalism would figure importantly in the presidential election of 2012, particularly in the campaign strategy of the Republican challenger, Mitt Romney. Prime among these indicators was the high level of popular concern that America had "lost its way" as evidenced by the response poll takers received to the "Is America on the right track?" question. When the question "All in all, do you think things in the nation are generally headed in the right direction, or do you feel things are off on the wrong track?" was asked by pollsters for CBS in February 2009, 81 percent of the respondents among 1,475 likely voters nationwide declared that the country was "on the wrong track." At that time, President Barack Obama had been in office for only two months and the sudden economic downturn had been under way for roughly five months. In October 2012, after the downturn had persisted for four years and Obama had nearly completed a term in office, opinion had shifted almost not at all as the same question brought 75 percent saying they thought the country was on the wrong track (Real Clear Politics 2012). Such extremely high numbers on this question typically indicate a major vulnerability on the part of the incumbent.

The issue of American exceptionalism ought to have offered a vein of gold for the Romney campaign to mine because variations of exceptionalist propositions could be counted on to play well with many of the groups they needed to mobilize. Tea Party members, for example, could be expected to respond well to warnings against a falling away from long-standing American patriotic virtues. Evangelicals would answer calls to remember that America was founded by devoted believers in a quest for religious freedom. Neoconservatives would respond to a candidate who promised what that group likes to call "a foreign policy of American greatness" dedicated to sharing America's unique gift of democracy with the world. Cultural conservatives would rise to a call to return to a golden age of pure values.

Moreover, Romney personally would find American exceptionalism congenial to his principles and faith since the Mormon religion upholds traditional, individual, and patriotic themes, and champions what conservatives call "family values." Mormonism is among the most exceptionalist of religions in that it preaches a concept of "chosenness" and teaches that its founding members were descendants of one of the lost tribes of Israel. A Utah state senator, Mike Lee, has said, "Mormons sort of have an extra chromosome when it comes to American exceptionalism. Mormons do have an added dose of a belief in American exceptionalism" (Bagley 2012).

Finally, Obama offered Romney an extraordinary opportunity and vulnerability when he declared at a press conference at the NATO summit in Strasbourg in April 2009 that he believed in American exceptionalism "just as I suspect Brits believe in British exceptionalism and Greeks believe in Greek exceptionalism" (White House Press Office 2009). This "Lake Wobegon" reading of exceptionalism, in which "all the [countries] are above average," was bound to infuriate true believers in America's specialness and so excite and delight the campaign consultants of all the many would-be Republican candidates.

All these factors would make exceptionalism a natural theme for Romney's campaign, and in any case, talking about America's uniqueness and importance in world history always offers a good way for any candidate to appear statesmanlike, thoughtful, deep-thinking and—the campaign designers hope—presidential. Curiously, however, the theme of exceptionalism did not figure very large in the 2012 campaign. To explore the possibility that American exceptionalism offered a number of missed opportunities to the Romney campaign, it is helpful to look at the Carter campaigns of 1976 and the Reagan campaign of 1980 and characterize how those candidates employed exceptionalist themes. First, however, one should consider how to think about exceptionalism and how it might function in campaigns and elections.

ON EXCEPTIONALISM, AMERICAN AND OTHERWISE

There is nothing exceptional about Americans believing themselves exceptional. The populations of many countries are seized with the conviction that they are unique, unparalleled, possessed by some great historical purpose, descended from divine origins, favored by their god, granted a divine mission to accomplish some great purpose, or in some other way destined to achieve vast or even transcendent ends. Obama's remark at Strasbourg thus was accurate, if impolitic.

Exceptionalism centers on exactly that proposition: that one's country (or subnational group) is uniquely important in history, that it is in some way chosen or has a mission that sets it apart. Anthropologists have observed that many tribes, including Stone Age peoples living in New Guinea, label themselves with a grand and universal title like "The Human Beings" and imagine themselves the original and most favored inhabitants of the globe (Turnbull 1972). Social anthropologists and historians have long observed that groups of many kinds and sizes hold and propagate shared propositions about their uniqueness and importance to maintain cohesion and strengthen bonds that unite their members.

It is possible to assemble out of the works of William H. McNeill (1982), David Kertzer (1988), Murray Edelman (1985), and Michael Kammen (1993) an approach to the study of exceptionalism based on anthropology and collective memory that might be called the "symbol, ritual, and myth approach." This approach begins with the empirical observation that the state is invisible. Although the state is tremendously powerful and can tax, imprison, draft, and even execute its citizens, it cannot be sensed by them directly. It has no look, taste, sound, smell, or feel and so it can be perceived only through its works and through various symbols such as flags, national buildings, monuments, statues, and maps. Famous among these for different countries are the Statue of Liberty, the Eiffel Tower, Buckingham Palace, the Brandenburg Gate, Red Square, and the Parthenon. Personifications also serve this function and include Uncle Sam, John Bull, and Emperor Hirohito.

Such symbols can be seen, but to be experienced more actively they can also be embedded in rituals, which are formalized, repeated activities in which people participate, usually in groups. The national anthem played before a baseball game is such a ritual. A presidential inauguration is another such ritual. A political campaign can contain many aspects of ritual. A stump speech, for example, has a number of formalized, repeated aspects and an audience recognizes the ritual moments when it is intended to applaud. A debate between or among political candidates has many ritual aspects as well. When members of societies gather together and act in patterned ways meaningful to them, they feel the bonds of solidarity among themselves strengthened.

These symbols and rituals are in turn linked together by dramatic narratives that can best be called political myths. Myths is an appropriate term not because the narratives are fairy tales but because they contain not strictly rational propositions that are, nonetheless, of profound and even transcendent importance (Tudor 1973). These myths convey the propositions that lie behind a sense of national exceptionalism. An example might make this theoretical concept clearer.

In Concord, Massachusetts, where the author went to high school, the 18th of April was a date of special significance on the civic calendar (Bellah 1967). "The eighteenth of April, in seventy-five" is a phrase persons raised in America will recall from the Longfellow poem, "The Midnight Ride of Paul Revere." (Longfellow 1864). Every year on that night there was a Patriots' Day dance at the high school while older people gathered at the Unitarian Universalist church by the Common in the old town center. At midnight, a man on horseback came galloping down the road from Lexington shouting "The British are coming! The British are coming!" and everyone would disperse to their homes around Concord, Acton, Carlisle, and Bedford to collect their muskets and begin a long, cold, and often wet tramp through the woods to the Old North Bridge over the Concord River near town. (Our family kept three replica muskets, one each for my father, my brother, and me.) Year after year we would walk all night to cover the nine miles from our house to the bridge,[1] being sure to arrive there shortly after dawn where we would find hundreds of others forming up on the side of the river across from town. Every year a set of Revolutionary War British soldier reenactors from Connecticut would appear with their elegant red coats and high black boots and every year a descendant of Colonel Buttrick would cry out, "Will you let them burn the town?" We would all shout "No!" and the few of us who had muskets that could make a sound would "exchange fire" with the British on the bridge. Two or three of them would fall down "dead," we would all cheer, then we would walk into town for a pancake breakfast put on by one of the civic clubs.

The symbols in this ritual included the muskets, the tricorn hats, the scraps of Minuteman uniform we pulled together, and the bridge itself. The ritual included the march, the words of Paul Revere and Colonel Buttrick, the exchange of fire, and the cheering. The narrative or political myth we were all reenacting was captured in a few lines spoken by 19th-century Concord resident Ralph Waldo Emerson on the occasion of the dedication of the statue at the bridge by which we would gather (Buell 2003, 5):

> By the rude bridge that arched the flood
> Their flag to April's breeze unfurled.
> Here once the embattled farmers stood
> And fired the shot heard round the world.[2]

The propositions that lie behind these symbols, rituals, and myths would be difficult to list exhaustively but the narrative surrounding "the Concord fight" features the ideas that America's foundation was the work of stalwart individuals acting in unison and inspired and united by the transcendent cause of freedom; that they struggled against long odds, inspired amateurs against trained professionals; and that their daring acts reach across time. Such propositions, with variations for culture, history, and geography, lie at the very core of most groups' sense of exceptionalism. The expression of these propositions is often the work of authors and artists such as Henry Wadsworth Longfellow, Ralph Waldo

Emerson, and Daniel Chester French, but the participation in the rituals involves the entire populace. In that way, rituals serve to propagate and reinforce beliefs that may be articulated by elites but in the end are held by almost all the citizenry.

Other symbols, rituals, and myths propagate other propositions of American exceptionalism. Plymouth, Massachusetts, is the site of annual rituals to parallel Concord's, though they convey other themes of American exceptionalism, including that America was founded in a quest for religious freedom, that (again) a few stalwart individuals were sustained by their faith, that they believed themselves to be chosen by God, and that the outcome confirmed their belief. The words of their minister and leader, Governor John Winthrop, became a central text of American exceptionalism: "For it must be considered that we shall be as a City upon a Hill. The eyes of all the world are upon us" (Winthrop 1630). This sermon was delivered mid-ocean on the way to the new world. His optimism and hyperbole are striking since at that time his tiny fleet was scattered and still weeks from landfall. In fact, the eyes of no one were upon them and they themselves did not know where they were or if they would survive. In words taken from the Sermon on the Mount and including a reference to the heavenly city of Jerusalem, the exceptionalist idea that America is a precious model toward which all the world shall move was established.

In other countries, the symbols, rituals, and myths that establish the nation's exceptionalism often have been expressed by their greatest literary figures. Homer did this for the Greeks. As Northrop Frye observed (Hart 1994, 85–86), the *Iliad* taught Greeks everything they needed to know about how to behave in battle, how to honor the gods, how to treat captives, how to lead in counsel, even how a king should implore the man who killed his son to return the body. The *Iliad* encapsulated the essence of "Greekness" and expressed Greek exceptionalism.

Caesar's heir commissioned Virgil to produce a similar work for Rome. His epic poem, the *Aeneid*, patterned on the *Iliad*, told the story of one Trojan prince as he escaped the burning city bringing his father, his son, and his household gods with him. Aeneas traveled west to Carthage, where he had an affair with and abandoned the Carthaginian queen (so explaining the inveterate hatred between the cities of Carthage

and Rome), then founded Rome and began to make war on the inhabitants of Italy. Virgil is explicit in laying out the essence of Roman exceptionalism in Book VI where he says "others will more delicately shape
breathing statues out of marble and trace out the paths of the stars in the
heavens, but to rule nations with power, to dictate the terms of peace, to
spare the conquered and to war down the proud—these shall be thy arts"
(Virgil).

What Homer did for the Greeks and Virgil did for the Romans,
Shakespeare did for the English, Victor Hugo for the French, and Tolstoy
for the Russians. Americans have had no such epic author, but American
leaders, from John Winthrop through Thomas Jefferson to Abraham
Lincoln, produced political rhetoric in the form of the sermon aboard
the *Arabella*, the Declaration of Independence, and the Gettysburg
Address that told narratives that outlined their core propositions of
American exceptionalism.

It may be that America has a greater need for national narratives than
other countries because it has faced geographic, demographic, cultural,
historical, and political issues that were not quickly resolvable. Unlike
Japan, for example, whose geographic extent is determined by the seas
that surround it, America's boundaries remained in flux all the way from
1620 through 1959. Unlike Korea, which is demographically uniform in
its ethnicity, America has "contained multitudes" and has needed figures
like Walt Whitman to explain us to ourselves. Unlike England, America
has not had a rich history of kings stretching back to Roman times, and
unlike many smaller states, America has urgently needed to explore and
explain its global purposes, especially since the end of the 19th century.
Narratives about America as model or America as the champion of
democracy or America as the "melting pot" have helped manage these
complex and interlinked issues.

THE CAMPAIGNS OF 1976 AND 1980

What do these observations about exceptionalism say regarding the
political campaigns of 1976, 1980, and 2012? First, they suggest that exceptionalism should figure in a campaign. An appeal to and an affirmation
of American exceptionalism is expected, subliminally at least, by the
people at whom the campaign is directed. If it is absent, the candidate

may seem shallow to them and the campaign may seem hollow. Exceptionalism should figure especially in a challenger's campaign since the challenger needs to excite a strong voter reaction to overcome the incumbent's advantage and needs to "invent himself" in the minds of the voters. He needs to create an identity for himself and lay down the logic of his foreign policy. All this can be done by speaking to America's purpose in the world.

Peggy Noonan, the campaign consultant who did most to help Ronald Reagan exploit American exceptionalism, remarked on the absence of any discussion of America's purpose and destiny in the Romney campaign. In June 2012 she complained that Romney's campaign was trying too hard to keep the focus on attacking Obama and warned that the campaign needed a larger context and purpose. "People want meaning, a higher and declared purpose," she wrote (Noonan 2012).

"With just more than 130 days to go, Romney has to start pulling from his brain and soul a coherent and graspable sense of the meaning of his run. 'I will be president for this reason and this. I will move for this and this. The philosophy that impels me consists of these things'" (Noonan 2012). In this column and many subsequent ones, she argued that the Romney campaign has "always been too small for the moment" (Noonan 2012). By invoking American exceptionalism, the Romney campaign could have addressed this need, while at the same time speaking to the neoconservatives, the Tea Party, the religious right, the cultural conservatives, the evangelical vote, and many others disposed to feel that America had lost track of its animating spirit.

Exceptionalism should figure in a political campaign especially in a year when exceptionalism is in doubt. In 1976, a year after the fall of Saigon, in a country thrown into recession by the oil shock of 1973, speaking to a society that had watched the demoralizing scandals of Watergate, the Church and Pike committee hearings into bungled CIA assassinations and attempted overthrows of foreign governments, and the revelations of bribery by Lockheed and others, Carter appealed directly and forcefully to American exceptionalism by declaring that America had lost its way and was behaving like an ordinary country, only worse. In 1980, a year after the Soviet invasion of Afghanistan and the continuing display of American impotence during the 444 days the hostages were held in our embassy in Iran, at a time of "stagflation" following the second oil shock, Reagan dealt with the prevailing sense of malaise by simply and boldly asserting American exceptionalism. "It's morning in America." he declared (Troy 2005, 153). By contrast, in 2012, with America exhausted by two unwon wars and an unwinnable war on terror, preoccupied in Central Asia while China overshadowed East and Southeast Asia, and saddled with a listless economy growing less than those of many African and Latin American countries, Romney offered a businessman's assessment: that he could provide better budgetary management. Carter and Reagan, as will be shown below, took up an opportunity that Romney missed.

Exceptionalism can be used to derive an identity for a candidate. Confronted with the crisis in American confidence of 1976, Carter depicted himself as "Jimmy," an honest, forthright, and dedicated person who promised frequently in his campaign speeches "I will never lie to you"[3] (PBS). He offered the country himself, replicating the "self-made man" narrative from American history when he appeared outside factories shaking hands and introducing himself as an unknown: "I'm Jimmy Carter and I'm running for president" (Greenstein 2004). Confronted with low morale and great uncertainty in 1980, Reagan presented himself as the quintessential man of the American West, a figure he had played in many movies. "America is standing tall," he declared, and he offered himself as an example of it doing so (Troy 2005, 153). Romney in 2012 did not derive an identity from American exceptionalism but rather presented himself as a successful businessman and a hugely wealthy manager of money, some of which he had inherited from his hugely wealthy father, also a politician. While Carter offered his person and Reagan offered his image, Romney offered his "five point plan" (MittRomneyCentral).

American exceptionalism can also be exploited to create a sense of a historic and magnificent backdrop to a campaign. Carter promised to lead us back into the paths that our forefathers were the first to tread. Reagan promised to prevail in the Cold War and push back the encroachments of godless Communism. Romney repeated his five-point plan.

Symbols and rituals central to American exceptionalism can be presented dramatically, even cinematically. Carter had no genius for this and there is no memorable image from his campaign. The single memorable image from his presidency is the handshake between Anwar Sadat and Menachem Begin on the White House lawn with Carter posed behind the two men. Reagan, by contrast, left the mental imprint of many cinematic instants: Reagan at the Normandy Landing, Reagan at the Korean DMZ, Reagan walking in Red Square. There is enduring political force in the image of Reagan at the Berlin Wall delivering the unforgettable line, "Mister Gorbachev, tear down this wall" (Boyd 1987). In all the decades of America dealing with hijackers and terrorists, no president has tapped into American exceptionalist sentiment the way Reagan did with the line he delivered after the 1985 *Achille Lauro* incident: "You can run, but you can't hide" (Reeves 2005). Reagan knew how to make the most out of the classic patriotic ritual of laying a wreath at the graves of American soldiers, and he was following the example of Lincoln at Gettysburg, yet adding cinematic value, when he went to Normandy and delivered his speech honoring "The Boys of Pointe du Hoq." Reagan had the help of fine handlers and producers and writers, but part of their genius was that they understood American exceptionalism and could see the power in a phrase like "city on a hill." When Peggy Noonan resurrected that phrase for Reagan, she was reaching back to 1630 from 1980. Three hundred and fifty years is a very long time in American history and proves the enduring power of such exceptionalist images. By contrast, the Romney campaign produced no memorable phrase or moment, unless it were the disastrous, secretly recorded remarks he delivered at a Republican party fundraiser in which he wrote off 47 percent of the electorate (Rutenberg 2012). That incident, plus the trip abroad to England and Israel that was intended to produce such phrases and moments must be painful for the candidate and his staff to recall.

American exceptionalism can be exploited by the use of a foil. Carter used Richard Nixon as a foil and deployed Henry Kissinger as Nixon's foreign affairs alter ego. He linked them both in his speeches to the CIA, Chile, Lockheed, and Watergate but also to détente and to inappropriately cordial relations with Ferdinand Marcos, Anastasio Somoza, and the Shah of Iran. He depicted both men as people who did not believe sufficiently in America's values and he used surrogates such as Tom Farer to brand Kissinger as "that cynical, ruthless child of Europe who hijacked America's foreign policy" (Farer 1980). All-American, Midwestern Gerald

Ford was harder to caricature as foreign, but Carter mocked him all the same when he called Henry Kissinger "the Lone Ranger of American foreign policy," since that left Ford to be his faithful Indian companion, Tonto. Carter also derived tactical advantage from this depiction of his adversaries. When he evoked American exceptionalism by championing human rights he could bring his Republican opponents under bracketing fire by appealing to those who found Nixon's dealings with Moscow under the terms of détente too accommodating of the totalitarians and at the same time appealing to those who found Nixon's close dealings with the shah, Marcos, and Somoza too supportive of ugly dictators.

Reagan treated the entire Soviet Union as his foil and he tapped into exceptionalist beliefs by declaring Moscow "the focus of evil in the modern world" (Busch 2001). Americans reacted with warm approval to the image of the United States standing up to the Evil Empire. His remarks effectively drained the remaining dregs of legitimacy from the nearly empty vessel of the Soviet Union, and they set the events of the revitalized Cold War before a dramatic backdrop of good and evil, endowing it with titanic shadows. (The effect was somewhat diminished when, three years later, Reagan had to announce that he no longer viewed the Soviet Union as a "focus of evil") (Meisler 1988).

Romney also sought a foil, but in doing so failed to sense the possibilities inherent in Americans' deep beliefs about themselves. (This is ironic since he was attacking his opponent for exactly that failing.) Romney displayed no larger sense of purpose than to snipe at his opponent, however, and in this endeavor he fell in line with a long train of others who had for many months been pressing the issue of Obama as a socialist, a Kenyan, an enemy of the Constitution, and a threat to America. This issue had been worked since 2007 by Sarah Palin, Michelle Bachmann, Mike Huckabee, Herman Cain, Rick Perry, Donald Trump, Rick Santorum, and most of all Newt Gingrich (Martin 2010). Romney himself wrote in his 2010 book *No Apology: The Case for American Greatness*, "This reorientation away from the celebration of American exceptionalism is misguided and bankrupt" (Romney 2010). Newt Gingrich outstripped Romney in this overworked effort, however, going so far as to costar in a movie about American exceptionalism. His costar was Callista Gingrich. Newt was his own producer and the effort was funded by an offshoot of the organization he headed, Citizens United Productions. Michelle Bachmann appeared in the film and Donald Trump appears in the trailer saying, "American exceptionalism is a really great term, and it's something that is very special to us. And by the way, we have to be very, very careful to protect it and cherish it because it can also disappear." The film was not scheduled for a wide release (CBS News 2011).

CONCLUSION

In summary, then, the Romney campaign missed significant opportunities to expand and deepen the appeal and impact of his candidacy and, surprisingly, it was the central theme of American exceptionalism that he failed to exploit. The chapter has had nothing to say about Obama's exploitation of American exceptionalism because he did even less in 2012 than his opponent to evoke and draw on exceptionalist ideas. As the incumbent, he faced less need to do so and as a matter of strategy he undoubtedly wanted to avoid revitalizing this overworked line of attack on him. It should be noted, however, that he made what appears to have been an offhand remark that could reveal a great deal about his personal understanding of American exceptionalism. He made it as long ago as November 2007 in an interview with James Traub of the *New York Times Magazine* (Traub 2007): "If you can tell people, 'We have a president in the White House who still has a grandmother living in a hut on the shores of Lake Victoria and has a sister who's half-Indonesian, married to a Chinese-Canadian,' then they're going to think that he may have a better sense of what's going on in our lives and in our country. And they'd be right." This remark, not repeated elsewhere in the campaign so far as the author could determine, suggests that Obama has rethought the nature of American exceptionalism. Although Obama never repeated this remark, so far as the author could determine, that moment of unscripted candor may begin to delineate a more resonant, more current, and more genuine meaning for the term "American exceptionalism," one that diverges dramatically from the clichéd meaning of the phrase. Instead of evoking scenes stretching from the Founding Fathers in Philadelphia to "The Greatest Generation" (as is typical when it is used by Reagan, Gingrich, or Romney), this reference to a grandmother in Kenya and a sister with a background in Indonesia and her husband who came to America from China via Canada reflects the life stories of many Americans alive today who would like to believe that they, too, helped make America unique and excellent. In that line of thought future campaigns may find golden ore to mine for electoral victory.

REFERENCES

Bagley, P. 2012. "Living History: Mormons' Exceptional Belief in American Exceptionalism." *Salt Lake Tribune,* June 23. Retrieved from http://www.sltrib .com/sltrib/news/54359356-78/mormons-god-american-exceptionalism.html .csp.

Bellah, R. N. 1967. "Civil Religion in America." *Daedalus* 96 (1): 1–21.

Boyd, G. M. 1987. "Raze Berlin Wall, Reagan Urges Soviet." *New York Times,* June 13. Retrieved from http://www.nytimes.com/1987/06/13/world/raze-berlin-wall -reagan-urges-soviet.html.

Buell, L. 2003. *Emerson.* Cambridge, MA: Harvard University Press.

Busch, A. 2001. *Ronald Reagan and the Politics of Freedom.* New York: Rowman and Littlefield, 197.

CBS News. 2011. "Newt Gingrich to Star in Citizens United Movie about 'American Exceptionalism.'" Retrieved from http://www.cbsnews.com/8301-503544_162 -20057495-503544.html.

Edelman, M. 1985. *The Symbolic Uses of Politics.* Champagne: University of Illinois Press.

Farer, T. 1980. *Toward a Humanitarian Diplomacy: A Primer for Policy.* New York: New York University Press.

Greenstein, F. I. 2004. *The Presidential Difference: Leadership Style from FDR to George W. Bush.* Princeton: Princeton University Press, 127–129.

Hart, J. L. 1994. *Northrop Frye: The Theoretical Imagination.* New York: Psychology Press.

Kammen, M. 1993. *Mystic Chords of Memory.* New York: Vintage.

Kertzer, D. 1988. *Ritual, Politics and Power.* New Haven: Yale University Press.

Longfellow, H. W. 1864. "The Midnight Ride of Paul Revere." In *Tales of a Wayside Inn.* Boston: Ticknor and Fields.

Martin, J. 2010. "The New Battle: What It Means to Be an American." *Politico,* August 20. Retrieved from http://www.politico.com/news/stories/0810/41273 .html#ixzz2GCd8vdTt.

McNeill, W. H. 1982. "The Care and Repair of Public Myth." *Foreign Affairs* 61 (1): 1–13.

Meisler, S. 1988. "Reagan Recants 'Evil Empire' Description." *Los Angeles Times,* June 1. Retrieved from http://articles.latimes.com/1988-06-01/news/mn -3667_1_evil-empire.

MittRomneyCentral. "Mitt Romney's Five Point Plan." Retrieved from http:// mittromneycentral.com/tag/five-point-plan/.

Noonan, P. 2012. "Once More, with Meaning." *Wall Street Journal,* June 22. Retrieved from http://online.wsj.com/article /SB10001424052702304898704577480853621956184.html.

PBS. *The American Experience: Jimmy Carter.* Retrieved from http://www.pbs.org /wgbh/americanexperience/features/transcript/carter-transcript/.

Real Clear Politics. 2012. December 10. Retrieved from http://www .realclearpolitics.com/epols/other/direction_of_country-902.html.

Reeves, R. 2005. *Ronald Reagan: The Triumph of the Imagination.* New York: Simon & Schuster, 277.

Romney, M. 2010. *No Apology: The Case for American Greatness.* New York: Macmillan, 263.

Rutenberg, J. 2012. "Romney Says Remarks on Voters Help Clarify Position." *New York Times,* September 8. Retrieved from http://www.nytimes.com/2012 /09/19/us/politics/in-leaked-video-romney-says-middle-east-peace-process -likely-to-remain-unsolved-problem.html?pagewanted=all&_r=0.

Traub, J. 2007. "Is (His) Biography (Our) Destiny?" *New York Times Magazine,* November 4. Retrieved from http://www.nytimes.com/2007/11/04/magazine /04obama-t.html?pagewanted=all&_r=0.

Troy, G. 2005. *Morning in America: How Ronald Reagan Invented the 1980s.* Princeton: Princeton University Press.

Tudor, H. 1973. *Political Myth.* London: Macmillan.

Turnbull, C. 1972. *The Mountain People.* New York: Simon & Schuster.

Virgil. *The Aeneid,* Book VI, lines 849–853 (author's translation).

White House Press Office, Press Release. 2009. April 4. Retrieved from http://www .whitehouse.gov/the-press-office/news-conference-president-obama -4042009.

Winthrop, J. 1630. "A Model of Christian Charity" in *Collections of the Massachu-setts Historical Society,* 3rd series (7), 31–38. Retrieved from http://history .hanover.edu/texts/winthmod.html.

NOTES

1. The organizers of the walk would strike a different commemorative medallion each year to distribute to the participants. The author finds he has kept six such medallions.

2. The stanza quoted is inscribed on the base of the Minuteman statue by Concord resident Daniel Chester French, a sculptor who also created the statue of Abraham Lincoln in the Lincoln Memorial in Washington.

3. The program begins quoting Carter: "I promised you four years ago that I would never lie to you. So I can't stand here tonight and say it doesn't hurt. About an hour ago I called Governor Reagan in California and I congratulated him for a fine victory. I look forward to working closely with him."

Chapter 12

President Obama's National Security and Counterterrorism Strategy and the Presidential Election of 2012

Leonard Cutler, Siena College

INTRODUCTION

In early May 2012, on the one-year anniversary of the death of Osama bin Laden, President Barack Obama made an unannounced visit to Afghanistan to sign a Strategic Partnership Agreement with President Hamid Karzai that established broad conditions for Afghan-U.S. relations after the departure of American fighting forces in 2014. The president spoke to an American television audience from Bagram Airbase as he thanked over 3,000 cheering troops assembled in an aircraft hangar that displayed several armored vehicles and the American flag. Mr. Obama said, "One year ago, from a base in Afghanistan, our troops launched the operation that killed Osama bin Laden. The goal I set—to defeat Al Qaeda, and deny it a chance to rebuild—is now within our reach" (Landler 2012). This was the president's first speech on Afghanistan in almost a year, and it came just before two major campaign rallies that served as the symbolic kickoff of Mr. Obama's reelection drive, which was designed in part to resonate with Americans' weariness with the war by emphasizing the withdrawal of 33,000 troops by September, leaving around 68,000 U.S. soldiers there, and a grand total of close to 100,000 NATO troops.

STRATEGIC PARTNERSHIP AGREEMENT

Although the agreement is vague with respect to specifics, this much we do know:

- American combat troops will be withdrawn by December 2014 and Afghan troops will be ready to take over principal responsibility for that nation's national security.
- The pact does not commit the United States to any specific troop presence or spending. It does allow the United States to maintain a limited support role in Afghanistan through 2024 to continue to train Afghan forces and to target operations against Al Qaeda. Estimates of the number of troops that could stay vary from as few as 10,000 to as many as 25,000 to 30,000.
- United States and NATO troops were to step back from a combat role to training and counterterrorism operations by mid-2013, a year earlier than originally expected.
- The United States pledged assistance for the next decade in developing the Afghan economy as well as public institutions.
- Afghanistan agreed to commit to inclusive and pluralistic democratic governance including free, fair, and transparent elections.
- The goal is not to build Afghanistan in America's image, or to eradicate every vestige of the Taliban, because these objectives would require too many years, dollars, and additional American lives.
- As part of an effort to broker a political settlement between the Afghan government and the Taliban, the Obama administration undertook direct discussions with the Taliban because many members from foot soldiers to leaders indicated an interest in reconciliation.

Despite the suggestion that various factions of the Taliban expressed interest in negotiations, the administration's leverage became all the more limited as the U.S. military presence phased down. The Taliban may have been willing to engage in talks without agreeing to anything while waiting it out to see what would happen after 2014. The Partnership Agreement was the administration's signal to the Taliban that waiting it out would not work since there would still be a NATO presence in Afghanistan after 2014. However, in reality, the shape and content of any negotiations would be directly linked to what happened on the battlefield, and therefore the Taliban did not commit to substantially diminishing its power, such as by disarming before 2014 (Brookings Institution 2012, 5–6).

Just a few weeks before the election the Obama administration virtually conceded that any strategy to end the war by engaging directly with the Taliban was essentially abandoned. This meant that any progress that would be made would come after 2014, once NATO forces withdrew and the Afghan government and military assumed full responsibility for the country. For a short period of time there had appeared to be a window of opportunity given preliminary talks earlier in 2012 in Qatar, but that effort fell apart when the Obama administration, confronted with bipartisan opposition from the Congress and within the Pentagon, could not make good on a proposed prisoner swap in which five Taliban leaders held at Guantanamo would have been exchanged for the sole American held by the insurgents. That trade was to have been an initial confidence-building measure that would have led to more serious negotiations. Any further attempt to revive negotiations thus would have to wait until after the presidential election, sometime later in 2013 (Rosenberg and Nordland 2012).

STRATEGIC COUNTERTERRORISM IN AFGHANISTAN

Under President Obama, Afghanistan had become the military's top priority in the war against Al Qaeda and the Taliban. The number of troops had surged, and counterinsurgency and nation-building had become the early core strategies. Obama's principal goal had been to promote good governance and legitimacy in the eyes of the local population (Cutler 2011).

Obama's strategy revolved around denying sanctuary to the insurgents. Training local security forces to hold territory so the insurgents could not return was pivotal. Building infrastructure and eliminating political corruption, thereby winning the "hearts and minds" of the population, was a key part of the plan. Local governments had to take the lead in any longer-term strategy since they had more legitimacy and were familiar with the language, culture, geography, history, and political landscape (Cutler 2011). Daniel Benjamin of the U.S. Department of State's new Bureau of Counterterrorism, in testimony before the House Foreign Affairs Subcommittee on Terrorism, Nonproliferation and Trade, insisted that what is pivotal for strategic counterterrorism is building partner capacity to help countries develop their own law enforcement and legal institutions to do a better job tracking, apprehending, arresting, prosecuting, and incarcerating terrorists, while at the same time respecting human rights and securing their borders (Benjamin 2012).

The Obama administration narrowed its goals in Afghanistan until it could make the case that America had achieved limited objectives in a war that was, in any traditional sense, unwinnable. Upon the redeployment of the 33,000 additional troops that President Obama originally ordered to Afghanistan to tamp down the Taliban, the administration declared that the surge had accomplished its mission. It reversed the momentum on the battlefield and dramatically increased the size and capability of the indigenous Afghan National Security Forces. This was considered a very important milestone for the United States in achieving its goals in Afghanistan.

The U.S. war against Al Qaeda has become a war against the Taliban and the Pashtun, the tribes living in both Afghanistan and Pakistan who have been successfully fighting foreign adversaries for several centuries. No one to date has ever effectively defeated the Pashtuns—not the British, the Soviets, or now, the Americans. The longer term commitment made by President Obama sent a message to the Afghans that Washington would not abandon them as it had after the Soviets were defeated, despite long-term and acute challenges the Taliban-led insurgency and its Al Qaeda affiliates present from sanctuaries within Pakistan. Afghanistan's close partnership with the United States and the NATO allies will continue well beyond the end of the transition period. A report released by the Pentagon last year detailed these concerns in addition to the endemic corruption and incompetence that have been the hallmark of the Karzai leadership and have alienated so many Afghans, accruing to the benefit of the Taliban (U.S. Department of Defense 2012, 6–7).

As the U.S. and NATO military and civilian presence and spending decrease, there will be a direct impact on the economy of Afghanistan. It remains highly questionable whether the Afghan government will be able to hold its own given the reduced American support, particularly since the strategic pact did not contain any U.S. dollar commitments. Therefore, what will be required is annual appropriation and authorization of funding by the U.S. Congress.

What further exacerbates the situation for the president is that this war is the longest in American history. Separate and apart from the loss of lives, American as well as Afghan, the war has cost over a trillion dollars, and, according to the Congressional Research Service (2012), it cost American taxpayers $198 billion for FY 2013 as compared to $43.5 billion as recently as FY 2008 (Cordesman 2012). Given the American public's desire to disengage from the Afghanistan front, continued support from the Congress could not be assured, particularly in an election year when the White House was up for grabs, as was control of both houses of Congress.

Two months after the Strategic Partnership Agreement was announced, Secretary of State Hillary Clinton represented the United States at a major international donors conference convened in Tokyo. The conference was attended by over 70 countries and organizations whose purpose was to pledge $16 billion in aid for Afghanistan over the next four years in the hope of stabilizing that country as foreign combat forces returned home. Secretary Clinton briefly visited with Afghan president Hamid Karzai before she formally attended the meeting in Tokyo.

On behalf of the Obama administration, Secretary Clinton declared Afghanistan to be the newest U.S. major non-NATO ally, and confirmed that the president was requesting at least one billion dollars from the Congress to assist Afghanistan to improve governance and finance management, and to safeguard the democratic process, rule of law, and human rights (especially the rights of women). The message to President Karzai was firm: the $16 billion would come with strict conditions that Afghanistan not fall victim to rampant government corruption and mismanagement. It was also reassuring that Mrs. Clinton emphasized that the partnership between the United States and Afghanistan would be enduring far into the future.

America remains a vital lifeline for Afghan president Hamid Karzai's control of the country and Prime Minister Nawaz Sharif's government in Pakistan. The United States needs Pakistan's cooperation to successfully withdraw troops from Afghanistan in 2013 and further down the road in 2014. Continued American economic and military aid is critical given the vulnerability that exists to the Pashtun Taliban, the feared Haqqani network, and the Lashkar-e-Taiba terrorist organization, all of which have links to Al Qaeda and are committed to the destabilization of both nations.

Increasing instability and turmoil would make it irresistible for outside actors, including Iran, Russia, China, and India, to cultivate their favored proxies to prosecute their objectives in Afghanistan, Pakistan, and the region. Pakistan, with a population of over 180 million people, has a very active insurgency, an expanding nuclear arsenal with a stockpile of over 100 nuclear warheads, and is developing light transportable nuclear weapons that can easily be brought to its border with India. Pakistan is perched at the crossroads of the Middle East and South Asia, which makes it susceptible to terrorist attacks, and its vulnerability to Islamist extremists presents a considerable concern and threat to U.S. national security, much more so than does Afghanistan.

The Defense Department report noted that the "share of overall violence has grown in eastern Afghanistan, a base for militants from the Haqqani network whose sophisticated attacks on Western targets may reflect a shift in military strategy" (U.S. Department of Defense 2012, 104–105). As the former chair of the Joint Chiefs of Staff, Admiral Mike Mullen, stated in 2011, the Pakistan-based Haqqani network continues to threaten a stable political solution in Afghanistan, and has become a proxy for Pakistan's intelligence services (Miller and DeYoung 2011, 1–2). In many ways, the Haqqanis are their own masters since they enjoy financial autonomy thanks to a tribal crime empire based on extortion, smuggling, and kidnapping. The Obama administration has officially designated the Haqqani network as a terrorist body, which bans Americans from doing any business with members of the group and blocks any assets it holds in the United States. It is a bitter irony that this action completely reverses the partnership that existed with the CIA during the Cold War when the American government hailed them as freedom fighters.

STRATEGIC COUNTERTERRORISM IN PAKISTAN

Divergent national security and strategic interests between the United States and Pakistan make cooperation between these governments very difficult. A major setback occurred in November 2011 when 24 Pakistani troops were accidentally killed in U.S. airstrikes during a cross-border attack. Pakistan cut off all land-based supply routes in Afghanistan, and none were permitted to reopen. Before the routes were closed, NATO convoys were paying an average of about $250 a truck, but the Pakistani government demanded $5,000 for each truck carrying supplies as a condition for permitting the United States and NATO access across its territory.

Thousands of trucks a day carried supplies from Pakistan to Afghanistan. The United States shifted deliveries to routes through Russia and other central Asian countries for providing the needed war supplies into Afghanistan. The impasse with Pakistan was not resolved at the May 2012 NATO summit in Chicago, and President Obama admitted that major tensions and real challenges continued to exist. Reopening the land route through Pakistan was vital to hauling vast stores of military equipment and vehicles out of Afghanistan during the next couple of years. After considerable backchannel negotiations between Thomas R. Nides, a deputy to Secretary of State Clinton, and Abdul Hafeez Shaikh, Pakistan's finance minister, Pakistan agreed to reopen the supply routes to the U.S.-led NATO force in Afghanistan when the United States formally apologized for the first time for the killing of the 24 Pakistani troops.

Through a series of emails, conference calls, and secret meetings, at least four drafts of the American apology went back and forth between the two countries. The two negotiators capitalized on their personal chemistry and shared business background to achieve success. They were able to contend with, and circumvent, significant resistance in their respective camps. Pakistan's army chief, General Ashfaq Parvez Kayani, rejected early American offers of an apology and senior White House officials were strongly opposed to offering any apology given strong anti-Pakistan sentiment. Money and geopolitics produced the necessary results (Walsh 2012).

The Obama administration also agreed to seek one billion dollars from Congress to reimburse Pakistan for the costs of operations against Al Qaeda and other terrorist groups. Secretary Clinton stated: "Foreign

Minister Khar and I acknowledged the mistakes that resulted in the loss of Pakistani military lives. We are sorry for the losses suffered by the Pakistani military.... I offered our sincere condolences to the families" (Schmitt 2012).

DRONE SECURITY POLICY

At the center of the current dispute between the United States and Pakistan is the use of targeted strikes against specific Al Qaeda terrorists in selected havens in Pakistan with remotely piloted aircraft, referred to as drones. The U.S. government has steadfastly insisted that such targeted strikes are legal, ethical, and wise. The government of Pakistan insists to the contrary that they are illegal, unethical, and unwise.

John Brennan, former assistant to the president for Homeland Security and Counterterrorism and current director of the CIA, has argued that these targeted strikes are legal pursuant to the Authorization for Use of Military Force (AUMF 2001) passed by Congress after the September 11 attacks. It authorizes the president to "use all necessary and appropriate force" against those nations, organizations, and individuals responsible for 9/11. The AUMF has been used by both the Bush and Obama administrations to justify, among other things, the use of unlimited detention against alleged terrorists (Cutler 2010, 79–82).

The Obama administration saw nothing in the AUMF that restricted any actions taken by the president, presumably directed against Al Qaeda and the Taliban, whether in Afghanistan or Pakistan. Further, the administration argued that there is nothing in international law that prohibits the United States from using lethal force against enemies outside of the active battlefield, at least when the nation involved consents, or is unable or unwilling to take action on its own against the threat. That would include the use of drones to achieve counterterrorism objectives in Pakistan.

Such targeted strikes, it is suggested, conform to the principle of necessity—the requirement that the target(s) have military value. Al Qaeda and the Taliban are legitimate military targets and it is wise to use remotely piloted aircraft in particular because of their ability to fly hundreds of miles over the most treacherous terrain, strike their targets with precision, and then return to base. Drones are also a wise choice because they reduce damage to American personnel and are more surgically precise, which might actually provide a clearer picture of the target, its surroundings, and most importantly, the presence of innocent civilians (Brennan 2012, 8–9).

It was learned through Michael Isikoff of NBC News that the Justice Department prepared a 16-page unsigned, undated "White Paper" that outlines the Obama administration's legal reasoning justifying targeted killings of terrorism suspects if an informed high-level official decides that the target is a high-ranking Al Qaeda figure or affiliate who poses an imminent threat of violent attack against the United States and that capturing him is not feasible. For a threat to be deemed imminent, it is not necessary for a specific attack to be under way. Therefore, the sweeping authority exists even if the target has never been charged with a crime or informed of the allegations against him, and even if the target is not located anywhere near an actual battlefield. More troubling is the contention that any limits on the government's claimed authority are not enforceable in any court. There is no judicial forum available to evaluate these constitutional considerations. According to this white paper, the government has the authority to carry out targeted killings without presenting evidence to a judge before the fact or after, and without acknowledging to the courts or the public or even the Congress that such authority was exercised (U.S. Department of Justice 2013).

Although more than 50 countries worldwide now use drones, the United States is the first nation to regularly conduct strikes employing them. It is clear that drones must be used responsibly, adhering to the most rigorous standards under both domestic and international law while respecting the national sovereignty of nations potentially affected by such attacks. The president has acknowledged that there have been instances where innocent civilians have been accidentally injured or even killed in these strikes, as well as members of allied military forces. Drones have become a provocative symbol of American power, impacting on national security and killing innocents in the process. The United States has established international precedent for sending drones over nations' borders to destroy enemies. The technology of the armed drone is exclusively that of the United States only on a temporary basis. It will, at some point in the near future, be available to America's adversaries. When that occurs, the U.S. government will want the credibility and legitimacy to be able to effectively restrict their actions.

U.S. drone strikes in the Federally Administered Tribal Areas (FATA) are deeply resented by the Pakistani population, and the government has publicly condemned these operations as illegal under international law and a violation of Pakistan's territorial sovereignty. Yet it has been argued that America's pursuit of fugitives linked to Al Qaeda in Pakistan has led to a two-faced policy toward Islamist militancy, which had Pakistani officials secretly accepting, and even in some cases encouraging American drone attacks, while condemning them in public as a violation of sovereignty (Walsh 2013). Nevertheless, a majority of international law experts would find the drone strikes in FATA to be illegal under international law, and also that they do not qualify as acts of self-defense under Article 51 of the U.N. Charter and thus violate Article 2(4), which upholds the territorial integrity of the state (Shah 2011).

In June 2012, the U.N. High Commissioner for Human Rights, Navi Pillay, announced that an investigation would be undertaken by the United Nations to focus on the rate of civilian casualties generated by the American drone campaign, and whether those casualties constituted human rights violations under international law. She said that indiscriminate killings and injuries of civilians under any circumstances were human rights violations and it was therefore necessary to bring into Pakistan the U.N. Special Rapporteur on Summary or Arbitrary Executions to investigate past strikes by U.S. military and intelligence forces (Munoz 2012).

At the 23rd Session of the U.N. Human Rights Council in 2013, Pillay said she was "profoundly disturbed at the human rights implications of the use of armed drones in the context of counter-terrorism and military operations." The High Commissioner's statement also criticized the failure of the United States to shut down the Guantanamo Bay Detention Center and said that "measures that violate human rights did not uproot terrorism; they nurture it" (*The Nation* 2013).

After a two-day dialogue with U.S. officials, the U.N. Special Rapporteur on Extrajudicial, Summary or Arbitrary Executions issued a report, which concluded that the United States failed to directly address any of his questions about legal concerns over drone strike killings in Pakistan. Rapporteur Christof Heyns presented his report at the 20th session of the U.N. Human Rights Council. The U.S. "government has continuously engaged in targeted killings in the territory of other states...and conducted raids and airstrikes as well as deployed unmanned aerial vehicles to target particular individuals...the government has not provided an official and satisfactory response, but has referred to a statement made by the Department of State Legal Advisor" (Heyns 2012, 21). The statement referred to is from Harold Koh, who served during President Obama's entire first term, and it includes the assertion that the government is engaged in an armed conflict against Al Qaeda, the Taliban, and associated forces, which the government considers to be legitimate targets under international humanitarian law, and the actions taken also to be consistent with the right of self-defense.

Nearly every top Al Qaeda figure killed by the United States since the 9/11 attacks has died in a remote-controlled strike by unmanned drone aircraft, with their deaths seen back in Washington by high-definition video transmission. An estimated 80 high-ranking terrorist leaders have been killed in such nations as Pakistan and Yemen in the past decade.

In August 2012, the UN Special Rapporteur on Human Rights and Counterterrorism, Ben Emmerson, stated that the U.S. government must allow an independent investigation of the legality of its drone strike counterterrorism policy. He insisted that the United States must expose its program to international scrutiny in order to evaluate the legality of the strikes, and that it was impossible to evaluate their legality until the U.S. government acknowledged their existence and permitted an investigation into their use. He prepared a report for the next session of the Human Rights Council to be held in 2013. If the United States continued to refuse to cooperate, Emmerson would recommend that the United Nations put the appropriate mechanisms in place through the Human Rights Council, the General Assembly, and the Office of the High Commissioner to investigate the targeted killings. Emmerson was working very closely with Christof Heyns and a number of member states to make U.S. drone attacks a priority on the international agenda (Judd 2012).

In the late spring of 2013, Special Rapporteur Emmerson held meetings in Washington with senior lawyers at the Department of State, Department of Defense, the Office of the Director of National Intelligence, the Central Intelligence Agency, and the President's National

Security Staff. At the conclusion of his visit he determined that more information about the drone program could be safely put in the public domain. He suggested that far too many important questions still remained unanswered with respect to transparency and accountability and that the results of his meetings would be provided to the U.N. General Assembly (U.N. News Centre 2013).

To determine whether the drone attacks carried out in Pakistan, which included the successful killing of Al Qaeda's second-in-command, the Libyan-born Abu Yahya al-Libi,[1] are wrongful under international law, a number of questions need to be answered, including but not limited to: (1) whether Pakistan freely consented to drone strikes on its territory; (2) whether the appropriate governing organ or agent of Pakistan sanctioned the drone strikes; (3) whether the United States exceeded the legitimate parameters of the attacks if they were authorized; and (4) whether the strikes are taking place in a legitimate theater of war (Afghanistan) or outside the conflict zone.

Jo Becker and Scott Shane (2012) argue that President Obama, by his own insistence and guided by John Brennan, signed off on and personally approved every drone strike against Al Qaeda in Yemen and Somalia and also on the more complex and risky drone strikes in Pakistan. The president had several reasons for becoming so immersed in lethal counterterrorism operations. A student of the just-war writings of Augustine and Thomas Aquinas, he believed that he should take moral responsibility for such actions, and he was well aware that bad strikes, such as several that occurred in Pakistan, can undermine America's image and strategic position (Becker and Shane 2012, 8).

Even prior to his election to the White House, Barack Obama in a 2007 campaign speech vowed to go after terrorist bases in Pakistan—even if Pakistani leaders objected. His rivals at that time, including Mitt Romney, Joseph R. Biden, Jr., and Hillary Clinton, all attacked him for his use of campaign rhetoric and bluster. Mr. Romney even said that Obama had become Dr. Strangelove. Though the attacks did not cost Obama the election, polls still showed that voters trusted the Republican Vietnam war hero, Senator John McCain (D-Ariz.) more than the Democratic one-term senator from Illinois.

It is evident that Mr. Obama as president has practiced what he preached. President Obama and his counterterrorism chief chose specific high-value targets for killing and reliance on a precision weapon, the drone, reflecting his pledge at the outset of his presidency to reject the Bush administration's false choice between America's safety and its ideals. In Pakistan, President Obama approved not only "personality" strikes aimed at named high-value terrorists, but "signature strikes" that targeted training camps and suspicious compounds in areas controlled by militants (Becker and Shane 2012, 12). In the last year of his first presidential term, President Obama enhanced the use of drone strikes in Pakistan, particularly in the northwestern region of that country to attempt to weaken the Al Qaeda–linked Haqqani terrorist network. Secretary of Defense Leon Panetta singled out this hard-core branch of the Taliban based in North Waziristan as a principal threat to the future of Afghanistan. The United States wanted Pakistan to take on the Haqqanis before the vast majority of American troops left the region by the end of 2014.

Unless the Pakistani Army is able to assert itself effectively, it is feared that the tribal region could be plunged into deeper chaos. If the insurgency increases in Afghanistan, it will expand into Pakistan's tribal areas where the Taliban will become more vigilant and self-assured. It is clear that even after 2014 the mutual dependency between the United States and Pakistan will not diminish, and the Afghans will have far more difficulty contending with the insurgents who carry out large-scale attacks on Kabul and other parts of that country.

THE STRATEGY OF FLEXIBLE PRAGMATISM AND THE ROMNEY CANDIDACY

President Obama's national security strategy with respect to dealing with the threat from Al Qaeda can best be characterized as flexible pragmatism. He is committed to ending America's war in Afghanistan while actually targeting the enemy more effectively. The light footprint approach in which the United States strikes from a distance with innovative technology makes it easier for the president to be tough at little cost to Americans, no longer requires the United States to engage in years-long enervating occupations, and, most importantly, did not adversely impact his political standing with the American public in an election year. However, the light footprint component of Obama's strategy seems to have worked best when dealing with nonstate actors, such as Al Qaeda, while it has created major problems when it was challenged by state actors who saw it as a direct violation of their national sovereignty. In both Afghanistan, and most notably Pakistan, there exists the messy situation of state and nonstate actors working in concert with one another.

What did this mean for the president as he sought reelection to office? In a nation that was tired of war, first in Iraq and then in Afghanistan, and yet still sought a projection of strength, President Obama was able to reposition his party on national security, and he scored well with a broad cross-section of the country as consistently measured by the polls going into the November 2012 election. He effectively neutralized the traditional Republican edge in the national security arena for the first time since the era of the Vietnam War. Mr. Obama consistently polled higher on the metric of perceived ability to be an effective commander-in-chief than his opponent, Mitt Romney. President Obama stressed rhetorically that he was a steady hand in a dangerous world where his leadership had been tested and proven. Mitt Romney was accused by the Obama team of outsourcing his foreign policy to neocon advisers who would lead a return to the reckless adventurism of the Bush administration based on a worldview that was stuck in a Cold War time warp.

Candidate Romney found himself with little maneuverability to strike a sharp political contrast with President Obama on counterterrorism policy related to Al Qaeda because of declining support among voters for the war in Afghanistan. The last thing Romney wanted to do was pigeonhole himself as a war hawk. At the same time, Romney could not appear to be a liberal dove advocating a precipitous withdrawal of American troops, which would alienate his Republican base. Mr. Romney embraced a timeline for near-total withdrawal by the end of 2014, plus leaving a small footprint of support forces—a position strikingly similar to Mr. Obama's. He advocated for Afghan forces taking over their own battle for independence from the Taliban and continuing and expanding drone strikes, just as Mr. Obama had. Romney also supported the raid that led to the killing of Osama bin Laden. The problem that he had was criticizing the president at the same time that he adopted a policy remarkably similar to that of the president.

To attempt to differentiate himself from President Obama, Mitt Romney vowed that under his leadership the coming era would be

"America's Century," with the United States retaining the world's biggest economy and strongest military. He would act to keep America safe in an era of rapidly evolving threats from shadowy terrorist groups and rogue nations. Mr. Romney believed that the real threat to the United States was Russia, not Al Qaeda.

As a presidential candidate Mitt Romney struggled in his attempt to present a coherent national security policy. Beyond his emphasis on American strength, which would thereby allegedly make for a safer world, the candidate failed to provide a comprehensive vision, instead touching on a few flash points where he perceived that he could score political points, most importantly regarding Iran, Syria, and Israel. Romney tried to give the impression that he would be tougher on Iran than the president, but he did not advocate for any real change of policy. He said that if Obama was reelected, Iran would have a nuclear weapon. Still, although Romney stated that he would consider using military force to prevent Iran from obtaining nuclear weapons, he consistently stopped short of promising to do so. Obama's position was the same. Romney insisted that Iran must halt all uranium enrichment but never said how he would enforce the demand, which had been made similarly by the United Nations Security Council. Although Romney supported, and the White House initially opposed, imposing sanctions on Iran's central bank, the measures taken with the president's approval disrupted Iran's currency and savaged the country's economy.

After three and a half years of attempting to halt Iran's nuclear program with diplomacy, sanctions, and even sabotage, the Obama administration and its allies imposed sweeping new sanctions to cut the country off from the global oil market. The European Union put in place a total embargo of all oil imports from Iran, which was the continent's sixth biggest supplier of crude oil in 2011. Even before these steps were taken, Iran conceded that its oil exports were down 20 to 30 percent. Its currency plunged over 40 percent against the dollar since late 2011.

The president's strategy prevailed with respect to the American public's perception of his strong leadership ability on national security issues related to the Persian Gulf. Still, Governor Romney consistently called for tougher sanctions on Iran than those that already existed, although he never did say how he would strengthen them. Less than a month before the election, in a major foreign policy address delivered at the Virginia Military Institute, the alma mater of former secretary of state George C. Marshall, the architect of the Marshall Plan that rebuilt Europe after World War II, the Republican nominee insisted that President Obama was a weak leader who was sitting on the sidelines rather than dealing with Iran directly, and that Iran's ties to the Syrian government further jeopardized and destabilized U.S. security interests in the Middle East.

In the last presidential debate, which was specifically designed to focus on foreign policy issues, Governor Romney repeated his attack on President Obama with respect to Iran. The subject of Iran's nuclear program came up consistently. Mr. Romney insisted Iran was closer to a bomb and that international sanctions needed to be tightened to be truly effective and that as president he would seek a war crimes indictment against Mahmoud Ahmadinejad for inciting genocide against Israel. But for all of the rhetoric on Iran, there were very few substantive differences between the two candidates. Both were in favor of strong international sanctions and the application of diplomatic pressure, and both endorsed the use of full military power to prevent Iran from getting a nuclear weapon.

On Syria, Governor Romney proposed that the United States take a more assertive role by working directly with other countries to help arm the Syrian rebels to defeat President Bashar Assad's tyrannical regime. He did not call for the United States to directly arm the rebels, but insisted that he would support other countries providing the opposition with enough military assistance to force Assad from power. President Obama was opposed to providing weapons to the rebels because his administration insisted that U.S. arms assistance would further militarize Syria and make it even harder to stabilize the country after Assad's eventual downfall. The administration was concerned about the nature of the rebels and their access to arms, particularly given the small but growing influence of Islamist extremists among them.

On Israel, the Romney campaign accused the Obama administration of badly misunderstanding the dynamics of the region, which supposedly had led to diminished U.S. authority and painted Israel into a corner. Romney insisted that the key to negotiating a lasting peace was an Israel certain about its security. This begged the question as to how, as president, Romney would achieve his goal. Furthermore, President Obama had sharply increased naval operations in the Gulf and helped to fund the development of new missile-defense systems in Israel. Obama never threatened to withhold U.S. aid to Israel because of its settlement activity; instead, he took U.S. financial assistance to Israel to record levels. The Obama administration cast the only UN veto during the president's first term against the one-sided anti-Israel UN Security Council resolution on settlements. Additionally, Obama derailed Palestinian attempts to unilaterally declare statehood at the United Nations. Most recently when a bus full of Israeli tourists were attacked by terrorists in Sofia Bulgaria, resulting in the death of seven of them, President Obama termed it a "barbaric terrorist attack" and immediately pledged his assistance to bring the perpetrators, alleged to be an Iran-sponsored Hezbollah guerilla group, to justice.

Despite encounters between Israeli prime minister Benjamin Netanyahu and President Obama that have been marked by misunderstandings, mutual suspicion, slights, and prickly tension, Netanyahu has insisted that his relationship with Obama is friendlier than it has been portrayed in the media, and that he and the president are people who appreciate each other's savvy and strength. In September 2011, when Obama received a late-night call requesting assistance in rescuing the Israelis trapped in the Egyptian embassy, Netanyahu called it a decisive and fateful moment, recalling that Obama said that he would do everything that he could—and he did. That assessment from Netanyahu did not place Mr. Obama in the position of losing the support of the American Jewish community in his bid for reelection to the White House in 2012 despite the fact that it did drop nine percentage points from 2008.

Reviewing documents issued by the Romney campaign on national security policy, including white papers and speeches delivered by the candidate, one is left to question why he principally criticized the president's style while, for the most part, avoiding any substantive critique of the president's policies. Romney merely vowed he would use power wisely, firmly, actively, and without a sense of false pride. "A Romney national security policy will proceed with clarity and resolve. Our friends and allies will not have doubts about where we stand and what we will do to safeguard our interests and theirs. Neither will our rivals, competitors, and adversaries" (Dreazen 2012).

His other areas of emphasis, including national defense, tended to replay standard Republican attacks on defense cuts or to fall in line with Obama's approach. Romney accused Obama of short-changing the military, and pledged to spend at least 4 percent of the nation's GDP on the Pentagon's base budget, a premise that would bring spending to levels that were unprecedented since the end of World War II. Romney never spelled out in detail what other spending he would cut, or what taxes, if any, he would increase to provide the estimated additional two and a half trillion dollars that would be required over the next decade. While Republicans tried to pin the looming defense cuts on Obama, GOP members in both the House and the Senate had voted for the reductions contained in the omnibus bill that raised the nation's borrowing authority and implemented cuts to reduce the growing federal deficit.

Defense spending was a critical local campaign issue in two pivotal swing states, Virginia and Florida, which had large military civilian workforces. It is of significance to note, however, that many Americans expressed their concern that Obama did not go far enough in cutting military spending and wanted cuts to go even deeper. Several polls leading up to the election found that, by a 41 to 21 percent margin, Americans thought the country spent too much on the military rather than not enough (Preble 2012). On November 6, President Obama won both swing states in his successful bid for reelection to office.

In a major foreign policy address to the Veterans of Foreign Wars, candidate Romney called for an independent investigation into claims the White House had leaked national security information for President Obama's political gain. He accused Obama of putting politics over national security by providing sensitive policy decisions to reporters affiliated with the *New York Times* (Becker and Shane) concerning the "Kill List" among other secrets. To bolster his criticism over the leaks of classified information, Romney specifically referenced comments from Senator Diane Feinstein, chair of the Intelligence Committee, who two days prior to the VFW Convention said that the White House had to understand that some of the leaks were coming from their ranks. Obama strongly rejected the leak accusations, which he also described as offensive.

If Romney had won the presidency he would have found his operational flexibility heavily constrained by a combination of politics, legal restrictions, international political realities, and the precedence of the presidential office. It is important to recognize that these constraints are a key to understanding why Obama continued most aspects of the Bush national security strategy. Because of our system of checks and balances, the Bush administration was frustrated in its attempts to expand the scope of executive actions in the field of national security, and the policies that emerged, particularly in the second term, enjoyed a degree of legitimacy and collective endorsement that made it difficult for Obama to abandon them. The Obama administration would continue almost all of its predecessor's policies, transforming what had seemed extraordinary under the Bush administration into the "new normal" of American counterterrorism policy (Goldsmith 2012).

POSTSCRIPT

In a normal presidential election, national security issues would register high with respect to the American voting public's evaluation of the party candidates. As pointed out in this discussion, Barack Obama consistently outscored his rival in terms of suitability as a commander-in-chief of the nation, while faring less favorably in terms of the economy. The 2012 presidential cycle was dominated by the unrelenting focus on the national economy, while critical national security concerns were pushed into the background. This is regrettable since several controversial substantive areas affecting America's role in the world were ripe for evaluation.

In his speech celebrating the one-year anniversary of the killing of Osama bin Laden, President Obama said that "this time of war began in Afghanistan, and this is where it will end." Afghanistan will most probably end in an unsatisfying manner for the vast majority of Americans because there will be no victory, a corrupt but marginally improved government will persist in Kabul after the presidential elections scheduled for April 2014, technical and support advisors assisting Afghan security forces will be fighting a weakening but still resilient and dangerous Taliban, and an unpredictable Pakistan will be aiding Afghan as well as Taliban forces.

A decision announced by the Pakistan government a week after the presidential election provides a cautiously optimistic sign concerning future reconciliation of Afghan/Pakistan efforts at facilitating peace talks in Afghanistan. A 12-point joint statement, issued by both governments, urged the Taliban and other armed groups to sever all talks with Al Qaeda and other international terror networks. The statement also emphasized that Pakistan and Afghanistan would work closely with other international partners to remove the names from the UN sanctions list of the potential negotiators among the Taliban and other groups to enable them to participate in peace talks.

Now numbering over 350,000 soldiers, which represents the biggest troop strength to date, the Afghan National Security Forces are faced with endemic desertions and low reenlistment rates that have required replacement of at least a third of its entire force every year. This means that the country's military recruitment centers have a combined quota of 5,000 new recruits every month. If that recruitment stopped, for any reason, the Afghan National Army would collapse.

The United States' consistent war goal has been and continues to be the destruction of Al Qaeda and the prevention of the use of Afghanistan as a base for attacks. When it comes to decimating Al Qaeda, Obama has been very willing to not only continue but also expand many policies of George W. Bush. The reality is that over a decade after 9/11, the war against Al Qaeda continues in such places as Pakistan, Yemen, and Somalia, not just in Afghanistan.

Several concerns remain with respect to the future role for the United States in Afghanistan during the second Obama administration. Despite the fact that Afghan forces outnumber the Taliban by over 10-to-1, and the assurance from the Obama administration that Afghanistan will be provided the weapons it requires to fight an insurgency, not a single Afghan army battalion is currently capable of functioning in the field without American advisors. In the worst-case scenario, if the Afghan forces collapse, will the United States reverse course and extend its military commitment or even expand its military support to avoid a Taliban victory?

Will the Afghan citizenry accept a newly elected government in Kabul in 2014 as a truly viable alternative to the Taliban, or will the attempt to transfer authority through a peaceful transition prove elusive? If so, can the United States continue to rely on its light footprint approach to produce its desired results? The light footprint approach to national security adopted by the Obama administration has obvious benefits: it is less expensive, takes fewer casualties, does not require extensive long-term occupation, does not call for nation building, and it is dedicated to wiping out specific terrorists and terrorist havens. However, it has real, practical limitations.

Perhaps the most enduring policy legacy of the past four years may well turn out to be the approach to national security counterterrorism that John Brennan calls the Yemen model, a mixture of drone strikes and Special Forces raids targeting top Al Qaeda leaders. The practice of targeted killing as a principal tool in the war against Al Qaeda has permitted the U.S. government to decide to target and kill any individual in the territory of any state if it concluded that individual constituted a threat to American national security interests. There exists a total lack of transparency regarding the legal framework and targeting choices for killings, and the dangerous precedent that such a practice represents remains a major concern in terms of both domestic and international law.

It is not surprising that drone strikes and targeted killings are very unpopular abroad, particularly in Pakistan where just 17 percent of Pakistanis supported them against leaders of extremist groups according to a Pew Research Center poll conducted late last year. Domestically, critics speak with different voices on this issue. Some Republicans in Congress have accused President Obama of adopting a de facto kill preference because he shut down the CIA's overseas prisons and does not want to send additional detainees to Guantanamo Bay, Cuba. Human rights advocates argue that some drone strikes have amounted to extrajudicial killings, execution without trial of suspected militants whose identities American officials often do not know and who may not pose a threat to the United States. Yet with the American public such strikes and killings remain popular. In a Gallup poll reported in March 2013, 65 percent of Americans questioned approved of strikes to kill suspected foreign terrorists, while only 28 percent were opposed. Interestingly, after a sharp rise of targeted strikes in Pakistan, which peaked at 117 in 2010, the number fell to 64 in 2011, 46 in 2012, and likely even fewer in 2013. In Yemen, where strikes shot up to 42 in 2012, strikes tapered to a minimal level after January 2013, according to *The Long War Journal*, which covers covert wars. For the record, such strikes and targeted killings eliminated Osama bin Laden and 22 of the 30 top leaders of Al Qaeda who were removed from the field (Shane 2013).

Into his second term, the president cannot continue to rely on non-existent "implied authority" in the AUMF, nor for that matter, the power of the commander-in-chief clause in Article II of the U.S. Constitution to justify his actions. The United States' war on terror is a bigger war than just the one front in Afghanistan. Potentially this means the president may decide to employ lethal force against anyone, and any targeted training camp or compound anywhere, to deal with any perceived threat to America's national security interests. While it may make sense to advocate for exercise of broad discretionary power when and where a serious threat to national security exists, such unchecked, unfettered power by any president is ripe for potential abuse, regardless of whether it is Barack Obama or his future successors.

In what may very well become a benchmark address focusing on his counterterrorism policy to guide the balance of his presidency, Barack Obama returned to the National Defense University in May 2013 to offer his vision of America's global role and his principal goal of defining our effort "not as a boundless global war on terror, but rather as a series of persistent, targeted efforts to dismantle specific networks of violent extremists that threaten America" (Obama 2013).

The president, who insisted that it is up to us to define the nature and scope of this struggle, lest it define us, emphasized the following components of his comprehensive counterterrorism strategy:

- The United States must involve itself in partnerships with other countries in gathering and sharing of intelligence, and the arrest and prosecution of terrorists.
- It is not possible for America to simply deploy a team of Special Forces to capture every terrorist. There are places where it would pose profound risks to our troops and local civilians, and times when putting U.S. boots on the ground may trigger a major international crisis. Therefore, lethal targeted action against Al Qaeda and its associational forces, including the use of drones, has been and will continue to be effectively employed.
- Drone strikes have saved lives and such actions are legal under domestic and international law. To say a military tactic is legal, or

even effective, is not to say it is wise or moral in every instance. Therefore, clear guidelines, oversight, and accountability that is now codified in Presidential Policy Guidance will be the new norm.

- The United States will continue to take strikes against high-value Al Qaeda targets but also against forces that are massing to support attacks on coalition forces. By the end of 2014, the United States will no longer have the same need for force protection, and that will reduce the need for unmanned strikes.

- Some drone operations will shift from the CIA to the Department of Defense, particularly those in Yemen, where the Pentagon's Joint Special Operations Command is already running a parallel drone program. It is fully expected that the Defense Department will assume control over all drone operations in less than two years, predicated on periodic six-month reviews to determine whether such operations were ready to be transferred to military control. The transfer of the Pakistan drone program will coincide with the withdrawal of combat forces from Afghanistan in 2014.

- Strong oversight of all lethal action means that Congress authorizes such use of force and is properly briefed on every strike that America takes, including the one instance when the United States targeted an American citizen, Anwar al-Awlaki. The president does not believe it would be constitutional for the government to target and kill any U.S. citizen with a drone, but when a U.S. citizen goes abroad to wage war against America, his citizenship should not serve as a shield to protect him.

- Proposals to extend oversight of lethal actions outside of war zones that go beyond reporting to Congress require serious consideration and thoughtful review. For example, the establishment of a special court to evaluate and authorize lethal action has the benefit of bringing the judiciary into the process, but it may raise serious constitutional questions about presidential and judicial authority. An independent oversight board in the executive branch may introduce a layer of bureaucracy into national security decision making, which may raise concerns related to confidence and trust.

It is refreshing to hear President Obama expressing an interest in instituting some form of independent review of how and when drone strikes would be conducted. Yet a special national security court with the power to approve death warrants for American citizens as well as all other individuals deemed to be terrorists away from the battlefield creates very real concerns. First and foremost, it negates the traditional role of the judiciary as the independent arbiter of the law. Judges render their decisions predicated on defined, settled sets of facts (evidence), not intelligence, and the vagueness of the notion of supposed imminent threat by a would-be terrorist, and whether, under the circumstances, capture instead of killing is feasible and preferable. It is absolutely essential that a national security court not become embroiled in deciding such disputes predicated on preference, because it then would lose its legitimacy, credibility, and independence and become an arm of the executive branch. It is well recognized that the Foreign Intelligence Surveillance Court (FISC), often described as a template for the creation of a special national security court, is considered a rubber stamp for the government, rarely rejecting applications presented to it.

- Fundamental to national security policy is sustained engagement through diplomacy and foreign assistance; not just military assistance, but assistance for training internal security forces, feeding the hungry, building schools, and creating reservoirs of goodwill that marginalize extremists.

- The Authorization to Use Military Force (AUMF) is now nearly 12 years old, and it is time to refine and ultimately repeal its mandate. This position is very consistent with those of leading Republicans and Democrats in the Congress who have expressed their concern that they have essentially given the president a blank check for using military force globally. As John McCain said in the Senate Armed Services Committee, the president's authority is no longer applicable to the conditions that prevailed in 2001 when the Congress passed the AUMF, and continuing to allow the Pentagon to have carte blanche authority to do what it wants militarily is of great concern. He was joined in this view by Chairman of the Committee Carl Levin and senators Lindsey Graham, Dick Durbin, and Bob Corker. All agreed that a major revision of the law or a new resolution would be the appropriate course of action for the Congress to take (McAuliff 2013).

In his quest to demonstrate that the United States is the principal nation responsible for maintaining global order, President Obama has pursued a power politics mindset while at the same time improvising, shifting, and adapting to the specific circumstances of the moment. He must be held publicly accountable, however, and be required to bring the use of drone attacks under the rule of law. Congress, as the president's constitutional partner in the exercise of national security policy, must provide the required oversight for the use of such strikes so American citizens know what military actions are being undertaken in their name. In order for Congress to perform this proper constitutional role, it must be provided the administration's standards, criteria, and guidelines employed to undertake targeted killings. While Congress needs to be provided a more informed and consultative role, it is far more difficult to expect greater transparency. The reality is that it is much easier to classify information than to declassify it. Former legal advisor to the State Department Harold Koh, in an address to the Oxford Union, stated that it (the administration) should make public its full legal explanation for targeting and drone strikes including all standards and processes for doing so. Although the Presidential Policy Guidance document cited by President Obama in his National Defense University speech is codified, it remains classified (Koh 2013).

The United States remains the preeminent power of the world. As a result, whenever a situation arises in which a potential hot spot could have global impact, it is the natural expectation that the president of the United States will intercede and thereby become part of the solution to the policy problem. Until he leaves office in January 2017, Mr. Obama has the authority as well as the ability to keep the United States safe and secure without violating the rule of law. It is up to him to demonstrate that he has the political will to do so because it can lead to a more lasting and effective legacy for his second term.

REFERENCES

Authorization for Use of Military Force (AUMF). 2001. *Public Law* 107-40; 50 USC 1541.

Becker, J., and S. Shane, S. 2012. "Secret 'Kill List' Proves a Test of Obama's Principles and Will." *New York Times,* May 29. Retrieved from http://www.nytimes.com/2012/05/29/world/obamas-leadership-in-war-on-al-qaeda.html.

Benjamin, D. 2012. "Assessment of the U.S. Department of State's Counterterrorism Strategy. Testimony, House Foreign Affairs Subcommittee on Terrorism, Nonproliferation and Trade." April 19. Retrieved from http://london .usembassy.gov/terror031.html.

Brennan, J. 2012. "The Ethics and Efficiency of the President's Counterterrorism Strategy." Council on Foreign Relations, April 30.

Brookings Institution. 2012. "Afghanistan Field Trip Report VII: The Overall Transition in Afghanistan's Foreign Policy." Trip Reports/Number 22 (May).

Congressional Research Service. 2012. "$83 Billion in Projected War Costs for 2013." January 17. Retrieved from http://www.afghanistanstudygroup.org/tag /congressional-research-service.

Cordesman, A. 2012. "The U.S. Cost of the Afghan War: FY 2002–FY 2013." Center for Strategic and International Studies (December).

Cutler, L. 2010. "Bush v. Obama Detainee Policy Post-9/11: An Assessment." *Strategic Studies Quarterly* 4 (2).

Cutler, L. 2011. "A Decade Later: An Assessment of U.S. Policy Since 9/11." *Jurist— Forum*, September 12. Retrieved from http://jurist.org/forum/2011/09 /leonard-cutler-decade-later.php.

Dreazen, Y. 2012. "How Obama and Romney Differ—and Don't—on Foreign Policy." *Atlantic,* June 8. Retrieved from http://www.theatlantic.com/interna-tional/archive/2012/06/how-obama-and-romney-differ-and-dont-on-foreign-policy/258283/.

Goldsmith, J. 2012. *Power and Constraint: The Accountable Presidency after 9/11.* New York: W. W. Norton.

Heyns, C. 2012. "Report of the Special Rapporteur on Extrajudicial, Summary or Arbitrary Executions, Addendum, Follow-Up Recommendations—United States of America." Human Rights Council, Twentieth Session. Agenda item 3 (June).

Judd, T. 2012. "US Should Hand Over Footage of Drone Strikes or Face UN Inquiry." *Independent,* August 20. Retrieved from http://www.independent.co. uk/news/world/asia/us-should-hand-over-footage-of-drone-strikes-or -face-un-inquiry-8061504.html.

Koh, H. 2013. "How to End the Forever War." Oxford Union, Oxford, UK, May 7. Retrieved from http://www.lawfareblog.com/wp-content/uploads /2013/05/2013-5-7-Koh-oxford-univ.

Landler, M. 2012. "Obama Signs Pact in Kabul, Turning Page in Afghan War." *New York Times,* May 1. Retrieved from http://www.nytimes.com/2012/05/02 /world/asia/obama-lands-in-kabul-on-unannounced-visit.html.

McAuliff, M. 2013. "Obama War Powers Under 2001 Law 'Astoundingly Disturbing,' Senators Say." *Huffington Post,* May 17. Retrieved from http://www .huffingtonpost.com/2013/05/16/war-powers-obama-administration_n _3288420.

Miller, G., and K. DeYoung. 2011. "Adm. Mullen's Words on Pakistan Come under Scrutiny." *Washington Post,* September 27. Retrieved from http://www .washingtonpost.com/world/national-security/adm-mullens-words-on -pakistan-come-under-scrutiny/2011/09/27/gIQAHPJB3K_story.html.

Munoz, C. 2012. "U.N. Demands Investigation of U.S. Drone Strikes in Pakistan." *The Hill's Defense Blog,* June 7. Retrieved from http://thehill.com/blogs /defcon-hill/policy-and-strategy/231593-un-demands -investigation.html.

Nation. 2013. "UNHCR Chief 'Disturbed' at Use of Drones in Pakistan." May 28. Retrieved from http://www.nation.com.pk/pakistan-news-newspaper-daily -english-online/national/28-May-2013/unhcr-chief-disturbed-at-use-of -drones-in-pakistan.

Obama, B. 2013. "Speech on Drone Policy." *New York Times,* May 23. Retrieved from www.nytimes.com/2013/05/24/us/politics/transcript_of_obama_speech_on _drone_policy.

Preble, C. 2012. "Romney's National Security Problem." *Cato Institute.* Retrieved from http://www.cato-at-liberty.org/romneys-national-security-problem/.

Rosenerg, M., and R. Nordland. 2012. "U.S. Abandoning Hope for Taliban Peace Deal." *New York Times,* October 1. Retrieved from http://www.nytimes .com/2012/10/02/world/asia/us-scales-back-plans-for-afghan-peace.html.

Schmitt, E. 2012. "Clinton's 'Sorry' to Pakistan Ends Barrier to NATO." *New York Times,* July 3, A1.

Shah, S. 2011. "Drone Strikes in Pakistan: Examining Consent in International Law." *Jurist—Forum,* December 15. Retrieved from http://jurist.org/forum/2011/12 /sikander-shah-drone-strikes.php.

Shane, S. 2013. "Targeted Killing Comes to Define War on Terror." *New York Times,* April 7, A1.

UN News Centre. 2013. "Independent UN Rights Expert Urges More Clarity on US Counter-Terrorism Policies." *UN News Service,* June 7. Retrieved from http:// www.un.org/apps/news/printnews.asp?nid=45119.

U.S. Department of Defense 2012. "Report on Progress Toward Security and Stability in Afghanistan." Washington, D.C. (April).

U.S. Department of Justice White Paper. 2013. "Lawfulness of a Lethal Operation Directed Against a U.S. Citizen Who Is a Senior Operational Leader of al-Qaida or an Associated Force." *NBC News,* February 6.

Walsh, D. 2013. "U.S. Shift Poses Risk to Pakistan." *New York Times,* May 25, A1.

Walsh, D. 2012. "Quiet Duo Forged Road Deal for U.S. and Pakistan." *New York Times,* July 27, A20.

NOTES

1. Perhaps the most well-known Al Qaeda figure killed in a drone strike before al-Libi was Anwar al-Awlaki, a United States citizen and a prominent member of the Yemen Al Qaeda affiliate who was killed in September 2011. The CIA had the

full support from Yemen's president, Abdu Rabbu Mansour Hadi, in its campaign to pursue the terrorist by any means necessary in order to stabilize Yemen. The significance of this targeted killing of an American citizen, in a country with which the United States was not at war, was made by the president (in secret) without the benefit of capture or a trial. It was originally the subject of a 50-page secret legal memorandum written in 2010 by the Justice Department's Office of Legal Counsel to justify the addition of U.S. citizen Anwar al-Awlaki to the government's "kill list."

Chapter 13

The Obama Administration's Homeland Security Record as a 2012 Campaign Issue

Tom Lansford, Jack Covarrubias, and Robert J. Pauly, Jr.,
University of Southern Mississippi–Gulf Coast

INTRODUCTION

From the very genesis of the Department of Homeland Security (DHS) in the wake of Al Qaeda's terrorist attacks against the United States on September 11, 2001, safeguarding the homeland from (and responding effectively to) catastrophic events has been as significant an American national security issue as any. Regardless of political party affiliation and control of the legislative branches of the U.S. government, achieving consensus on homeland security has been far less challenging than is the case with most, if not all, other issues in American politics since the events of 9/11. Consequently, in comparing the George W. Bush and Barack H. Obama administrations, aside from occasional rhetorical distinctions, differences in approaches to defending the United States from terrorist threats in particular have been minimal in practice.

With respect to presidential electoral politics, bipartisanship was especially evident regarding the issue of homeland security during the 2012 campaign pitting Democratic incumbent Obama against Republican challenger Mitt Romney, former governor of Massachusetts. Such was the extent of consensus between America's principal two political parties on homeland security priorities by the end of Obama's first term in office that the issue proved more contentious during the Republican primaries than in exchanges between Obama and Romney in their race for the White House.

When Obama first ran for president in 2008, defeating Republican challenger and Arizona senator John McCain handily, he was emphatic in declaring unacceptable the Bush administration's establishment and maintenance of a detention facility at the U.S. military base at Guantanamo Bay, Cuba, for prisoners in the context of the global war on terrorism. It was a signature homeland security issue for Obama, who pledged to close the facility expeditiously upon assuming office. However, in practice, Obama did not close the detention center, nor did he reverse or alter significantly many other Bush administration approaches to securing the American homeland from terrorist attacks, most notably those conceived and perpetrated by Al Qaeda and its affiliates. Examples included: (1) the continued pursuit of Al Qaeda leader Osama bin Laden, who was killed in a U.S. Navy SEAL operation in May 2011 in Abbottabad, Pakistan; (2) reliance on the USA Patriot Act (especially as it pertains to monitoring of cell phone and e-mail traffic by the National Security Agency); and (3) the realization that trying prisoners detained at Guantanamo Bay in American civilian criminal courtrooms rather than via military tribunals was more difficult to put into practice than it had been to promise.

With these introductory observations as a point of departure, this chapter is designed to review the role of homeland security in the 2012 presidential election from the perspectives of both contending parties, in light of the strains of continuity and change in the policies of the Bush and Obama administrations in that issue area. This chapter does so through the presentation of three related sections. The first section examines the Obama administration's development and implementation of homeland security policies from 2009 to 2012 and identifies strains of continuity and change in comparing the approaches used by Obama and his immediate presidential predecessor. The second section examines the similarities and differences between the Republican candidates' positions on homeland security, as articulated during the primaries in the winter and spring of 2012. The third section examines the convergences and divergences between Obama's and Romney's positions on homeland security, as expressed during the general election campaign.

U.S. HOMELAND SECURITY POLICIES, FROM BUSH TO OBAMA, 2001–2012

Throughout the history of the United States, the issues of homeland security and national security have been interconnected in many ways. Although the 9/11 attacks brought the term "homeland security" more directly into the American public consciousness, both through the proliferation of that term in the vernacular of public officials at the local, state, and federal levels as well as among the media, there have always been—and will remain—myriad connections between safeguarding U.S. security interests at home and abroad. As John Lewis Gaddis observes, "Americans…have generally responded to threats—particularly to surprise attacks—by taking the offensive, by becoming more conspicuous, by confronting, neutralizing and if possible overwhelming the sources of danger rather than fleeing from them. Expansion, we have assumed, is the path to security" (Gaddis 2004, 13). That point was not lost on either the Bush or Obama administrations, both of which faced the related (and often quite daunting) challenges of clarifying institutional lines of authority between the nascent DHS and historically entrenched entities such as the Central Intelligence Agency (CIA) and Department of Defense (DOD), as well as the relationships between federal, state, and local bodies that must work together as effectively as possible in the face of a catastrophic or lesser terrorist attack.

The Bush administration responded to the events of 9/11 on two related domestic and international security policy tracks. On the international front of what Bush quickly characterized as a global war on terrorism, the United States prosecuted Operation Enduring Freedom, which resulted in the elimination of the Islamic extremist Taliban regime in Afghanistan and the dispersion of Al Qaeda's leadership, albeit without the killing or capture of Bin Laden, between October and December 2001.

On the domestic front, Bush pushed for the establishment of the DHS, a process that was completed in just over one year through congressional passage of the Homeland Security Act of November 2002 (Department of Homeland Security). The relationship between the two was specified clearly in the October 2007 *National Strategy for Homeland Security*, in which Bush stressed:

> Many of the threats we face—pandemic diseases, the proliferation of weapons of mass destruction, terrorism, and natural disasters—also demand multinational effort and cooperation. To this end, we have strengthened our homeland security through foreign partnerships, and we are committed to expanding and increasing our layers of defense, which extend well beyond our borders, by seeking further cooperation with our international partners. As we secure the Homeland, however, we cannot simply rely on defensive approaches and well-planned response and recovery measures. We recognize that our efforts must also involve offense at home and abroad. We will disrupt the enemy's plans and diminish the impact of future disasters through measures that enhance the resilience of our economy and critical infrastructure before an incident occurs. (Bush 2007)

Coupled with the USA Patriot Act, which was passed by Congress and signed into law by Bush in October 2001, the creation of the DHS demonstrated a general bipartisan consensus on the need for improvements in the ways in which the American national government safeguarded the security of the homeland and its citizens therein. However, these developments also left open the potential for disagreements between Democrats and Republicans, whether in the Congress, executive and judicial branches of the national government, and officials at the state and local levels, over the related evolution of the DHS and enforcement of the Patriot Act. Above all, the most contentious such issues grew out of a debate over the extent of freedom Americans are willing to sacrifice and the types of tactics employed against adversaries they will accept to mitigate terrorist threats to national security, primarily but not exclusively, within the borders of the United States. The Bush administration's emphasis on the primacy of security over civil liberties and the use of enhanced interrogation techniques against captured members of terrorist groups provided the impetus for proponents and opponents of that stance to focus on that issue in most, if not all, of the campaign cycles that have unfolded since.

As Nancy Baker asserts, the 9/11 attacks and possibility of comparable strikes in the future "posed an enormous challenge to each level and branch of government, especially the executive. President Bush and his administration could have pursued a number of possible courses of action. When Bush framed the crisis as a war against terrorism, the homefront became a battlefront and the markers of an open society—a free press, individual protections in criminal proceedings and privacy from government snooping—were conceptually transformed by the administration into opportunities for the enemy" (Baker 2003, 563).

Differences between the Bush administration and its critics, most notably those on the far left of the Democratic Party and libertarians affiliated with Republicans such as Texas congressman Ron Paul, arose over the following three sets of issues, all of which still retain at least some political merit as Obama approaches the midpoint of his final term: (1) tracking terrorists with tools (largely Internet- and cell phone–based) that can also access the communications traffic of all Americans; (2) gathering intelligence by interrogating suspected terrorists with enhanced interrogation techniques characterized by some as "torture"; and (3) detaining captured terrorists at Guantanamo Bay, denying them speedy trials, and eventually trying them before military tribunals rather than in civilian courts.

For the Bush administration, each of these issues proved to be a significant factor in implementing three interconnected sets of U.S. strategies—those associated with homeland security, national security, and counterterrorism.[1] The administration's second *National Strategy for Homeland Security*, for example, presents four central objectives: "Prevent and disrupt terrorist attacks; Protect the American people, our critical infrastructure, and key resources; Respond to and recover from incidents that do occur; and Continue to strengthen the foundation to ensure our long-term success" (Bush 2007). All of these were topics for debate in the Bush-era congressional elections of 2002, 2004, and 2006, as well as in the presidential election of 2004. On balance, Republican-Democratic differences over homeland security played to the former party's advantage in two of those three elections (2002 and 2004), as evidenced most significantly by Bush's victory over Democratic senator John Kerry of Massachusetts in the 2004 presidential race. However, in 2006, the Democrats capitalized on rising public discontent over the Bush administration's use of what some characterized as torture of terrorist detainees to gain intelligence, as well as concerns over the president's emphasis on an increasingly costly war in Iraq while Al Qaeda leader Bin Laden remained at large, to help gain control of both the House of Representatives and Senate from the Republicans. As Representative Nancy Pelosi (D-CA), who was elected by her Democratic peers as Speaker of the House in January 2007, noted on election night in November 2006: "Tonight is a great victory for the American people. Today the American people voted for change, and they voted for Democrats to take our country in a new direction.... And nowhere did the people make it more clear that we need a new direction than in the war in Iraq" (Branigan 2006).

Obama, who was elected as junior U.S. senator from Illinois in 2004, echoed the sentiments of Pelosi and others on the political left, first in 2006 and then during his successful run for the Democratic nomination in the 2008 presidential election. Obama struck on common themes during both the primaries against fellow Democrats and then the presidential race in which he defeated Republican nominee John McCain comfortably. Most significantly, he was emphatic in myriad campaign speeches in condemning the Bush administration for declaring detainees in the war on terror as enemy combatants, using enhanced interrogation techniques to secure intelligence from many of those individuals, and holding them indefinitely without trial at Guantanamo Bay, and pledging to close the facility if elected president. In an April 2008 Democratic Candidate Forum at Messiah College in Grantham, Pennsylvania, for example, Obama stressed that:

> We have to be clear and unequivocal. We do not torture, period. That should be our position. That will be my position as president. That includes renditions. We don't subcontract torture. Torture does not end up yielding good information—most intelligence officers agree with that—but it is also important for our long-term security to send a message to the world that we will lead not just with our military might but we are going to lead with our values and our ideals. That we are not a nation that gives away our civil liberties simple because we're scared. We're always at our worst when we're fearful. Fear is a bad counsel and I always want to operate out of hope and out of faith. (Democratic Candidates 2008)

Similarly, in a June 2007 appearance during the run-up to the 2007–2008 primaries, Obama suggested:

> Why don't we close Guantanamo and restore the right of habeas corpus, because that's how we lead, not with the might of our military, but the power of our ideals and the power of our values. It's time to show the world we're not a country that ships prisoners in the dead of night to be tortured in far-off countries. We're not a country that runs prisons which lock people away without ever telling them why they're there or what they're charged with. (Obama 2007)

Obama echoed both sets of the above sentiments throughout his campaign against McCain, which provided a foundation for his administration's development and implementation of homeland security policy and strategy more broadly and the means through which to counter terrorist threats to the United States in particular. Over the course of Obama's first term in the White House, his administration addressed the issue of homeland security generally and the relationship between homeland security and national security in three related strategic documents: the February 2010 *Quadrennial Homeland Security Review Report*, May 2010 *National Security Strategy*, and June 2011 *National Strategy for Counterterrorism*. In each case, the approaches employed by the administration were implemented in ways one could characterize as both convergent and divergent with the criticisms Obama had for Bush during the 2008 presidential campaign.

In the context of the 2010 *Quadrennial Homeland Security Review Report*, the Obama administration identified the following five "missions" central to safeguarding the security of the American homeland: (1) "Preventing Terrorism and Enhancing Security"; (2) "Securing and Managing Our Borders"; (3) "Enforcing and Administering Our Immigration Laws"; (4) "Safeguarding and Securing Cyberspace"; and (5) "Ensuring Resilience to Disasters" (Department of Homeland Security 2010). The first of those objectives in particular is directly connected to the Obama administration's *National Security Strategy* and *National Strategy for Counterterrorism*, both of which afforded politicians of all political affiliations and American voters opportunities to assess how the president's policies compared with his campaign promises. As U.S. secretary of Homeland Security Janet Napolitano noted in the introduction to her department's report, "Just as today's threats to our national security and strategic interests are evolving and interdependent, so too must our efforts to ensure the security of our homeland reflect these same characteristics" (Department of Homeland Security 2010).

That spirit of interdependence is also evident in the 2010 *National Security Strategy*. As Obama stresses in the introduction to the document, America's "long-term security will come not from our ability to instill fear in other peoples, but through our capacity to speak to their hopes. And that work will best be done through the power of the decency and dignity of the American people—our troops and diplomats, but also our private sector, nongovernmental organizations, and citizens" (Obama 2010). Homeland security challenges in particular are addressed in depth in the opening pages of the third section of the 60-page document, which is entitled "Advancing Our Interests." Most significantly, that section asserts: "At home, the United States is pursuing a strategy capable of meeting the full range of hazards and threats to our communities.... Security at home relies on our ability to prevent and deter attacks by identifying and interdicting threats, denying hostile actors the ability to operate within our borders, protecting the nation's critical infrastructure and key resources, and safeguarding cyberspace" (Obama 2010).

As with the above two strategic documents, the June 2011 *National Strategy for Counterterrorism* recognizes the need for synthesis between approaches to homeland security and national security. Most significantly, with respect to coordination, the strategy stresses that U.S. counterterrorism efforts "require a multidepartmental and multinational effort that goes beyond traditional intelligence, military and law enforcement functions. We are engaged in a broad, sustained, and integrated campaign that harnesses every tool of American power—military, civilian, and the power of our values—together with the concerted efforts of allies, partners, and multilateral institutions" (Obama 2011). Further, the document emphasizes the connection between domestic and international terrorist threats, noting that the Obama administration's most important responsibility is "to protect the American people at home and abroad. This includes eliminating threats to their physical safety, countering threats to global peace and security, and promoting and protecting US interests around the globe" (Obama 2011).

In each of its three overarching strategic security documents, the Obama administration implemented approaches to safeguard U.S. homeland security through actions that leave scholars clear opportunities to assess the extent to which the president followed his campaign promises fully, partially, or not at all with respect to the treatment of members of Al Qaeda and its affiliates in prosecuting the war on terrorism. Ultimately, examples drawn from Obama's first term demonstrate mixed results on three issues in particular: the emphasis of war efforts in Afghanistan relative to those in Iraq; the tactics used to confront Al Qaeda and its affiliates across the world; and the treatment of terrorists detained in the above struggles.

With respect to the first of these issues, Obama did shift America's focus, following through on his pledge to withdraw (nearly) all U.S. military forces from Iraq by December 2011 and raising the force level in Afghanistan as high as 100,000 in March 2010. It should be noted, though, that Obama simply followed the extant Bush-era agreement to withdraw U.S. forces by the end of 2011. Regarding the second issue, Obama did indeed switch tactics, although public perceptions of the results were mixed. While Obama ended the Bush administration's rendition program and extraction of intelligence from captured terrorists through enhanced interrogation techniques, he expanded U.S. drone attacks on members of Al Qaeda and its affiliates. Rather than capture and attempt to gain intelligence from such suspects, America simply killed them (and, in many cases, others unfortunate enough to be in the vicinity of a bombing), leading to criticism of the administration and perhaps reducing the potential intelligence that could have been gained through other means. Lastly, as pertains to the third issue, Obama did not keep his promise to close the U.S. detention facility, which remained open for business throughout his first term. Collectively, these issues provided a foundation for the 2012 presidential campaign that followed, a topic addressed in greater detail in the forthcoming sections of this chapter.

THE REPUBLICAN PRIMARIES

Although homeland security was not a major issue in the Republican primaries, in many ways the most substantive debates and discussions on the topic during the 2012 election cycle occurred during the race for the GOP nomination. The primary contest itself was mainly a contest, as Colin Dueck described it, "between Mitt Romney and the alternatives—a race between the Mitts and the non-Mitts" (Dueck 2012).

During the primaries, a succession of non-Mitts was able to outperform Romney in specific states or lead in opinion polls for brief periods. However, Romney was able to steadily accumulate delegates and ultimately secured the nomination in May 2012, following the Texas primary. In the areas of foreign and homeland security policy, however, the race took on a different complexion. The general perception was that there was a consensus among most of the candidates on the broad components of foreign policy and homeland security. For example, all of the primary candidates took a hard line on border security and more stringent immigration controls. They all endorsed construction of a fence along the U.S.-Mexican border. Minnesota representative Michele Bachmann even promised to build two fences while Georgia businessman Herman Cain pledged to install an electric fence to deter illegal immigrants (Peoples 2011).

Texas representative Ron Paul was the most conspicuous outlier within the crowded field of candidates, leading to perceptions of Paul versus the "non-Pauls" on issues of foreign and homeland security policy (Dueck 2012). However, candidates for the GOP presidential nomination actually differed over several important components of contemporary U.S. homeland security policy. Specific differences emerged in four broad policy areas: the size and scope of the Department of Homeland Security (DHS); the USA PATRIOT ACT (Patriot Act) and civil liberties; enhanced interrogation techniques; and the status and detention of suspected terrorists at Guantanamo Bay.

The primaries revealed policy commonalities between the more moderate GOP candidates and the small-government, Libertarian wing of the party, led by Paul. For instance, while the majority of the crowded field of Republican candidates generally supported the creation of DHS, during the September 7, 2011, debate at the Ronald Reagan Library, moderate candidate and former Utah governor Jon Huntsman contended that DHS had created an atmosphere of "a fortress security mentality that is not American" and needed to be reformed (*New York Times* 2011). Paul called for the abolishment of individual agencies within DHS, including the Transportation Safety Administration (TSA) and the Federal Emergency Management Agency (FEMA). At about the same time, conservative Texas governor Rick Perry was critical of the creation of the department, asserting that it was "unprincipled" for Republicans to back the new organization (*New York Times* 2011). Conversely, former Pennsylvania senator Rick Santorum defended his vote to establish DHS.

The primary campaign also revealed divisions over the Patriot Act. Paul and Huntsman were critical of the measure for its expansion of government surveillance powers. Tea Party enthusiasts within the GOP roundly denounced the measure. Tea Party–backed candidate Bachmann was forced to repeatedly defend her 2011 vote to reauthorize the Patriot Act to her conservative backers. On the other hand, Santorum and the former Speaker of the House, Newt Gingrich, praised the measure as a necessary response to defend against terrorism. Gingrich even called for an increase in the government's investigatory capabilities under the act.

Paul, who consistently argued that the surveillance and arrest powers of the government needed to be curtailed, emerged as a staunch civil libertarian in most matters pertaining to homeland security. The more moderate Huntsman typically adopted centrist positions on civil liberties. Other candidates expressed a willingness to curtail civil liberties in exchange for enhanced security. For instance, in the November 22, 2011, GOP debate in Washington, D.C., Santorum endorsed profiling by the Transportation Safety Administration (TSA) at airports. When asked if he would support ethnic or religious profiling, the former senator responded, "Obviously, Muslims would be—would be someone you'd look at, absolutely" (Halperin 2011). Paul vehemently disagreed with Santorum, pointing out that profiling was "digging a hole for ourselves. What if they look like Timothy McVeigh?" (Halperin 2011). Cain called for the "targeted identification" of potential suspects at airports to avoid "oversimplifying" screening efforts by concentrating on one group (Halperin 2011).

Meanwhile, Romney had called for the wiretapping of mosques and increased surveillance of some Muslims as a counterterrorism tool. He maintained this position through the primaries in what biographer Ronald B. Scott described as an attempt to appeal to the conservative wing of the GOP (Scott 2011, 118–122). Gingrich also supported an expansion of electronic surveillance. Paul steadfastly opposed the expansion of government surveillance initiatives, including wireless wiretapping, arguing that that such programs violated the right to privacy inherent in the Fourth Amendment.

Divisions over torture and enhanced interrogation techniques were also evident through the campaign. Paul and Huntsman were vocal in their opposition to torture, including waterboarding, while Gingrich specifically condemned waterboarding. In 2007, Paul had introduced unsuccessful legislation that would have forbidden the use of evidence obtained through torture. In his 2011 book, *Liberty Defined*, Paul wrote:

> If we are fearful enough, we are willing to tolerate what might otherwise be regarded as immoral means of dealing with the enemy. For example, the use of torture to combat evildoers has been accepted by a large number of otherwise reasonable Americans as a result of those who purposely, successfully used fear as a tactic to achieve their mischievous goals. And now we are moving toward the acceptance of assassination of American citizens as necessary to provide national security. (Paul 2011, 10)

Bachmann and Santorum argued that waterboarding was a necessary tool to extract information. Santorum asserted that without waterboarding, many of the nation's successes against Al Qaeda would not have been possible. During the November 12, 2011, primary debate in Spartanburg, South Carolina, Bachmann and Cain both stated they would reauthorize waterboarding (GOP Debate 2011). Perennial frontrunner and former Massachusetts governor Mitt Romney joined Cain in asserting after the debate that waterboarding was not torture. In response, Arizona senator and former GOP presidential candidate John McCain condemned the candidates' approach and declared that he was "very disappointed by the statements…supporting waterboarding. Waterboarding is torture" (Farber 2013). Although he generally refrained from commenting on the Republican debates, in the aftermath of the Spartanburg event, President Obama declared that the GOP contenders were "wrong" and that "waterboarding is torture. It's contrary to America's traditions.… That's not who we are" (Farber 2013).

Debate over the treatment of those detained in the war on terror extended beyond interrogation methods. Bachmann, Gingrich, and Romney explicitly rejected extending constitutional rights or civil liberties, including Miranda rights, to enemy combatants or foreign terrorist suspects. Paul was the only GOP candidate who embraced the extension of U.S. legal or constitutional protections to enemy combatants.

Through the long primary season, Paul repeatedly stressed his support for the closure of Guantanamo Bay. His sentiments on the detention facility were perhaps best expressed in a 2009 interview with Fox News in which the congressman declared, "Sure, it [Guantanamo Bay] should be closed because we don't need it. It was unnecessary, the way these prisoners were captured were very questionable. They haven't had really due process. So, the real thugs that need to be tried, they ought to be tried" (Paul 2009). Paul went on to argue that terrorists should be detained and tried through the existing legal system, a process that he asserted had worked well in the past, including the apprehension and trial of those involved in the 1993 attack on the World Trade Center. Huntsman also called for the closure of the detention facilities at Guantanamo.

By May, Romney had won the GOP nomination, ultimately securing 43 states and 1,462 delegates. Santorum placed second with 6 states and 234 delegates, and Paul was third with 4 states and 154 delegates. During the primaries, Romney emphasized his experience in counterterrorism and homeland security while head of the 2002 Winter Olympics in Salt Lake City. However, his approach to homeland security did not substantively differ from that of his closest rivals, Santorum and Gingrich. Furthermore, once the general campaign began, there emerged few differences between Romney and Obama on homeland security.

THE GENERAL ELECTION

Homeland security was less of a major issue in the 2012 presidential election than it had been in 2008, when then-candidate Obama vigorously criticized a range of the policies of George W. Bush and pledged to end or rescind them. A poll comparing the most important issues in 2008 and 2012 among older voters found that job growth, rising health care costs, Social Security and Medicare, government competence, and the national deficit were rated most salient in 2012. In 2008, it had been government competence, Social Security and Medicare, rising health care costs, education, and terrorism. Concern over terrorism dropped from fifth to ninth place in the poll (In Choosing a President 2012). Meanwhile, a 2011 Gallup poll found that 56 percent of Americans opposed cuts to homeland security, but higher percentages opposed reductions in funding for education (67 percent), Social Security (64 percent), Medicare (61 percent), and national defense (57 percent).[2]

In the 2008 campaign, then-candidate Obama was highly critical of several components of contemporary U.S. homeland security policy. At the time, the Democratic candidate pledged to end the use of enhanced interrogation techniques (such as waterboarding), close the detention facility at Guantanamo, clarify the status of foreign detainees and provide them the right to challenge their detention through civilian courts, and revise the Patriot Act. In a June 2007 speech, Obama declared, "We're going to close Guantanamo. And we're going to restore habeas corpus.... We're going to lead by example—by not just word but by deed. That's our vision for the future" (White 2007). Obama also pledged to end wireless wiretapping and restrict other aspects of domestic surveillance. As part of his campaign stump speech, Obama promised Americans that he would end the use of "wiretaps without warrants" (Broache 2008).

Once in office, Obama signed Executive Order 13491, which prohibited torture and some enhanced interrogation techniques. The prohibition gained some Republican support, including notably Arizona senator and former GOP presidential candidate John McCain and South Carolina senator Lindsey Graham. The new president also endeavored to close the detention facility at Guantanamo Bay through an executive order. However, Congress blocked the implementation of the order by repeatedly denying funds to close the center and transfer the detainees, beginning with a 90–6 vote in May 2009. Meanwhile, in May 2011, Obama signed an extension of the Patriot Act in spite of his criticism of various aspects of the measure while a candidate. In extending the act, Obama aligned himself with conservative congressional Republicans over the objections of civil libertarians in both parties. In January 2012, Rebecca MacKinnon, a senior fellow at the new America Foundation, described the administration's approach in the following manner:

> As a presidential candidate in 2008, Barack Obama pledged to reform the Patriot Act and rescind the FISA Amendments Act, but as president he reversed his position. The Obama administration has fought bipartisan efforts in Congress to bring the change he once championed. The

result is the "new normal": surveillance, often of questionable legality and sometimes clear illegality, against which Americans have little effective recourse, on the rare occasions that we even know that violations are taking place. (MacKinnon 2012)

The policy convergences on homeland security between Obama and leading Republicans constrained Romney's ability to articulate a clear strategy or vision that was different from that of the president. As noted, Romney supported the extension of the Patriot Act and the broader surveillance programs of the Obama administration. To this extent, Romney aligned himself with the existing bipartisan consensus on homeland security and rejected the Ron Paul/civil libertarian wing of the GOP (and liberals).

Throughout the campaign, President Obama sought to avoid any impression of weakness in the war on terror or homeland security and consistently emphasized his record. The president also benefited from the lack of any primary challenge, thereby forestalling potential questions or criticisms from the left wing of the Democratic Party over his homeland security policies. On the other hand, Romney had to defend himself against challenges from both the left and right during his nomination effort.

There were some minor specific differences on homeland security policy, but none provided either candidate the opportunity to articulate a homeland security strategy that was dramatically different from that of his opponent. Neither candidate wished to appear weak or "soft" on homeland security or terrorism. For instance, during their October 22, 2012, debate on foreign policy, both candidates endorsed the use of drones to target suspected terrorists. When asked about the use of drones, Romney declared: "I support that entirely and feel the president was right to up the usage of that technology and believe that we should continue to use it to continue to go after the people who represent a threat to this nation and to our friends" (Ponnuru 2012). While the candidates did adopt different positions on foreign and security policy, including defense spending and policy toward Iran over its nuclear program, there was a strong convergence on homeland security.

The Republican nominee did continue to emphasize his support for maintaining the detention facility at Guantanamo Bay. He also specifically called for improvements in cybersecurity to protect the nation's infrastructure and security apparatus. The former governor asserted that cybersecurity would be one of his top priorities during his first 100 days in office. In a 2011 white paper, Romney had contended that Obama had not developed a comprehensive cybersecurity policy and had failed to effectively integrate the efforts of the various agencies involved in cybersecurity (Romney 2011).

Romney's inability to clearly differentiate his approach to homeland security from that of the president was part of a larger problem his campaign faced in terms of its ability to develop an alternative vision and strategy on foreign and security policy. This deficiency led to criticism from fellow Republicans. For example, in the aftermath of the campaign, Louisiana governor Bobby Jindal offered the following criticisms:

> The honest truth is, look, Governor Romney's campaign I don't think laid out a specific vision that connected with American voters. Governor Romney is an honorable person, and he should be thanked for his many years of public service, but his campaign was largely about his biography and his experience.... But time and time again, biography and experience are not enough to win an election. You have to have a vision; you have to connect your policies to the aspirations of the American people. I don't think the campaign did that. As a result, I think this campaign became a contest about personalities. (Wilson 2012)

During the campaign, Obama highlighted his record on homeland security and counterterrorism. During his first term, authorities were able to foil a number of terrorist attacks, including the 2009 Christmas Day airline bombing (undertaken by Umar Farouk Abdulmutallab, the so-called "underwear bomber") and the 2010 attempted car bombing in Times Square. Of course, Obama's greatest success in the war on terror was the killing of Osama bin Laden on May 2, 2011. The death of the Al Qaeda leader was used by the Obama campaign to highlight the president's ability to make difficult decisions. Several campaign ads questioned whether Romney would have authorized the raid against bin Laden. One spot included a 2007 quote from Romney that it was not worth it to move "heaven and earth spending billions of dollars just trying to catch one person" (Feller 2012). The ads brought swift condemnation from the Romney campaign and Republicans who charged that Obama was politicizing national security (McCain described the campaign effort as "shameless" and "diminishing the memory of September 11") (Feller 2012).

CONCLUSION

The lack of significant political departure between President Obama and Romney on homeland security issues can be viewed as reality trumping political expediency during the campaign. With Obama being forced to take foreign policy measures that lined up well with the Republican Party, Romney had little room to maneuver to a stance that would significantly differentiate his position without alienating conservatives. Likewise, Americans increasingly turned inward to domestic issues, leaving homeland security issues as important but secondary to other bread and butter issues. For the election, homeland security did not serve as the traditional departure point between the two parties, thereby robbing Romney of the traditional Republican strength on security issues. Given the rise of security-related concerns during the Obama administration after the 2012 election, including the NSA wiretapping issue and the expansion of internal issues within Iraq after the U.S. military departure, the 2012 election could prove the exception to the rule rather than an indicator of a sea change in the importance of homeland security concerns during national elections.

REFERENCES

Baker, N. 2003. "National Security versus Civil Liberties." *Presidential Studies Quarterly* 33 (3) (September): 563.

Branigan, W. 2006. "Democrats Take Majority in House; Pelosi Poised to Become Speaker." *Washington Post,* November 8). http://www.washingtonpost.com/wp-dyn/content/article/2006/11/07/AR2006110700473.html.

Broache, A. 2008. "Obama: No Warrantless Wiretaps If You Elect Me." *CNET,* January 8. Retrieved from http://news.cnet.com/8301-10784_3-9845595-7.html.

Bush, G. W. 2007. "National Strategy for Homeland Security." White House (October). Retrieved from http://www.dhs.gov/xlibrary/assets/nat_strat_homelandsecurity_2007.pdf.

Democratic Candidates Compassion Forum. 2008. *On the Issues,* April 13. Retrieved from http://www.ontheissues.org/Archive/2008_Dems_Compassion_Forum_Homeland_Security.htm.

Department of Homeland Security. "Creation of the Department of Homeland Security." Retrieved from http://www.dhs.gov/creation-department-homeland-security.

Department of Homeland Security. 2010. "Quadrennial Homeland Security Review Report: A Strategic Framework for a Secure Homeland." February. Retrieved from http://www.dhs.gov/xlibrary/assets/qhsr_report.pdf.

Dueck, C. 2012. "The GOP Primaries and Foreign Policy." *Real Clear Politics,* January 26. Retrieved from http://dyn.realclearpolitics.com/printpage/?url=http://www.realclearpolitics.com/articles/2012/01/26/the_gop_primaries_and_foreign_policy_112921-full.html&showimages=1.

Farber, D. 2013. "John McCain Hits GOP Hopefuls over Waterboarding." *CBS News,* November. Retrieved from http://www.cbsnews.com/8301-503544_162-57324283-503544/john-mccain-hits-gop-hopefuls-over-waterboarding/.

Feller, B. 2012. "Obama Campaign Using Osama Bin Laden Killing as 2012 Campaign Tool." *Huffington Post,* April 28. Retrieved from http://www.huffingtonpost.com/2012/04/28/obama-campaign-bin-laden_n_1461431.html?.

Gaddis, J. L. 2004. *Surprise, Security and the American Experience.* Cambridge: Harvard University Press.

"GOP Debate: Herman Cain, Michelle Bachmann Would Reinstate Waterboarding." 2011. *New York Daily News,* November 13. Retrieved from http://www.nydailynews.com/news/politics/gop-debate-herman-cain-sen-michelle-bachmann-reinstate-waterboarding-article-1.976916.

Halperin, M. 2011. "Transcript: CNN National Security Debate." *Time,* November 23. Retrieved from http://thepage.time.com/2011/11/23/transcript-cnn-national-security-debate/.

"In Choosing a President, What Issues Matter Most to Older Voters?" 2012. *AARP,* March 8. Retrieved from http://www.aarp.org/politics-society/government-elections/info-03-2012/survey-2008-2011-elections.html.

MacKinnon, R. 2012. "We're Losing Control of Our Digital Privacy." *CNN,* January 29. Retrieved from http://www.cnn.com/2012/01/26/opinion/mackinnon-sopa-government-surveillance/.

New York Times. 2011. "The Republican Debate at the Reagan Library: Transcript." September 7. Retrieved from http://www.nytimes.com/2011/09/08/us/politics/08republican-debate-text.html?pagewanted=all&_r=0.

Obama, B. H. 2007. "Remarks at 'Take Back America' Conference in Washington, D.C." *On the Issues,* June 18–20. Retrieved from http://www.ontheissues.org/2008/Barack_Obama_Homeland_Security.htm.

Obama, B. H. 2010. "National Security Strategy" (May). Retrieved from http://www.whitehouse.gov/sites/default/files/rss_viewer/national_security_strategy.pdf.

Obama, B. H. 2011. "National Strategy for Counterterrorism" (June). Retrieved from http://www.whitehouse.gov/sites/default/files/counterterrorism_strategy.pdf.

Paul, R. 2009. "Interview." *Fox News,* May 21. Retrieved from http://www.foxnews.com/story/2009/05/21/ron-paul-makes-case-for-closing-gitmo/.

Paul, R. 2011. *Liberty Defined: 50 Essential Issues That Affect Our Freedom*. New York: Hachette Book Group.

Peoples, S. 2011. "Immigration Debate Heats Up in GOP Primary." *Huffington Post: Politics,* October 20. Retrieved from http://www.huffingtonpost.com /2011/10/20/gop-primary-immigration_n_1021627.html.

Ponnuru, R. 2012. "Why Drones Stayed out of Sight in the 2012 Campaign." *Bloomberg,* November 5. Retrieved from http://www.bloomberg.com/news /2012-11-05/why-drones-stayed-out-of-sight-in-the-2012-campaign.html.

Romney, M. 2011. "An American Century: A Strategy to Secure America's Enduring Interests and Ideals." October 7. Retrieved from http://mittromney.com/sites /default/files/shared/AnAmericanCentury-WhitePaper_0.pdf.

Scott, R. B. 2011. *Mitt Romney: An Inside Look at the Man and His Politics*. Guilford, CT: Lyons Press.

White, E. 2007. "Obama Says Gitmo Facility Should Close." *Washington Post,* June 24. Retrieved from http://www.washingtonpost.com/wp-dyn/content/article /2007/06/24/AR2007062401046.html.

Wilson, R. 2012. "At Republican Confab Romney Gets the Blame." *National Journal,* November 14. Retrieved from http://www.nationaljournal.com/politics/at -republican-confab-romney-gets-the-blame-20121114.

NOTES

1. These three sets of strategies are as follows: the July 2002 *National Strategy for Homeland Security* and October 2007 *National Strategy for Homeland Security*; the September 2002 *National Security Strategy* and March 2006 *National Security Strategy*; and the February 2003 *National Strategy for Combating Terrorism* and the September 2006 *National Strategy for Combating Terrorism*.

2. There were partisan differences in the poll; only 38 percent of Republicans supported cuts to homeland security, while 47 percent of Democrats did; Frank Newport and Lydia Saad, "Americans Oppose Cuts in Education, Social Security, Defense," Gallop Poll (January 26, 2011); online at http://www.gallup.com/poll/145790/Americans-Oppose-Cuts-Education-Social-Security-Defense.aspx.

Chapter 14

U.S. Foreign Policy and Global Change in the 2012 Presidential Election

Chris J. Dolan, Lebanon Valley College

THE 2012 PRESIDENTIAL ELECTION AND A WORLD IN TRANSITION

President Barack Obama's reelection in November 2012 could be seen as a public affirmation of his foreign policy goals and objectives. Although international issues are usually relegated to the back burner in presidential elections, foreign policy and national security were significant factors in both the Obama and Romney campaigns (Cohen 2012; Indyk 2012). This was ironic given that the two political parties were resolutely focused on addressing domestic unemployment, economic recovery, deficits and the debt, and health care reform. Obama did highlight his numerous accomplishments, including the rescue of the global economy, killing of bin Laden, military withdrawals from Iraq and Afghanistan, diplomacy with Iran over its nuclear weapons program, collaboration with Russia on non-proliferation of weapons of mass destruction, and extending an olive to branch to China in promoting regional security cooperation (Indyk et al.

2012). Obama could even claim that his foreign policy accomplishments had the immediate effect of improving America's global image (Pew Global Attitudes Project 2012a). In addition, Obama was eager to bulk up the national security credentials of the Democratic Party.

Throughout the election, Republican candidate Mitt Romney criticized Obama for pursuing a foreign policy of accommodation and for facilitating the diminishment of American global power (McGregor 2012). Romney made the conventional argument that Obama was a weak and naïve president who often apologized for America's so-called historical errors and for failing to support traditional allies like Israel. His rhetorical critique was that U.S. foreign policy under Obama should be condemned for "leading from behind" (Baker and Cooper 2012).

In the election and over the course of the Obama presidency, a number of complex and dynamic global challenges have threatened to undermine and complicate America's foreign policy interests. The overthrow of Ukrainian president Viktor Yanukovych and the annexation of Crimea by Russia represent some of the most critical threats to the security of Europe since the end of the Cold War. Russia's aggressive move in Crimea and influence within Ukraine has reminded Obama that NATO's level of commitment to European security will be put to the test as Russia pushes back against the historical trajectory of NATO expansion and European Union enlargement. Also, China's rise as a military power and its tensions with Japan, South Korea, and the Philippines could alter the strategic balance of power throughout Asia and the Pacific. In response to the rising significance of Asia in global economics and politics, Obama's decisions to continue moving U.S. forces to the Pacific and establish a military presence in Australia reflect not only the reconfiguration of U.S. strategic interests but a shifting global order. In addition, the rising death toll in the Syrian civil war and the struggle with Russia to bring that conflict to an end, the faltering Israeli-Palestinian peace talks, and the resurgence of violence in Egypt could destabilize the Middle East.

Obama has set forth a largely realist foreign policy course that mixed pragmatism with caution unmodified by grand strategy, missionary triumphalism, and political ideology. But the broader, more comprehensive charge raised by Romney and Republicans during the election was whether U.S. global power and influence under Obama is in decline. Or, were global events that remain largely outside the direct control of the president simply too complex to simplify in the heated 2012 presidential election?

POLITICS OF THE "PIVOT"

During the 2012 election and in his first term, President Obama tried to move his foreign policy agenda with a "pivot" to Asia and the Pacific. He has done so by highlighting the significance and economic rise to prominence of China. As president he moved to sustain existing alliances with Japan, South Korea, Australia, and the Philippines while building new and stronger partnerships with Myanmar, Cambodia, Indonesia, and Vietnam. He even framed his visits to Myanmar and Cambodia as part of a broader agenda of highlighting transitions toward market development and democracy throughout the region (Nakamura 2012).

Obama's argument throughout the 2012 election was that Romney would return to George W. Bush's aggressive unilateralism, which overextended the U.S. military, and his deregulatory policies that contributed to the global recession of 2008 (A. Berman 2012; Sanger 2009). Obama accused Romney of being "stuck in a Cold War time warp" who failed to perceive the significance of rising nations in Asia and would therefore be reckless with such issues as trade, finance, and security (Joyner 2012). Romney attacked Obama for placing the United States "at the mercy of events instead of shaping events," suggesting that U.S. global power was on the decline because the president is a weak commander-in-chief (Rucker 2012). While the United States and most leading economies were able to avoid the calamitous effects of the global breakdown by coordinating monetary policies and promoting common interests, the global reputation of the United States was being questioned by the movement of economic power to Asia and the Pacific (Ikenberry 2008, 2011a). Under his leadership, Obama would be forced to navigate between managing global change and setting a foreign policy that would continue to promote U.S. global leadership.

The Asia-Pacific region did not dominate foreign policy issues in the 2012 election, although the role of U.S. global leadership in relation to China certainly did. With the "pivot" strategy, Obama sought a broad engagement strategy to build support and establish alliances throughout

Asia and the Pacific while extending U.S. economic interests into this vital region. The Obama administration was concerned that state development and other export-led models of growth would gain more acceptance and legitimacy, especially in emerging economies and developing states (Bijian 2005; Ikenberry 2008, 2011b). The ultimate goal was to check attempts by rising powers, such as China and India, from reshaping global trade, finance, regulation, and development in ways that could undermine U.S. global economic interests (Nathan and Scobell 2012).

When China was discussed in the 2012 election, the campaigns focused mainly on the U.S. relationship with the country as a foreign creditor and in terms of trade. Although Obama complained to the World Trade Organization about allegations of China's trading improprieties, Romney attacked him of not being tough enough on China for violating intellectual property and patent protections (Presidential Debate Transcript 2012). Romney even accused the president of doing nothing as thousands of American jobs disappeared because of China's unfair trade and monetary practices and manipulation of its currency to make Chinese exports cheaper and more competitive. Romney stated, "It's time to stand up to the cheaters and make sure we protect jobs for the American people" (LaFraniere 2012). The Obama campaign shot back in an ad claiming that Romney's private equity firm invested in a Chinese company that exploited low-wage labor.

While the United States and China have kept their differences at bay, the Obama administration maintains that China's economic arrival has not yet transformed it into a globally responsible actor (Zakaria 2011). The United States hoped China's rise to economic influence would create incentives for it to adhere to liberal norms and rules (Rasul-Ronning 2012). As a result, there is growing suspicion between the United States and China regarding each other's interests and intentions. The Obama administration is worried that China will seek to invest its massive economic resources and savings in military programs designed to reshape and recast the strategic balance of power in the region (Zakaria 2011). The concern is China using the nuclear crisis in North Korea and raising the stakes over disputed islands as part of a broader attempt to chip away at U.S. allies and American influence (Bumiller 2012; Keck 2014; Tisdall 2012). The Obama administration knows that others in the region—especially Japan, South Korea, the Philippines, Vietnam, and Taiwan—are relatively supportive of America's effort to check and balance Chinese influence (Fackler 2012). To counter China's strategic maneuvering, Obama signed a basing agreement with the Philippines in 2014 in the wake of Typhoon Yolanda to enhance U.S. military presence throughout the region (Keck 2014).

CONTENDING WITH THE MIDDLE EAST

The Middle East dominated the 2012 presidential election and frustrated Obama's attempt to shift the focus of U.S. foreign policy toward Asia and the Pacific. Recognizing that the region continues to hold the most peril in U.S. foreign policy, Obama made attempts to improve America's image. In his 2009 speech at Cairo University, he stated, "I've come here to Cairo to seek a new beginning between the United States and Muslims around the world, one based on mutual interest and mutual respect, and one based upon the truth that America and Islam are not exclusive and need not be in competition" (Obama 2009). He followed up on his commitment with the military withdrawals from Iraq and Afghanistan, hoping to address the criticism that the U.S. does not take the interests of others into account and rushes too quickly to use force (Kohut 2010).

As a way of distinguishing himself from his Republican opponent, Obama also abandoned the notion of a comprehensive "war on terrorism" (Gordon and Trainor 2012; Klaidman 2012; Sanger 2012). Obama's focus would be narrowly targeted at terrorists operating in Pakistan, Afghanistan, and Yemen. Afghanistan was even deemed a "major non-NATO ally" of the United States, which would facilitate security cooperation between the two states well after the completion of the Afghan presidential election held in April 2014 when the United States began relinquishing control of the country's security (Rosenberg and Bowley 2012). But it was the killing of Osama bin Laden that earned him the most accolades and significantly raised his national security profile (Gordon and Trainor 2012; Klaidman 2012; Sullivan 2012).

On the Israeli-Palestinian peace process, expectations were high given that Obama promised to make it his top foreign policy priority (Indyk and Lieberthal 2012). However, he sent mixed messages to both sides. Israeli leaders protested when Obama threw his support behind a diplomatic solution calling for all sides to return to 1967 borders and make land swaps to compensate for disputed territory (Landler and Myers 2011). When special Mideast envoy George Mitchell told Israeli prime minister Benjamin Netanyahu that the United States favored just a partial settlement freeze, this opened Obama up to charges that he was biased against the Palestinians (Indyk and Lieberthal 2012). While Obama's initial recommendations did seem like valid and rational attempts at making progress, he misunderstood the extent to which internal dynamics constrained the ability of negotiators and mediators to make such concessions. As a result, each side became frustrated with a president who they had believed was genuinely committed to a real and lasting peace (Harnden 2011).

Romney even plunged himself into the volatile issue. During a campaign trip to Israel, he offended Palestinian leaders by claiming that cultural differences are the reason why Palestinians are economically less successful than Israelis (Parker and Oppel 2012). The Romney campaign also attacked Obama for not visiting Israel and not recognizing Jerusalem as the capital of the Jewish state even though his failure to visit was not historically unusual (Kessler 2012). Much of the Republican criticism was premised on Obama's first-term visits to Egypt, Turkey, Iraq, and Saudi Arabia and not the Jewish state (Black and Tran 2009; Kessler 2012). When Obama did eventually make his first visit as president to Israel and the West Bank in March 2013 to shore up the peace process, it was described by Republicans as "maintenance trip" (Macaskill 2013).

The strain between Obama and Netanyahu might have been relieved if Obama had been more successful in convincing Arab states and negotiators that seeking a genuine peace was America's primary concern during the 2012 election. Many in the Arab world became suspicious of Obama in the wake of his hesitancy to close the detention facility in Guantanamo and after he began publicly embracing Israeli negotiating positions as his campaign against Romney drew to a close in November 2012 (Indyk and Lieberthal 2012). In April 2014, U.S. secretary of state John Kerry even threatened to "walk away" from negotiations as the peace process reached its closest point of collapse after Israel's refusal to release Palestinian prisoners and the Palestinians voting to join 15 international organizations that would draw them closer to enhanced UN recognition (Stearns 2014). It should be noted that Netanyahu and Abbas were not willing to compromise on many of the finer points throughout the process, especially halting Israeli settlements in the occupied territories and Palestinian security guarantees for Israel (Greenberg 2011; Stearns 2014).

THE ARAB SPRING IN ELECTORAL POLITICS

The reverberations of the Arab Spring were felt throughout the 2012 presidential campaign season as Obama sought to chart a course emphasizing democracy throughout the region. Although the NATO intervention in Libya put Obama on the side of a popular uprising, the violent civil war in Syria, terrorist attacks against the U.S. Consulate in Benghazi, Libya, and instability in Egypt factored into campaign politics and threatened Obama's attempts at redirecting U.S. global priorities (Lizza 2011).

During his first term, Obama was selective in his response to violence directed at protesters by key regimes across the region. While he eventually abandoned support for Egyptian president Hosni Mubarak and Tunisian president Zine el-Abidine Ben-Ali, Obama neglected to push for reforms in Bahrain and did not protest Saudi military intervention that backed up the Bahraini monarchy's crackdown on protests by the Shiite majority (Black 2011; Lizza 2011). Obama's lack of response to the Saudi intervention could be interpreted as an attempt to counterbalance Iranian interests in the Persian Gulf. Seeing an opportunity to remove longtime nemesis Muammar Qaddafi from power, he backed U.S. participation in NATO-led air strikes in Libya and supported the rebel National Transition Council. However, Obama has meandered in pushing for the removal of President Bashar al-Assad in Syria even though at least 150,000 have been killed (Surk 2014; Warrick 2011). While Obama's slow embrace of popular movements placed the United States on a course that acknowledges the movement away from autocracy, his selectivity reflected a desire to safeguard U.S. strategic interests in the Middle East (Gerges 2012).

The NATO intervention in Libya was a key feature in Obama's foreign policy strategy and was used by Democratic allies to fend off Republican campaign attacks that Obama was "leading from behind" (Boyle 2011).

It was a signal that the United States would defer to longstanding alliances and multilateralism as opposed to launching unilateral strikes (Lizza 2011). In Libya, the Obama administration influenced the UN Security Council to pass Resolution 1973 to protect the civilian population from attacks by Qaddafi's forces and participated in NATO operations supporting rebel forces that ultimately forced him from power (Sargent 2011). Most important, it was in U.S. interests to be on the side of a popular uprising against a dictator. As Obama stated, "America has an important strategic interest in preventing Qaddafi from overrunning those who oppose him. A massacre would have driven thousands of additional refugees across Libya's borders, putting enormous strains on the peaceful—yet fragile—transitions in Egypt and Tunisia. The democratic impulses that are dawning across the region would be eclipsed by the darkest form of dictatorship, as repressive leaders concluded that violence is the best strategy to cling to power" (Obama 2011).

The escalating violence in Syria gave Republican critics reason to attack the administration for failing to lead. Obama's initial decision against using force to oust President Bashar al-Assad in Syria reflected a measure of caution and selectivity regarding the extent to which his administration would support antiregime forces during the Arab Spring (Black 2011; Knickerbocker 2011). Although sanctions have choked Assad and UN officials have called for safe zones to protect civilian noncombatants, the escalating violence increased pressure on the West to topple Assad. However, peace efforts by the UN and the Arab League led by Kofi Annan quickly unraveled as the violence spread throughout Syria with massacres and atrocities taking place in areas suspected of being sympathetic to antiregime forces (Blomfield 2012).

The specific issues of arming rebel groups and Syria's chemical weapons featured prominently as foreign policy issues in the 2012 election, especially after Obama enunciated his "red line" warning about the use of chemical weapons by the Syrian regime. On August 20, 2012, the president stated, "We have been very clear to the Assad regime, but also to other players on the ground, that a red line for us is we start seeing a whole bunch of chemical weapons moving around or being utilized. That would change my calculus. That would change my equation" (see Kessler 2013). Although the president was somewhat vague on which options the

United States would seek, the implication was that the president might launch air strikes against regime targets in response to the potential use of chemical weapons. In response, candidate Romney accused the president of "sitting on the sidelines" and promised, if elected president, to arm rebel groups fighting government forces with heavy weapons (Macaskill 2012). In attempting to shift away from the president's policy of leaning on Saudi Arabia and Qatar to support the rebels and containing the civil war from spreading throughout the region, Romney was hoping that a more forceful stance would distinguish him from the president and bulk up his foreign policy credentials.

Given Russia's support for the Assad regime, the difficulties and constraints in launching air strikes became abundantly clear to the president (Weaver 2012). Russia has close ties with Assad and had, along with China, vetoed three different Security Council resolutions authorizing engagement. With his hands tied, Obama launched a major diplomatic effort to encourage Russia to abandon its military support for Assad and consent to some measure of multilateral action in order to obviate the spread of violence throughout the region (Klapper 2012).

Although both Syria and Libya factored heavily in the 2012 election, there were strategic considerations in Syria that were not present in Libya. The Obama administration was concerned that regime change could drive Islamists who constitute a sizable portion of the rebel forces into power should the Assad regime collapse. The intervention by Hezbollah from Lebanon in support of the Syrian government, rising numbers of refugees fleeing the violence, and the role of Al Qaeda could draw Turkey, Jordan, Israel, and Iraq into the war. Even more dangerous was the rise of the barbarous Islamic State in Iraq and Syria, which emerged from Al Qaeda and strengthened during the Syrian civil war and amidst sectarian chaos in Iraq. Obama's response was to piece together a coalition of Kurdish militias and Western and Arab states to launch airstrikes and coordinate ground attacks against key targets in Iraq and Syria. Unlike Libya, where Qaddafi lacked broad-based regional support, Assad enjoys support from both Iran and Russia (Warrick and Sly 2012).

After his reelection, Syria continued to factor into the president's foreign policy calculus. Following reports that the Syrian government used chemical weapons on August 21, 2013, killing more than 1,400 people in a rebel area near Damascus, Obama sought to build support among G-20 nations for air strikes (Spetalnick and Anishchuk 2013). Moreover, the president claimed "I didn't set a red line. The world set a red line" (see Kessler 2013). However, after a British parliamentary vote against air strikes and with 48 percent of Americans opposing force, the president embraced a more diplomatic course (Pew Research Center 2013).

Although his Republicans critics claimed the president backtracked from the original "red line" statement he uttered during the 2012 campaign, Obama could at least point to his threat to use force as a factor pressuring Syria in dismantling its chemical weapons program. He even accepted an offer from Russian president Vladimir Putin to help remove and destroy the weapons by mid-2014, effectively taking air strikes off the table during the dismantlement process (Gordon 2013; Baker 2014). The UN Security Council unanimously adopted Resolution 2118 requiring Syria to follow a strict timeline enforced by the Organization for the Prohibition of Chemical Weapons (OPCW) to destroy its chemical arsenal and weapons production facilities. However, progress has been slow amid accusations by the United States of foot dragging and by the United Kingdom that the Syrian government intends to hold back its stockpiles in case of a partition or invasion (Black 2012). As of February 2014, only 4 percent of Syria's chemical weapons components had been removed for destruction (Zirulnick 2014).

During the 2012 election and beyond, upheaval in the Middle East extended well past Syria. On September 11, 2012, the U.S. consulate in Benghazi, Libya was attacked, resulting in the deaths of U.S. ambassador Christopher Stevens and three U.S. consular officials, and the U.S. Embassy in Cairo was stormed by a militants. Almost immediately, Romney accused the president of sympathizing with the attackers by stating, "It's disgraceful that the Obama administration's first response was not to condemn attacks on our diplomatic missions, but to sympathize with those who waged the attacks" (see Weiner 2012). He added, "An apology for America's values is never the right course" (see Baker and Parker 2012). Romney was responding to an embassy statement released hours before the protests and the attack in Benghazi began to quell tensions following the public release of an anti-Muslim Islam video.

Obama quickly accused Romney of distorting the chain of events and politicizing the tragedy by stating that "Governor Romney seems to have a tendency to shoot first and aim later.... And as president, one of the things I've learned is you can't do that—that, you know, it's important for you to make sure that the statements that you make are backed up by the facts, and that you've thought through the ramifications." A bipartisan Senate report later deemed the Libyan terror group Ansar al-Sharia responsible for the Benghazi terrorist attacks and blamed the attacks on poor security at the consulate and lack of communication among intelligence, state, and defense officials, and absolved the Obama administration of covering up the attacks. However, Republicans placed blame on former secretary of state Hillary Clinton as the official who was responsible for security lapses in Benghazi as she weighed a possible run for the presidency in 2016 (Goldman and Gearan 2014).

The eruption of violence reflected a broader challenge for Obama in resetting U.S. foreign policy toward the Middle East following years of U.S. support for repressive regimes and in the immediate wake of the wars in Iraq and Afghanistan. Obama has struggled to strike the right balance between supporting popular movements and securing American interests as Islamist parties rose to power in a number of nations (Black 2011; Lizza 2011; Zuckerman 2012). The transition to popular rule proved to be a major hurdle confronting Obama, especially since the United States has a long history of backing repressive governments that kept Islamists in check and helped to stabilize the region.

Obama was forced to confront this reality in the middle of the 2012 election, especially when the Islamist government came to power in Egypt. Some Republican legislators made statements and conservative groups supportive of the Romney campaign ran ads linking the Obama White House and State Department officials to the Muslim Brotherhood (Mann 2012; Fox 2012a, 2012b). These campaign and partisan accusations were connected to what many believed was the Obama administration's support of the parliamentary election results leading to the victory of the political wing of the Muslim Brotherhood and its candidate, Mohammed Morsi, in the 2012 presidential election in the wake of the overthrow of Hosni Mubarak in 2011. Obama did not object when the Egyptian military under the leadership of popular defense minister General Abdul-

Fattah el-Sisi overthrew and jailed Morsi and launched a violent crack-down on the Muslim Brotherhood (Kagan 2013).

After the military-backed government resigned in February 2014, el-Sisi announced his intention to run for the Egyptian presidency. The challenge for Obama was whether or not to openly embrace el-Sisi, who led the overthrow of his country's first freely elected government (Kirkpat-rick 2014). Although the United States is not omnipotent, the Obama administration can wield a considerable degree of power in Egypt with its annual $1.3 billion aid package to the military and influence over how the International Monetary Fund and other global donors distribute funds to Egypt (Kagan 2013). The question was whether and how the Obama admin-istration would leverage that influence over an el-Sisi government.

Obama's struggles in responding to events in Egypt overshadow a broader reality that did not surface during the 2012 election. Surveys indicate that democracy continues to be the preferred form of govern-ment in a number of Arab nation-states with Muslims demonstrating widespread support for multiparty elections, freedom of expression, and political rights for women (Pew Global Attitudes Project 2012b). However, to varying degrees, many prefer that Islam play a role in political life. Most citizens in Pakistan, Jordan, and Egypt believe their laws should follow the Quran while majorities or pluralities in Tunisia and Turkey believe laws should at least acknowledge and adhere to general Islamic principles (Pew Global Attitudes Project 2012b). While Obama attempted to address America's image, U.S. foreign policy remains unpopular throughout the Arab world, and few believe the United States supports democracy in the Middle East, including just 37 percent in Egypt and roughly 3 in 10 in Tunisia (Pew Global Attitudes Project 2012b).

The challenge is whether Obama would or should scale back public diplomacy activities or curtail foreign aid to key states in the region, especially those in which American diplomatic missions and other peace operations are inherently exposed. Attacks on the U.S. consulates and embassies in Libya and Egypt forced the United States to confront the nature of the American presence. Scaling back U.S. operations would dramatically harm America's ability to build cultural exchange programs that help build and sustain social and political institutions in key states experiencing the transition away from autocracy toward popular rule.

Given the violence that took place at the height of the 2012 presidential election and campaign season, members of Congress weighed in by proposing cuts to U.S. bilateral aid to key states, including Egypt, the second largest recipient (R. Berman 2012). For example, influential House Republicans moved to curtail a $450 million package for Egypt to demonstrate their opposition to the newly elected Morsi government (Cooper and Landler 2012; Myers 2012). While Romney's blunt criticism of Obama failed to resonate with voters, the Republican opposition contended that the uprisings did create political opportunities to demand a harder stance on Islamist governments and show support for Israel (Sink 2012).

The most important challenge for any U.S. president is addressing the tension and contradiction in U.S. foreign policy between promoting so-called democratic principles and strategic interests. Obama tentatively supported popular movements in Tunisia, Libya, Egypt, and Syria, but failed to do so in Yemen, Saudi Arabia, Bahrain, and Jordan. This raises the question of whether continued U.S. support for police states and repressive monarchies that hold back domestic political reforms and check liberalization is a realistic long-term foreign policy strategy. It remains to be seen if autocratic regimes will continue to be immune from popular demands. No matter what the future holds for the region, Obama has opted for a cautious and selective course. In the absence of a long-term and consistent foreign policy that more effectively balances the tensions and contradictions between strategic interests and democratic principles, U.S. influence in the region is likely to diminish under Obama and his successors. This will have dire consequences for the prospect of a genuine peace among the Palestinians and Israelis.

RUSSIAN RESURGENCE AND NUCLEAR PROLIFERATION

At the height of the 2012 presidential election, the Obama campaign criticized Romney for claiming that Russia was the "number one geopolitical foe" of the United States and that "resetting" relations with the country would harm U.S. interests (see Willis 2012). It did not help the president when Romney reacted negatively to comments made by Obama to then Russian president Dmitri Medvedev in early 2012 regarding U.S. missile defense that "After my election, I have more flexibility," to which

Medvedev responded, "I understand. I will transmit this information to Vladimir" (Willis 2012). Following Russia's annexation of Crimea in March 2014 after the overthrow by pro-Western demonstrators of the Russian-backed government of Ukrainian president Viktor Yanukovych, Romney was now in a position to say "I told you so," even publicly criticizing Obama that same month for being naïve about Putin's intentions. Echoing sentiments made by U.S. senator John McCain that Obama is the "most naïve president in history," Romney criticized the president's "faulty judgment about Russia's intentions and objectives" raised during the 2012 election (see Shear and Baker 2014).

Relations with Russia were already tense over Syria and after Putin decided to grant Edward Snowden (the National Security Agency contractor who was accused of leaking materials and information regarding the vast global network of electronic surveillance of communications) temporary asylum in Russia. The clear challenge confronting the president in his second term is whether or not to view Putin's Russia as an enemy or adversary. In response to Russia's move in Crimea and the massing of Russian troops on its border with Ukraine, the United States and European Union implemented sanctions against Russian policymakers and businesspersons. Obama even dismissed Russia as a "regional power," which operates "not out of strength, but out of weakness" (see Shear and Baker 2014). While Russian annexation of Crimea demonstrates the continued relevance of European security after the Cold War, any move that entices Ukraine toward NATO and the EU could be interpreted by Russia as a move by the West to gobble up yet another former Soviet republic and ally. However, the United States and NATO might still be drawn into a conflict given Russia's embrace of what seems to be a long-term strategy of thwarting Ukraine from moving outside its sphere of influence. The most dangerous scenario is the possibility of a Russian invasion on behalf of pro-Russian separatists in eastern Ukraine (Loyola 2014; MacFarquhar 2014).

The president's political hands are tied because he depends on Russian cooperation on critical threats facing both nations. After the 2013 Boston Marathon bombings, in which four people were killed and over three hundred were injured in attacks by Chechen radicals, Obama and Putin pledged more cooperation on counterterrorism measures (LaFranchi 2013). Also, key to resetting relations with Russia was lessening tensions resulting from the Bush administration's decision to deploy a missile defense system in Poland and the Czech Republic. In March 2010, Obama and Medvedev signed the New Start Treaty, which committed the United States and Russia to reducing their nuclear weapons arsenals (Shear 2010). Therefore, Obama must work with Russia and not perceive its refusal to cooperate on select issues as indicators of an adversarial relationship. Both states share common interests in the fight against global terrorism and in preventing terrorists from obtaining weapons of mass destruction. The United States and Russia cannot afford to get along without each other.

One of the most important issues that demands U.S.-Russia cooperation is the Iranian nuclear program. At the start of his presidency, Obama attempted to engage Iran in multilateral talks; however, when this failed, he sought options to directly pressure President Mahmoud Ahmadinejad with warnings and consequences (Indyk, O'Hanlon, and Lieberthal 2012). When Iran's new moderate president, Hassan Rouhani, came to power in 2013, his government promised Iranians that it would seek to ease Western sanctions by working with the United States to solve the nuclear issue. This was a positive step after years of resistance and defiance from former leader Mahmoud Ahmadinejad (Ahmed 2013). In an interim accord, Iranian negotiators pledged to comply with P5+ nations (United States, United Kingdom, France, China, Russia, plus Germany) to halt work on the Arak nuclear reactor where spent fuel contained plutonium and consent to IAEA inspections. Although Iran would not close the facility, the United States agreed to convert it to a light water reactor to reduce worries about its potential use for military purposes. And despite the ongoing crisis in Ukraine, Obama has been able to persuade Russia that it is in its interests to remain engaged in the nuclear talks.

However, despite opposition from the Obama White House, Republicans endorsed a bill that would broaden sanctions on Iran to pressure it into dismantling its nuclear facilities. Moreover, progress in the nuclear talks did not assuage Republicans who believe Iran represents a security threat to Israel (Rubin and Gladstone 2014). During the 2012 election, Romney and Republican legislators indicated they would back Israeli military strikes against Iranian nuclear sites (Sherwood 2012).

At the same time the Obama administration was negotiating with Iran, it has been frustrated by North Korea's repeated attempts to enhance its nuclear program. During his first term, North Korea successfully weaponized most of its plutonium, reprocessed spent fuel rods, test fired short-range missiles, conducted underground nuclear tests, and revealed the existence of a new enrichment facility. In response, the UN approved Security Council Resolution 1874, which condemned the nuclear test, imposed new sanctions, and banned arm sales to the reclusive regime. In exchange for suspension of the enrichment program, the United States met with North Korean officials in China and attempted to restart the six-party nuclear talks that collapsed in 2008. After the death of dictator Kim Jong Ill in December 2011, his son Kim Jong Un assumed control of the regime and subsequently test launched a long-range missile, sent an operational satellite into space, and conducted a third nuclear test (Sang-Hun 2013). North Korea went further by threatening to launch preemptive strikes against South Korea, detaining American missionary Kenneth Bae, and temporarily closing the Kaesong industrial park. Furthermore, a March 2014 UN Human Rights Council report revealed the existence of an extensive system of concentration camps and torture facilities to starve, imprison, and execute prisoners inside North Korea (DeTrani 2014).

Obama's approach to dealing with the North Korean nuclear issue has and will continue to evolve. While it has enough room to engage in direct talks with the regime, it eventually embraced an approach that former secretary of state Clinton referred to as "strategic patience in close consultations with our six party allies" (see Snyder 2013). Obama and the new government of South Korean president Park Geun-hye have sought greater coordination and cooperation through trilateral U.S.-South Korea-China dialogue on common issues and challenges posed by North Korea while at the same time going ahead with joint U.S.-South Korea military drills (Bradshaw 2014). The approach rests on the assumption that North Korean provocation and self-imposed isolation would lead China to pressure the regime into denuclearizing its stockpiles. In other words, Obama believed direct dialogue with North Korea would not produce any tangible benefits and might come at great risk. As former secretary of defense Robert Gates stated, the United States "would not buy this horse for a third time" (see Snyder 2013).

INTO THE GREAT WIDE OPEN

Throughout the 2012 electoral contest, President Obama sought to distance himself from Mitt Romney by painting his Republican opponent as a unilateralist who would return to the aggressive foreign policies of former president George W. Bush. His "pivot" to Asia was made in response to a rising China and to shore up the strategic balance of power in the region and designed to reassure Japan, the Philippines, South Korea, and Australia (Clinton 2011; Lieberthal 2011). Obama took political credit for ordering the daring raid that killed Osama bin Laden, nuclear talks with Iran, withdrawing U.S. forces from Afghanistan and Iraq, and preventing global economic catastrophe (Klaidman 2012). His campaign focused on the successful NATO intervention in Libya, which was conducted with UN authorization and without American casualties. There is much to suggest that Obama helped to restore the American brand in the face of Republican campaign criticism.

However, some of the criticism leveled against Obama by Romney during the 2012 election and by congressional Republicans might stick to the president. Romney's tough tone on Russia and his criticism of Obama for attempting to reset relations will likely reverberate for many years. Russia's annexation of Crimea and unrest in eastern Ukraine means that the United States confronts what is likely the most significant foreign policy challenge since the end of the Cold War. The reality is that the United States must continue to be deeply engaged in the security of Europe.

Moreover, there may be ramifications for what Romney claimed is an Obama foreign policy lacking a comprehensive global blueprint (Laidi 2012). The charge was that U.S. global power has been declining under Obama because his foreign policy lacks guidelines based on American principles. Romney and his Republican allies often accused the president of apologizing for U.S. global action and lacking a national security strategy focused on military strength. Given China's rise to prominence within this broader political narrative, the scope of U.S. military power and economic influence in Asia and the Pacific will continue to be put to the test by America's rivals and Obama's political opponents.

Interestingly, although Obama warned voters in the 2012 election that Romney would return America to the Bush era, there is surprising continuity between the foreign policies of the Bush and Obama administrations. Obama has continued with and expanded domestic and offshore oil drilling operations to the point where the United States is now forecast to overtake Saudi Arabia as the world's leading oil producer and become a net exporter of oil (Rosenthal 2012). He also expanded U.S. counterterrorism operations as part of his focus on Al Qaeda (Harnden 2010). Obama has been very aggressive in his use of drones in carrying out secretive strikes against suspected militants (including U.S. citizens) identified on so-called "kill lists" (Harris 2012). Obama implemented controversial NSA electronic surveillance programs and continued with the use of rendition, detentions, and the "state secrets" doctrine to prosecute suspected terrorists and enemies (Becker and Shane 2012; Nakashima 2014). Although he has sought to recast America's global image, Obama's actions are consistent with the role of war president.

The reality of navigating U.S. foreign policy through a shifting and changing global order appears to be overshadowing his 2012 campaign promises and policy achievements. Although the United States has largely recovered from the global recession and financial crisis, many Americans simply have not experienced the benefits of that recovery as the U.S. transitions toward a "new normal." The political brinkmanship between Obama and congressional Republicans continues to impact the budgetary outlook for the world's largest economy and defense posture of the world's strongest military. The president's campaign promise to deliver on comprehensive immigration reform legislation is an indication that gridlock and divided government continue to withhold progress on consequential issues. Obama is no longer an inexperienced president with a short foreign policy resume. Like any second-term president, he is focused on promoting his legacy and shaping the direction of U.S. foreign relations. Therefore, Obama's success in foreign policy should be measured against both his campaign promises from the 2012 election and in relation to broader global events that exist far beyond the control of any American president.

REFERENCES

Ahmed, A. 2013. "Iran's Rouhani." *Al-Jazeera,* August 4. Retrieved from http://www
.aljazeera.com/video/middleeast/2013/08/2013843428202796.html.

Baker, P. 2014. "Pressure Rising as Obama Works to Rein in Russia." *New York Times,* March 2, A1.

Baker, P., and H. Cooper. 2012. "Sparring over Foreign Policy, Obama Goes on the Offense." *New York Times,* October 22, A1.

Baker, P., and A. Parker. 2012. "A Challenger's Criticism Is Furiously Returned." *New York Times,* September 12, A1.

Becker, J., and S. Shane. 2012. "Secret 'Kill List' Proves a Test of Obama's Principles and Will." *New York Times,* May 29, A1.

Berman, A. 2012. "Mitt Romney's Neocon War Cabinet." *Nation,* May 2. Retrieved from http://www.thenation.com/article/167683/mitt-romneys-neocon-war -cabinet#.

Berman, R. 2012. "House Conservatives Call for Stripping Aid to Libya, Egypt from Spending Bill." *Hill,* September 12. Retrieved from http://thehill.com/blogs /global-affairs/middle-east-north-africa/249071-house-conservatives -consider-stripping-foreign-aid-to-libya-from-spending-bill.

Bijian, Z. 2005. "China's 'Peaceful Rise' to Great-Power Status." *Foreign Affairs* (September/October), 18–24.

Black, I. 2011. "Barack Obama Signals Selective US Response to 'Arab Spring.'" *Guardian,* May 19. Retrieved from http://www.guardian.co.uk/world/2011 /may/19/barack-obama-response-arab-spring.

Black, I. 2012. "Syria Insists Chemical Weapons Would Only Be Used against Outside Forces." *Guardian,* July 23. Retrieved from http://www.guardian.co .uk/world/2012/jul/23/syria-chemical-weapons-own-goal.

Black, I., and M. Tran. 2009. "Barack Obama Pledges New Beginning between US and Muslims." *Guardian,* June 4. Retrieved from http://www.guardian.co.uk /world/2009/jun/04/barack-obama-speech-cairo-israel.

Blomfield, A. 2012. "Syria: Kofi Annan Claims Peace Plan Can Be Revived." *Telegraph,* July 9. Retrieved from http://www.telegraph.co.uk/news/world- news/middleeast/syria/9387409/Syria-Kofi-Annan-claims-peace-plan-can-be -revived.html.

Boyle, M. 2011. "Obama: 'Leading from Behind' on Libya." *Guardian,* August 27. Retrieved from http://www.theguardian.com/commentisfree/cifamerica/2011 /aug/27/obama-libya-leadership-nato.

Bradshaw, J. 2014. "North Korea Needs 'Strategic Reshaping.'" *Asia Times,* April 8. Retrieved from http://www.atimes.com/atimes/Korea/KOR-01-080414.html.

Bumiller, E. 2012. "Words and Deeds Show Focus of the American Military on Asia." *New York Times,* November 10, A6.

Clinton, H. 2011. "America's Pacific Century." *Foreign Policy,* October 11. Retrieved from http://www.foreignpolicy.com/articles/2011/10/11/americas_pacific _century.

Cohen, R. 2012. "The Foreign Policy Divide." *New York Times,* October 1. Retrieved from http://www.nytimes.com/2012/10/02/opinion/roger-cohen-the-foreign -policy-divide.html.

Cooper, H., and M. Landler. 2012. "Egypt May Be Bigger Concern Than Libya for White House." *New York Times,* September 13. Retrieved from http://www.nytimes.com/2012/09/14/world/middleeast/egypt-not-libya-may-be-bigger-challenge-for-white-house.html?pagewanted=all.

DeTrani, J. R. 2014. "Six-Party Legacy Emboldens North Korea." *Asia Times,* April 4. Retrieved from http://www.atimes.com/atimes/Korea/KOR-01-040414.html.

Fackler, M. 2012. "Dispute over Islands Reflects Japanese Fear of China's Rise." *New York Times,* August 21, A1.

Fox, L. 2012a. "Michelle Bachmann Sticks to Accusations About Muslim Brotherhood." *US News and World Report,* July 19. Retrieved from http://www.usnews.com/news/articles/2012/07/19/michele-bachmann-sticks-to-accusations-about-muslim-brotherhood.

Fox, L. 2012b. "New Ad Implies Obama Is Cozy with Muslim Brotherhood." *US News and World Report,* September 20. Retrieved from http://www.usnews.com/news/blogs/washington-whispers/2012/09/20/new-ad-implies-obama-is-cozy-with-muslim-brotherhood.

Gerges, F. 2012. *Obama and the Middle East: The End of America's Moment?* New York: Palgrave-Macmillan.

Goldman, A., and A. Gearan. 2014. "Senate Report: Attacks on U.S. Compounds in Benghazi Could Have Been Prevented." *Washington Post,* January 15. Retrieved from http://www.washingtonpost.com/world/national-security/senate-report-attack-on-us-compound-in-benghazi-could-have-been-prevented/2014/01/15/5e197224-7de9-11e3-95c6-0a7aa80874bc_story.html.

Gordon, M. 2013. "U.S. and Russia Reach Deal to Destroy Syria's Chemical Arms." *New York Times,* September 14, A1.

Gordon, M., and B. Trainor. 2012. *The Endgame: The Inside Story of the Struggle for Iraq, from George W. Bush to Barack Obama.* New York: Pantheon.

Greenberg, J. 2011. "Netanyahu Visit Deepens Israeli-Palestinian Impasse." *Washington Post,* May 25. Retrieved from http://www.washingtonpost.com/world/middle-east/netanyahu-visit-deepens-israeli-palestinian-impasse/2011/05/25/AGEHkSBH_story.html.

Harnden, T. 2010. "Barack Obama Declares the 'War on Terror' Is Over." *Telegraph,* May 27. Retrieved from http://www.telegraph.co.uk/news/worldnews/barackobama/7772598/BarackObama-declares-the-War-on-Terror-is-over.html.

Harnden, T. 2011. "Benjamin Netanyahu Rebukes Barack Obama over 1967 Plan." *Telegraph,* May 20. Retrieved from http://www.telegraph.co.uk/news/worldnews/middleeast/israel/8527226/Benjamin--Netanyahu-rebukes-Barack-Obama-over-1967-plan.html.

Harris, P. 2012. "Drone Wars and State Secrecy—How Barack Obama Became a Hardliner." *Guardian,* June 2. Retrieved from http://www.guardian.co.uk/world/2012/jun/02/drone-wars-secrecy-barack-obama.

Ikenberry, G. J. 2008. "The Rise of China and the Future of the West: Can the Liberal System Survive?" *Foreign Affairs* (January/February), 23–37.

Ikenberry, G. J. 2011a. *Liberal Leviathan: The Origins, Crisis, and Transformation of the American World Order*. Princeton: Princeton University Press.

Ikenberry, G. J. 2011b. "Future of the Liberal World Order." *Foreign Affairs* (May/June), 56–68.

Indyk, M. S. 2012. "Foreign Policy and the 2012 Presidential Election." *Brookings*, November 8. Retrieved from http://www.brookings.edu/blogs/up-front/posts/2012/11/08-us-election-foreign-policy-ath.

Indyk, M. S., and K. G. Lieberthal. 2012. "Scoring Obama's Foreign Policy: A Progressive Pragmatist Tries to Bend History." *Foreign Affairs* (May/June), 29–41.

Indyk, M. S., K. G. Lieberthal, and M. O'Hanlon. 2012. *Bending History: Barack Obama's Foreign Policy*. Washington DC: Brookings Institution Press.

Joyner, J. 2012. "What Would Romney's Foreign Policy Look Like?" *Atlantic* September 12. Retrieved from http://www.theatlantic.com/politics/archive/2012/09/what-would-romneys-foreign-policy-look-like/262303/.

Kagan, R. 2013. "Time to Break Out of a Rut in Egypt." *Washington Post*, July 5. Retrieved from http://www.washingtonpost.com/opinions/in-egypt-its-past-time-for-the-obama-administration-to-use-what-power-the-us-has/2013/07/05/86e0bd0a-e5a2-11e2-aef3-339619eab080_story.html.

Keck, Z. 2014. "US-Philippines Reach Deal on US Military Access." *Diplomat*, March 14. Retrieved from http://thediplomat.com/2014/03/us-philippines-reach-deal-on-greater-us-military-access/.

Kessler, G. 2012. "Obama Knocked for Not Visiting Israel." *Washington Post*, August 6. Retrieved from http://www.washingtonpost.com/blogs/fact-checker/post/obama-knocked-for-not-visiting-israel/2012/08/03/9420de6e-dce3-11e1-8e43-4a3c4375504a_blog.html.

Kessler, G. 2013. "President Obama and the 'Red Line' on Syria's Chemical Weapons." *Washington Post*, September 6. Retrieved from http://www.washingtonpost.com/blogs/fact-checker/wp/2013/09/06/president-obama-and-the-red-line-on-syrias-chemical-weapons/.

Kirkpatrick, D. 2014. "General Who Led Takeover of Egypt to Run for President." *New York Times*, March 26, A4.

Klaidman, D. 2012. *Kill or Capture: The War on Terror and the Soul of the Obama Presidency*. New York: Houghton-Mifflin.

Klapper, B. 2012. "US: Russia Sending Syria Attack Helicopters." *Washington Post*, June 12. Retrieved from http://www.washingtonpost.com/world/national-security/us-russia-is-sending-syria-attack-helicopters/2012/06/12/gJQARMRqXV_story.html.

Knickerbocker, B. 2011. "Syria Violence Puts Obama in Diplomatic, Political Tough Spot." *Christian Science Monitor*, April 23. Retrieved from http://www.csmonitor.com/USA/Foreign-Policy/2011/0423/Syria-violence-puts-Obama-in-diplomatic-political-tough-spot.

Kohut, A. 2010. "Reviving America's Global Image." *Pew Global Attitudes Project,* March 5. Retrieved from http://www.pewglobal.org/2010/03/05/reviving -americas-global-image/.

LaFranchi, H. 2013. "Can Cooperation on Boston Bombings Bridge US-Russia Distrust? It Will Be Hard." *Christian Science Monitor,* April 29. Retrieved from http://www.csmonitor.com/USA/Foreign-Policy/2013/0429/Can-cooperation -on-Boston-bombings-bridge-US-Russia-distrust-It-will-be-hard.-video.

LaFraniere, S. 2012. "China and Its Trade Practices Are Coming to the Debates." *New York Times,* October 15, A13.

Laidi, Z. 2012. *Limited Achievements: Obama's Foreign Policy.* New York: Palgrave-Macmillan.

Landler, M., and S. L. Myers. 2011. "Obama Sees '67 Borders as Starting Point for Peace Deal." *New York Times,* May 11, A1.

Lieberthal, K. G. 2011. "The American Pivot to Asia." *Foreign Policy,* December 21. Retrieved from http://www.foreignpolicy.com/articles/2011/12/21/the _american_pivot_to_asia.

Lizza, R. 2011. "The Consequentialist: How the Arab Spring Remade Obama's Foreign Policy." *New Yorker,* May 2. Retrieved from http://www.newyorker .com/reporting/2011/05/02/110502fa_fact_lizza#ixzz2BwrodG31.

Loyola, M. 2014. "At Moscow's Mercy." *Foreign Policy,* April 7. Retrieved from http:// www.foreignpolicy.com/articles/2014/04/07/at_moscows_mercy_nato_obama _russia_ukraine.

Macaskill, E. 2012. "Mitt Romney: Arm the Syrian Rebels." *Guardian,* October 8. Retrieved from http://www.theguardian.com/world/2012/oct/08/mitt -romney-arm-syrian-rebels.

Macaskill, E. 2013. "Obama's Visit to Israel Criticised as a 'Maintenance Trip' without Peace Plan." *Guardian,* March 14. Retrieved from http://www .theguardian.com/world/2013/mar/14/barack-obama-israel-trip-peace.

MacFarquhar, N. 2014. "Russia Plotting for Ukrainian Influence, Not Invasion, Analysts Say." *New York Times,* April 9. Retrieved from http://www.nytimes. com/2014/04/10/world/europe/russia-plotting-for-ukrainian-influence-not -invasion-analysts-say.html?hp.

Mann, J. 2012. *The Obamians: The Struggle inside the White House to Redefine American Power.* New York: Viking.

McGregor, J. 2012. "Mitt Romney's Foreign Policy Speech: A Leadership Moment?" *Washington Post,* October 8. Retrieved from http://www.washingtonpost.com /national/on-leadership/mitt-romneys-foreign-policy-speech-a-leadership -moment/2012/10/08/041decae-1185-11e2-be82-c3411b76800a9_story.html.

Myers, S. L. 2012. "U.S. Move to Give Egypt $450 Million in Aid Meets Resistance." *New York Times,* September 29, A11.

Nakamura, D. 2012. "Obama, in Burma Speech: 'We Always Remained Hopeful About You.'" *Washington Post,* November 19. Retrieved from http://www .washingtonpost.com/world/asia_pacific/obama-to-praise-burmas-journey -toward-democracy/2012/11/18/4aa0176a-31f1-11e2-bfd5-e202b6d7b501_story .html?hpid=z4.

Nakashima, E. 2014. "Obama Says New NSA Proposal Alleviates Privacy Concerns About Surveillance." *Washington Post,* March 25. Retrieved from http://www .washingtonpost.com/world/national-security/obama-says-new-nsa-proposal -alleviates-privacy-concerns/2014/03/25/c6911126-b431-11e3-8cb6 -284052554d74_story.html.

Nathan, A., and A. Scobell. 2012. "How China Sees America: The Sum of Beijing's Fears." *Foreign Affairs* (September/October), 30–44.

Obama, B. 2009. "Remarks by the President on a New Beginning, Cairo University, Cairo, Egypt." White House, Office of the Press Secretary, June 4. Retrieved from http://www.whitehouse.gov/the-press-office/remarks-president-cairo -university-6-04-09.

Obama, B. 2011. "Remarks by the President in Address to the Nation on Libya." White House, Office of the Press Secretary, March 28. Retrieved from http:// www.whitehouse.gov/the-press-office/2011/03/28/remarks-president-address -nation-libya.

Parker, A., and R. A. Oppel. 2012. "Romney Trip Raises Sparks at a 2nd Stop." *New York Times,* July 31, A1.

Pew Global Attitudes Project. 2012a. "Global Opinion of Obama Slips, International Policies Faulted." June 13. Retrieved from http://www.pewglobal.org/2011 /05/17/arab-spring-fails-to-improve-us-image/.

Pew Global Attitudes Project. 2012b. "Most Muslims Want Democracy, Personal Freedoms, and Islam in Political Life." July 10. Retrieved from http://www .pewglobal.org/2012/07/10/most-muslims-want-democracy-personal -freedoms-and-islam-in-political-life/.

Pew Research Center for the People and the Press. 2013. "Public Opinion Runs Against Syrian Airstrikes." September 3. Retrieved from http://www.people -press.org/2013/09/03/public-opinion-runs-against-syrian-airstrikes/.

"Presidential Debate Transcript, Boca Raton, Florida." 2012. October 23. Retrieved from http://www.cfr.org/elections/presidential-debate-transcript-florida -october-2012/p29323.

Rasul-Ronning, Z. 2012. *Conflicted Power: Obama's US Foreign and Strategic Policy in a Shifting World Order.* Bloomington, IN: AuthorHouse.

Rosenberg, M., and Bowley, G. 2012. "U.S. Grants Special Ally Status to Afghans, Easing Fears of Abandonment." *New York Times,* July 7, A9.

Rosenthal, E. 2012. "U.S. to Be World's Top Oil Producer in 5 Years, Report Says." *New York Times,* November 12. Retrieved from http://www.nytimes.com /2012/11/13/business/energy-environment/report-sees-us-as-top-oil-producer -in-5-years.html.

Rubin, A., and R. Gladstone. 2014. "West See Unity on Iran Despite Crisis in Ukraine." *New York Times,* March 18, A10.

Rucker, P. 2012. "Romney Continues Attack on Obama's Foreign Policy." *Washington Post,* September 13. Retrieved from http://www.washingtonpost.com /blogs/post-politics/wp/2012/09/13/mitt-romney-casts-obama-as-weak-on -foreign-policy/.

Sanger, D. E. 2009. *The Inheritance: The World Obama Confronts and the Challenges to American Power.* New York: Broadway.

Sanger, D. E. 2012. *Confront and Conceal: Obama's Secret Wars and Surprising Use of American Power.* New York: Crown Publishers.

Sang-Hun, C. 2013. "North Korea Learning to Make Crucial Nuclear Parts, Study Finds." *New York Times,* September 23, A10.

Sargent, G. 2011. "Obama Explains Libya Mission to Congress." *Washington Post,* March 21. Retrieved from http://www.washingtonpost.com/blogs/plum-line /post/obama-explains-libya-mission-to-congress/2011/03/03/ABU9377_blog .html.

Shear, M. D. 2010. "Obama, Medvedev Sign Treaty to Reduce Nuclear Weapons." *Washington Post,* April 8. Retrieved from http://www.washingtonpost.com /wp-dyn/content/article/2010/04/08/AR2010040801677.html.

Shear, M., and P. Baker. 2014. "Obama Answers Critics, Dismissing Russia as a 'Regional Power.'" *New York Times,* March 25, A8.

Sherwood, H. 2012. "Mitt Romney Would Support Israeli Military Strike Against Iran, Says Aide." *Guardian,* July 29. Retrieved from http://www.theguardian .com/world/2012/jul/29/mitt-romney-backs-israel-strike-iran.

Sink, J. 2012. "Poll: Romney's Remarks on Middle East Unrest Viewed Negatively." *Hill,* September 17. Retrieved from http://thehill.com/blogs/blog-briefing -room/news/249873-poll-romney-criticism-of-embassy-attack-response -viewed-negatively-.

Snyder, S. 2013. "U.S. Policy Toward North Korea." Council on Foreign Relations (January). Retrieved from http://www.cfr.org/north-korea/us-policy-toward -north-korea/p29962.

Spetalnick, M., and A. Anishchuk. 2013. "Obama Rejects G20 Pressure to Abandon Syria Air Strike Plan." *Reuters,* September 6. Retrieved from http://www .reuters.com/article/2013/09/06/us-russia-g-idUSBRE98315S20130906.

Stearns, S. 2014. "Kerry: US Commitment to Mideast Peace Not Open-Ended." *Voice of America News,* April 5. Retrieved from http://www.voanews.com /content/kerry-time-for-reality-check-in-mideast-peace-process/1886161 .html.

Sullivan, M. 2012. "Questions on Drones, Unanswered Still." *New York Times,* October 13. Retrieved from https://www.nytimes.com/2012/10/14/public -editor/questions-on-drones-unanswered-still.html.

Surk, B. 2014. "Death Toll from Syria's 3-Year Conflict Exceeds 150,000, Activists Say as Fighting Rages On." *US News and World Report,* April 1. Retrieved from http://www.usnews.com/news/world/articles/2014/04/01/activists-syria -conflict-death-toll-hits-150-344.

Tisdall, S. 2012. "China and Japan: A Dangerous Standoff over the Senkaku Islands." *Guardian,* September 17. Retrieved from http://www.guardian.co.uk /commentisfree/2012/sep/17/china-japan-dangerous-standoff.

Warrick, J. 2011. "Clinton Defends U.S. Response to Crackdown in Syria." *Washington Post,* August 16. Retrieved from http://www.washingtonpost.com/world

/national-security/clinton-defends-us-response-to-crackdown-in-syria
/2011/08/16/gIQA3jloJJ_story.html.

Warrick, J., and L. Sly. 2012. "U.S. Officials: Iran Is Stepping Up Lethal Aid to Syria."
Washington Post, March 3. Retrieved from http://www.washingtonpost.com
/world/national-security/us-officials-iran-is-stepping-up-lethal-aid-to-syria
/2012/03/02/gIQAGR9XpR_story.html.

Weaver, M. 2012. "Syria Conflict: Obama Urged to Be Tougher with Assad."
Guardian, November 7. Retrieved from http://www.guardian.co.uk/world
/middle-east-live/2012/nov/07/syria-obama-tougher-assad-live.

Weiner, R. 2012. "Romney Calls Obama Administration Response to Libya Attacks
'Disgraceful.'" *Washington Post,* September 12. Retrieved from http://www
.washingtonpost.com/blogs/post-politics/wp/2012/09/12/romney-calls
-obama-response-to-libya-attacks-disgraceful/.

Willis, A. 2012. "Mitt Romney: Russia Is America's 'Number One Geopolitical
Foe.'" *Telegraph,* March 27. Retrieved from http://www.telegraph.co.uk/news
/worldnews/us-election/9168533/Mitt-Romney-Russia-is-Americas-number
-one-geopolitical-foe.html.

Zakaria, F. 2011. "The Dangerous Chip on China's Shoulder." *Time,* January 12.
Retrieved from http://www.time.com/time/magazine/article
/0,9171,2042361,00.html.

Zirulnick, A. 2014. "Behind Syria's Calculations on Missing Chemical Weapons
Deadline." *Christian Science Monitor,* February 5. Retrieved from http://www
.csmonitor.com/World/Security-Watch/terrorism-security/2014/0205
/Behind-Syria-s-calculations-on-missing-chemical-weapons-deadline-video.

Zuckerman, M. B. 2012. "Barack Obama's Middle East Miscalculation." *US News
and World Report,* January 20. Retrieved from http://www.usnews.com
/opinion/mzuckerman/articles/2012/01/20/barack-obamas-middle-east
-miscalculation-.

Contributors

Douglas M. Brattebo is Associate Professor of Political Science and Director of the James A. Garfield Center for the Study of the American Presidency at Hiram College. Among the courses Brattebo teaches are Ethics in U.S. Foreign Policy, Introduction to American Government, The American Presidency and the Executive Branch, The Virtues, Leadership, and Legacy of Abraham Lincoln, and Engaged Citizenship. One of his most recent publications is a chapter, "Closed for Repairs So It Can Reengage with the World: Prospects for Reforming the Republican Party," in *The American Election 2012: Contexts and Consequences*, edited by R. Ward Holder and Peter B. Josephson.

Tom Lansford is a Professor of Political Science. His research interests include foreign and security policy, and the U.S. presidency. Dr. Lansford is the author, coauthor, editor, or coeditor of more than 40 books, and the author of more than one hundred essays, book chapters, and reviews. His books include *A Bitter Harvest: U.S. Foreign Policy and Afghanistan* (2003), *The Historical Dictionary of U.S. Diplomacy Since the Cold War* (2007), and *9/11 and the Wars in Afghanistan and Iraq: A Chronology and Reference Guide* (2011). His more recent edited collections include *America's War on Terror* (2003; 2nd ed., 2009), *Judging Bush* (2009), and *The Obama Presidency: A Preliminary Assessment* (2012).

Jack Covarrubias is the Director of the Center for Policy and Resilience and a member of the governing board of the National Social Science Association. His experience bridges academia and the military where he has focused on the American foreign policy experience and homeland security. His most recent works include the edited volume *The Obama Presidency: A Preliminary Assessment* (2012) and the coauthored work *Fostering Community Resilience: Homeland Security and Hurricane Katrina* (2010).

Neal Allen is an Assistant Professor of Political Science at Wichita State University. He is the author of "Living, Dead and Undead: Nullification Past and Present" in *American Political Thought* and "Scandal and the Politics of Race: From Martin Luther King, Jr. to Barack Obama and Beyond," in *Scandal!: An Interdisciplinary Approach to the Consequences, Outcomes, and Significance of Political Scandals*.

David J. Bonanza is a political science research analyst with a bachelor of science summa cum laude in business economics from the University of South Florida. He is an honorary member of Pi Sigma Alpha ("The National Political Science Honor Society"), and his professional experience includes analytical roles with *Fortune* 100 companies in the banking and telecommunications industries. He has coauthored the text *Politics in Florida* (3rd ed.) and chapters in Larry Sabato's books *Pendulum Swing* (2011) and *The Year of Obama* (2009); he has also assisted with the production of many other publications, including a featured column on political news website Sayfie Review.

Richard S. Conley is Associate Professor of Political Science at the University of Florida (Gainesville). His research interests include the presidency, Congress, and comparative executive-legislative relations. He is author of *The Presidency, Congress, and Divided Government: A Postwar Assessment* (2003), as well as historical dictionaries on the presidencies of Ronald Reagan and George H. W. Bush, William Clinton, and George W. Bush. His current research includes a book on prime ministerial leadership in Canada from Diefenbaker to Harper. His articles on American and comparative politics have appeared in journals including *Presidential Studies Quarterly, Congress and the Presidency, Political Science Quarterly, Political Studies,* and *Comparative Political Research*.

Leonard Cutler (PhD, New School for Social Research) is Professor of Public Law, Chair of the Department of Political Science, and Director of the Center for the Study of Government and Politics at Siena College, Loudonville, New York. Cutler is also on the board of Albany Law School. His areas of expertise include constitutional law, criminal law and procedure, and national security and counterterrorism. His research has appeared in edited volumes and journals, and he has authored several books including, most recently, *The Rule of Law and Law of War* (Edwin Mellen) and *Developments in National Security Policy of the United States Post 9/11* (Edwin Mellen). He contributed a chapter on counterterrorism policy in *The Obama Presidency, A Preliminary Assessment* (SUNY Press, 2012). Cutler has provided testimony to the Judiciary Committee of the U.S. Senate on "Restoring the Rule of Law," and the President's Task Force on Detainee Disposition on issues related to war powers, NSA surveillance, and the Authorization for the Use of Military Force (AUMF).

Byron W. Daynes is Professor of Political Science at Brigham Young University and a William J. Clinton Distinguished Fellow. Dr. Baynes has published many works including Raymond Tatalovich and Byron W. Daynes, eds., *Moral Controversies in American Politics,* 4th ed. (Armonk, NY: M. E. Sharpe, 2011); Byron W. Daynes and Glen Sussman, *White House Politics and the Environment* (College Station, TX: Texas A&M University Press, 2010); Byron W. Daynes and Glen Sussman, *The American Presidency and the Social Agenda* (Upper Saddle River, NJ: Prentice Hall, 2001); Glen Sussman and Byron W. Daynes, *U.S. Politics and Climate Change: Science Confronts Policy* (Boulder, CO: Lynne Rienner Publishers, 2013).

Chris J. Dolan is Professor of Politics and Director of Global Studies at Lebanon Valley College in Annville, Pennsylvania. He is the author or coauthor of *Striking First, In War We Trust,* and *The Presidency and Economic Policy* as well as numerous articles in political science and international studies journals and chapters in edited books. His research interests include U.S. foreign policy, U.S. national security, international relations theory, and globalization.

Michael K. Gusmano's research interests include the politics of health care reform, comparative health systems, aging, health and health care inequalities, and normative theories of policy analysis. In addition to his appointment at the Hastings Center, Dr. Gusmano holds adjunct appointments at Columbia University and Yale University. His most recent book, *Health Care in World Cities* (Johns Hopkins University Press, 2010), documents the implications of national and local health care policies for access to care in New York, London, and Paris. He holds a PhD in political science from the University of Maryland at College Park and a master's in public policy from the State University of New York at Albany. He was also a postdoctoral fellow in the Robert Wood Johnson Foundation Scholars in Health Policy program at Yale University (1995–1997). Dr. Gusmano is the president of the American Political Science Association's *Organized Section on Health Politics and Policy*. He serves on the editorial boards for the *Journal of Health Politics, Policy and Law*, *Health Economics Policy and Law*, and *The Hastings Center Report*.

Chad Kinsella is an Assistant Professor of Political Science at Lander University with a focus on electoral politics including a recently published article, "The Political Geography of the South: A Spatial Analysis of the 2008 Presidential Election," in the *American Review of Politics*.

Susan A. MacManus is a Distinguished University Professor, University of South Florida. For the last six election cycles, she has served as political analyst for WFLA-TV (Tampa NBC affiliate). She was a blogger for TBO.com during the 2004 and 2006 election campaigns and has been the featured columnist for sayfiereview.com (Florida's leading political website) since 2008. MacManus has published many works on politics including, most recently, *Politics in States and Communities*, 15th ed., with Thomas R. Dye (Prentice Hall, 2014), and *Florida's Politics*, 3rd ed., with Aubrey Jewett, Thomas R. Dye, and David Bonanza (Florida Institute of Government, 2011). She served as Chair of the Florida Elections Commission from 1999 to 2003 and as an advisor to the Florida Division of Elections. In 2008, MacManus was appointed by the U.S. Election Assistance Commission to two working groups: the Election Management Guidelines Development Working Group on Elderly and Disabled Voters in Long-Term Care Facilities and the Working Group on Media and Public Relations.

Jewerl Maxwell is Dean of Academic Initiatives and Associate Professor of Political Science at Gordon College. He holds an MA and PhD from Miami University, and a BA (summa cum laude) in history, political science, and public affairs from Muskingum University. Dr. Maxwell coauthored *Tough Times for the President: Political Adversity and the Sources of Executive Power* (2012) with Ryan Barilleaux. Dr. Maxwell teaches courses in the American presidency, campaigns, and constitutional law.

Robert J. Pauly, Jr. is Associate Professor of International Policy and Development at The University of Southern Mississippi. His research interests focus broadly on the fields of U.S. foreign policy, national security, and homeland security, with emphasis on American policy toward the states of the greater Middle East. He is the author of five books and nearly 40 academic articles, essays, and book chapters, including, most recently, the *Ashgate Research Companion to US Foreign Policy* (2010). He analyzes U.S. foreign policy and national security issues during a weekly appearance on the Gulf Coast Mornings radio show on 104.9 FM in Biloxi, MS.

Steve A. Stuglin (PhD, Georgia State University) is an award-winning teacher and currently an instructor of communications at Georgia Highlands College. His research interests include political rhetoric, public policy, and corporate management, with a focus on the relationships between storied institutions. He has written extensively on the relationship between the domestic auto industry and the presidency and presented these findings in numerous conference presentations, including at meetings of the National Communication Association, the Southern States Communication Association, and the Rhetoric Society of America. His recent chapter on the 2008–2009 government intervention in the auto industry appeared in *The Obama Presidency: A Preliminary Assessment* (SUNY).

Andrew Travis holds a BA in Political Science from Cedarville University (with highest honor), where he served as a Research Assistant for the Center for Political Studies. He has completed some PhD coursework in Political Science at the University of North Carolina at Chapel Hill, studying American political behavior and identities. He currently works at a market research firm in Maryland.

Shirley Anne Warshaw is Professor of Political Science at Gettysburg College and the Harold G. Evans Professor of Eisenhower Leadership Studies. She received her PhD from the Johns Hopkins University, MBA from the Wharton School of Finance and Commerce of the University of Pennsylvania, and BA from the University of Pennsylvania. Prior to joining the Gettysburg College faculty, Dr. Warshaw worked in Pennsylvania state government and served in the Governor's Office under two governors. Dr. Warshaw has written seven books on presidential decision making and numerous book chapters and articles. Her books include *The Clinton Years* (2004), *The Keys to Power: Managing the Presidency* (1999; 2004, 2nd ed.), *The Domestic Presidency: Decision Making in the White House* (1997), *Powersharing: White House–Cabinet Relations in the Modern Presidency* (1996), *Reexamining the Eisenhower Presidency* (1994), *The Eisenhower Legacy* (1992), and most recently, *The Co-Presidency of George W. Bush and Dick Cheney* (Stanford University Press 2009).

Stephen D. Wrage is a professor of Political Science at the U.S. Naval Academy in Annapolis. He specializes in ethics and American foreign policy and is the author of a number of widely used case studies of actual ethical quandaries experienced by officers in the American military. In 1991 he held a Pew Faculty Fellowship in International Affairs at the Kennedy School of Government. In 1995 he spent a Fulbright year teaching at the National University of Singapore and has written about that severely controlled society for the *Washington Post*, the *Los Angeles Times*, the Asian *Wall Street Journal*, and the *Atlantic Monthly*. In 2004 he published *Immaculate Warfare*, a study of the ethical, practical, and command issues raised by precision-guided munitions. His latest book is *Spirits Talking: Thomas Jefferson, John Adams and Abigail Adams Argue Right and Wrong in the Affairs of States*. It is a set of dialogues laying out three theoretical perspectives on issues in ethics and international affairs.

Index